Managed Evolution

Stephan Murer · Bruno Bonati · Frank J. Furrer

Managed Evolution

A Strategy for
Very Large
Information Systems

Springer

Dr. Stephan Murer
Credit Suisse
8070 Zürich
Switzerland
stephan.murer@credit-suisse.com

Dr. Frank J. Furrer
Guldifuess 3
8260 Stein am Rhein
Switzerland
frank.j.furrer@bluewin.ch

Bruno Bonati
Bruno Bonati Consulting
Bernoldweg 4a
6300 Zug
Switzerland
bruno@bonati-consulting.com

This publication is the result of the long professional careers of the authors in the management, architecture and design of very large information systems. The content is the result of the personal experience of the authors and represents their personal views on the subject matter. Although numerous examples from the Credit Suisse AG very large information system are used, the content never constitutes any view, opinion, or obligation for Credit Suisse AG.

ISBN 978-3-642-43131-9   ISBN 978-3-642-01633-2 (eBook)
DOI 10.1007/978-3-642-01633-2
Springer Heidelberg Dordrecht London New York

© Springer-Verlag Berlin Heidelberg 2011
Softcover re-print of the Hardcover 1st edition 2011
This work is subject to copyright. All rights are reserved, whether the whole or part of the material is concerned, specifically the rights of translation, reprinting, reuse of illustrations, recitation, broadcasting, reproduction on microfilm or in any other way, and storage in data banks. Duplication of this publication or parts thereof is permitted only under the provisions of the German Copyright Law of September 9, 1965, in its current version, and permission for use must always be obtained from Springer. Violations are liable to prosecution under the German Copyright Law.

The use of general descriptive names, registered names, trademarks, etc. in this publication does not imply, even in the absence of a specific statement, that such names are exempt from the relevant protective laws and regulations and therefore free for general use.

Cover design: WMXDesign GmbH, Heidelberg, Germany

Springer is part of Springer Science+Business Media (www.springer.com)

Foreword

Information technology requirements at today's companies have soared, placing IT at the heart of everything that companies do. IT enables businesses to conduct their core activities and connects a wide range of internal experts with a variety of external clients. IT services have evolved rapidly and broadly from simple desktop support to complex systems and networks so critical to success that, without them, companies would come to a standstill.

The success of IT is rooted in the need to actively help shape an organization's overall strategy, and thus to understand and anticipate changing client requirements. On the one hand, this collaboration is based on an equal partnership with the business side of the company – a partnership that requires a solid foundation of trust and leadership. On the other hand, it means that IT must be agile not only in its processes and systems, but also in its mindset. Together with comprehensive technical expertise and proven talent, this heightened level of agility requires interdisciplinary and integrated thinking. In the end, this is the essence of a world class IT organization.

The dynamic interplay of an equal partnership with the business and a heightened level of agility are crucial factors for a Managed Evolution strategy as described in detail on the following pages. It is this dynamic interplay which forms the basic principle that guides IT in everything it does. This principle allows IT to develop and implement a vision, and gives it the freedom to drive a company forward. This is the spirit of this book, which provides theoretical explanations and practical examples to show how an agile IT architecture, guided by a trusted partnership with the business, can ensure a company's long-term success.

Zürich, Switzerland
April 2010

Karl Landert
Chief Information Officer Credit Suisse

Preface

Context

Modern society is fundamentally dependent on highly complex *infrastructures*. Examples of infrastructures include energy distribution, transportation systems, communications networks, financial services, governments, the military, airline reservation systems and traffic control.

All of these infrastructures depend in one way or the other on *information systems*. Information systems are mission-critical. A malfunction or failure of the system partly or totally inhibits the operation of the infrastructure. Such malfunctions or failures can potentially cause damage, chaos, loss or serious disturbances.

Many of these systems belong to a special class of systems, introduced in this book: The *very large information systems*. They have some common main characteristics: They consist of a large set of rich functionality and are exposed to a continuous flow of new requirements, resulting in a high rate of change. Typically, very large information systems have grown over decades and as a consequence have accumulated significant portions of so called *legacy parts*. As a result, very large information systems exhibit massive and increasing *complexity*. This

> "It is generally agreed that increasing complexity is at the heart of most difficult problems facing today's systems architecting and engineering"
> *Mark W. Maier, Eberhardt Rechtin, 2002*

is the cause of many problems in adapting, evolving, maintaining and operating these systems. Unfortunately, the need to continuously add new functionality, to adapt to new technology, to serve additional locations, absorb growth and to add more users to the systems inevitably increases complexity.

Challenge

Driven by user, technology and market requirements, very large information systems must continually be transformed to ensure the competitiveness of the *business* they serve. In spite of a high rate of change the systems must at all times guarantee the desired quality attributes, such as stability, availability, dependability and security. Deficiencies or failures in such non-functional areas may seriously damage the business. In addition, the continuous aging of the system results in obsolescence of parts of the system. Such legacy parts resist modifications, are expensive to maintain, eventually reach the end of their lifecycle and must therefore be replaced.

An economic requirement is the need for continuously improving the *efficiency* of the system: The cost and time to market for the implementation of new functionality as well as the operational cost are under constant pressure.

The development of very large information systems covers implementing new requirements on time and budget, managing system complexity and reducing development and maintenance cost – all at the same time. This is a demanding task incurring considerable risk. Today it can often be observed that organizations tackle these challenges by developing the very large information systems opportunistically. In an *opportunistic approach* the two drivers for investments are new business requirements and the promise of new technologies. Very often the need to take proper care of the existing system is disregarded. The continuous addition of new functionality and new technology leads to ever growing *complexity*. This approach inevitably leads into the *complexity trap*. The very large information system becomes inflexible, costly and unreliable. It no longer fulfils the stakeholder expectations. The system reaches a dangerous dead end. The resulting questions are: Is there an alternative? Which is the adequate strategy for very large information systems?

The Message in This Book

This book shows one proven way to meet the challenges of the development over time of mission-critical, very large information systems that include significant legacy parts. It takes the reader from the analysis of the issues of very large information systems to an assessment of the different strategic approaches. The recommended strategy, in the experience of the authors, is *Managed Evolution*. Managed evolution leads to a continuous improvement and sustainable lifecycle evolution of very large information systems. It also improves *agility* in the form of reduced time to market and lower cost for adapting to new requirements. The elements and the implementation of this strategy, including the main processes, instruments and metrics are described in this book.

The authors believe that managed evolution is applicable to any very large information system. The reason is that all very large information systems obey the same laws: Requirements growth, structural decay, technology obsolescence and growing complexity lead to quality, efficiency and cost challenges. The experience of the authors is based on work with very large information systems in the financial industry, an early adopter of information technology. In their opinion, these concepts will become relevant to other industries that adopted information technology later.

All the recommendations, conclusions and findings about managed evolution are based on the experience of the authors with this approach. The approach has been successful over more than a decade for a very large information system in the financial services industry.

Side-Stories

Modern financial institutions use *information systems* to deliver their services to customers. Transactions in most cases happen electronically and not physically anymore. The assets have largely been converted to "bits in Information systems". This development has left financial institutions heavily dependent on their information systems.

> "Today's banking operation consists mostly of managing and moving data about money"

The managed evolution approach documented in this book has been developed and applied by the authors at Credit Suisse[1], a global bank. Some key practical results mainly from Credit Suisse are used in this book as *sidestories* to illustrate important concepts.

Intended Audience

This book is a management book, not an engineering text and not a banking story. It explains the added value delivered by the managed evolution of very large information systems compared to other strategic approaches The intended audience of this book is: Managers and IT architects who deal with very large information systems from a strategic perspective, developers and project

> "Poor architecture creates a litany of problems, including:
> - Redundant applications, processes, and data
> - Needless IT rework
> - Redundant hardware and software (Infrastructure)"
>
> David Marco, 2004

---

[1] see http://www.credit-suisse.com for more information.

managers who perform work on such systems and business managers who want to understand how the long term evolution of their systems impacts their business and its future.

Structure of the Book

The book contains four parts:

- Chapters 1–4 introduce structure, properties, challenges and architecture of very large information systems. The focus is on the *system*, including system analysis, system architecting and system engineering with respect to managed evolution,
- Chapters 5–7 focus on the *organization* behind the very large information system. This includes business-IT alignment, people, culture, organization and measurement for the successful execution of managed evolution,
- Chapter 8 summarizes and concludes the book with an outlook.
- Finally references are listed, a glossary and a list of abbreviations of the most important terms are provided and an extensive index concludes the book.

Acknowledgments

First of all, special thanks goes to our reviewers Paolo Conti, Jennifer Costley, Monika Dunant, Claus Hagen, Oliver Kling, Karl Landert, Hans Neukom, Eric Newcomer, Werner Schaad, Daniel Schmutz, Peter Schnorf, Ernst Sonderegger, Andrea Steiner, Claude Täschler, Hanspeter Uebelbacher, and Carl Worms for their excellent and constructive comments and contributions. They have invested their valuable time and greatly improved both the content and the comprehensiveness of the book.

We highly appreciate the professional English language check and the final read-through of the full manuscript done by Rob Robinson. Native German speakers – as all three authors are – will never be able to reach this level of perfection. Rob, thanks very much for the improvement of the readability of the book.

Thanks also to Niels Peter Thomas, Alice Blanck and Ulrike Stricker-Komba from Springer Verlag in Heidelberg for their careful and competent guidance during the managed evolution of this book. It was a pleasure to work with Springer Verlag, Heidelberg.

During our many years of work in Credit Suisse architecture we greatly appreciated the discussions, solution finding and problem solving with our colleagues. We have learned a lot from them and express our sincere gratitude. Without their valuable work, this book would not have been possible. We would especially like to mention: Matthias Bärtsch, Walter Chiastra, Marianne Forchini-Schmid, Stephan Hug, Andreas Geppert, Marc Günthardt, Ulv Grönquist, Haiyan Hasse-Ye, Roger Hüsser, Roger Karrer, Daniel Kernberg, Thomas Koch, Daniel Koller, Cornelia Kradolfer, Heinrich Krause, Ricardo Polisano, Ernst Siegrist, Roger Süess, Claude Täschler, Roger Weber, Andreas Weigel, Gritta Wolf, and Jacqueline Yang.

Thanks also go to Doris Itschner, Yvonne Wyssling, and Monica Wyssling for managing the time schedules of the authors during the nearly 2 years of work.

Last but not least, our thanks also go to all the authors of the listed references for their excellent literature (see references in Sect. 9.1 at the end of the book) which allowed us to build on their extensive shared knowledge and experience.

About the Authors

Stephan Murer was born 1963 in Switzerland. He graduated with an information technology engineering diploma and a PhD. in computer science from the ETH in Zürich in 1992. After that he continued his academic career at the International Computer Science Institute of the University of California, Berkeley. 1994 Stephan joined Credit Suisse, where he held a number of different positions. In 2000 he completed his MBA from the University of St. Gallen. Since 2000 he has been managing director and chief architect, responsible for the overall design of Credit Suisse's Information systems. Stephan Murer can be reached at stephan.murer@credit-suisse.com.

Bruno Bonati was born 1949 in Switzerland and studied Economics at the University of St.Gallen. He graduated as lic.oec.HSG in 1973. After graduation he worked in several companies and in 1996 he became Member of the Executive Board and Head of IT and Operations in Credit Suisse. In 1997 Credit Suisse started the managed evolution strategy in IT and developed the Service Oriented Architecture for the Swiss IT Platform.

In 2005 after retirement from Credit Suisse he worked as an independent consultant for IT and Banking. He has been the senior consultant for BIAN, the Banking Industry Network an independent organization led by large banks and vendors with the goal to develop SOA in banking and to enable the standardization of services in banking. He is a member of several non executive boards of directors, among them Swisscom IT Services and is chairman of the Zuger Kantonalbank. Bruno Bonati can be reached at bruno@bonati-consulting.com.

Frank J. Furrer was born 1945 in Switzerland and studied electrical engineering at the Swiss Federal Institute of Technology in Zurich (ETH Zurich). He graduated as Master of Science in 1969. After graduation he worked as a research assistant at the Institute of Technical Physics at the Swiss Federal Institute of Technology in Zurich (Prof. Dr. E. Baumann) and earned his PhD. in advanced communications engineering in the year 1975.

In the following years he worked in several consulting firms. 1997 he started his own consulting practice, focussed on applications architecture and security for very large information systems. Frank J. Furrer is the author of several books on industrial communications and information system security and works as an independent consultant. Frank J. Furrer can be reached at frank.j.furrer@villa-aurora.ch.

Contents

**Part I Structure, Properties, Challenges and Architecture
of Very Large Information Systems**

1 Very Large Information System Challenge 3
   1.1 Background 3
   1.2 Complexity of Very Large Information Systems 5
   1.3 Properties of Very Large Information Systems 9
   1.4 Strategic Approaches for Very Large Information Systems 14
       1.4.1 Opportunistic Approach 17
       1.4.2 Replacement Approach 19
       1.4.3 Greenfield Approach 22
   1.5 The Core Idea of Managed Evolution 23
   1.6 Elements of Managed Evolution 30
   1.7 Where to Start with Managed Evolution 32

2 Architecture Management 35
   2.1 What is IT Architecture and Why Is It Important
       to Managed Evolution 35
   2.2 Architecture Principles 37
   2.3 Architecture Layers and Models 39
   2.4 Business Architecture 42
   2.5 Application Architecture 45
   2.6 Technical Architecture 57
   2.7 Vertical Architectures 60
   2.8 Architecture As an Activity: The Architecture Process 65
   2.9 Architecture Organization: Federated Architecture Process 71

3 Integration Architecture 79
   3.1 Enabling Managed Evolution 79
   3.2 Challenges for Integration Architecture 81

		3.3	Composing Systems from Components	83
			3.3.1 Functional Composition	84
			3.3.2 Desktop Integration	85
			3.3.3 Process Orchestration	86
			3.3.4 Layering Components	86
		3.4	Choosing the Right Interfaces	91
			3.4.1 Adequate Degree of Coupling	92
			3.4.2 Adequate Integration Scope	94
			3.4.3 Avoid Redundancy	95
			3.4.4 Formal Syntax and Rich Semantics	96
			3.4.5 Adequate Granularity and Reuse	99
			3.4.6 Bridging Technical Heterogeneity and Network Distance	100
			3.4.7 Use Industry Standards Where Applicable	101
		3.5	Interfaces and Service Contracts	102
			3.5.1 Interfaces and Services	103
			3.5.2 Non-Functional Properties of Services	106
			3.5.3 Contracts as Active Relationships	107
			3.5.4 Service Versioning	109
		3.6	Service Management Process	111
		3.7	Service Delivery Infrastructure	116
		3.8	Consuming Foreign Services	119
		3.9	Evolutionary Decomposition of Monolithic Systems	124
4	**Infrastructure**			129
	4.1	Managed Evolution of Infrastructure		129
	4.2	Technology Portfolio		131
	4.3	Platforms		138
		4.3.1 Platform Concept		138
		4.3.2 Platforms as Infrastructure Service Providers		139
		4.3.3 Application Development Support Processes		141
		4.3.4 Platforms Operation Processes		142
		4.3.5 Platform Management Processes		146
		4.3.6 Application Platforms and Runtime Platforms		148
	4.4	Operations		152
		4.4.1 Operational Challenge of Managed Evolution		153
		4.4.2 Componentization for Operations		153
		4.4.3 Autonomic Computing		155
		4.4.4 Configuration Management Database		158

Part II Organization and Management Processes for the Execution of Managed Evolution

5	**Business-IT Alignment**		163
	5.1 Managed Evolution and Business-IT Alignment	163
	5.2 Limitations of Hierarchical IT Governance	167

		5.3 Matching Roles: Balance of Power	168
		5.4 Governance Models for Project Portfolio Management	173
		5.5 Business-IT Alignment Processes	178
		5.5.1 Strategic Business-IT Alignment Process	178
		5.5.2 Project Portfolio Management Process	183
		5.5.3 Project Management Process	185
6	**People, Culture and Organization**		187
	6.1	People and Skills	187
	6.2	Culture and Values	192
	6.3	IT Organization	196
		6.3.1 IT Organization Embedding	196
		6.3.2 Interaction of IT Functions	198
		6.3.3 Strengthening System-Wide Consistency Through Organization	201
		6.3.4 Checks and Balances	202
7	**Measuring the Managed Evolution**		203
	7.1	Introduction	203
	7.2	Measuring Change Drivers and Enablers	205
	7.3	Measuring System Properties	210
	7.4	Measuring Managed Evolution Strategy	216
	7.5	Impact Factors on Agility	224

Part III Summary, Conclusions and Outlook

8	**Conclusions and Outlook**		229
	8.1	Summary of Key Points	229
	8.2	Outlook	232

References	235
Glossary	247
Abbreviations	257
Index	259

List of Figures

Fig. 1.1	Parts and connections in a system	6
Fig. 1.2	Growth of number of connections between parts of a system	8
Fig. 1.3	Boundary of a very large information system	10
Fig. 1.4	Growth of Java code base in Credit Suisse	13
Fig. 1.5	System evolution coordinate system	16
Fig. 1.6	Evolution curve with the desired system state	18
Fig. 1.7	Core idea of managed evolution	24
Fig. 1.8	Problem statement – original slide 1998	28
Fig. 1.9	Solution space – original slide 1998	28
Fig. 2.1	Architecture layers	41
Fig. 2.2	The Credit Suisse business component map – original slide	45
Fig. 2.3	Categories of the Credit Suisse 2009 domain model	49
Fig. 2.4	The Credit Suisse 2009 domain model	50
Fig. 2.5	Business component map and application domain model relationship	52
Fig. 2.6	BOM abstraction and aggregation levels in Credit Suisse	54
Fig. 2.7	Credit Suisse enterprise level business object model	55
Fig. 2.8	Business object model of the domain "customer and partner"	58
Fig. 2.9	Technical domain model	59
Fig. 2.10	Vertical architecture areas	61
Fig. 2.11	Credit Suisse security architecture	63
Fig. 2.12	Architecture process	65
Fig. 2.13	Credit Suisse federated architecture functions	75
Fig. 3.1	Four integration contexts	84
Fig. 3.2	Component layering	87
Fig. 3.3	Connections (usage) between components	89
Fig. 3.4	Front solution components	90
Fig. 3.5	Component business object "address"	99
Fig. 3.6	Technical and application integration	101
Fig. 3.7	Interface and service	103

Fig. 3.8	Service versioning	110
Fig. 3.9	Service management process	112
Fig. 3.10	Service management system elements	115
Fig. 3.11	The Credit Suisse enterprise service bus CSXB	119
Fig. 3.12	Usage of exchange infrastructure (CORBA)	120
Fig. 3.13	Commercial off-the-shelf software integration	121
Fig. 3.14	Mainframe application disentangling	127
Fig. 4.1	Infrastructure strategy	131
Fig. 4.2	The two dimensions of the technology portfolio	132
Fig. 4.3	Mainstream technology	133
Fig. 4.4	Platform process map	140
Fig. 4.5	Technical components of a platform	142
Fig. 4.6	Development tool chain	143
Fig. 4.7	Platform systems management ecosystem	144
Fig. 4.8	Synchronized lifecycles of platforms and business applications	146
Fig. 4.9	JAP adoption history	148
Fig. 4.10	Platforms	149
Fig. 4.11	Java platform reference architecture for Internet applications	150
Fig. 4.12	Autonomic component	157
Fig. 4.13	Automatic discovery of components	159
Fig. 5.1	Hierarchical governance model	168
Fig. 5.2	Committees, roles and processes in the governance model	170
Fig. 5.3	Credit Suisse CIO basket	171
Fig. 5.4	Business basket governance model	174
Fig. 5.5	Domain basket governance model	175
Fig. 5.6	360° Application domain analysis	177
Fig. 5.7	Result of the domain assessment for domain BAS	177
Fig. 6.1	Positioning of the three IT disciplines	195
Fig. 6.2	Boundaries and interfaces between core IT functions	199
Fig. 7.1	Measurement for managed evolution	204
Fig. 7.2	Efficiency of the architecture communication process	207
Fig. 7.3	IT architecture survey result example 1	208
Fig. 7.4	IT architecture survey result example 2	208
Fig. 7.5	CORBA-based services reuse statistics	213
Fig. 7.6	System evolution mechanism	217
Fig. 7.7	Measurement periods for time to market and development cost	219
Fig. 7.8	Credit Suisse Switzerland use case point measurement method	220
Fig. 7.9	Credit Suisse Switzerland time to market and development cost for 17 quarters	223
Fig. 7.10	Credit Suisse Switzerland agility measurements for 17 quarters	223
Fig. 7.11	Agility for projects using and not using special engineering	225

List of Tables

Table 2.1	Application landscape architecture principles for multi-country capability	40
Table 2.2	Description of Credit Suisse enterprise level business objects	56
Table 2.3	Credit Suisse IT architecture review checklist (Extract)	69
Table 3.1	Semantic specification of "colour red"	98
Table 3.2	Extract of the DSS service call syntactical specification (XML Schema)	105
Table 3.3	SLA for the service "getCustomer"	108
Table 3.4	Definition of the information type "date"	116
Table 4.1	Technical product architecture and lifecycle status	137
Table 4.2	Technical product version record	137
Table 4.3	OLA for JAP Application Platform	145
Table 6.1	Employee rating in the Credit Suisse Career Tracks	191
Table 6.2	The Credit Suisse career tracks	191
Table 7.1	Credit Suisse Switzerland IT architecture scorecard	214

List of Side Stories

Side-Story 1.1: Credit Suisse Global Banking System 12
Side-Story 1.2: Credit Suisse and Clariden-Leu Merger 20
Side-Story 1.3: Credit Suisse Decision for Managed Evolution 26
Side-Story 2.1: Multi-Country Capability Architecture 39
Side-Story 2.2: Credit Suisse Business Component Map (BCM) 44
Side-Story 2.3: Credit Suisse Domain Model with the
 Main Design Considerations 48
Side-Story 2.4. Relationship Between CDM and BCM 51
Side-Story 2.5: Credit Suisse Business Object Model 53
Side-Story 2.6. Credit Suisse Security Architecture 62
Side-Story 2.7. Credit Suisse Architecture Communication Process 67
Side-Story 2.8. Credit Suisse Check List for Architecture Reviews 68
Side-Story 2.9: Credit Suisse IT Architecture Organization 74
Side-Story 3.1: Credit Suisse Global Front Systems 89
Side-Story 3.2: Semantic Color Specification 97
Side-Story 3.3: Service Definition Using Business Objects 98
Side-Story 3.4: Formal Syntax Specification of an Interface Using XML
 Schema 104
Side-Story 3.5: Example of a Credit Suisse Service Level Agreement 108
Side-Story 3.6: Credit Suisse Service Management System IFMS 114
Side-Story 3.7: The Credit Suisse Integration Infrastructure CSXB 118
Side-Story 3.8: Banking Industry Architecture Network (BIAN) 122
Side-Story 3.9: Disentangling the Mainframe Applications (DiMA) 126
Side-Story 4.1: Credit Suisse Technology Portfolio Management 136
Side-Story 4.2: Credit Suisse Operation Level Agreement 144
Side-Story 4.3: JAVA Application Platform Adoption 147
Side-Story 4.4: Credit Suisse Java Application Platform (JAP) 149
Side-Story 5.1: Credit Suisse Basket Governance Model for CIO Basket ... 170
Side-Story 5.2: Credit Suisse Domain Assessment 2009 176
Side-Story 5.3: Credit Suisse Switzerland Architecture Program 2010 182

Side-Story 6.1: Credit Suisse Strategic IT Training 188
Side-Story 6.2: Credit Suisse Career Tracks 190
Side-Story 7.1: Credit Suisse Career Tracks 206
Side-Story 7.2: CORBA-Based Service Seuse 212
Side-Story 7.3: Credit Suisse Switzerland Architecture Scorecard 214
Side-Story 7.4: Credit Suisse Switzerland UCP Measurement 219
Side-Story 7.5: Credit Suisse Switzerland Agility Measurements
 for 17 Quarters 222
Side-Story 7.6: Credit Suisse Single Factor Analysis for Agility 225

Part I
Structure, Properties, Challenges and Architecture of Very Large Information Systems

Chapter 1
Very Large Information System Challenge

Summary This chapter introduces the notion and the properties of a very large information system. Complexity is one key property of such systems. The source and the consequences of complexity are elaborated. The complexity trap is introduced which leads a very large information system over the years to become unmanageable, i.e. delivering less and less business value per investment and becoming less and less modifiable. The complexity trap is shown to be an unavoidable consequence of opportunistic evolution of very large information systems. Alternative evolution strategies of system replacement and of greenfield approach are demonstrated to be applicable only in very specific situations, such as mergers. The only successful and sustainable evolution strategy for very large information systems is managed evolution. Managed evolution is introduced and its context, motivation, paradigms and elements are described as a tour d'horizon. The individual topics are refined in the following chapters of the book.

1.1 Background

Information technology has become an indispensable tool for almost any kind of business. It has gained particular importance for industries whose exclusive business it is to deal with information. This might be in the field of producing content such as the media, transporting content such as the telecom industry, or processing special kinds of information, such as the finance industry. Typically, information technology accounts for 15% of a financial services company operating expenses and up to a quarter of the employees are information system specialists. Wrong operational or strategic decisions may threaten the success of such a business. With the level of integration and automation we see in modern business processes, failures in systems have far reaching consequences. It is fair to say that in many aspects the modern world is dependent on reliable, properly operating systems.

Some industries, like banking, airlines, or the military were very early adopters of information technology [Neukom_04]. These industries started building such systems 50–60 years ago. The mid-1950s witnessed the emergence of commercial computers. Since then, more industries continued to extend the functionality of the

> "Legacy components may contain genuine value. More often enterprises resist the investment to rewrite or migrate legacy systems, thus putting at risk the business that the systems support since the business is forced to align to the system and not vice versa"
> Willem-Jan van den Heuvel, 2007

systems and kept integrating more and more data. Very often the growth has led to very complex systems that are hard to understand, difficult to maintain and strongly resist extensions. These systems contain a massive amount of implicit knowledge that is hard to extract and manage, because the initial designers are no longer available and the documentation is not as good as it should be. Such systems are known as *legacy systems* ([Heuvel_07], [Brodie_95], [Masak_06]). Very often "legacy" has a negative connotation in this context. It is, however, important to recognize that only systems that have been used successfully over many years earn the title "legacy". So, at least at the time of their inception, they were usually successful designs. As time went by and more and more functionality was packed into the systems, often the initial structure proved to be no longer viable, or the second and third generation of engineers no longer understood the initial design, so that more and more design noise was introduced. As a consequence many of the early adopters of information technology sit on complex legacy systems that are hard to maintain and difficult to evolve. Often they are built on technologies that are no longer mainstream, causing an increasing skills shortage and little support from the market.

Organizationally this leads to tension between the IT function and its business customers who have a hard time to understand why it is so slow and expensive to fulfill new business requirements in legacy systems. If the system is outdated, questions are why it can't be replaced at reasonable cost and why it costs more and more to run the systems, although they read that information technology is getting ever cheaper and more powerful. Often the specialists don't have the language to explain these issues, leading to a situation of bad communication and, eventually, mistrust. Modern organizations try to overcome this issue by setting up an institutionalized communication and decision framework, known under the term *IT Governance*.

This situation of a strong dependency on systems that are hard to understand and difficult to manage exists today in many organizations. Depending on the definition, the majority of all software in use would qualify as legacy. The three authors have spent the better part of their professional life managing this situation in the context of a large bank. While doing this, they developed a number of strategic, managerial and technical insights and methods that they found worth sharing with the community.

The remainder of the book deals with very large information systems. So, there is a need to define the term *very large information system* for the purpose of this book. A very large information system is a system consisting of a large number of components and many dependencies, being dynamically developed, with parts of considerable age and high importance for the business it serves. Such systems are inherently hard to manage for various reasons which will be shown later in the book. One aspect which is particularly hard to manage is system *complexity*.

This book is written from the perspective of an organization that mainly develops its own systems. This is the main background of the authors. Nevertheless, the authors have observed similar behaviour with very large information systems that were written as software products to be sold on the market ([Buxmann_08]). In such software development companies business requirements are not directly absorbed by the development organization. Instead, an intermediate product management function, which defines new releases according to customer requirements from the market, exists.

1.2 Complexity of Very Large Information Systems

Systems have grown significantly over the last 60 years ([Neukom_04]). Their complexity has exploded from isolated computers to global systems. Complexity is a difficult and intriguing concept. Many scientific disciplines define complexity for their own use, such as computational complexity, mathematical complexity, complexity in systems engineering or complexity in living organisms. In *systems theory* ([Schöning_08], [Evans_04], [Flood_93], [Maier_02], [Weinberg_01], [Adamsen_00]) – which is the scientific discipline for understanding very large information systems – basically the following definition of complexity is common:

> "Scale changes everything"
> Linda Northrop, 2006

Consisting of many different and connected parts

The two important concepts here are *part* and *connection* (Fig. 1.1). The parts of very large information systems are *applications* providing the business functionality and data and *technical components* constituting the *infrastructure*. The connections between the parts generate *dependencies*, such as *data flows* or *control flows*.

The main challenge for successfully developing a complex system is dealing with its *connections*: A change in a part of the system may propagate via connections to other parts of the system and possibly force a change on the connected parts. In a very large information system the connections cause the following *dependencies* among the parts:

- *Functional* dependencies: A change in the functionality of a part may have unknown, unforeseen and possibly damaging consequences for other parts. Example: A bank wants to change the structure of its product catalog. The product catalog contains information about the bank's products, interest rates, applicable fees, etc. Banking *products* are, e.g., account and deposit keeping, execution of payments and stock exchange transactions for customers, issuing credit and debit

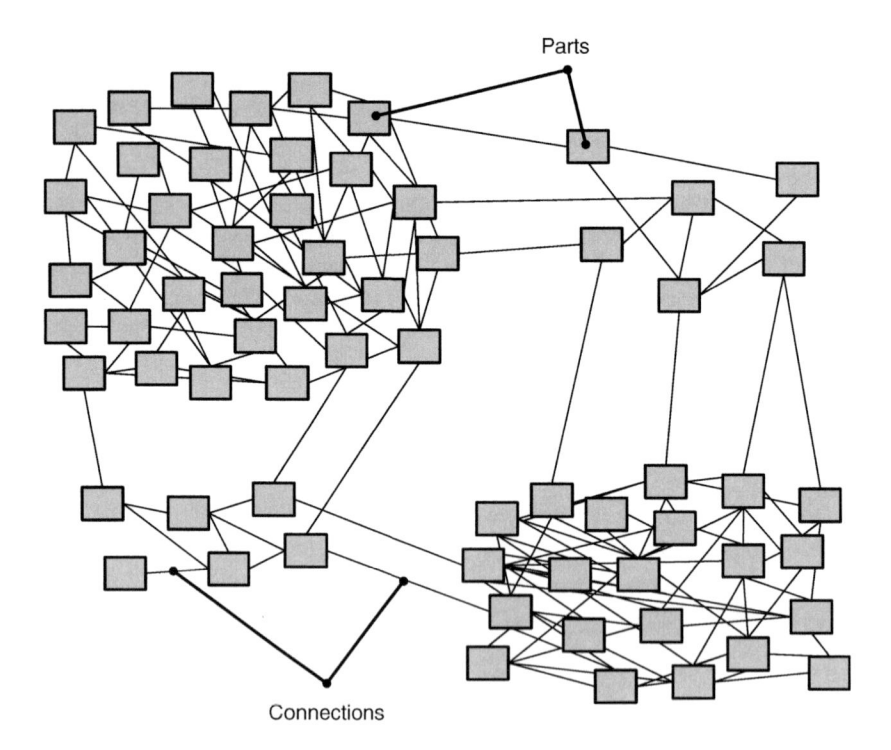

Fig. 1.1 Parts and connections in a system

cards, granting loans and mortgages, etc. Before this planned functional change, all processing applications had their own, different implementation of product representation. The centralized provision of this information forces all the processing applications to reprogram their functionality and to use the information provided by the central service – resulting in a massive functional change in a large number of applications. The consequence of larger functional changes is a careful migration plan, so that applications can be modified over time and "old" and "new" functionality can coexist over the migration period.

- *Semantic* dependencies: The meaning of a term or data element must be explicitly clear and unambiguous among all users of the term or data element. If the provider of the data element changes or extends the meaning, all users of the data element must be made aware of this and possibly adapt their processing. As an example, for a long time the only currency used for bookkeeping in banking systems was the local currency, such as Swiss Francs in Switzerland: All data elements "amount" implicitly were local currency. Globalization forced systems to allow for different bookkeeping currencies – the "amount" now could represent Swiss Francs, American Dollars, English Pounds, Euros. The implicit semantic meaning was lost! Unambiguous semantic had to be redefined by the extension of the data element "amount" to "currencyCode, amount". Each amount was categorized by its currency code. Currency codes are standardized

1.2 Complexity of Very Large Information Systems

worldwide by the International Standards Organization (ISO), thus establishing global semantics for amounts. The consequence is that all terms and data used in the system must be semantically defined.

- *Temporal* dependencies: A change in a part of the system may require changes in other parts of the system at the *same* time. The consequence of this *temporal dependency* is that the system cannot operate properly as long as *all* changes have not been consistently implemented in the affected parts. Example: A few years ago the IBAN (International Banking Account Number) was introduced. This format for account numbers unified the numbering system globally and made routing and processing much simpler. All banks had to convert to IBAN and the system was only globally usable when the last bank had adopted IBAN. The consequence is careful planning of changes that have temporal dependencies.
- *Technical* dependencies: The parts of very large information systems are connected through different technologies for the exchange of data or the propagation of control flows. The interconnection technologies transport, route and convert the information between the applications and also between different technical platforms. Unfortunately, different systems and different vendors use different standards, such as for formatting data or for the interchange protocols. Interoperability must therefore be enabled by conversion and transformation, thus creating a dependency on the underlying technology. Another area of technical dependency is the building blocks of the run-time environments, such as operating systems, data base technology and compilers. The risk of this technical dependency is that applications may have to be adapted whenever technical infrastructure components change.
- *Operational* dependencies: During execution time of the applications, each application or component is dependent on other applications, components or infrastructure elements. If one of those fails or becomes unavailable, the application may not function properly anymore. Example: Many banking applications running on decentralized servers need access to the customer information located on one server. If this server is temporarily unavailable, these applications stop. The consequence is to identify such operational dependencies and to eliminate them through suitable mechanisms, such as managed redundancy.

Each connection in the system generates dependencies, very often more than one dependency at the same time, such as a functional and an operational dependency. If the connections are not properly managed, the number of connections may get out of hand and the number of dependencies may grow to a state where the system becomes highly inflexible. The complexity of very large information systems increases with the number of connections and with the number of dependencies generated by each connection. If this fact is not managed, the system complexity may reach a point that is no longer manageable and where the system's evolution is at an end.

The number of parts grows with increasing size of the system. The number of possible connections between the parts grows even faster. Each new part can potentially be connected to all existing parts. The number of connections in this worst case increases faster than linear when the number of parts becomes larger: In this case it becomes $n*(n-1)/2$, meaning that it increases in the order of n^2 as illustrated in Fig. 1.2. Complex systems may, therefore, have a very large number of connections making their evolution very hard to understand, plan, document, execute and control.

Experience shows that continuously grown very large information systems have more parts than necessary, often due to redundancy, and also more connections than necessary often related to overlapping control or

> "For every 25% increase in the complexity of the problem space, there is a 100% increase in the complexity of the solutions space" [Glass's Law]
> R. Woodfield, 1979/Roger Sessions, 2008

data flows, as well as too many and often tight dependencies generated by the connections. At the start of any evolution phase, the system architects, engineers and developers are in many cases confronted with an overly complicated system with too many parts, connections and dependencies, resulting in a *system complexity* which is hard to understand, difficult to document and risky to change.

One difficult architecture and engineering requirement in such a situation is *simplification*. The system architects must try to reduce the number of parts and the number of connections in the system. There is, however, a lower limit to the number of parts and to the lowest number of connections in a system. This lower limit is

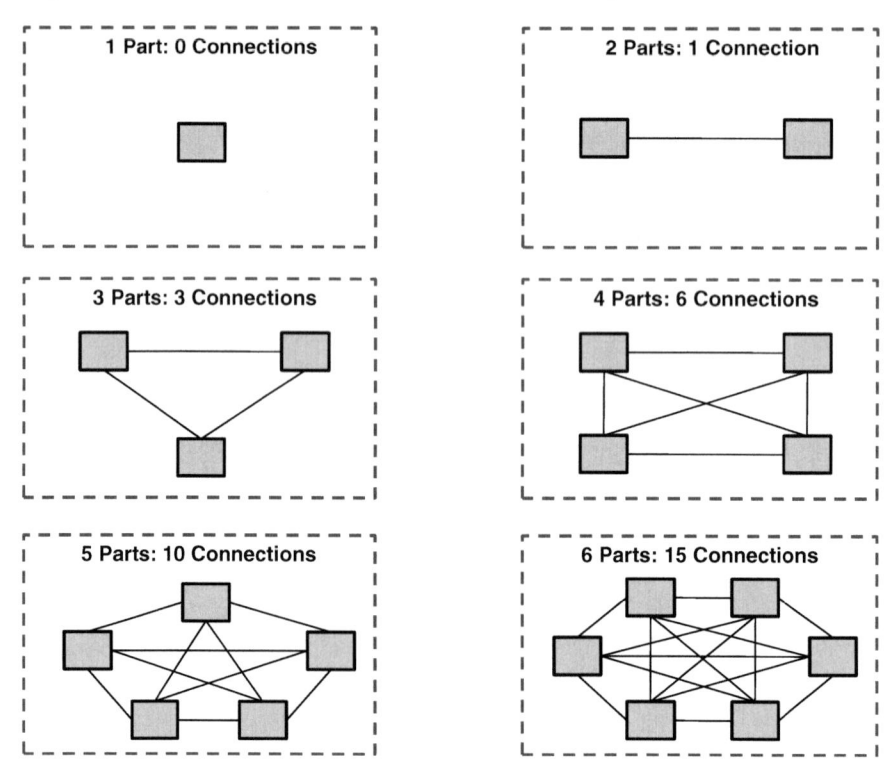

Fig. 1.2 Growth of number of connections between parts of a system

given by the functionality of the system: The system will not be able to work properly if one more part or one more connection is removed.

Once the number of parts and the number of connections have been reduced as much as possible, the *topological system complexity* is as low as possible. An interesting approach and process to systematically find the solution with the least topological complexity for a given set of specifications has been proposed by Roger Sessions ([Sessions_08], [Sessions_09]). Roger Sessions also introduces a system complexity metric that measures both the topological system complexity as a consequence of the number of parts and connections and the functional complexity as a consequence of the amount of functionality. This system complexity metric shows the impact of minimizing the number of parts and connections while architecting a solution for a given set of requirements.

The next step in mastering system complexity is properly managing the dependencies, such as introducing loose coupling ([Kaye_03]). The often multiple *dependencies* created through the connections – functional, semantic, temporal, technical or operational dependencies – must be implemented *intelligently*. This is where the power of a well-designed application architecture (Sect. 2.5) and integration architecture (Chap. 3) comes into play.

Although Fig. 1.2 shows the worst case for the number of connections between parts, the fact remains, that very large information systems consist of a very large number of parts and therefore have a very large number of dependencies too. Modern information systems are connected to the Internet, which creates potentially limitless dependencies. In practice, the main external dependencies are to suppliers and customers systems. It is therefore important to understand these dependencies and to define the system boundary in such a way as to have control over the most impacting external dependencies, specifically dependencies over which the organization has no or only limited governance.

With respect to managed evolution, the *system boundary* of the very large information system under consideration must be defined such that no important parts and no important dependencies remain unmanaged, that is are not governed by the concepts of integration architecture (as defined in Chap. 3). A useful guidance is the *density* of dependencies generated by the connections (Fig. 1.3): Regions with a high density of dependencies should be within the system boundary. Thus, the cuts should be made where few dependencies are present. Interfaces crossing the system boundary are particularly hard to manage and require special attention.

For managed evolution it is important that organization and governance are aligned to the system boundary. If this is not the case, then the whole system cannot be transformed by managed evolution, because interests of different stakeholders will force divergence.

1.3 Properties of Very Large Information Systems

System complexity resulting from a large number of parts that are dependent on each other via their connections (see Sect. 1.2) is the most obvious *property* of

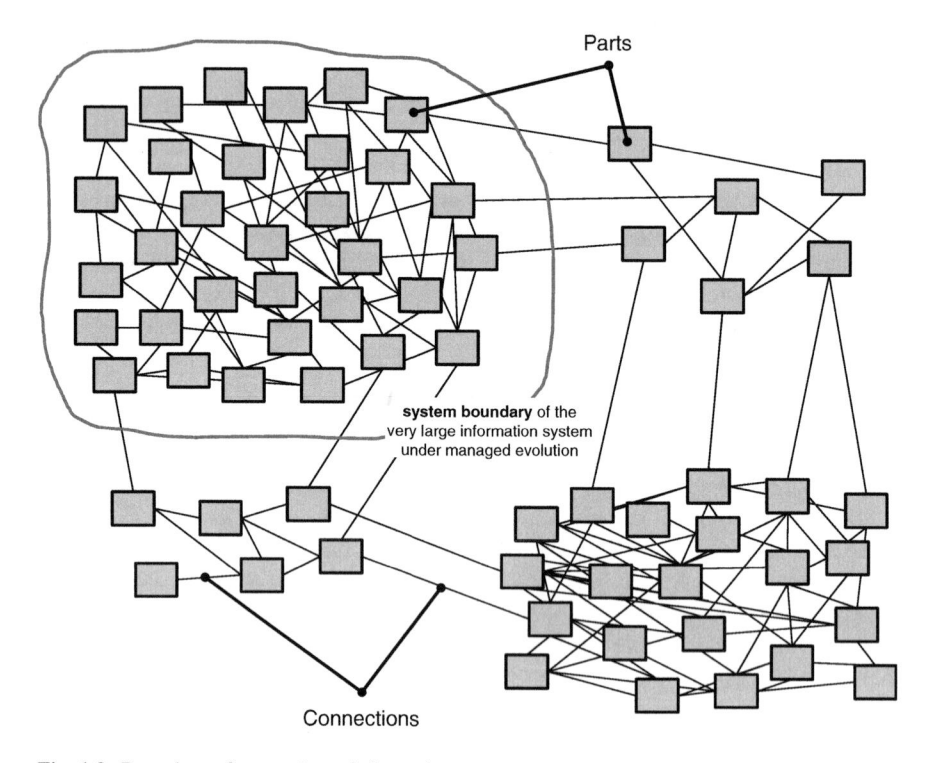

Fig. 1.3 Boundary of a very large information system

a very large information system. However, a very large information system cannot be characterized by its system complexity alone. A number of other properties have to be considered which contribute to the challenge to manage very large information systems. The properties include functional size, percentage of legacy code, rate of change, system value, mission criticality, diversity of its technology base, governance and organization. The properties are explained here and their influence on different evolution approaches is shown later.

The second property of very large information systems is their *functional size*. Functional size can be expressed in a number of ways, such as the number of source lines of code (SLOC, see [Boehm_00]), the number of function points (#FP, see [Garmus_01]), or the number of use case points (#UCP, see [Anda_08]). As a rule of thumb, systems with more than a few Million SLOCs are considered very large information systems in the context of this book. Size matters because the size of individual parts is limited and therefore large systems consist of many parts and connections.

Systems grow over many years to become very large information systems. Therefore such systems contain substantial amounts of *legacy code*: The third property is the functional size of the legacy part of the very large information system, which can again be measured as shown above. Therefore, substantial parts of the system need to be completely replaced or reengineered because of aging technology and structural erosion. Typically, a system cannot efficiently be extended without structural change for more than 10 years. Again, this is a rule of thumb and depending on the business context, the change rate and the long-term vision of the initial architects, the point of structural breakdown may be reached after 5 or after 20 years. The important point is that the system has gone beyond this point. Legacy code has eventually to be replaced because legacy parts resist modifications to an extent where it is no longer economically feasible to add functionality to them. In many cases, the high operational cost and the lower reliability of such legacy parts become inacceptable for the organization.

The fourth property impacting systems is today's high, business-driven *number of changes*. The change rate impacting the system may be difficult to absorb and to implement without compromising other system properties, such as availability, security or performance. The business depends on a timely implementation of modifications. The system may become a limiting factor for business growth and business strategy implementation if this is not the case.

A consequence of size and age is the *value* of the system, which is the fifth property: During the many years of evolution, continuous investments have been made, adding new functionality and increasing the value of the system year by year. Very large information systems therefore have a high replacement cost for a fully functional system replacement, including non-functional properties. As an example, the replacement cost of a very large financial services system is considered to be three to five billion Swiss Francs.

Very large information systems in most cases serve and enable viable businesses that cannot operate when the system is unavailable. This leads to a considerable degree of *mission criticality*. Mission criticality is therefore the sixth property of the system. Mission criticality is often expressed as the non-availability time span that is acceptable to the business. Another indication for mission criticality is the number of users that are dependent on the availability of the system. Modifications to such systems introduce an element of *risk*: Any change may jeopardize the mission by degradation of the system properties, such as availability or stability. Large changes constitute a larger risk.

The seventh property is infrastructure proliferation: Due to their size and age very large information systems have heterogeneity of the *technology base*, which is damaging to flexibility. The system relies on a number of different technologies that generate dependencies between infrastructure and applications. Underlying infrastructure technology can only be changed or modernized in controlled, limited steps because of the impact on the application landscape.

The eighth property is the type of *governance*: As very large information systems live longer than organizational structures and because such systems are serving large organizations, fragmented governance structures and distributed company organizations result. The type of *governance* is a property that strongly impacts the applicable evolution approach. Systems are often under federated governance, meaning that the ownership and responsibility for system parts is assigned to different parts of the organization with no or little centralized control. Global changes are difficult due to conflicting interests of owners and distributed budget ownership. Coor-

> "Imagine, we started out doing SOA and ended up fixing our enterprise governance along the way"
> Eric A. Marks, 2008

dinated development of very large information systems under federated governance is impossible without a certain degree of central control.

Similar to governance, the structure of the IT *organization* constitutes the ninth important property of the very large information system. The system is owned and operated by a large, federated organization. Different parts of the system are often under governance, ownership, budget authority and responsibility of different organization units with no or little centralized control. Strict centralized control is not an option in such situations.

As a summary, we define *very large information systems* as:

Functionally rich, having a long development history, containing significant legacy parts which need to be replaced or reengineered, being exposed to a high rate of change, having high replacement cost, thus representing a high value to their owners, relying on heterogeneous technologies, being mission critical, having a large number of stakeholders resulting in a federated governance and often in a distributed IT organization.

Most successful, long-term users or vendors of information technology have very large information systems in operation and under development. One well-known example is the US air traffic control system ([Duke_05], [Hite_04], [Farrell_08]). But one can find such systems in every large bank or telecom operator, but also with successful software vendors such as Microsoft, Oracle or SAP. All these systems face the challenge of change and evolution and need a sustainable evolution approach.

Today this challenge can mainly be experienced in industries that have a long-standing tradition of relying heavily on information technology. It is, however, very probable that successful players in industries that have only recently built very large information systems, like large e-commerce and web-companies, will find themselves in the same situation 5–10 years from now.

As an example of a very large information system the Credit Suisse system is described in Side-Story 1.1.

Side-Story 1.1: Credit Suisse Global Banking System

This side story gives an example of a very large information system. Actually, the authors have spent the better part of their professional careers shaping this system. Most of what they write about in this book is based on this experience.

Credit Suisse is a global bank headquartered in Switzerland, operating around the globe. Its main hubs are Zürich, New York, London, Hong Kong and Singapore. In total there are branches and subsidiaries in over

50 countries. Credit Suisse is organized as a global bank with three client-facing business units: *Asset Management* serving institutional investors, *Investment Banking* serving the capital markets, and *Private Banking* serving wealthy individuals and families. For a number of years Credit Suisse has implemented a "one bank" strategy providing a number of shared services, including IT from a centralized shared services organization. Credit Suisse has 48'000 employees around the world, of which roughly 20% work for the information technology unit.

Integrated banks need global processes and tightly integrated systems in order to always be able to understand key figures for bank management in real time and to be able to react quickly across all global markets. This is a challenge, because the needed functionality is extremely rich, as represented by an application portfolio consisting of more than 5'000 business applications. A large part of these applications have been developed in-house, as only a limited market for such systems exists. The total code base of Credit Suisse exceeds 100 million source lines of code written mainly in Java, C#, C++ and PL/1. As an example, the growth of the Java code is shown in Fig. 1.4. The impressive growth is partly due to new functionality, but also due to a refactoring of PL/1 applications to Java. Data is stored in thousands of production databases. Several ten thousands of interfaces connect the applications.

The system is not standing still. Hundreds of projects, with a total yearly cost of more than one billion Swiss francs keep changing the system. We estimate that roughly 10% of the whole system is being replaced every year. These changes result in more than 3'000 production changes every week.

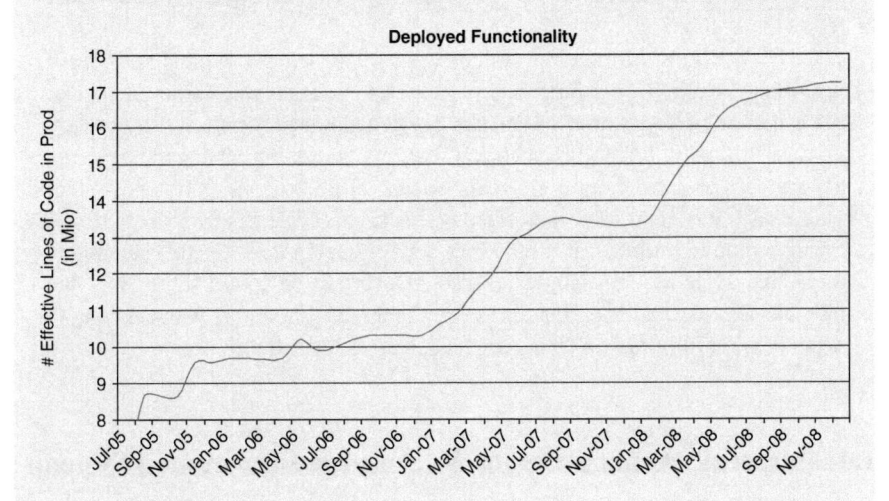

Fig. 1.4 Growth of Java code base in Credit Suisse

Despite the fast change, the sensitive nature of the business requires that the highest standards of availability, business continuity and security are met. Many of the business services are offered to the customers through Internet banking applications. Many hundreds of thousands of clients trust these applications to conduct business and have their data protected by the quality of Credit Suisse's infrastructure and applications. Experience shows that Credit Suisse's systems – as all Internet-facing systems – are being attacked every day from the Internet. Regulators expect the highest availability standards, as Credit Suisse's systems are seen as critical for the continuous operation of the financial markets in many regions.

Servers are hosted in a number of data centers around the globe with major hubs in Switzerland, the US, the UK and Singapore. Applications are run on more than 22'000 servers. Data is held on more than 7'600 terabytes of storage. Internal staff uses 70'000 personal computers all connected to the internal network across 500 buildings worldwide. Often local operations are required for regulatory reasons or reduced latency to the exchanges. To be competitive, low-latency trading systems must be able to react to changes in the market with latencies of a few milliseconds in order to execute client-trading orders immediately following a favorable price change.

As a bank, Credit Suisse's main production factor has always been intelligent handling of information about assets, such as private banking, investment banking and asset management for its customers. Therefore, Credit Suisse has been an early adopter of information technology, with roots all the way back to the 1970s [Neukom_04]. This poses the general challenge that parts of the system are outdated and need to be replaced. Credit Suisse applies the managed evolution methodology to continuously improve and renew its systems.

Credit Suisse's information system is in many ways a typical very large information system. It is functionally very rich, consists of a large number of parts that are tightly connected and has a significant legacy part. It is absolutely mission critical in many dimensions, even beyond the borders of the bank. Its history goes back over almost 40 years; so that it fulfills the property of a system whose parts have partially exceeded their useful lifecycle. As the system serves a very dynamic business, it is still very actively being developed. The authors think that systems with similar characteristics can be found throughout the financial services industry, but also within other early adopters who are heavily dependent on information technology, such as airlines or defense.

1.4 Strategic Approaches for Very Large Information Systems

Typically organizations start to realize the challenge posed by very large information systems when it gets harder and harder to implement new business requirements and to maintain production stability at the necessary levels. Technically, the data

1.4 Strategic Approaches for Very Large Information Systems

models no longer properly reflect the business, the number of connections grows beyond control and outdated technologies pose unnecessary risks. Other indicators include lack of skills for old technologies and applications, incomplete or missing documentation, unfulfilled service level agreements and decreasing levels of user satisfaction. Very often, this is accompanied with a crisis of the whole organization. The system no longer delivers, as it should. People start talking about the system having reached the end of its *lifecycle*. Often a vigorous debate splits the organization: Some want to fully replace the system by a new one with the same functionality. This approach is known as the "greenfield" approach. Some don't see the problem and just want to continue as before. This, more often than not, is an amorphous collection of projects driven purely by uncoordinated business requirements.

At the latest, when the system has reached this dangerous state, the discussions about system evolution strategies should become serious. A fairly diverse literature related to *evolution* of systems exists ([Mens_08], [Lankhorst_05]). Some authors focus on the evolution or modernization of the legacy part of the system ([Ulrich _02], [Masak_06], [Heuvel_07], [Brodie_95], [Yang_03], [Miller_98],

> "The modernizing efforts of the NAS (US National Airspace System), called the Advanced Automation System (AAS), was suspended in 1994 because of software-related problems, after missing its initial deadline by several years and exceeding its budget by several billions of dollars"
> Bernd Bruegge, Allen H. Dutoit, 2000

[Warren_99], [Seacord_03]). The existing literature falls into two categories. The first category describes a desired architectural state of a system. The second category presents methods, processes and technologies for the modernization of legacy systems. Common to both is the emphasis on *system architecture*. The approach taken in this book combines and extends the material from the literature in the sense that a sustainable evolution strategy, which at the same time delivers new functionality and continuously modernizes the legacy parts of the very large information system, is presented.

A history of failed very large information system developments exist – although only few of them have been extensively published, see e.g., ([Charette_05], [Jones_95], [Bruegge_00], [Neukom_09a], [Neukom_09b], [Sessions_09], [Glass_97]).

In order to understand the dynamics behind the evolution of a system it is useful to show the evolution in two dimensions as in Fig. 1.5.

The x-axis in this graph denotes the *business value* of the system measured by the amount of useful functionality provided by the system. Along the y-axis, the *agility* of the information system is shown, as measured by the effort to add a certain amount of functionality to the system[1]. Agility is a property of the system

---

[1] The metrics are introduced in Chap. 7 (Measuring the Managed Evolution).

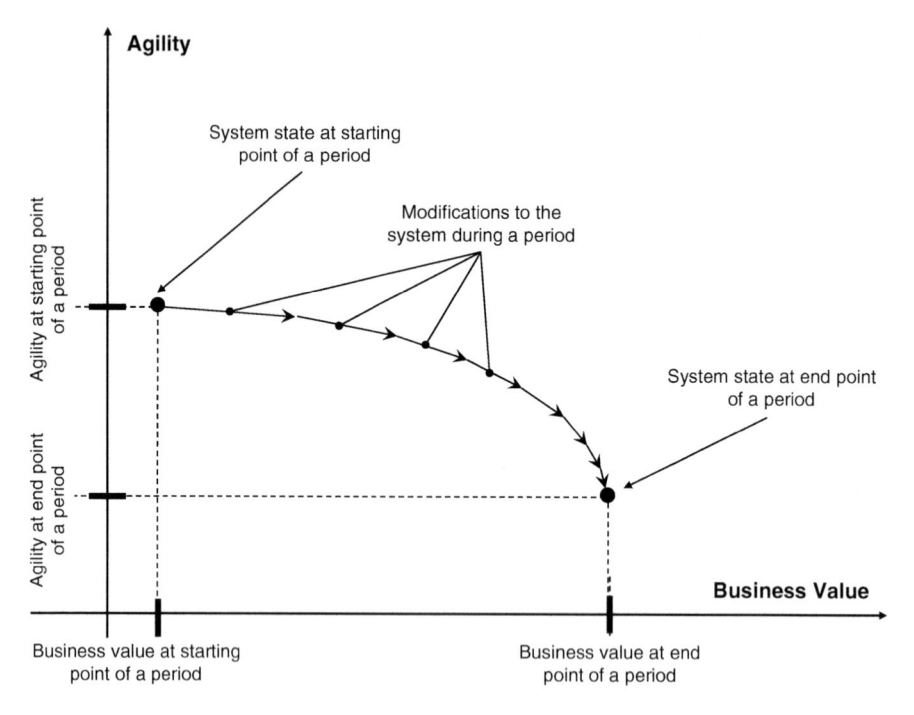

Fig. 1.5 System evolution coordinate system

as a whole and expresses the effort that must be invested to implement a "unit of change". "Unit of change" will be introduced and quantified in Chap. 7.

The arrows in Fig. 1.5 represent the *modifications* to the system. After each completion of a modification, the state of the system at a certain point in time is represented by a value on the business value axis and a value on the agility axis. Modifications in most cases increase the functionality of the system. The less intended effect of modifications is often that the same modifications decrease the agility of the system, with architecture erosion being one important reason.

As shown in Fig. 1.5 early modifications deliver a lot of functionality – represented by the horizontal length of the arrows – at the cost of a minor reduction of agility by slightly eroding the *architectural integrity* of the system. After many modifications this develops into a tailspin, ending in a situation where little functionality can only be added at high cost. The situation shown in Fig. 1.5 is typical for many systems that have evolved over a number of years with purely business driven modifications. The approach of *opportunistically* implementing business requirements cannot lead to a sustainable state. Such a way of developing systems obviously leads to disaster.

1.4.1 Opportunistic Approach

The main characteristic of the *opportunistic approach* to system evolution is a purely business-requirements driven project portfolio with little or no consideration for agility issues. Business requirements are implemented in the system where it takes least effort in money and time from the point of view of the project instead of where it should be from a conceptual integrity point of view. This small-scale approach focuses on the business' functional requirements and neglects non-functional properties and the overarching functionality, such as legal, audit and regulatory compliance support. The opportunistic approach is a "laissez faire" strategy, which requires the least effort and governance from all involved stakeholders.

> "The force of entropy means that uniform disorder is the only thing that happens automatically and by itself. If you want to create a completely ad hoc IT-architecture, you do not have to lift a finger.
> It will happen automatically as a result of day-to-day IT activity"
> Richard Hubert, 2002

This opportunistic approach produces some typical results, such as uncoordinated "*silo*"-*applications*[2] with massive redundancy and divergence in functionality, interfaces and data. This leads to excessive complexity. Such silo-applications are difficult to *integrate* and therefore incomplete and inconsistent vital *business information*, such as risk, customer data, and audit trails results. In addition, the development projects become increasingly *inefficient* because more and more effort is needed to integrate, synchronize and reconcile the data of the silo-applications. The *technology portfolio* is too broad, partially outdated and has substantial end-of-life problems. Due to outdated and widely diversified technology platforms and due to the high degree of overlaps in functionality and data of the silo-applications high *operating cost* results. Finally, hard to manage *operational dependencies* impair the availability and dependability of the system.

> "Complexity is difficult to manage, and most interesting systems are complex. The compounding of systems into systems of systems tends to introduce new complexities in the form of unexpected overlaps of parts and unexpected behaviour of previously well-behaved systems"
> Tim Weilkiens, 2006

The opportunistic approach drives the system into the *complexity trap*: As more and more functionality is added without regard to architectural principles for very large information systems, the system complexity increases continuously. More and more parts and dependencies are introduced in an uncoordinated way. As a consequence, the conceptual integrity and the agility of the system continuously decrease.

---

[2]"Silo"-applications are stand-alone, vertical stacks of applications and infrastructure, resulting in much redundancy and divergent technology portfolios ([Graves_08]).

The implementation of new functionality requires more and more effort. In parallel, the maintenance and operating cost of the system also increase steadily. The opportunistic approach leads to the disastrous evolution curve shown in Fig. 1.5. Once the system has progressed sufficiently on the downward evolution curve, difficulties start. The implementation of business requirements is slow and costly, the system becomes unstable and operating cost explodes. So, following an evolution curve as generated by the opportunistic approach is obviously not a good idea.

Figure 1.6 shows the *desired system state* in addition to the opportunistic system evolution curve. The desired state features a high agility and a high business value. To reach this desired state an *evolution strategy* for the very large information system must be developed, specified and consequently executed. The question here is to define an adequate strategy to solve the issues for the development over time of very large information systems.

A system in the very low agility and low business value state as shown in Fig. 1.5 must be brought back to a viable state as shown in Fig. 1.6. The system evolution curve must be corrected by the nearly vertical arrow, transforming the system into the desired state. Basically, this transformation can be executed by two approaches: The *replacement approach* and the *greenfield approach* which are described in the next two sections.

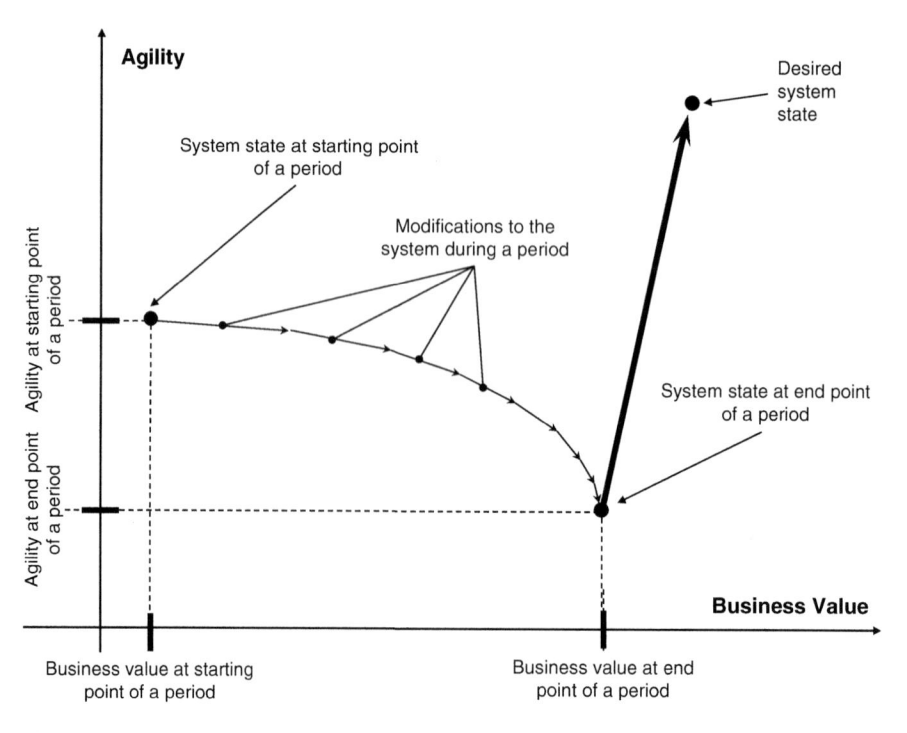

Fig. 1.6 Evolution curve with the desired system state

1.4.2 Replacement Approach

Because over the years the opportunistic approach has lead to a system with low agility and stagnating business value (Fig. 1.6) it is tempting to try to replace the system as a whole in order to reach the desired state: The replacement approach promises to get rid of the old, problematic system and to get a new, "perfect" one. The prerequisite for the success of this approach is the availability of a suitable system which replaces the complete functionality. There are several possible approaches to replace the system which shall be explained in the following.

If a *standard software package* with the required functionality and performance is available on the market, then it is possible to replace the system by this package. Unfortunately, more often than not, such packages cover only part of the required functionality. In such cases one has to take into consideration that the *integration costs* for the package into the existing IT environment are significant. Experience shows that the integration costs are easily three times the initial licensing costs. In practice it is often possible to replace parts of the system, such as enterprise resource planning (ERP) by standard software. For many very large information systems, however, no standard software covering the complete requirements is available. Therefore, replacement by standard software as a whole is often not feasible.

If no standard software package is available which fulfils the functional and performance needs of the business, one option could be to migrate to an *existing system* of another organization. This has successfully been done across various industries in merger and acquisition situations. After a merger or an acquisition there often is a strong business case for harmonizing processes and combining information systems. This encourages migrating of one party of the merger to the system of the other party. The selection of the target system is not only a technical or functional, but also a political decision. It is an observation that in most cases the system of the acquirer becomes the new common system. Very strong *governance* is for many reasons the key success factor in such situations. The skills and resources of the common system are available and can be prioritized, supporting successful migration. If these prerequisites are met, experience shows that a successful migration is possible within a reasonable time frame. The challenges of functional and technical size can be solved by good project management and by the assignment of sufficiently experienced staff. The downside of this approach, however, is that often the maintenance of the target system tends to be neglected because all resources are focused on the migration project. This may create new problems after the migration has been completed. This approach is only successful if the business adapts its products and processes to the target system because some capabilities of the old system may no longer be available. Another success factor for such a project is to postpone other modifications. Migrating and at the same time trying to implement functional changes is a high risk. Therefore, the project must be kept as short as possible, in order not to jeopardize other business opportunities. A successful merger example is given in Side-Story 1.2.

The case that an organization migrates to the existing system of another organization without a merger or acquisition background is theoretical. At least the authors do not know of any successful replacement as described above without the pressure of an acquisition or merger background. Such an attempt most probably fails for the following reasons: It is hardly possible to create sufficient motivation and governance for the migration of the old system and for holding off additional requirements during the migration project. The stakeholders of the target system want to develop their system in pace with new business requirements, whereas the stakeholders of the system to be replaced will not accept the implementation freeze for the duration of the migration project. They also oppose the need to adapt their accustomed products, processes and customer interactions to the target system. Resistance from both the business users and the IT department of the system to be replaced are expected.

Another merger-like scenario that allows for a successful replacement is the common development of a system by a number of partners. Successful examples exist in various industries, where medium and small organizations *outsource* their IT operations to a common, often jointly owned, service provider. The common service provider develops, maintains and operates the IT services required by its customers. This is successful in the long term for outsourcers with systems of limited complexity and with a moderate rate of change. Organizations with larger, more complex systems and at the same time the need to differentiate their offerings cannot – or can only partially – go down this path. Outsourcing non-differentiating functions, such as enterprise resource planning and human resource management is possible.

The key challenge with this model is that partners not benefitting from a specific change to be made at the request of one partner may resist the change. This may jeopardize the business opportunities of the requesting partner. In the experience of the authors, such conflicts of interest make governance very difficult and have actually led to the end of some commonly operated systems in the past.

Side-Story 1.2: Credit Suisse and Clariden-Leu Merger

In the discussion about realistic strategies for very large information systems the authors stated that, as an exception, a *replacement approach* is feasible in a merger or similar situation. In this case, the systems of one or multiple partners in the merger are being replaced completely by the proven system of one of the partners within a limited time frame.

In the year 2005 Credit Suisse decided to merge five independent private banks it owned into one new bank named Clariden-Leu (http://www.claridenleu.ch). Historically, this structure was caused by a number of acquisitions by Credit Suisse over many years and the strategy to keep the independence of these banks and their brands to cater to different customer segments.

All banks were internationally active and had branches in the main private banking hubs, such as Zurich, Singapore or Nassau. In 2005 the board reached the conclusion that this was no longer the most effective way forward and that a new structure was necessary. Three of the five banks already used the system of the mother company, Credit Suisse. Two banks had their own systems.

After some strategic considerations about operational independence from the mother company versus higher synergies, the decision was taken to bring all their banking operations to the strategic systems of Credit Suisse in the various locations. Technically that meant that the two banks with independent systems had to be migrated onto the existing Credit Suisse system. At the same time all five banks were merged into one unit. After the merger, the combined bank had roughly 100 billion Swiss Francs of assets under management from customers around the world.

The main challenge was that each bank had a rich history of special products, agreements and even individual solutions for clients. All in all this resulted in 1'500 different requirements, which had to be described, decided and implemented. The key to success was stringent project governance. Special requirements were scrutinized very thoroughly and only few extensions to the existing system or isolated special-purpose applications got approval. The project was to be completed within 18 months after the decision to go ahead. The objective was reached by successfully merging the various locations throughout 2007, with Switzerland being the most complex location completed in September 2007. The project was structured into 40 subprojects. More than 250 different applications had to be replaced and their data migrated. New infrastructure had to be deployed to roughly 2'000 workplaces around the world. All users had to be trained with the new applications without interrupting the daily business. More than 1'000 specialists were involved in the project.

This project was the last in a series of Credit Suisse system merger projects that followed the consolidation of the Swiss banking market in the 1990s. All these projects were technically and economically successful for the following reasons:

- The target system of Credit Suisse is mature, providing rich functionality, including multi-entity capability and was operated and developed by a capable support organization.
- The good business case and top management involvement in governance helped to drive the necessary reprioritization of projects to create the capacity for the execution of the migration projects.
- Short decision paths and strictly limited project duration helped in keeping the scope; i.e. not deviating from the focus.

1.4.3 Greenfield Approach

Section 1.4.2 described potentially successful situations for a replacement approach based on an available solution. If no such solution is available, one might be tempted to build a complete replacement on the *green field*. In a replacement approach the existing business processes and products have to be adapted to the capabilities of the available solution. In a greenfield approach, however, the development starts from specifications which are an improvement of the existing system capabilities.

The idea to build a new system from scratch – to start on a "green field" – in order to get rid of all the deficiencies of a legacy system is tempting: It seems possible to implement all the new functions desired, to base the system on the newest organizational set up and to use modern technology. In addition it is a big incentive and motivation for the IT crew to build a "perfect new world".

However, for very large information systems this is a very difficult approach. In various industries there are examples of failed greenfield approaches: In fact, the authors witnessed two major greenfield projects in their environment that completely failed. The author's assessment of the greenfield approach is based on these negative experiences and failed projects. One problem is that the duration of such a project is long: It takes at least 3–5 years – even with an optimistic plan. During the project duration the organization has to fully support the development and maintenance of two systems: All business requirements have to be implemented on both systems in parallel. If the decision is to implement new functionality only in the greenfield project, the pressure from the business side on the project increases with each postponed business requirement. The consequence is, that the adaption of the system to respond to new business requirements is more or less stopped for half a decade – until the completed greenfield system is put into operation.

An additional complication is that the technology base cannot be frozen for such a long development time: What appears to be the most modern technology at the start of the greenfield project may look fairly outdated at the completion of the project.

An idea often mentioned in this approach is to use the emerging, new system only for one business unit in the organization and to migrate all the other business units to the new greenfield system at the end of the project. The authors have no knowledge of a successful implementation of this unit-wise approach. It can be assumed that this procedure would make it even more difficult: In this case there would not be parallel development of two systems. The differing business requirements for the two systems would lead to a progressive divergence between the two systems, resulting in massive difficulties when the business functionality of the old system has to be migrated to the new system. A greenfield approach also creates a very difficult situation from a human resources perspective. The people and skills for the maintenance of the existing system have to be retained until the lights of the replaced system are switched off. In parallel, a whole new crew of people and skills for the development of the greenfield system must be built up and managed.

In addition, there is a motivation issue: People working on the new greenfield system are motivated and have a

> "A system replacement very often replaces known deficiencies of the old system by unknown and worse deficiencies of the new system"

good personal perspective for their future, whereas the "old system people" are obliged to maintain and develop a system with "no future". From a cost perspective the organization has to sponsor two systems in parallel that causes a lot of pressure on the projects. If the process to adapt continuously to new business requirements is not extremely strong and disciplined, the risk becomes very high that the greenfield system becomes outdated during its development and does not fulfill the stakeholders expectations when it is put into operation. The expectations are that the greenfield system is at least as good as the replaced system from Day One on! An additional problem is documentation: The documentation of the system to be replaced may (and usually is) poor and incomplete, which requires a massive amount of reverse engineering. And finally there is the risk that known old problems – present in the system to be replaced – are replaced by new, mostly unknown problems in the greenfield system.

The conclusion by the authors is that a greenfield approach is extremely difficult for very large information systems because it massively disrupts the working of the organization.

1.5 The Core Idea of Managed Evolution

So what should those do that can neither merge nor buy, who will not take the risk of a greenfield approach and have understood that the opportunistic approach does not work? Clearly, the answer must be based on an *evolutionary approach* because total replacements are impossible as explained above. Evolution means that the system changes gradually. There is no end of life for the system as a whole. Only parts are being replaced. Isn't this back to square one? Wasn't it exactly the evolutionary approach that led to an inefficient information technology system in the first place? Not if the concept of *managed evolution* is introduced: It combines the continuous delivery of new business value with the continuous improvement of agility.

The evolution of systems is driven by a number of external forces, especially a continuous flow of requirements for the implementation of new functionality and new technology, resulting in a considerable *rate of change* and at the same time the need to continuously enhance the efficiency of the system.

Figure 1.7 shows a different evolution curve that leads to the desired system state with more business value and higher agility at the *same* time. Higher agility will allow for creating more business value at lower cost and in shorter time, which will in turn allow for more investments creating even more value and so on. How can such a positive effect in a very large information system be created and sustained?

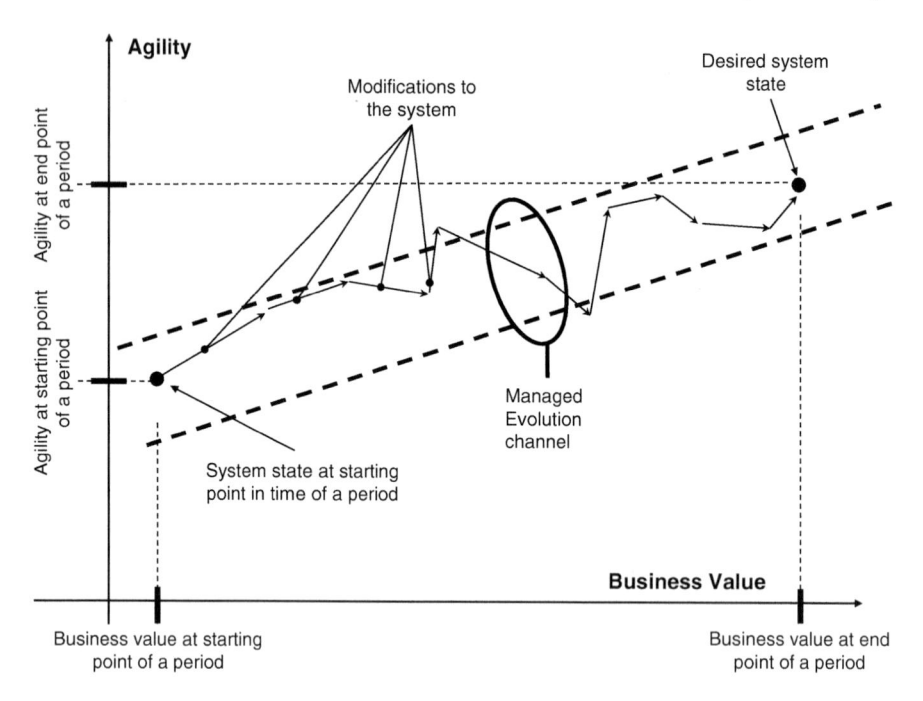

Fig. 1.7 Core idea of managed evolution

The solution is that most modifications should increase both business value *and* agility at the same time. This leads to a set of modifications, where even over a short period both values get continuously better. By doing so, no radical, risky projects are needed to bring the system back to a reasonable level of agility. This is symbolized by the *evolution channel* in Fig. 1.7. The idea of "managed evolution" is on the one hand to evolve the system without needing radical moves and on the other hand to manage this evolution such that the result of the portfolio of modifications remains within the managed evolution channel.

Examining the set of modifications in Fig. 1.7 more closely, one can see three categories of modifications:

1. Modifications with a moderately upward tilted slope arrow: These are the typical business modifications which deliver the requested functionality and at the same time implement the overall IT target architecture within their respective project scope. Each project is forced by the architecture process (see Sect. 2.8) to implement their deliverables in conformance with the set of IT standards, thus incrementally increasing the architectural quality of the system and resulting in a gain in agility. The additional effort for IT strategy conformance (see Sect. 5.5.1) compared to pure business requirements implementation may slightly slow down such modifications, but helps agility of the overall system. Whenever time-to-market considerations permit, this is the preferred way to deliver new business value.

1.5 The Core Idea of Managed Evolution

2. Modifications with a downward tilted arrow represent the situation where business value has to be implemented at the expense of agility. This should be avoided, where possible, but it happens in practice. As long as it is done on purpose and for good reasons, there is little problem with it.
3. Modifications with a steeply upward tilted arrow are modifications that are designed particularly to improve the agility of the system. Typical examples of such modifications are improving interfaces, reengineering data bases, removing redundant data and functionality, or moving applications to contemporary technology.

The desired improvements in architectural and conceptual integrity can be met by adhering to three *principles* of managed evolution:

1. Choose adequate, risk-managed *evolution steps*. Keep the number and volume of changes in any period to a safe, controllable level.
2. Balance the *investment* into the system between the development of new functionality, such as the implementation of business and stakeholder requirements, and the improvement of the agility, such as technology modernization, reengineering, architecture improvement.
3. Use adequate *metrics* to measure and control the progress towards the managed evolution objectives.

The core idea of managed evolution is the control of the portfolio of modifications such that over a certain period of time the executed modifications remain *within* the evolution channel of Fig. 1.7. In order to control the progress of the managed evolution strategy a quantitative framework is necessary. This metrics framework is described in Chap. 7 ("Measuring the Managed Evolution"). The specific choice of the two measurable system properties *agility* and *business value* is typical for very large information systems in industries with a high rate of change and a very high dependency of the business and its customers on the system, such as the financial industry. An important idea here is the view of *"multidimensional optimization"*: A number of measureable system properties – in our case the two properties agility and business value – are optimized at the same time according to a specified optimization objective (introduced in Sect. 1.5). A 3-dimensional or even n-dimensional optimization could be applicable to other types of systems or to other needs of the responsible organization. For other industries relying on very large information systems, other choices of system properties may be adequate as strategic metrics. As an example, in a large airline/hotel reservation system instead of the business value the cost per unit transaction, such as responding to an enquiry for seat availability and seat price on a certain flight, may be adequate. Instead of agility, a good metric may be the total response time per unit transaction, such as responding to the same query.

The purpose of this book is to explain what is needed to implement managed evolution for a very large information system in a large, global organization. Later in this book the necessary elements of managed evolution will be outlined.

The *decision* to follow managed evolution has far reaching consequences for an organization. In Side-Story 1.3 the sequence of events which led to the decision for managed evolution at Credit Suisse is described.

Side-Story 1.3: Credit Suisse Decision for Managed Evolution

Between 1985 and 1995 Credit Suisse successfully acquired different banks in Switzerland. The biggest of these acquisitions was Schweizerische Volksbank. Through this merger of the second largest Swiss bank (Credit Suisse) and the fourth largest (Schweizerische Volksbank) the new unit became a very large bank. The two merging banks both had their own, independent systems.

The decision with respect to the two systems was to exploit synergies and to migrate Swiss Volksbank IT to the Credit Suisse IT platform, keeping the data of the two banks strictly separated. The reason for this decision was the idea to develop each bank with a different business strategy. With this setup the applications were nearly identical – with growing divergence introduced over time because of individual enhancements. Data was still kept completely separate.

The impact on the system of this very demanding merger project, which lasted 2 years, was manifold: First, all skilled resources had been allocated to the project (with extra pay for the successful execution of the merger project). The second impact was a significant increase in complexity that caused more and more availability problems for the existing systems. With all the resources absorbed in the merger project, the maintenance and enhancement of the existing systems had been neglected. At the end of the merger project the resulting system could not support the business requirements and business changes in a satisfactory manner anymore. Heavy outages, bad response times and long lasting development projects were among the worst consequences.

Because of the difficulties after the merger project, a *greenfield approach* (see 1.4.2) had gained many influential supporters. A project was started, but was abandoned after 2 difficult years. An organizational split of the business into different business units requesting different IT approaches followed, which made the situation even worse. Which were the reasons for this failure? First, the greenfield approach was launched with a poor analysis of the issues of the existing, legacy system. The common understanding was that the existing complexity was too high to be significantly reduced. However, the complexity had never been analyzed beyond this superficial statement. The project leaders viewed the system as being at the end of its lifecycle. A further issue was that it seemed not possible to define and build the new system with modern technologies, because the developers that had the business know-how were only able to write the code in the technologies they were familiar with. So the system was going to be built based on old, familiar technologies.

1.5 The Core Idea of Managed Evolution

In addition, the attempted greenfield approach was not embedded in the overall IT strategy. All the issues like governance, organization, culture and skills development were not considered in this greenfield project (see Sect. 1.3). After a while it became clear, that it would have taken a considerable amount of time to complete the greenfield system. Based on this insight, coupled with the impatience of the business side that requested that new functions be implemented immediately, the pressure on delivery increased dramatically. The final fact that halted the project was cost development: The gap between reported cost figures and budgeted cost, as well as the gap between planned project completion time and expected completion time increased continuously for the worse. The initial Credit Suisse estimate was a project duration of 7 years and a cost of one billion Swiss Francs. The project seemed to become a never ending, incredibly expensive story! The problems of the system started to become serious for Credit Suisse. No underlying IT strategy existed at that time.

One group of stakeholders still opted for a greenfield approach, this time proposing a new, very modern core banking system that, however, only existed as a blueprint. One business unit tried to implement an existing standard third party software package in its own business area. However, after several months of studies and project work it was recognized that the functional coverage was not sufficient and the integration issues were too difficult. Why was this outcome possible after the bad experience with the failed earlier greenfield approach? One main reason was that the *governance* for the system strategy for Credit Suisse at the top management level was not yet strongly developed. Strategic decisions were often delegated to the business units which kept changing over time and only took care of their own immediate requirements.

Finally, the idea of *managed evolution* grew in the retail banking unit of Credit Suisse. The idea was to solve the biggest issues of the Swiss IT platform with a strategic approach by developing the existing systems gradually. Due to the evident and continuous success of managed evolution, this idea has become the cornerstone for information technology system strategy for the entire global Credit Suisse IT organization.

In November 1998 the board met in a historic meeting to decide on the IT strategy. Two of the seminal slides presented and discussed are shown in Figs. 1.8 and 1.9.

The Credit Suisse Group executive board decided at the time that the *managed evolution* approach must be applied to all business units on the Swiss IT platform and no other strategies were allowed.

At the same time market forces drove the requirement to bring banking services to the Internet with a very short time to market. This, together with increasing availability problems caused by the complexity of the existing system became the driver for managed evolution.

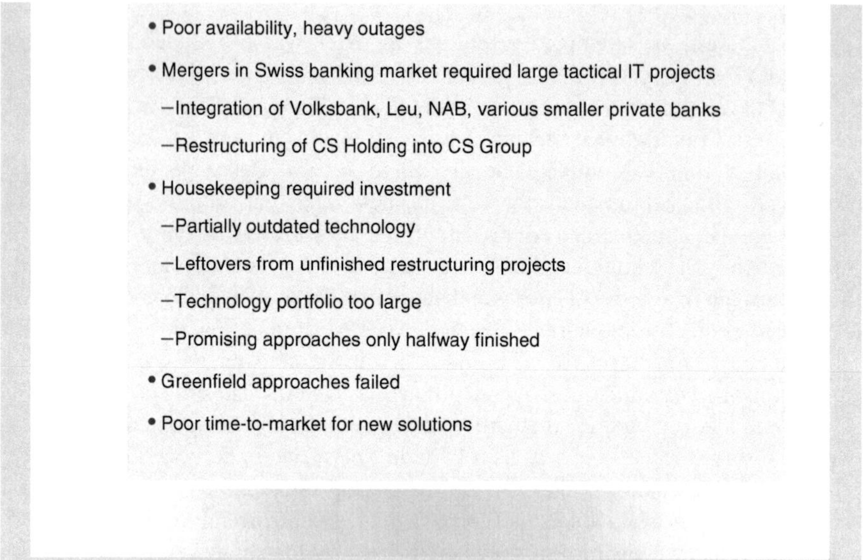

- Poor availability, heavy outages
- Mergers in Swiss banking market required large tactical IT projects
  - Integration of Volksbank, Leu, NAB, various smaller private banks
  - Restructuring of CS Holding into CS Group
- Housekeeping required investment
  - Partially outdated technology
  - Leftovers from unfinished restructuring projects
  - Technology portfolio too large
  - Promising approaches only halfway finished
- Greenfield approaches failed
- Poor time-to-market for new solutions

Fig. 1.8 Problem statement – original slide 1998

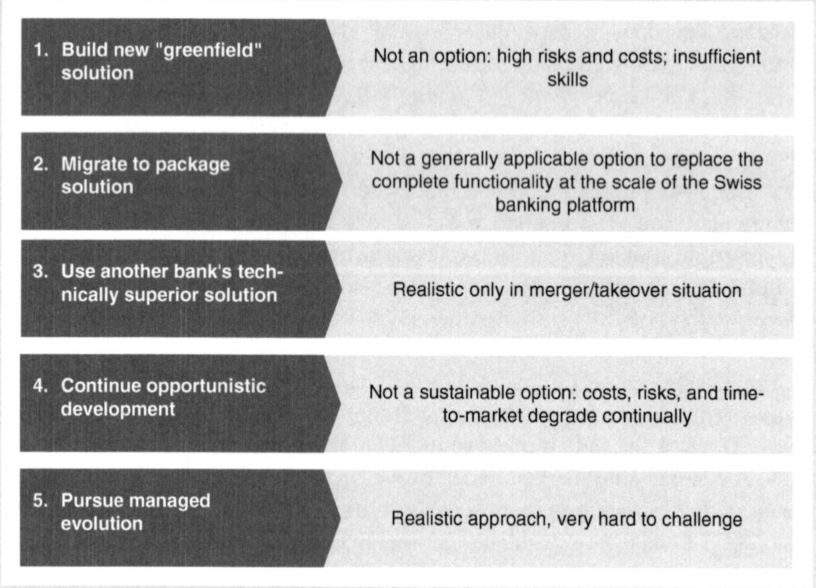

1. Build new "greenfield" solution	Not an option: high risks and costs; insufficient skills
2. Migrate to package solution	Not a generally applicable option to replace the complete functionality at the scale of the Swiss banking platform
3. Use another bank's technically superior solution	Realistic only in merger/takeover situation
4. Continue opportunistic development	Not a sustainable option: costs, risks, and time-to-market degrade continually
5. Pursue managed evolution	Realistic approach, very hard to challenge

Fig. 1.9 Solution space – original slide 1998

1.5 The Core Idea of Managed Evolution

Managed evolution was defined in 1998 with the following strategic direction:

- *Open architecture*, with well-defined interfaces and components; acceptable effort and risk to replace components.
- Strong IT *architecture leadership*.
- *Investment protection*: Existing platforms are perceived as assets, particularly with respect to know-how and people.
- *Risk awareness*: Step-by-step evolution enables effective risk control in very large projects.
- Flexibility enables easy adaptation to the bank's needs (=system *agility*).
- Systematic *lifecycle management* enables different development speeds in different parts of the platform.
- Target system remains a moving target.

Managed evolution was launched with a large *rearchitecture program*. The six projects constituting the rearchitecture program were chosen based on an extensive analysis of the critical weaknesses of the existing system. The first project was to standardize the data warehouses and the management systems. The second major project was the technical renovation that merged the two platforms of Credit Suisse and of Swiss Volksbank – in the meantime these two banks had been completely merged business-wise – in order to reduce the complexity from two systems to one. However, the new single system had to become multi-entity capable, because some other banks had been acquired in the meantime which should be kept as own brands and also run on the system. The third project restructured the core banking system in a way that the systems became available 7×24 h, a prerequisite to provide Internet banking on the core system.

The most innovative project, which also had the biggest impact on the modernization of the system, was building a new front end system architecture which was connected by a *service layer* to the back end systems. Developing this service layer was a challenging project and suffered from a lot of ups and downs with performance issues of commercial middleware components. The project was driven by the high complexity caused by the many existing point-to-point connections and the business requirements to build new delivery channels very quickly. Already at that time, implementing a standardized interface layer for access to backend functionality was the chosen direction. The last of the six projects was to implement an *application architecture* strategy and function. The main tasks of application architecture were to develop a *domain model* (Side Story 2.3) and to partition the tightly coupled existing application landscape. For the designers of the managed evolution strategy it was clear that *architecture management* and a strategic *project portfolio management* were key ingredients for success.

1.6 Elements of Managed Evolution

As outlined above, managed evolution is essentially about steering a *portfolio* of modifications for the very large system in a coordinated way. Modifications are executed through projects. So, the first element of managed evolution is an efficient *project portfolio management* process. Without adequate information about projects modifying the system and efficient ways to influence them, managed evolution cannot be executed. These requirements for a project portfolio management have a massive influence on how budgets are allocated and finally lead to a new *business-IT alignment*, both on the strategic and on the operational level (see Chap. 5).

Another important element of managed evolution is strong and continuous *architecture management* for the full system (see Chap. 2). Architecture management produces and maintains IT *target architecture*, consisting of blueprints, principles and IT standards. One particularly important result of application architecture is the *domain model* (see Side Story 2.3), which divides the overall system into domains, both into technical domains and application domains. In the project portfolio management process, the domain model is used to organize projects in such a way that all projects affecting a certain domain can be governed together, thus avoiding redundant or even counterproductive work. This is especially important, when many independent business sponsors have requirements for the same domain, such as for the extension of the same applications.

Integration architecture (Chap. 3) plays a key role in supporting the managed evolution. Its main deliverable is a target architectural design that divides the application landscape into *components* and a process that manages the *interfaces* between components. Typically domains may serve as a first level of the component map. As the authors have claimed above, managed evolution is the only way forward, because the very large information system is too big to be replaced in one go. Integration architecture decomposes the system into partitions that are isolated from each other by *managed interfaces* and small enough to be reengineered in one piece. The question of how to decompose a monolithic system into components without violating the principles of managed evolution – that is without replacing it completely – merits a separate discussion later in this chapter (see Sect. 1.7).

One particular integration challenge is the dependency of applications on *infrastructure*. Technically, a lot of this can be resolved by introducing various kinds of abstraction layers (Chap. 4). But the pure technical abstraction layer doesn't prove to be sufficient in practice. A higher level concept that includes a technology stack and processes for lifecycle management, development and operation of applications based on that stack is needed for sustainable success in this area. One possible concept is the *platform architecture* that defines this abstraction layer between applications and infrastructure (see Sect. 4.3). Platforms are constructed from technology products such as operating systems, databases, network devices, middleware and system management agents. As a whole, these components form the *technology portfolio*. Technical architecture defines a target technology portfolio such that no unwanted overlaps exist in the portfolio and that the lifecycle is

1.6 Elements of Managed Evolution

managed properly. No inappropriate risk must be taken with immature, off-market, or end-of-life technologies. In the spirit of managed evolution, it is important to understand architecture definition as a process, because the target architecture needs to be reviewed and aligned regularly to reflect new technical developments or changes to the business strategy.

Once the target IT architecture is defined, proper *architecture implementation* ensures convergence of the reality towards the IT target architecture (Chap. 2). Besides targeted investments in architecture programs, the main instruments for this are regular reviews of all projects for alignment to the IT target architecture and for opportunities to improve the system's architectural properties in the context of business driven projects. In the graphical abstraction of Fig. 1.7 this process ensures that every arrow, representing a modification, is twisted upward to an extent that makes economical sense.

A decisive part of this business-IT alignment is the alignment of business and IT strategy (Chap. 5). During each information technology strategy cycle all applications in the application portfolio and all infrastructure technologies in the technology portfolio are reviewed and assessed for architectural health and appropriate business functionality, domain by domain. This result is then compared with expectations about future business requirements ("Fit-for-Future") as derived from the *business strategy*. This analysis results in an *investment plan* that defines investment levels for each domain according to its architectural fitness and its importance towards fulfilling the expected business requirements. Within these investment levels, project portfolios are then developed for each domain.

Depending on the architectural health and the overall business spending in each domain, a complementary portfolio of agility-improvement projects is defined. The set of projects aimed at improving agility or IT architecture in general constitutes the *architecture program*. In Fig. 1.7 these projects are the ones with the steeply upward pointing arrows. They complement the portfolio of business driven modifications such that the overall portfolio of modifications stays inside the evolution channel. Details of an appropriate investment split between business driven modifications and the architecture program are discussed in Sect. 1.6. In general, the architecture program focuses its investments into domains (defined in Sect. 2.5) with little business requirements, but heavy structural challenges.

A further key element of managed evolution is the *organization* owning the very large information system. The organization has to develop certain skills, cultural values and organizational properties to be successful at managing the evolution of a very large information system (Chap. 6). One particularly important aspect of an evolutionary approach is that knowledge and skills about the existing system must be valued and preserved, as it is the indispensable base for future developments. On the other hand, the culture has to be changed in such a way that people trust the deliverables of other people in the organization and abandon the traditional "silo-thinking" where each unit does everything by itself in an independent way. It also requires adaptations in processes and in the structure of the organization (Chap. 6). The modularization of the system leads to more reusable components. This means that the different organization units producing and using the components become more dependent on each other.

The final elements of managed evolution are *measurement* and *control* (Chap. 7). The results of the evolution of the very large information system must be measured and tracked. Deviations of the desired evolution strategy must be identified and corrected. The effectiveness of the managed evolution instruments must be assessed. This requires the measurement of characteristic attributes of the very large information system and of the impact of the instruments of managed evolution. It also includes measuring architecture and the different processes that are decisive for the success of the managed evolution.

Figure 1.7 shows the managed evolution channel with a slight upward angle, representing that business value should grow and agility should improve at the same time over the period under consideration. The interesting question here is: Which percentage of the available budget should be invested in projects improving agility and which percentage in the development of business functionality? No generally accepted figures are available. However, the author's believe that the following split of the yearly IT solution delivery *budget* (which is the budget for delivering new functionality including adaptive maintenance, but excluding the corrective maintenance and operations), is the base for a sustainable managed evolution strategy:

- Roughly 80% for the implementation of new business functionality (*x*-axis: Creation of business value),
- Roughly 20% for improving agility.

The 20% budget not only includes the specific architecture programs for the improvement of IT efficiency and agility, but also the architecture-related efforts in projects implementing new functionality (raising the slope of individual project arrows in Fig. 1.7).

1.7 Where to Start with Managed Evolution

The concept of managed evolution was developed under the pressure to evolve, maintain and sustain very large information systems. As such, the concept of managed evolution is much younger than the systems to which it applies. Managed evolution of a particular system has therefore to start at some point in time – much later after the system was developed.

Most organizations only start to rethink their strategy under pressure. Pressure in this case means that the organization has recognized that it is in the tailspin of ever more expensive projects that do not deliver what they should and that create more and more collateral damage in the existing system (Fig. 1.6). Very often this situation is recognized in the event of a *crisis*, like a major project failure or substantial instability issues with the running system. Some organizations are more sensitive than others, so that the size of the crisis may vary. Once the

1.7 Where to Start with Managed Evolution

organization has decided to embark on a managed evolution strategy, there are a few steps to take.

The first challenge is to get the scope of the very large information system right. Definition of scope denotes the drawing of the system boundaries, i.e. defining what belongs to the very large information system under consideration and what is out of scope. If the scope is too small – that is, if tightly connected components are not part of the same scope – the strategy won't work because major dependencies remain unmanaged. If the scope is too large, unnecessary coordination overhead is created among parts of the system that are only loosely coupled. As obvious as it sounds, it is not easy to get the scope right, because the legacy system may no longer be aligned to the current organization of the business. In any case, the scope must be chosen by *architectural criteria* rather than organizational or other criteria.

The second challenge is to start *modularizing* the very large information system in a pragmatic manner. The components and interfaces should support a defined business value or a required technical improvement. It does not make economic sense to modularize a system in an area where no change is requested. The agility of the system already improves dramatically if the most important interfaces of the system are implemented according to the integration strategy. The basic idea here is to have a strategic plan for the overall modularization of the very large information system and to implement this plan incrementally.

> "Until the management recognizes a strategic objective to become "service-oriented", the full benefit of a Service Oriented Architecture will not be realized"
> Norbert Bieberstein, 2008

The third challenge is to adapt *governance*, strategy, processes and organization to the appropriate scope. A strong *architectural leadership* across the whole scope is needed. Prioritization of projects and definition of architecture programs have to be done with the whole scope in mind. The development organization has to be reshaped to align to architectural domains.

The fourth challenge is *cultural*. The concept of managed evolution implies that the whole is more than the sum of its parts. It means that everybody touching one part of the system should keep the consequences for the whole system in mind. People have to be aware that the overall design quality of a very large information technology system is defined by a myriad of microscopic design decisions being taken by hundreds or thousands of developers. A culture of "think big – act local" is needed. To a certain extent, this quality can be reinforced by good control processes. But control is limited to handling exceptions. The other cultural aspect is trust. If reuse is to be fostered, project managers and developers have to trust the providers of prerequisite components. Again, good planning will help, but can't replace trust and commitment to live up to promises. The last cultural aspect is long-term thinking. In managed evolution, every component may live as long as it fulfils its purpose. So, long-lived components are valuable components. Strong communication, leadership and appropriate incentives help to implement these cultural values in the organization.

Finally, the fifth challenge is initial *funding*. Managed evolution starts with initiating a program addressing the challenges outlined above. This program will need funding on top of the ordinary project portfolio. In the beginning, it is a challenge to convince sponsors that this money is well spent for the future. The experience of the authors is that this challenge may best be tackled in the context of an extraordinary event, like a merger or a crisis.

Chapter 2
Architecture Management

Summary Architecture management plays a key role in the sustainable success of managed evolution. Architecture management defines the target architecture, a number of models, a set of technical standards and guiding principles for the evolution of the system. It defines and operates processes to evolve architecture standards, to communicate them to the organization and to ensure their implementation. Strong review activities on projects enforce adherence to the standards. Architecture metrics finally allow the progress of key indicators to be measured. A federated architecture organization is essential for powerful architecture management in a very large organization.

2.1 What is IT Architecture and Why Is It Important to Managed Evolution

The Oxford Advanced Learner's Dictionary ([Oxford_05]) defines architecture as follows:

1. The art and study of designing buildings: to study architecture
2. The design or style of a building or buildings: the architecture of the eighteenth century, modern architecture
3. (Computing) The design and structure of a computer system

Similarly, IEEE (Institute of Electrical and Electronics Engineers in [IEEE_00]) defines IT architecture as:

"The fundamental organization of a system embodied in its components, their relationships to each other, and to the environment, and the principles guiding its design and evolution"

The definitions above show two facets of architecture. On the one hand we have "architecture" as an *activity*, art, or profession (Point 1 in the definition), on the other hand we call the results of the architect's work "architecture" (Points 2 and 3 in the definition).

Understanding IT architecture as an *activity*: In the *architecture process*, architecture is developed, design questions are answered and architectural standards are implemented in the system. In a very large information system, the architect's work at the highest level is very similar to the work of a city planner. The architect defines guidelines and IT standards comparable to city zoning plans, setting constraints for building in certain areas. Reviews and approvals of designs are comparable to implementation permits, just as city planners issue building permits for construction projects. The architect plans and builds the necessary infrastructure to allow for a managed evolution of the city – via IT strategy and architecture driven investment programs.

Understanding architecture as design and *structure*: Architecture consists of its systems, representing the current state of the architecture and of documents defining structure, standards, concepts, principles and roadmaps that govern the future evolution of the system.

It is important to understand that *every* system has an architecture, be it an implicit or an explicit one. If the architecture is implicit we have no way to control, analyze, reason about, evolve and communicate it. It is the role of the architect to establish explicit architecture of the system and to communicate it well to all involved parties.

As described in Chap. 1, there are two ways to improve agility in the managed evolution strategy: One way is to invest into explicit *architecture programs*, the other is to steer every single project into a direction that improves the overall agility (Fig. 1.7). Both approaches only work if there is a clear and explicitly communicated *target architecture*. This is particularly important in a very large information system where thousands of developers make thousands of small design decisions every day. The sum of these micro-decisions determines the overall direction of the system's evolution. So, if more people understand and support the target architecture it will be implemented at lower cost. It is a waste of energy if, due to bad communication or bad understanding, design decisions point in opposite directions and annihilate each other. In addition to that, a control element is required to detect and react on deviations from the target architecture. Furthermore, investment programs to build the necessary infrastructures or to remove duplicate functionality and data are needed.

"Architecture is something of a black art in the IT world. Architects learn on the job, bringing years of experience in design and technology to the business problems they tackle. It's not an easy task to impart architecture knowledge"
Ian Gorton, 2006

Fully aware of the fact that architecture and design takes place on a number of different abstraction layers, such as from the detailed design of a data center network all the way up to an abstract enterprise-wide business object model, we avoid a general discussion on IT architecture, which can be found in a number of excellent books, such as [Masak_05], [Masak_07], [Mens_08], [Gorton_06], [Lankhorst_05], [Abramowicz_07], [Erl_04], [Woods_03], [Garland_03], [Britton_01], [Cummins_09], [Bernstein_09]. We rather focus on elements of IT architecture as far as they are necessary to support managed evolution of very large information systems. In our experience, the key elements to manage the architecture of very large information systems are the following:

- A set of fundamental *principles* guiding the architecture,
- A *structure* that helps divide the very large information system into more tractable pieces,
- A management *process* to develop, communicate, implement and control architecture,
- A federated *organization* that implements the architecture process aligned to the target structure of the system.

In the following we will describe these elements in more detail and add examples from our own experience to illustrate the concepts in a non-trivial case.

2.2 Architecture Principles

Fundamental to the architecture of a very large information system is a set of *architecture principles* to be applied across the whole system. This set of principles should be small and address a couple of key questions, such as the position on technology diversity. It is important that the principles can be described briefly and communicated well across the IT organization. As every developer is making his or her own *micro-architecture* decisions, it is fundamental that these principles are broadly understood, accepted and consistently followed.

Managed evolution as the central architectural principle at the heart of this book is one of the prime architecture principles for very large information systems.

Almost a *meta-principle* to be clarified is that IT architecture is *not* an exact science. There are many conflicting goals and interests in designing a system. Short time-to-market or low-cost development may lead

> "'Architecture', in a broad sense, is the synergy of art and science in designing complex structures, such that functionality and complexity are controlled"
> Marc Lankhorst, 2005

to high operational cost. Design for highest performance may reduce flexibility in parameterization and vice versa. Inserting additional layers of abstraction may increase runtime overhead, but reduce development, maintenance and future enhancement cost. Higher security requirements must be carefully implemented in order not to lead to reduced user comfort and potentially to lower availability and higher operating cost. It is important to be aware of and *accept* those trade-offs. One-dimensional optimization typically leads to sub-optimum solutions.

Compliance oriented governance does not necessarily lead to the desired results in architecture. In order to properly handle the trade-offs, both experience and good quantitative models are needed.

If the system supports a dynamic business, then flexibility and agility with regard to business organization and expansion is a must. Applications tend to live longer than the structure of the organization, the legal environment, or the global footprint. Therefore, flexibility principles with respect to certain dimensions are needed. Here are a few requirements that the authors have encountered across a number of different industries:

- *Multiple entities*: Several legally independent organizations should be able to co-exist in the same system in order to leverage scale effects. Each entity needs a certain degree of independence in order to be able to position itself in the market. It is crucial to set the right degree of independence and to implement flexibility accordingly. Typical topics in this include independent pricing of products and services, appropriate separation of data among legal entities and flexible support for different business organizations and processes.
- *Multiple countries*: The system should be able to support international growth by flexibly accommodating new countries, new markets and new business. Key topics in this area include the support of different languages, different currencies, different legal and regulatory environments and operation across multiple time zones, particularly if your system is based on a daily online/batch cycle.
- *Multiple channels*: Sales channels have become more heterogeneous, especially if the organization sells a purely virtual product that lends itself well for electronic distribution. So, flexibility with respect to different sales channels, direct or indirect, physical or electronic is fundamental to a successful long-term architecture.

Depending on your business, other principles regarding flexibility of the value chain, scalability and the like are needed.

Some principles should address and clarify the *technology risk* appetite. They define the structure of the *technology portfolio*. The principles should answer questions such as: How must the technology portfolio be aligned to technology market mainstream in order to profit from the technology ecosystem? How aggressively shall new and risky technologies be brought in? What is the position on desirable, or not so desirable, diversity in the technology portfolio? Where should exceptions to the principles be allowed? Chap. 4. (Infrastructure) explains the underlying rationale and processes for technology management in more detail.

One fundamental architectural choice to be made is the question of whether components of the system should be bought and integrated or whether the system will be based mainly on proprietary development. This choice is dependent on the size of the organization, on the market of relevant software, on the capabilities of the organization building the system and many other criteria. In the experience of the authors, any very large information system has both types: Proprietary development and buy and integrate components.

The following Side-Story 2.1 explains how a generic requirement is reflected in architectural principles to be applied across the application landscape.

Side-Story 2.1: Multi-Country Capability Architecture

Credit Suisse has IT operations in many locations, some of them large and some of them rather small. However, the customers expect the same high quality service, independently from the location of their bank branch. It is, however, not feasible to install and operate the rich functionality of a large location in all the small locations worldwide.

Therefore, in order to provide richer functionality to the smaller locations and to increase processing volume, Credit Suisse intends to use its Swiss system for global business. This brings a number of challenges, such as handling multiple legal entities, dealing with the specifics of different countries, adapting to different laws and regulations, providing products for local markets and supporting local languages. Traditionally the existing applications do not support international business.

Instead of operating a large number of individual IT installations in many countries, IT services will be offered out of a small number of hubs. A team of specialists defined the required multi-country capability of the IT system, including applications, presentation, reporting, etc. These requirements impact existing applications. Before transforming thousands of applications, the architecture team derived clear and comprehensive principles from the generic requirement. A representative choice of the application landscape architecture principles covering the multi-country capability is listed in Table 2.1.

The principles in Table 2.1 were approved by the architecture steering committee and communicated to the development community. In addition, specific implementation guidelines were published for each of the multi-country application landscape architecture principles, such as the BOUID format specification <BOUID = numeric4>. The complete set of multi-country application landscape architecture principles allows application developers to work on many applications in parallel and to implement the multi-country capability in a short time and with full interoperability.

2.3 Architecture Layers and Models

Models are essential elements of very large information system architecture. They allow the architect to manage complexity and to document the system consistently and precisely. Models help simplify reality by abstraction. The first purpose is the *structuring* of the large number of parts in the

> "Models must not be regarded as rather inconsequential artifacts of software development but instead as the core products"
> Anneke Kleppe, 2009

Table 2.1 (Side-Story 2-1) Application landscape architecture principles for multi-country capability

Principle name	Principle text	Remarks
Multi-Entity Capability (MEC)	The entity in MEC (the "E" in MEC) is the *Business Operation Unit* (BOU). Each BOU is uniquely identified by its Business Operation Unit Identifier (BOUID) • Each Business Operation Unit belongs to exactly one legal entity • Each Business Operation Unit is associated with exactly one country • A BOUID is assigned only once, i.e. BOUIDs are never reused • A legal entity can span several BOUs and countries	The BOU is the central concept because it allows unambiguous linking of metadata, data and functionality to a unit operating in exactly one organizational (legal) entity and in one jurisdiction (Country). Reuse of BOUIDs is not allowed because otherwise the historical and archive data would become ambiguous
Data Affiliation	All customer- and employee-related data must refer to the BOU of its legal owner. All database structures storing such data must have an attribute <BOUID> which identifies the context	Points to the laws and regulations protecting the data
Data Separation	The customer- and employee-identifying data must be separated from the content they refer to. All applications must work properly without client-identifying data.	This is necessary for cross-border anonymization. Instead of the client-identifying data, secure, reversible cryptographic techniques are used, generating a code which allows the processing of the data without exposing the client
Data Authorization	Data access protection must be enforced according to the national laws and regulations and according to the contractual obligations of the different BOUs	
MEC Control	All components have to be designed, implemented and deployed in such a way that new business units can be easily supported, ideally by updating configuration tables	Assures the flexibility for adding new business units
Interfaces	All interfaces over which business operation unit specific data is passed must include the BOUID field	Applies in fact to most interfaces

2.3 Architecture Layers and Models

system (see Sect. 1.2) and the second purpose is shaping the connections. The focus in this book is on models that are important on the enterprise architecture level ([Lankhorst_05]). For the implementation of functionality and data structures, additional models (notably the logical and the physical models) are required, which will not be discussed in this book. Refer to [Schmidt_99], [Simsion_05], [Nicola_02] and many other texts for more information on logical and physical modeling.

When working with different models, like domain models, business object models and others, the models must be kept *consistent* at all times. Models evolve gradually along the managed evolution path, thus becoming complex over time. Keeping models consistent among each other require special methods. Very helpful instruments are rich metamodels ([Marco_04], [Frankel_03], [Knöpfel_05], [Inmon_08], [Wegener_07]) underlying each model and automatic model checkers ([Baier_07]) being made available to all model developers.

The most important models for structuring are the *layer models* (Fig. 2.1), the *domain models* (Side-Story 2.3 and Fig. 2.9) and the *business functional map* (Side-Story 2.2). The set of models required for architecture management will be described in this chapter, starting with the *layer model*.

It is very common to manage enterprise architecture as three separate layers. A *business architecture layer* describes the entities, processes and functions on

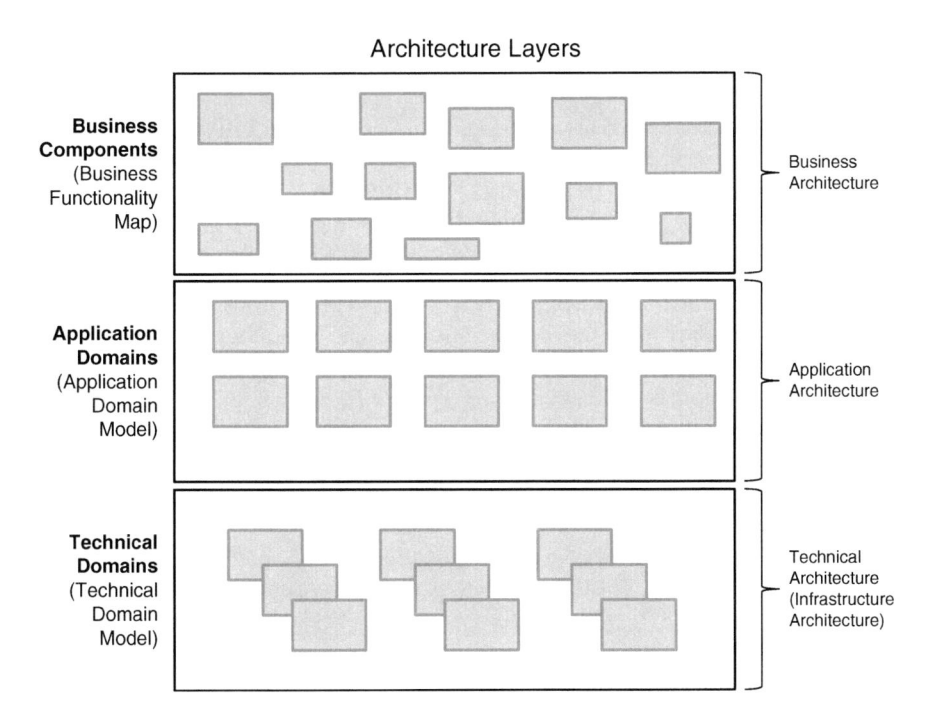

Fig. 2.1 Architecture layers

a business level. An *application architecture layer* describes how business requirements are implemented in applications. And a third layer, the *technical architecture layer* deals with the underlying infrastructure (see Fig. 2.1).

Business architecture is structured according to a *business functional map*. Technical and application architecture are both structured by their *domain models* which are presented later in this book.

2.4 Business Architecture

Systems implement products, processes and services of real businesses. Therefore it is not surprising that the system architecture should be derived from overarching *business architecture*. In the literature a number of different definitions for business architecture can be found. As for all architectures, business architecture is at the same time an activity and a well-structured documentation of a current or future state. The OMG's[1] business architecture working group defines this aspect of business architecture as "A blueprint of the enterprise that provides a common understanding of the organization and is used to align strategic objectives and tactical demands". Depending on the *framework*, business architecture covers aspects like strategy, products, processes, information, capabilities, knowledge and organization. Good background information on business architecture can be found in ([Zachmann_08], [OMG_08], [Sandoe_01], [Gharajedaghi_06], [Moser_07], [Knittel_06], [Ross_06]).

> "An enterprise system is an extraordinary complex application of information technology designed to support organizational processes in a highly integrated fashion"
> Kent Sandoe, 2001

For the purpose of system architecture the important aspects of business architecture are the following:

- *Information/Semantics*: Systems serve to store and process business information. To implement such systems, precise structure and *semantics* for the business information must be defined ([McComb_04]). Typical tools for this are information models, glossaries and ontologies ([Sowa_00]). Although it would be useful to capture semantics formally for system implementation, current practices are informal text-based definitions. The direct counterpart to this in application architecture is

> "The world is changing fast and, for better or worse, *semantics* is at the heart of it"
> Dave McComb, 2002

---

[1]Object Management Group.

2.4 Business Architecture

the *business object model* ([Nicola_02]), formalizing the information model in a more implementable way.

- *Functionality*: The business functionality is provided by the applications. A structured *business functionality m*ap can be used to analyze the application landscape for functional overlaps, gaps and misalignments. Often the business functionality is linked to the information architecture, describing what information is used by which business functionality. Side-Story 2.2 gives an example for such a map. This is similar to the domain model and the application portfolio, although experience shows that the structure of the application domain model might look quite different from a business functionality map, as the structuring criteria are different. You may want to keep functionality grouped around the same data or being offered in one package together in the same application domain, for example.
- *Processes*: Business uses well-defined processes to provide their services to the clients and to manage the internal processing. With the focus on business *process engineering* and flexible orchestration of services into workflows, understanding the business processes is important. From the business processes we can identify the process steps common to multiple processes. These can then be provided as services for flexible orchestration. Generally, good business process definitions can be found nowadays for well structured operational areas of the business, where they are being used successfully to systematically improve efficiency by continuously capturing process data, analyzing it and improving the process based on the data.
- *Organization and roles*: Organizations are structured and have clearly defined roles which execute their assigned tasks. For many decisions in IT architecture it is important to understand the organization and the roles of people in the organizations. Examples for this include access control systems or the design of portals, where all functionality for a particular role is presented in an integrated way.

Most business architecture frameworks capture the information described above in one or the other form. In the experience of the authors there typically is a *precision gap* between business architecture and IT architecture. While business architecture definition tends to be loose at times, IT architecture must be more precise, so that it can be implemented in systems. Often large enterprises don't have a central owner for all aspects of business architecture across all areas. Therefore the coverage may be patchy and the business architecture is defined implicitly by the behaviour of the people and systems behind a business process. Increased regulatory scrutiny, such as the Sarbanes-Oxley act ([Marchetti_05]) and improved formal optimization methods, such as Lean Six Sigma ([George_04], [George_05]), have lead to more formal documentation of business architecture in recent years.

Most large organizations do not have an explicit function that is responsible for the overall evolution of business architecture. So, in practice, business architecture to the extent necessary for the underlying IT architecture is often maintained by the IT architecture organization.

The main structural model in *business architecture* is the *business functional map*. As an example, the business functional map – in the form of a business component map – of Credit Suisse is described in Side-Story 2.2.

Side-Story 2.2: Credit Suisse Business Component Map (BCM)

Recently the strong growth of trading activities revealed functional and performance deficits in the Credit Suisse trading and operations application landscape in the Swiss hub. Some of the applications were quite old (more then 20 years) and the extensions required by the very active business could only be implemented with difficulty.

In 2006 Credit Suisse IT management decided to define a new, modern Trading and Operations Target Application Landscape (TOTAL). This alignment was to be based on a *business component map* ([IBM_05a]). Business component map development follows a modeling methodology introduced in 2006 by IBM: *Business Component Modeling* (BCM). In this context, *business components* are the modular building blocks that make up the specialized enterprise. Each component has a business purpose which is the reason for its existence within the organization and conducts a mutually exclusive set of activities (IT-supported, manual, or mixed) to achieve its business purpose. Each business component is based on its own governance model and provides/receives *business services*.

A team consisting of Credit Suisse experts and IBM consultants was formed and worked for 4 months in close cooperation. IBM brought three generic business component maps (for generic retail, private and investment banking) to the table as a starting point. At the end of the definition phase, the Credit Suisse *Business Component Map* (BCM) as shown in Fig. 2.2 was delivered.

Business component modeling – resulting in the business component map as its main deliverable – has proven its value as a methodology to define a functional alignment between business and IT, including a view into the future. After this activity, the planned target architecture for the trading and operations landscape was defined from a functional point of view.

The BCM (Fig. 2.2) has successfully been used to identify functional redundancy, such as overlaps, multiple implementations and to plan a roadmap for the implementation of the target architecture. Several major development programs have subsequently been launched at Credit Suisse to transform the current trading and operations application landscape into the desired target architecture.

The BCM methodology has proven to be so powerful that it is now used globally in Credit Suisse in various areas and for several uses.

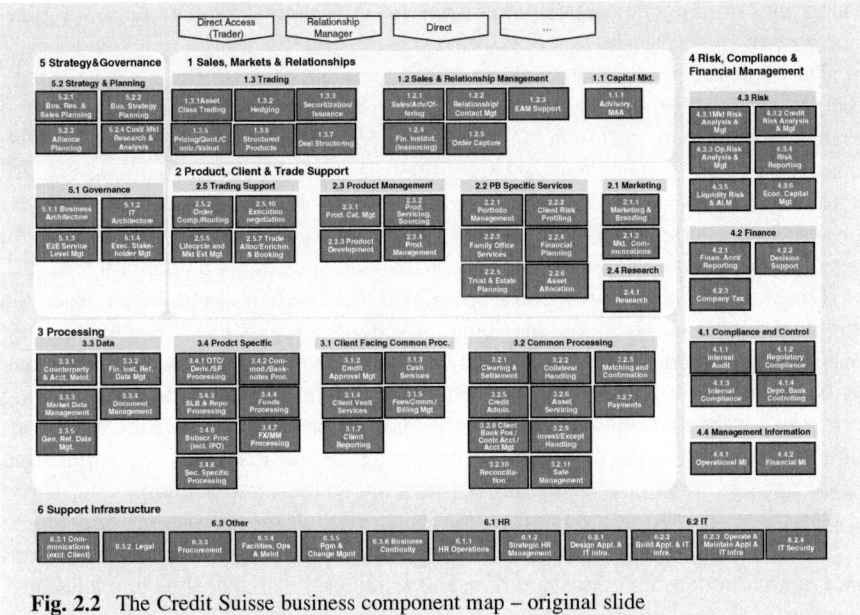

Fig. 2.2 The Credit Suisse business component map – original slide

2.5 Application Architecture

All business applications in the system form the *application landscape*. For the purpose of this book, an application comprises a set of *functionality*, the corresponding *data* and includes *interfaces* to other applications in order to achieve a specific business purpose. Applications consist of one or several software components designed to support business processes and to fulfill specific needs of users. A component consists of programs, data structures, configuration information and associated documentation.

The application landscape is partitioned into *application domains*. Each application belongs to one or more domains. Application domains are *subsets* of the application landscape characterized by a high cohesion from the business point of view. Central to an application domain are its business entities and business functions. Depending on the size of the application landscape one may introduce multiple levels of structure with domains and *subdomains*. In the experience of the authors, up to two dozen domains can be handled on the top level. Within a

> "From the perspective of the underlying science and engineering knowledge base, software is the least well understood and the most problematic element of large scale systems"
> Linda Northrop, 2006

domain up to twenty subdomains and 50–100 applications per subdomain can be handled. Experience shows that in a typical application landscape the domain model is not evenly populated, but the two level structure is sufficient to manage landscapes of many thousands of applications, as is typical for very large information systems.

The choice of application domains is an important strategic choice. It goes with the assumption that applications in the same domain can be more tightly coupled than applications in different domains. Typical architectural rules that go with domain borders include that databases may be shared inside a domain, but not across. Sharing data across domains requires that additional quality criteria be imposed on interfaces that are offered for use outside the providing domain. In very large information systems these rules may again be defined on multiple levels.

The choice of the domain model also expresses certain assumptions about the structure of a business. Should the domains be defined regionally, along the process, or aligned to products? Domain model decisions are long-term decisions and have to be taken carefully. The model must be kept stable as a fundamental guiding principle for the managed evolution of the application landscape and the infrastructure. The domain model will over time influence the reality in the application landscape by more closely coupling applications in the same domain.

The domain model decomposes the *functionality* and persistent *data* of the application landscape into smaller, manageable containers. The subdomains contain non-redundant functions and data and together they cover the complete functionality and data universe of the application landscape. This is an ideal view, without taking into consideration the actual functionality of the existing applications. The modeling approach can be seen as first preparing a list of all functions (on a suitable level of granularity, such as "maintain customer address and customer contract information") and data (again on a suitable level of granularity, such as "customer master data"). Second, all entries in this complete, consistent list of functions and data are then uniquely assigned to the best-suited subdomain.

Assigning all entries in the list to the most appropriate subdomain requires some rules:

1. Strong *cohesion* of the functions and data within a subdomain: Cohesion is a measure of how related functionality and data are gathered together and how well the parts inside a subdomain work as a whole. Cohesion is the glue holding a subdomain together. Weakly cohesive subdomains are a sign of bad decomposition. Each subdomain must have a clearly defined scope and not be a grab bag of unrelated functionality and data ([Spinellis_09]).
2. Low *coupling*: Coupling is a measure of the dependency between subdomains – the amount of "wiring" to and from them. Good partitioning results in little coupling and so the subdomains become less dependent on each other. Obviously, coupling required by the cooperation among applications in one subdomain and applications in other subdomains or the environment are necessary – but unnecessary wiring should be avoided by good subdomain decomposition ([Spinellis_09]).
3. Comprehensive *business-IT alignment*: Because cohesion is mainly rooted in the way business conducts its processes, the business cohesion strongly supports good decomposition. This synergy must be exploited, which automatically leads to a comprehensive business-IT alignment, especially if "business terminology" is used as much as possible in the domain model. A good domain model also

2.5 Application Architecture

separates dedicated *business* functionality, such as payments or trading from *general* functionality, such as enterprise resource planning, electronic archive, communication channels.

One trap to avoid while constructing a domain model is thinking in products: If a domain model is structured around products, synergies in their production or processing will not be identified. The domain model must become – and remain – the functional and high-level data model of the ideal organization. As such it survives business strategy changes, company reorganizations, mergers and acquisitions and forms a stable, reliable base for the evolution of the application landscape.

Developing a domain model is a highly cooperative, consensus-based effort of business and IT resources under the strong leadership of application architecture. As such, it involves a broad range of experts.

The domain model benefits four areas:

1. *IT architecture*, supporting complexity management, providing the structural foundation for the *enterprise service oriented architecture* (integration architecture), defining the rules for various disentangling programs for *legacy applications* and providing the "ideal", redundancy-free functional and data *model of the organization*. Once all applications have been assigned to the "best fit" subdomain, redundancy and misfits can easily be identified. A big complexity reduction potential is made accessible!
2. *System evolution*: Enabling independent development, deployment and operation of *components* improves the agility of the system. Better locality and isolation of applications in domains reduces effort for coordination of changes touching many applications. Higher software quality due to reduced cross-component impacts will result. Generation of new, unwanted or unknown *redundancy* is avoided.
3. *IT management*: Leads to improved *transparency* by using domain-based management and reporting and creation of a powerful domain architect organization with defined responsibilities assigned to architectural roles.
4. *Business reasons*: Better understanding of the IT landscape is achieved with domain-model based investment planning, resulting in better coordination and less effort duplication. Complexity reduction leads, as a direct consequence, to shorter time to market and lower development cost for new functionality. Finally, there is an improvement in business-IT alignment.

The domain approach enables the possibility to define *domain-specific architectures* ([Duffy_04]) and *domain specific languages* (DSL, [Kleppe_09]) based on the domain's business concepts, such as business objects. Together, this leads to *domain specific modeling* (DSM, [Kelly_08]). Domain-specific modeling raises the level of abstraction beyond current modeling approaches and increases application productivity.

> "Throughout the history of software development, raising the level of abstraction has been the cause of the largest leaps in developer productivity"
> Steven Kelly, 2008

A successful domain model requires the full and consistent implementation of five elements:

1. The *structure* (Fig. 2.4): The main topic of this Side-Story 2.3,
2. A *representation*: Mapping of all domains/subdomains and applications, including their information flows, attributes and properties in an on-line repository,
3. A *"federated architecture organization"*, including the domain architects and other cross-business unit, cross-domain architecture roles (see Sect. 1.9),
4. A set of *processes* for the evolution, maintenance and optimization of the *application* landscape based on domains, including change request management for the domains, management of the domain architects, processes for the periodic domain assessment,
5. Strong and dedicated *governance* supporting and leading the domain architecture and the domain activities.

Side-Story 2.3: Credit Suisse Domain Model with the Main Design Considerations

Between 1995 and 2005 the amount of information and know-how related to the application landscape of Credit Suisse became far too large to be understood and controlled by any single person or even a team. Over the years, solutions were developed without always being correctly aligned with the existing application landscape. This led to unnecessary complexity, like unknown and unwanted redundancy, to silo'ed applications, to a loss of conceptual integrity, strong architecture erosion and various other issues.

In addition, starting in 2006 the strategy of Credit Suisse was oriented towards *"OneBank"*, i.e. the global integration and cooperation of all business units (Private banking, retail banking, corporate banking, asset management, investment banking) into one business model under one common brand. This again increased the challenge of managing the combined application landscapes.

This situation called for the development of a *model* of the "target system for the integrated bank (One Bank)". Such a model could then be used to partition, organize, understand and control the consolidation and the evolution of the very large application landscape. A central architecture team was mandated to develop the model – this was the start of the Credit Suisse *Combined Domain Model* (CDM). The combined domain model relied on an earlier application domain model developed and used in Credit Suisse private banking. Part of the organization therefore was familiar with domain models and had experienced their value for the management of the application landscape.

2.5 Application Architecture

> "The key to controlling complexity is a good domain model"
> Eric Evans, 2004

Due to the large size and the many different stakeholders, the development of the domain model was started with an enterprise model. This enterprise model is shown in Fig. 2.3: It consists of seven categories. Category 1 "Partners and Persons" covers all the parties with which the bank is exchanging services or information. This is done via category 5 "Communication and Collaboration". The categories 2 "Finance, Investment & Sales", 3 "Trading and Markets" and 4 "Cash and Asset Operations" are the "production lines" of the bank – here the products and services are "manufactured". Categories 6 "Accounting, Controlling and Reporting" and 7 "Enterprise Common Services" cover enterprise support functions, such as human resource management, compliance to all legal and regulatory requirements, enterprise content management etc. Note that the business context of this domain model is *banking* – other industries will have different domain models.

Once the enterprise model (Fig. 2.3) was agreed, a high-level decomposition of the functionality and data was laid down. The next step was to define and assign *domains*.

Again, the collaborative effort of business and IT resources – this time on a detailed level – was required. The current domain model of Credit Suisse is shown in Fig. 2.4: It contains 22 domains (and covers the full business

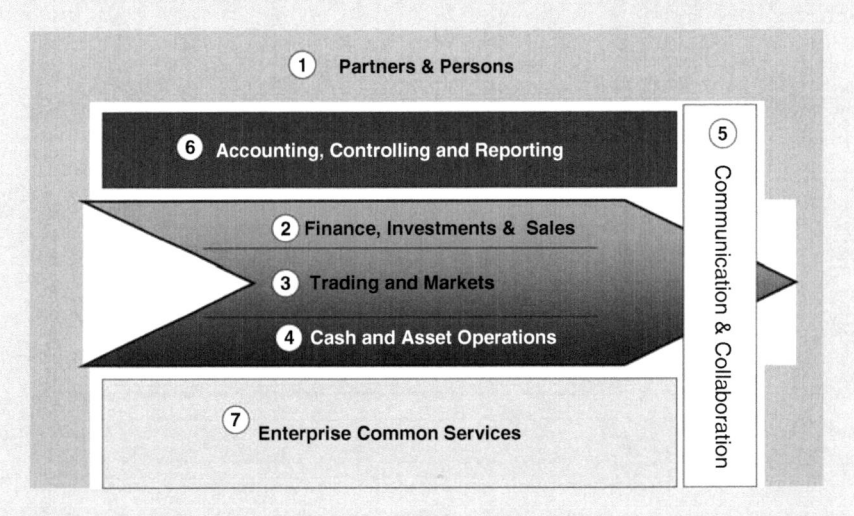

Fig. 2.3 Categories of the Credit Suisse 2009 domain model

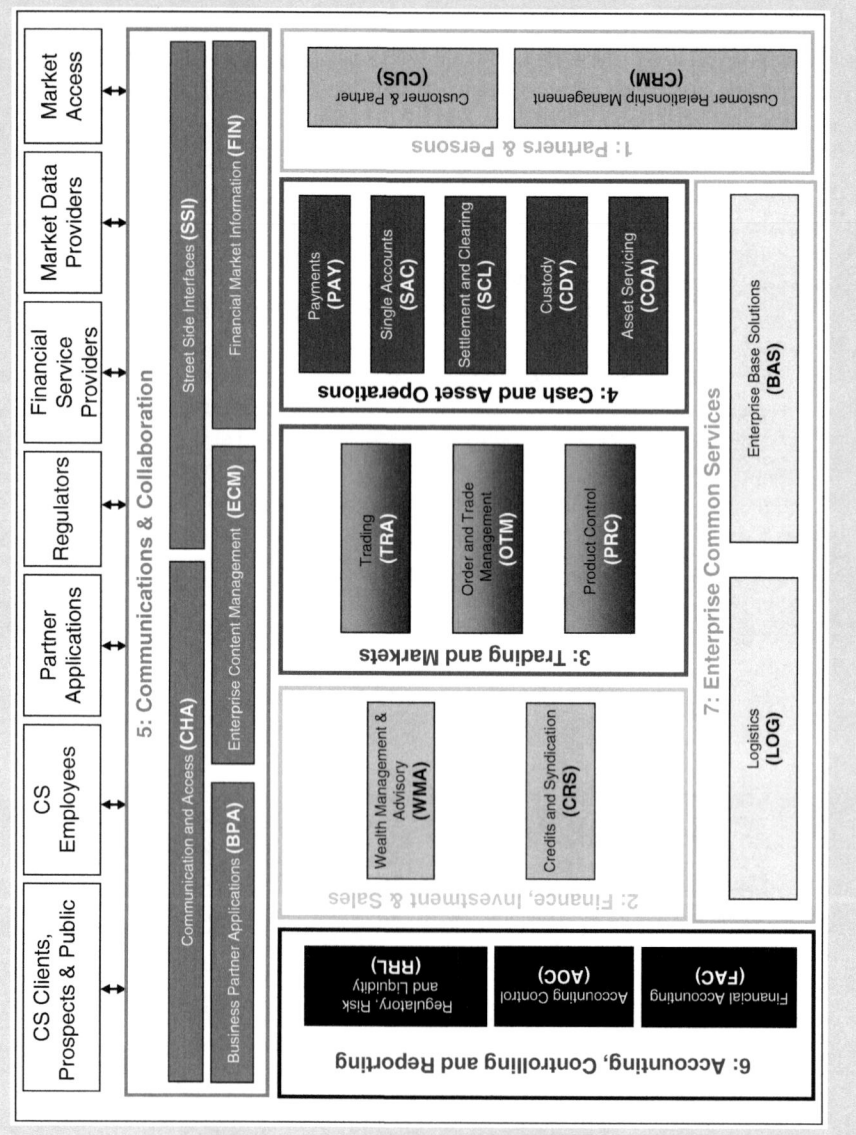

Fig. 2.4 The Credit Suisse 2009 domain model

2.5 Application Architecture

offering of Credit Suisse worldwide). The domain model has proven to be an invaluable tool for a number of processes.

The domain model became the key structural ordering element: Most applications were assigned to subdomains. An inventory and planning tool was introduced which listed all applications, together with a large number of properties and attributes of the individual applications and the *information flows* between the applications.

The *domain model* (see Side-Story 2.3) is linked to the *business component map* as presented in Side-Story 2.2. They are, however, not the same. Side-Story 2.4 explains their relationship.

Side-Story 2.4. Relationship Between CDM and BCM

In the middle of Fig. 2.5 a list of functions and data is shown: This list contains the *complete functionality* and all the *data* required to operate the business. The list is unstructured. There is only one such list: The list is complete, free of redundancy and consistent – it represents the "atomic" breakdown of the business to be supported by the system. An *atomic business function* is the lowest level of functionality in a system that is still recognizable to the business (see [Sessions_09], [Sessions_08]). Note that all the functions and data are included, not only the IT-supported functions and data, but also the functions executed manually and the data used in manual processes.

On the left side of Fig. 2.5 the *BCM (Business Component Map)* is presented. The BCM relates to the list of functions via a mapping of individual functions into the business components. The mapping rules are according to the business view. The aggregation into business components is optimized for reuse in business processes. It is therefore possible that some basic functionality or data required to operate the system (such as reference data, access protection functions, etc.) is not mapped to the BCM, but only to the domain model.

On the right side of Fig. 2.5 the *CDM (Combined Domain Model)* is drawn. The CDM relates to the list of functions and data via a mapping of individual functions and data elements into the domains. The mapping rules are according to optimal IT implementation. All functions and data are uniquely assigned. Following the principle of functional and data business cohesion this partitioning provides the foundation for the optimized, effective and efficient IT implementation of the business functionality and data.

52   2 Architecture Management

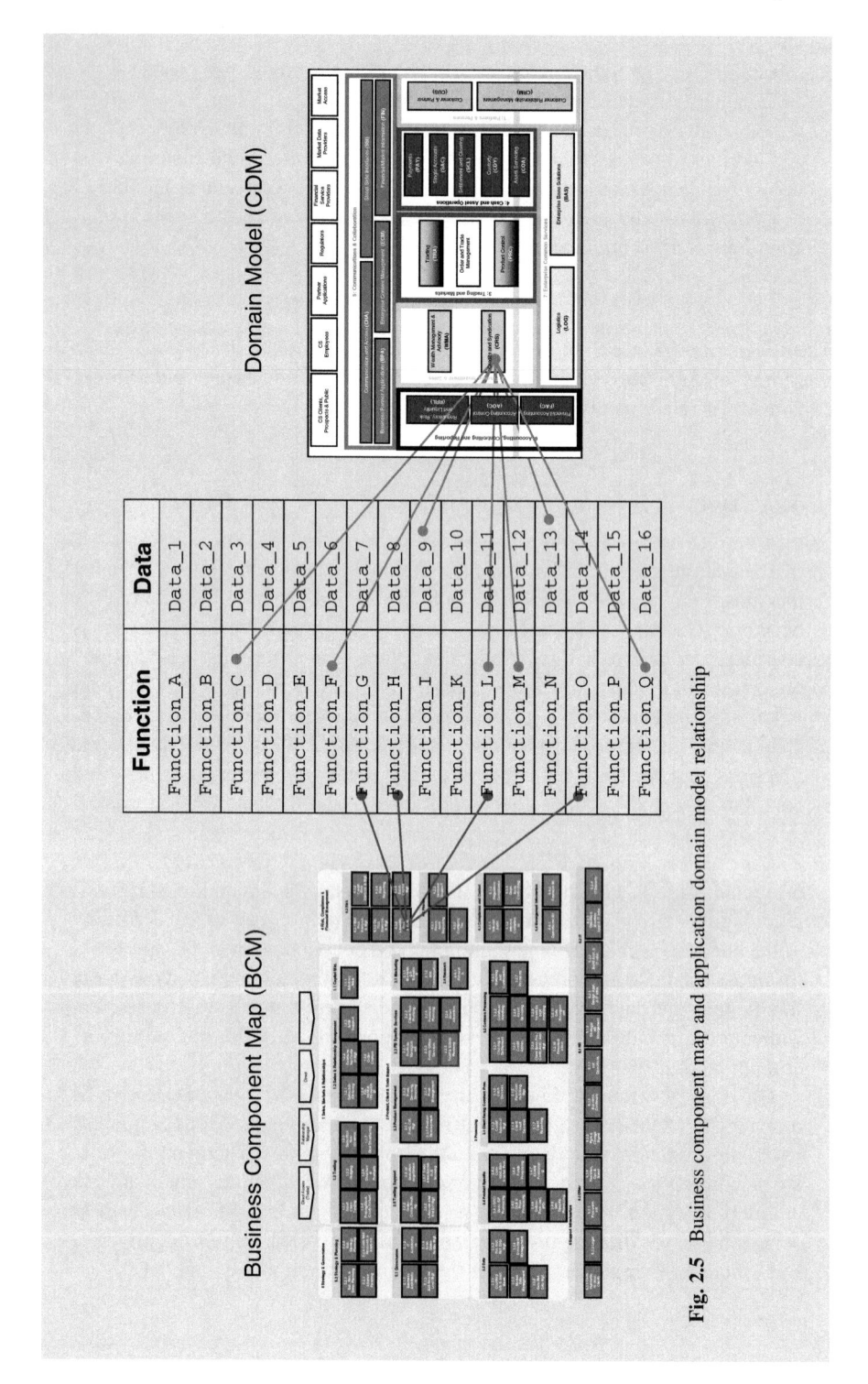

Fig. 2.5 Business component map and application domain model relationship

Business component maps and domain models are *structural models*. Structural models are necessary, but not sufficient to model an information system. In a very large information system with many stakeholders and a distributed system development activity the *semantics* – the exact *meaning* ([Vygotsky_02], [Portner_05]) of all concepts, terms and expressions used in the system – must be defined ([McComb_04]) so that all architects, programmers and users of the system rely on a common semantic definition of the shared objects. Semantic ambiguity is one of the prime reasons for redundancy in systems. The same concept is implemented slightly differently in different domains. Unclear semantics lead to integration problems because two sides of an interface do not share the understanding of data fields. They may, for example, assume different units of measurement. This creates the need for *semantic models*.

Semantics can be modeled on different levels of consistency. The simplest form is a *glossary* of terms, including allowable values, units etc. Often used semantic definition instrument are *taxonomies*, which specify the hierarchy and the meaning of terms used in an enterprise ([Stewart_08]). A *business object model* defines semantics on an even higher level of consistency. All business entities are modeled as objects, including their definitions, attributes,

> "As people start forming communities and attacking a problem, their approaches to the solution will vary. As these groups separate, they must develop more detailed communication within each subgroup, and the language diverges. New words aren't usually invented, rather new meanings are imposed on the words and phrases already being used"
> Dave McComb, 2004

operations and relationships ([Daum_03a], [Lhotka_08]). The richest level of specification is *ontologies* ([Fensel_07], [Allemang_08], [McComb_04]). An ontology is a logical model, defining all the objects, attributes and relationships in a formal, machine-readable way. Ontologies – especially based on the standardized Web Ontology Language OWL – form the base of the semantic web and thus of future, semantically interoperable business systems ([Dietz_06], [Lacy_05], [Stuckenschmidt_05], [Haase_06], Financial Ontology: [Montes_05]). The advantage of ontologies is that they can be fully checked for internal consistency.

As an example, a small extract of the Credit Suisse business object model (BOM) is presented in Side-Story 2.5. The business object model is an important instrument of application architecture.

Side-Story 2.5: Credit Suisse Business Object Model

Business object models (BOMs), [Daum_03a], [Lhotka_08]) are highly industry-specific models of the business concepts, their properties and their relationships. Developing a sound, useful business object model for a very large information system is a major endeavor which requires the massive collaboration of both business knowledge and IT knowledge resources.

A business object model captures the essence of a business in a formal way and forms the basis for consistent IT implementation.

> "A sound conceptual model documents that the participating analysts and engineers have understood the problem"
> Berthold Daum, 2003

In order to keep the BOM manageable[2], Credit Suisse used three levels of *aggregation* and three levels of *abstraction* (Fig. 2.6).

The *aggregation levels* (from top to bottom) are "enterprise level", "domain level" and "component level". Enterprise level business objects – labeled eBOs – are at the top level. eBOs are valid for the complete enterprise. The eBOs are refined by top-down transformation rules to the domain level (see Side-Story 2.3), where the domain business objects dBOs are maintained. The domain business object model dBOM is the core knowledge base of banking concepts and their relationships. The lowest level of aggregation is the "component business objects", i.e. the cBOs. cBOs are modeled when individual components are defined. cBOs are then used as the basis for implementation.

The *abstraction levels* are "conceptual", "logical" and "physical". The BOM only handles the conceptual levels. The lower abstraction levels are deduced and refined from the conceptual models.

Figure 2.7 shows the enterprise level BOM of Credit Suisse: All the key concepts are captured and represented. All the dBOs – on the domain level – are refined from the eBOs by adhering to clearly specified refinement rules that are automatically checked by a model checker.

		Enterprise Level	Domain Level	Component Level
Abstraction Level	Conceptual Level	Enterprise Business Object Model	Domain Business Object Model	Component Business Object Model
	Logical Level		Logical Domain Model (optional, recommended)	Logical Data Model
	Physical Level			Physical Data Model

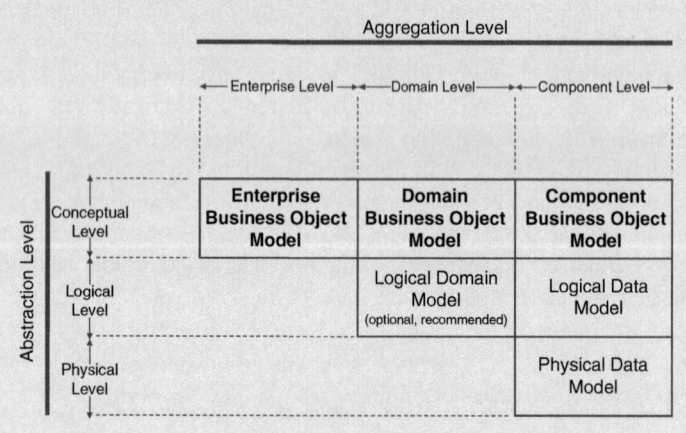

Fig. 2.6 BOM abstraction and aggregation levels in Credit Suisse

---

[2]The Credit Suisse BOM contains 21 Enterprise Business Objects (eBOs), in the order of 500 Domain Business Objects (dBOs) and several thousand Component Business Objects (cBOs).

2.5 Application Architecture

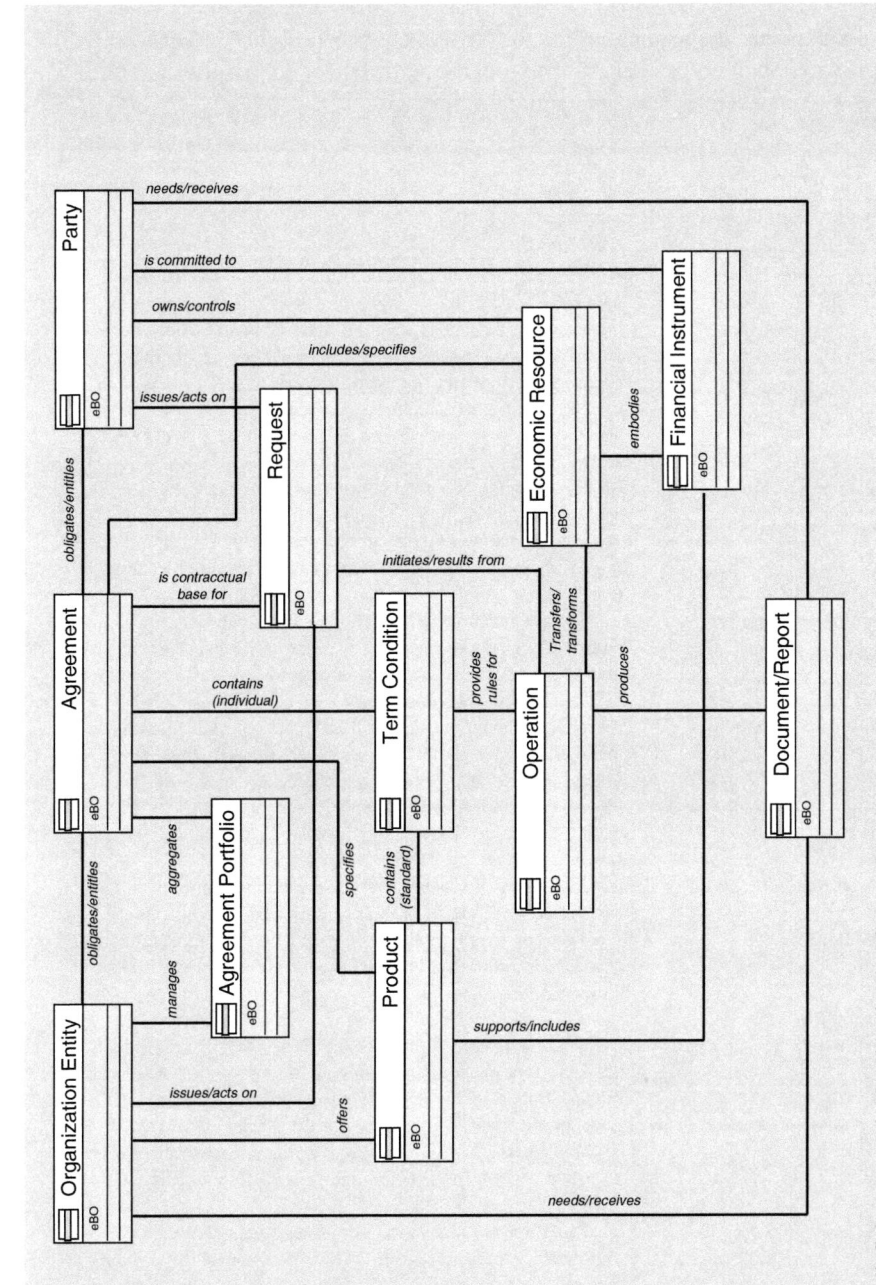

Fig. 2.7 Credit Suisse enterprise level business object model

A condensed specification of the eBOs is given in Table 2.2. The full specification of eBOs contains the properties (attributes), the associations and the BO management and versioning information.

Table 2.2 Description of Credit Suisse enterprise level business objects

Enterprise level business object eBO	Description
Organization Entity	An OrganizationEntity is any unit within Credit Suisse. These units may be ordered in a legal hierarchy, according to a line management hierarchy (or matrix) or in an organization chart
Party	Any internal or external entity with which an OrganizationEntity exchanges information, documents, goods or services based on an Agreement or a relationship. The entity can be a physical or legal person, a corporation, a government unit, a group of persons and any combination of these
Agreement	An explicit or implicit contract between two or many Parties, specifying rights, obligations and responsibilities of all Parties involved. Agreements have either a predefined validity in time (e.g. a credit duration) or have an indefinite temporal validity (e.g. a cash account)
AgreementPortfolio	The set of Agreements for which the bank has a responsibility based on this AgreementPortfolio to supervise and/or manage risk, investments, performance or other metrics and to report them to the stakeholders and authorities
FinancialInstrument	A FinancialInstrument is a standardized trading or exchange vehicle that defines rights and obligations of a Party using the FinancialInstrument. The value and price of a FinancialInstrument can be obtained from market makers (Party)
Product	A banking service or banking product offered and delivered by an OrganizationEntity to one or several Parties
TermCondition	Standard terms (e.g. prices or rates) and conditions (e.g. credit usage) for Products and specific details of individual Agreements
Request	A Request is any trigger (demand) to execute an action (Operation), exchange information (DocumentReport) or generate, modify or terminate an Agreement
Operation	Transaction performed generally in the context of an Agreement triggered by the arrival of a Request (e.g. order) and resulting in the transfer or exchange of EconomicResources, exchange or modification of information, or change of Agreement
EconomicResource	An EconomicResource is a value under the control of a Party. EconomicResources have measurable properties that can be used by valuation methods to determine their value, e.g. their monetary value
Document/Report	A DocumentReport is a container for information of any form (electronic, paper, message etc.) and of any content (text, figures, pictures, sound, film etc.). A DocumentReport can either be raw information or can be an assembly or aggregation of information from various sources and/or DocumentReports compiled and presented according to a defined set of rules

The "working level" of the BOM is the *conceptual domain level*. Each domain refines and specifies its key business concepts, attributes, associations and operations in their domain business object model dBOM.

As an example, the dBOM of the domain Customer and Partners ("CUS", see Side-Story 2.3) is shown in Fig. 2.8 (without associations). Any project building a solution in the domain CUS – or using domain business objects from the domain CUS – has to start with the CUS domain objects and refine (enrich) them while constructing the component business objects cBOs.

One of the most demanding tasks related to the business object model of a very large information system is the *model consistency*. If the model is not consistent, it may cause more harm than benefit! The hierarchical consistency is assured by a clearly specified set of rules for how a dBO is enriched from an eBO and how a cBO is enriched from a dBO, including the refinement of associations, attributes and operations. Overall consistency as an example assures uniqueness in the namespace for all elements of the model. In a very large information system, business object model consistency can only be assured by a common repository and an automated model checker.

2.6 Technical Architecture

Technical architecture is the underlying layer of infrastructure comprising all elements of IT infrastructure such as hardware, system software, databases, networking components, system management software, database management systems and middleware components. Typically, this layer is not fundamentally dependent on the purpose the system is used for. We call the set of technology components used in this architecture layer the *technology portfolio*. Most of the elements in the technology portfolio can be found underneath any kind of very large information system. There is a gray zone between applications and infrastructure, which is commonly, but not very precisely, called *middleware*. These are technology components that can be considered part of the application or infrastructure in its own right. Depending on the maturity of the organization and the kind of applications on top of the infrastructure, this boundary may be chosen at different levels ([Masak_07], [Woods_03], [Britton_01]). Efficient organizations generally try to move this boundary upwards by standardizing more and more of the middleware and providing it as a set of common services to the applications. It is also a historic development in computing that ever more powerful abstractions have been developed and used over time. Examples include operating systems, virtual machines, databases and transaction monitors. More about the concepts and principles on how to manage the technology portfolio can be found in Chap. 4 (Infrastructure).

The infrastructure layer introduced in Fig. 2.1 is organized as *technical domains*: The technical domains form the basis for managing the *technology portfolio*. In the federated architecture organization each technical domain is managed by a *technical domain architect*. It is the role of the domain architect to define standards and

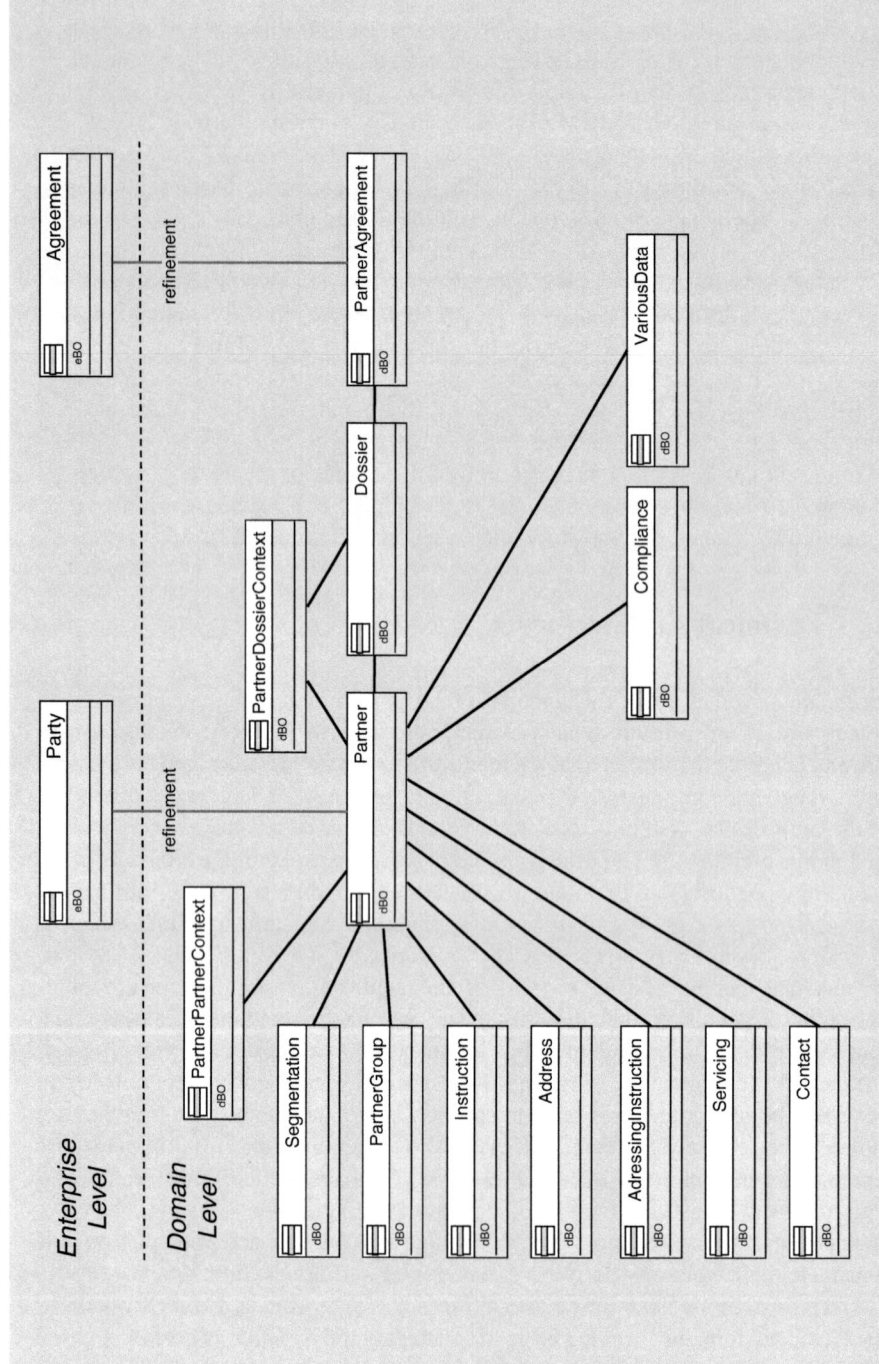

Fig. 2.8 (Side-Story-25) Business object model of the domain "customer and partner"

2.6 Technical Architecture

roadmaps for all the technical components and platforms in his or her domain. Careful, continuous and predictable management of the technology portfolio is fundamental for managed evolution. Replacement of a substantial part of the technology portfolio within a short timeframe is typically impossible due to the application adoption effort. Porting and retesting the large number of applications relying on a particular technical component in very large information systems is just too expensive. If the change in the technology portfolio is gradual and predictable, the applications can adapt within their natural lifecycles paced by the changing business needs.

The choice of technical domains is an important architectural decision reflecting the market segmentation for infrastructure products. A proven technical domain model is shown in Fig. 2.9. This technical domain model contains 11 *technical domains*:

1. *Platforms*: The platforms are specifically defined, engineered and implemented to present the infrastructure services to the applications. Platforms integrate software and hardware components and processes;
2. *Application Development Environments*: Tools and processes needed for the modelling, development, test, integration and documentation of applications;
3. *Integration Software*: Technical components for the communication between applications. Often this is known under the term middleware in the market;

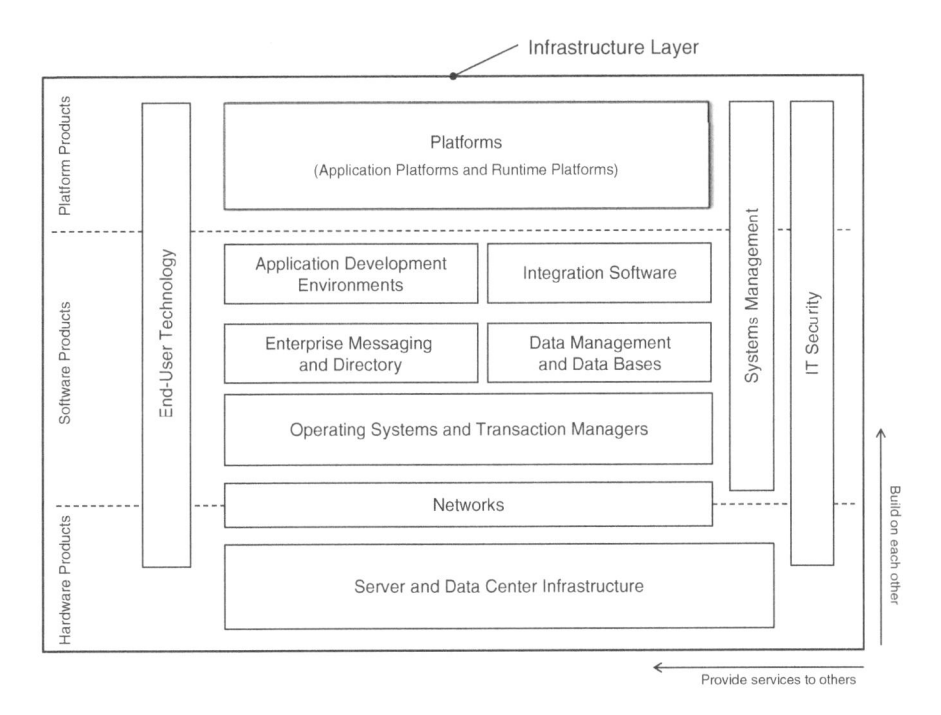

Fig. 2.9 Technical domain model

4. *Enterprise Messaging and Directory*: Enterprise infrastructure for employee and customer communication, including e-Mail, directory services, instant messaging;
5. *Data Management and Data Bases*: Databases and their management systems (e.g. database server software, database client drivers), database development tools (e.g. Schema modelling tools);
6. *Operating Systems and Transaction Managers*: Server operating systems, server virtualization, web and application servers (e.g. JEE container), transaction managers;
7. *Systems Management*: Systems and software required for monitoring, management, performance analysis and operating of the very large information system, such as capacity and performance management, configuration and inventory management, incident management;
8. *IT Security*: All the systems and software for the protection of the assets, such as security administration, data encryption, Internet boundary protection;
9. *End User Technology*: Tools provided to the end user to improve personal productivity, such as personal computers, office applications, collaboration technologies, mobile access and printing;
10. *Networks*: All the products to connect systems on the data transmission level, both within the information system and also across the boundaries, such as to the Internet;
11. *Server and Data Center Infrastructure*: Data center hardware and physical infrastructure, including emergency back up power, cabling, cooling, server hardware and storage facilities.

The technical domains (Fig. 2.9) are organized in three layers: "Hardware products", "software products" and "platform products". Products in higher layers build on top of products in the lower layers. Platforms form the highest layer, providing integrated infrastructure services to the applications. Some technical domains cover more than one layer because software and hardware are closely linked to each other. The technical domain *end-user technology* is such an example, because it contains all the necessary hardware and software products to deliver the end-user services and is in itself a platform.

2.7 Vertical Architectures

Some architecture aspects relate at the same time to business, application and technical architecture and have to be managed across all layers on the level of the entire global system. Such architectures are termed *vertical architectures* (see Fig. 2.10).

Integration architecture is an important prerequisite for the managed evolution. The integration architecture (see Chap. 3) consists of principles, processes and technical solutions for managing the distribution and heterogeneity of the application

2.7 Vertical Architectures

Business Architecture
Business model based on the utilization of optimal processes and organizational structures
-> *which functions, processes and organizations?*

Application Architecture
Well-structured application landscape established according to common principles
-> *which applications and components?*

Technical/Infrastructure Architecture
Standardized application platforms based on standardized technical components
-> *which IT infrastructure?*

Integration Architecture
Standardized interfaces and infrastucture for the integration of applications

System Management Architecture
Cost-efficient and dependable operation of the IT systems

Security Architecture
Protection of the information assets in the system

Vertical Architecture X

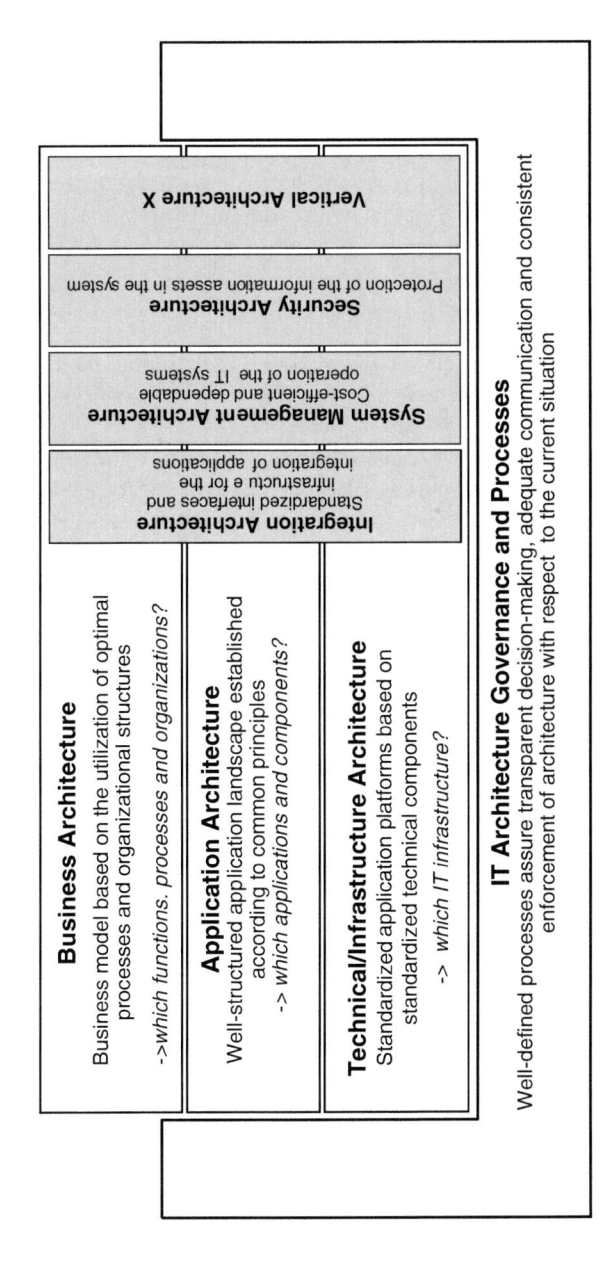

IT Architecture Governance and Processes
Well-defined processes assure transparent decision-making, adequate communication and consistent enforcement of architecture with respect to the current situation

Fig. 2.10 Vertical architecture areas

landscape and the underlying technologies. Most importantly it defines the concept of interfaces, a process to manage interfaces and technologies to implement interfaces across heterogeneous technology platforms and application domains. This is particularly important for the managed evolution, since under this concept only parts of functionality or technology of the entire system can be replaced. So managing the interfaces among these parts, allowing for an independent lifecycle for each part is fundamental for the success of managed evolution of very large information systems. This is recognized by most architects of large systems under the term "Service-Oriented Architecture" (SOA), see ([Erl_04], [Masak_07], [Woods_03], [McGovern_06], [Chappell_04], [Woods_06]), although the contemporary SOA-discussion is still too much focused on the technology rather than *interface management*. It is really crucial to see integration architecture as a vertical architecture that overlaps all three architecture layers in the following ways:

- It overlaps with *business architecture* where services should be integrated in a flexible way to easily create new views on business objects or be orchestrated into new implementations of business processes,
- It overlaps with *application architecture* where the syntax and semantics of the interfaces and general principles of where and how to interface are defined,
- It overlaps with *technical architecture* where it defines the underlying integration technologies, such as middleware, and methods.

Other vertical architectures depend strongly on the context of the system. In the context of banking, where confidentiality of data and flawless operation without interruptions or data losses are mandatory for success, *security architecture* and *systems management architecture* have proven to be essential vertical architectures (Fig. 2.10). One can imagine, however, application areas like numeric simulation systems to define performance architecture or military systems to define resilience architecture. More generally, vertical architectures represent important non-functional aspects of very large information systems which are of universal impact across the whole system.

As a more detailed example, the Credit Suisse security architecture is described in Side-Story 2.6.

Side-Story 2.6. Credit Suisse Security Architecture

Security is an important property of a system of a financial institution. Customer data and client transactions must be well protected against unauthorized access. Because a large percentage of transactions are executed electronically in today's modern banking and at the same time attacks from the outside become more and more frequent and dangerous dependable security architecture is mandatory.

2.7 Vertical Architectures

Today the security of systems is a well studied and fast progressing field. A great number of security concepts, mechanisms, tools and methods exist. To assure sufficient security in a very large information

> "Being able to detect, contain and eradicate security incidents is in many respects equivalent to defusing explosives – the sooner and better you do it, the less impact a security-related incident is likely to have"
> Linda McCarthy, 2003

system, a suitable, consistent and complete set of security measures must be defined, implemented, enforced and controlled: An important means to do so is the *security architecture*.

Security architecture ([Killmeyer_06]) is not described as objects and relationships: Security architecture consists of objectives, concepts, standards and security services that must be implemented throughout the complete system – hence the name "vertical architecture". Vertical architectures – especially security architecture – are not static architectures: The range and scope of threats is ever-increasing, including more sophisticated cyber-crime (see e.g. [Deloitte_10], [CERT_04]). Therefore, the Credit Suisse security architecture and the protection measures are continuously improved and adapted. This is in the responsibility of a global group of security architects, directly reporting to the Chief Architect.

The structure of the Credit Suisse security architecture is shown in Fig. 2.11: It consists of three horizontal *functional layers* – the transportation layer, the transformation layer and the manipulation layer. A typical transaction starts in the manipulation layer in one part of the system, is propagated down through the transformation layer, transported via the transportation layer and arrives in another part of the system where it runs up through the

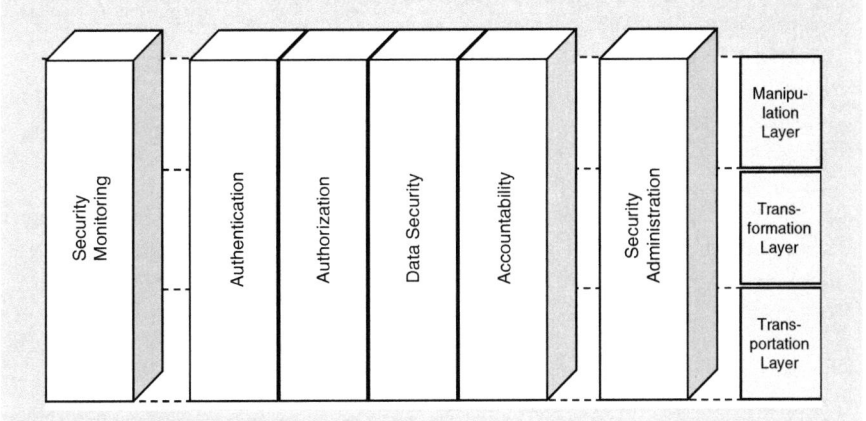

Fig. 2.11 Credit Suisse security architecture

transformation layer and is consumed and processed in the manipulation layer. Each layer is subject to various possible attacks.

The security architecture defines six *security technology towers* (Fig. 2.11): Four of them are *security mechanisms*, i.e. authentication, authorization, data security and accountability. The last two are *security controls*, i.e. security administration and security monitoring (see [Proctor_02], [Umar_04], [McCarthy_03] for details). The individual security technology towers provide the concepts, standards, processes, technologies and services for:

Authentication: Reliable identification and verification of the identity of system users, system components (servers and applications) and external partner systems,

Authorization: Granting (or denying) access of users and system components to resources based on the verified identity of a requestor and relying on explicit access control policies;

Data Security: Protection of data stored in the system or transmitted between systems against any unauthorized access or eavesdropping;

Accountability: Generation of a complete audit trail for all security-relevant transactions, including attacks and incidents;

Security Monitoring: Continuous supervision of the system activities related to security, including detection of real or attempted security breaches, such as intrusions and unauthorized accesses;

Security Administration: Management of identity credentials for authentication and access rights for authorization for all users, systems and resources.

For each functional layer the respective security technology towers specify security components. The security components must strictly be implemented in all parts of the Credit Suisse very large information system. Security is the subject of regular assessments by internal IT risk and audit, and is periodically scrutinized by independent external experts.

The impact of vertical security architecture on managed evolution is twofold: First, the weakest point in the very large information system determines to a large extent the overall security level of the system. It is therefore mandatory, to assure and maintain a consistent level of security throughout the complete very large information system, thus preventing security loopholes. Strong vertical security architecture allows the definition, implementation, checking and auditing of the security mechanisms implemented in the system. Second, individual applications and projects take advantage of the deployed security infrastructure and do not have to spend repeated effort and time on "reinventing security solutions".

2.8 Architecture as an Activity: The Architecture Process

One view of IT architecture is to see it as one of the *management processes* governing a very large information system. The purpose of that process is defining a target architecture and to steer the evolution of the system towards this target architecture. As shown in Fig. 2.12 the *architecture process* can be separated into four *subprocesses*:

1. Architecture development
2. Architecture communication
3. Architecture implementation
4. Architecture controlling.

The architecture *definition* process results in ratified architecture standards, models, target architectures and guidelines, which are mandatory for all development work within scope. The process starts with studies, prototypes and pilot projects. Pilot projects apply non-standard technology in production applications in order to understand general applicability. The evaluation result is subsequently used for decision making. In the ideal IT organization described in Chap. 6, there are two areas where architecture decisions are made: In the architecture function within the application development units and in the infrastructure architecture

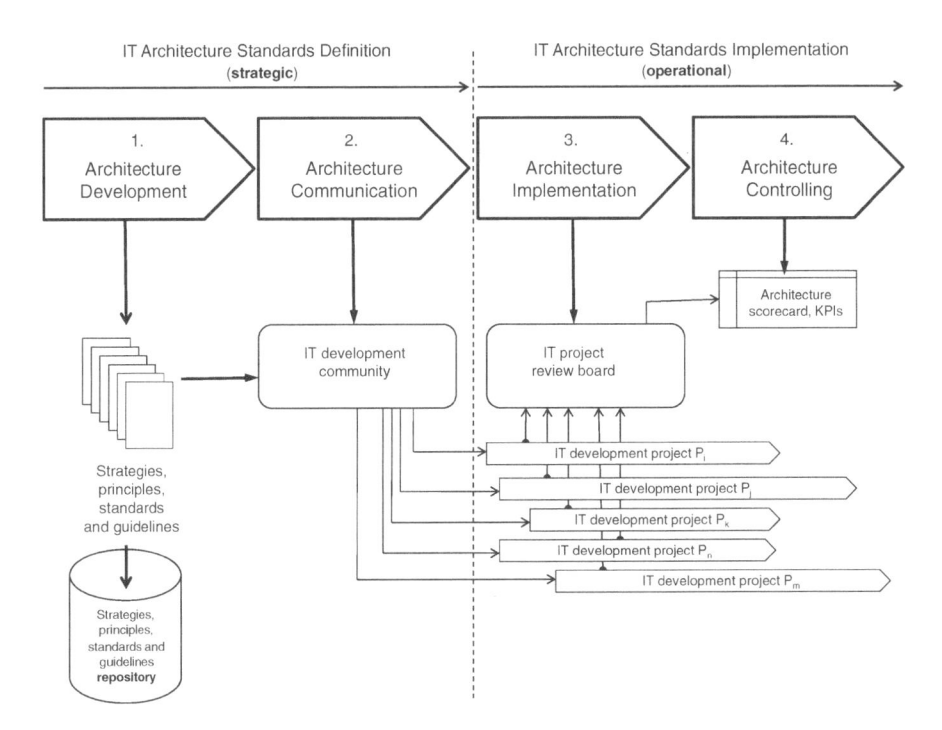

Fig. 2.12 Architecture process

function. These groups should have in place standing steering committees with representation across the architecture communities within their units. These steering committees are responsible for reviewing and approving all major architect decisions regarding strategies, programs, etc.

In addition, an IT-wide architecture steering committee led by the Chief Architect should be established to ratify the major decisions of the underlying committees. This IT-wide committee is also responsible for establishing overall strategy and many of the overarching elements of architecture management described in this book.

It is important to reinforce the binding nature of the decisions of these bodies by having well-defined membership and charters, regular scheduled meetings and published documentation and minutes. Where appropriate, the decisions should be documented as official standards for the IT organization.

The most important architecture strategies and decisions should be taken to the IT management committee for discussion and decision. For this to be effective, the Chief Architect should establish as part of the architecture planning cycle an agenda of key decisions required to support the managed evolution and guide these decisions through the governance process so they can be properly positioned for success with his or her peers.

The efficient operation of these steering bodies requires investment in syndication of the proposed decisions with the relevant committee members and other influential stakeholders prior to the meeting. In our experience, without such syndication and the integration of the resulting feedback into the proposal, many decisions will be sent back for further work or be rejected altogether.

As architecture work starts with every single developer, *architecture communication* is a very important first step to steer the system towards the target architecture. Architecture communication starts with a well structured *architecture documentation* that documents all the standards, guidelines, target architectures and the like. It is crucial that multiple targeted views of the same set of standards exist for different roles in the development process. The Java software developer will generally not be interested in testing standards for mainframe software developers and vice versa. Architecture needs to be communicated over multiple channels including documentation on the web, formal developer education, question and answer sessions with the architects and management leadership by the senior architects. It is important that communication is not a one-way channel, as widespread acceptance in the community is paramount to success. The general experience shows that resources invested into good communication pay back several times in the architecture implementation process.

> "Critical structural decisions are often made on the side, without executing proper control – for example, an engineer might quickly write a small batch program to synchronize data between two systems, and 10 years later, a small army of developers is needed to deal with the consequences of this ad-hoc decision"
> Dirk Krafzig, 2005

As an example the Credit Suisse architecture communication concept is presented in Side-Story 2.7.

Side-Story 2.7. Credit Suisse Architecture Communication Process

Architecture knowledge has become quite extensive in Credit Suisse. Much of it is documented in the form of binding IT standards. One key requirement is to make this knowledge available to the community in a suitable form. This is the objective of the *architecture communication process*. At Credit Suisse architecture communication happens through a number of different channels, such as classroom learning, consulting in projects, regular brush-ups, written communication and up-to-date webpages.

Classroom learning starts with the *architecture boot camp*: Each new hire entering a Credit Suisse Private Banking development department goes through a 2-day boot camp where the basics of Credit Suisse IT architecture are presented. Another instrument is *Fit-for-Architecture*, a full-day course mandatory to all solution architects at periodic intervals. In fit-for-architecture, new developments in architecture and IT standards are communicated. More than 20 architecture events in the form of auditorium and video broadcast lectures to a larger audience presenting new developments or emerging concepts are carried out each year.

Written communication includes the IT standards. In addition, some periodic publications, such as *InsideIT*, *Transfer* and an *architecture newsletter* are available. These publications are comprehensive and address a large audience.

Last but not least, architects from central architecture and domain architects are involved as consultants in every important project, bringing their expertise into the project at an early stage and accompanying the projects until their completion.

Formal project reviews by central architecture (see Table 2.3) are also used as a communication channel: Any architecture deficiency found during a review is discussed with the project architects, thus educating them on the job.

The *architecture implementation process* ensures that the standards and guidelines are adhered to and that exceptions to standards are managed at the appropriate level. If we presume that the system is changed by the portfolio of projects, this is best ensured by *reviewing* all projects at well-defined points in the project lifecycle with regard to their adherence to architecture standards, the quality of their design and the fit into the remainder of the application landscape. *Project reviews* are executed according to a fixed procedure and are based on formal review sheets. Side-Story 2.8 shows part of the architecture review check list used in the project reviews by Credit Suisse. In addition to that, senior architects are appointed as solution architects for critical projects, where substantial architecture impact is to be expected.

The other element of the architecture implementation process is the design and the sponsoring of *architecture programs*. Architecture programs are collections of IT architecture-driven projects that implement infrastructure in support of the target architecture, restructure applications that are no longer structurally fit for extensions and help retire outdated technology solutions and applications.

Side-Story 2.8. Credit Suisse Check List for Architecture Reviews

Every project of a certain size (measured by its development cost) or of architectural importance is reviewed four times according to the Credit Suisse project methodology by a team of IT architecture reviewers. Credit Suisse Private Banking uses two project methodologies: The classical *waterfall model* and the Rational Unified Process (RUP). For each project, the adequate methodology is chosen.

As an example, the waterfall model reviews correspond to the four project phases:

- *PC*: Project concept. The initial project concept is described in a document. It contains the basic project justification, the main project objectives and the project setup.
- *PO*: Project offer. The planned implementation – possibly including some options – is described in a document. Risk analysis and project planning is presented.
- *RO*: Realization offer. The project documents its activities, the solution architecture, the interaction with other applications and projects and the impact on the application landscape. The project planning and risk analysis is refined.
- *RC*: Request for conclusion. The project reports on the achievements, the open issues and the recommendations for the future.

The review is conducted by 2–5 reviewers based on an IT architecture project review checklist. Table 2.3 shows a short check list extract covering general questions, setup and banking applications. The full checklist covers all systems management, infrastructure, etc. Reviewers agree on common findings, resulting in a consolidated review report being communicated to the project. The conclusion of the review report is either "OK" which means that the project can continue as proposed, or "OKA" ("Auflagen" in German, hence "OKA"), which means that the project has to accept obligations, or "NOK" (Not OK) meaning that the project cannot enter the next phase before the raised issues are resolved and reviewed again.

The most important part of the review report is the *obligations*: Here the reviewers express requirements for architectural integrity of the modifications done by the project to the application landscape. Any obligation entered by the reviewers is recorded in a centralized obligation management system and is tracked. The mechanism of associating obligations by architecture reviewers to projects is important for managed evolution: It assures that each project is contributing to – or at least not damaging – the architectural integrity of the application landscape and thus improves the agility of the system (as shown in Fig. 1.7.).

2.8 Architecture as an Activity: The Architecture Process

Table 2.3 (Side-Story 2.8) Credit Suisse IT architecture review checklist (Extract)

IT Architecture Project Review Board of the 27.05.2009	OK	OKA	NOT OK	Reasons for NOK
Evaluation Architecture		X		

Architecture Reviewers	Date	Findings	Condition	Deadline
Hans Muster Peter Beispiel Jürg Modell	19.05.2009	The proposed data migration concept leads to unmanaged data redundancy	Propose a new data migration concept which completely eliminates data redundancy	PO

Exceptions, accepted deviation from standards
none

Conditions of Previous Reviews	Y	N	I	Comment / Statement
Have the conditions of the previous review(s) been met?			X	No open conditions
If conditions have not been met, discuss further actions with KSCD				

Review Details

Part 1: Sufficient/adequate documentation of architecture relevant requirements/descriptions

Nr.	PC	PO	RO	RC	Legend: Y = Yes / N = No / I = Irrelevant	Y	N	I	Comment / Statement
V01	X	X			Has the relevance for the strategy been described ■ Overall strategy/IT strategy ■ Strategy of domain/area				
V02	(X)	X	X		Have the functional requirements been described in a way that allows to derive and assess the implications on the IT-architecture and design?				
V03	(X)	X	X		Are the non-functional requirements described in a way that allows to derive and evaluate implications for the IT architecture and design.				
V04	(X)	X	X		Is the architecture relevant information available and are the relevant architecture decisions documented, e.g. concerning ● Available options (PO) ● Integration into overall system ● Interfaces to other projects/domains/applications ● Application and technical solution ● Security concept, risks ● Systems management, production ● Phase out of 'obsolete' architecture (e.g. technical or application components)				
V05		(X)	X		Entries in Information System and Dictionaries: ■ Application parameters entered in the applications inventory? ■ Portfolio of technical standards (TIA) updated?				

(continued)

Table 2.3 (Side-Story 2.8) (continued)

Part 2: General setup, integration/delineation

Nr.	PC	PO	RO	Legend: Y = Yes / N = No / I = Irrelevant	Y	N	I	Comment / Statement
G02	X	X	(X)	Integration into the overall system/ avoidance of redundancies ■ Are the boundaries/interactions with other projects, processes, domains, applications and infrastructures clear and appropriate? ■ Are potential redundancies, overlaps e.g. concerning infrastructures, services reasonable? Justified? Accepted? ■ Is there a mix of old and new architecture? Reasonable? Justified?				
G03		X	X	Migration to standard architecture / phase out of obsolete architecture/standards: ■ Are the necessary actions for a migration to standard architecture planned, described and appropriate? ■ Is it documented how/when old architecture will be phased out?				
G04	(X)	X	(X)	Options: ■ Are the proposed options appropriate and complete? ■ Is the proposed option reasonable?				
G05	(X)	X	X	Risks: ■ Have all risks relevant for architecture been identified? ■ Have they been mitigated accordingly?				
				etc.				

The fourth architecture process – *architecture controlling* – measures progress towards the target architecture. Typically this process is implemented as a balanced scorecard ([Kaplan_96], [Niven_06], [Kaplan_06]) of key performance indicators measuring various indicators (see Side-Story 7.3), including the following:

1. Standard *deviation indicators* measure on the one hand, whether the exception management process is sound and, on the other hand, whether the standards are appropriate to fulfil a majority of the needs.
2. Strategy *adoption indicators* measure how new architecture elements are being accepted in the projects. This is particularly important if the strategy requires the retirement of a widely used technology or interface. There, careful observation of the progress and immediate reaction to deviation from the plan are crucial for success.
3. Architecture *process quality indicators* measure stakeholder feedbacks, review efficiency, decision making efficiency, documentation quality and the like.

All performance indicators need to be reviewed regularly by the architecture process owner and the appropriate changes must be made to the other parts of the architecture.

2.9 Architecture Organization: Federated Architecture Process

Very large information systems are typically managed by large organizations. In order for the architecture process to be effective it needs to be embedded properly within the organization. The roles and responsibilities described below need to be defined and implemented.

At the top of the architecture organization there is the *chief architect* responsible for the architecture across the whole, global system. Alternatively, the chief architect is replaced by a committee of senior architects that make decisions. Given the strategic importance of architecture for managed evolution, the chief architect should, ideally, directly report to the CIO (Chief Information Officer) or other manager in charge of the overall IT organization in the company. Key tasks of the chief architect include the following:

- Lead the global architecture organization in its functional and regional dimensions
- Chair the chief architect's council that decides on architectural standards and concepts
- As a direct report to the Chief Information Officer (CIO) the chief architect represent architecture in the IT management team
- Lead the global architecture process, with a particular focus on reviewing projects for architectural alignment
- Drive improvement of architecture, propose IT architecture changes
- Provide IT architecture frameworks and standards
- Lead definition of strategy and roadmap for IT architecture
- Sponsor a project portfolio to help implement architectural standards and concepts, such as the execution of architecture programs
- Approve exceptions to standards where necessary.

Typically the chief architect is supported by a team that facilitates the architecture process by preparing the meetings, recording the decisions, facilitating communications like web conferencing or preparing events and measuring key performance indicators. In addition to that, a group for each of the architecture layers or vertical areas (application architecture, technical architecture, security architecture, etc.) directly reports to the chief architect. The heads of these groups take responsibility for the respective architecture area in the sense

> "The idea of Federated Enterprise Architecture is a practical way to employ architectural concepts in complex, multiunit enterprises; however, there is nothing magic happening. Someone has to figure out and actually create and manage what is to be federal, that is, centralized, optimized relative to the overall enterprise (or cluster), integrated, reused, etc. and conversely, someone has to figure out what is not to be federated, that is, what is to remain local, sub-optimized relative to the enterprise, unique to the business units"
> John Zachman, 2006

that they are experts in the field, define relevant architectural concepts and standards for approval by the Chief Architecture Steering Committee and sponsor projects in their area. Typically the architecture area heads also chair teams of experts throughout the organization that help prepare architecture decisions.

Depending on the organization and on the importance of using the latest technology, the chief architect may also lead a research group that helps facilitate innovation in the system. This team would usually be aligned to the external research and industrial community in order to understand relevant technical developments and be able to transfer those into the organization. They generally work with advanced technology studies, prototypes and pilots in order to evaluate new technologies for general use in the system. The leader of the group is responsible for the *innovation portfolio*.

In order to avoid the "ivory tower syndrome", it is important that all architects in these groups also perform real project work. Very often these architects act as solution architects in projects of high architectural importance. It has proven to be a good split of work, if these people dedicate one third of their time to projects and two thirds of their time to enterprise architecture work. In the experience of the authors, the chief architect's direct organization should roughly represent 1% of the staff in the overall IT organization.

According to the size of the organization, the chief architect's organization can be federated and have divisional (= business unit) or regional chief architects with the same responsibility for a business unit or a region of the IT organization as the chief architect has for the entire company. This organization is well suited for large IT organizations with a business unit or regional structure that share substantial parts of their systems. This is typically the case if all business units are in the same business and share a single domain model, or if the business units are heavily dependent on each other, by sharing a single infrastructure. To sum it up, the architecture organization needs to have the same scope as the system that is managed as a whole, which is tightly coupled and governed by the same principles.

In a two-level chief architect's organization the architecture area groups can be distributed to the business units or the regions according to the main user principle or be kept centrally. Typically each business unit's chief architect has his own architecture process group supporting the process in his business unit or region.

As architecture should be governed along the domain model, *domain architects* are needed that are responsible for all aspects in their domain with the following key tasks:

- Maintain, develop, communicate and enforce the *target architecture* for the assigned domain. Define roadmaps and strategies to move towards the target domain architecture,
- Together with the other domain architects continue to develop the overarching domain model, decide on assigning technical products or applications to the appropriate domains,

2.9 Architecture Organization: Federated Architecture Process

- Maintain the necessary data and object *models* for the assigned domain, align to overarching models, drive prototypes, pilots and reengineering projects in the domain,
- Regularly assess domain fitness, define necessary remediation steps.
- Maintain architectural information about the domain in order to facilitate system-wide analyses,
- Review all projects that affect the domain,
- Lead all solution architects in the domain.

Domain architects need to be senior architects with a broad background, a deep understanding of their domain and outstanding leadership skills. Domain architects should report to the head of the developer group responsible for developments in the domain. As the enterprise-wide architects, domain architects should be deeply involved in projects. In the experience of the authors, a good split between project and architecture governance work for the domain architects is 50% each. All domain architects together typically represent another 1% of the overall IT staff as a good benchmark, including one domain architect and one deputy for each domain.

There are two kinds of domain architects: *Technical domain architects* have responsibility for the architecture in a technical domain. Their second reporting line is into the head of technical architecture. *Application domain architects* have responsibility for application architecture in the domain and have a second reporting line into the head of application architecture. The responsibilities of application and technical domain architects are slightly different because technical domains are mainly buy-and-integrate, whereas application domains are often in-house development-based. One major role of technical domain architects is to understand and act on market trends. In contrast, application domain architects are more focused on the dialog with their business partners to understand requirements.

In the two-level chief architect model, each business unit has their own domain architects for all the domains relevant to the business unit. All business units work with the same domain model. If there are multiple domain architects for the same domain, but in different business units, one of them is the lead domain architect, in charge of system-wide issues in a domain.

The third and largest group of architects is the *solution architects*. Depending on the setup of the development organization, they are grouped in pools or assigned as secondary roles to experienced developers. Each project should have a solution architect assigned, in charge of the technical solution behind the project. Solution architects need to be well trained and guided in order to understand the relevant guidelines and standards applicable to their project. They need good leadership and communication skills to guide the work inside their project team and to communicate with the larger architecture organization to ensure a proper fit of their project work. As explained in Chap. 1 steering every project vector a little bit into the direction of better agility is the most effective way to evolve the system in the right direction. Solution architects are key enablers of this process, as they make most of the micro-architecture design decisions, which if added together constitute the architectural progress. Solution architects are also responsible to fix issues that come up during the project reviews. But, one needs to be realistic here: Project reviews can identify bad design or certain design flaws. But they cannot turn bad design into good design by means of architecture obligations. The ultimate factor for good design quality is the quality of the work of the solution architects. If they don't master their jobs, the whole organization doesn't work. The architecture process can only help by providing templates and standards that reduce the design space and by reviewing the project results in order to ensure quality. Therefore, a focus is needed on the selection and the development of solution architects. Chap. 6 (People and Culture) will elaborate more on this aspect. Typically, solution architects constitute a few percent of the total IT staff.

Side-Story 2.9: Credit Suisse IT Architecture Organization

Information technology within Credit Suisse is organized as a global unit, serving all business units, with the CIO reporting to the CEO of the company. As information technology is crucial to the bank's success, roughly 20% of the bank's staff belongs to the information technology unit. The bulk of the IT staff, on the one hand, belongs to four business-aligned departments building and maintaining applications for the three core businesses: investment banking; private banking; and for the shared services area. On the other hand, all infrastructure activities and the operation of data centers and applications sit with the technology infrastructure department. Credit Suisse is managed in the four regions Americas, Europe Middle East Africa, Asia Pacific and Switzerland. Each region is managed by a regional CIO in charge of local IT matters, such as human resources, regulatory reporting and day-to-day operation (Fig. 2.13).

The architecture organization is federated and includes a small central team in charge of global tools and processes to maintain the necessary data to manage architecture. These systems include an application and technology portfolio, which holds the current architecture of the global system as well as the formal target architecture, organized along the application and the technical domain model (see Side-Story 2.3). Other central teams manage *security architecture* and *integration architecture*. This reflects the view that security in a globally integrated system is only as good as its weakest link. Integration architecture maintains the necessary standards and interface contracts to enable interoperability across the enterprise. The central organization is lead by the bank's *chief architect*. The chief architect directly reports to the bank's CIO in charge of the information technology unit. The chief architect runs a global architecture steering committee to set standards and guidelines across the bank. In addition to that he/she also runs a global architecture program bundling bank wide *IT architecture investments*, as

2.9 Architecture Organization: Federated Architecture Process 75

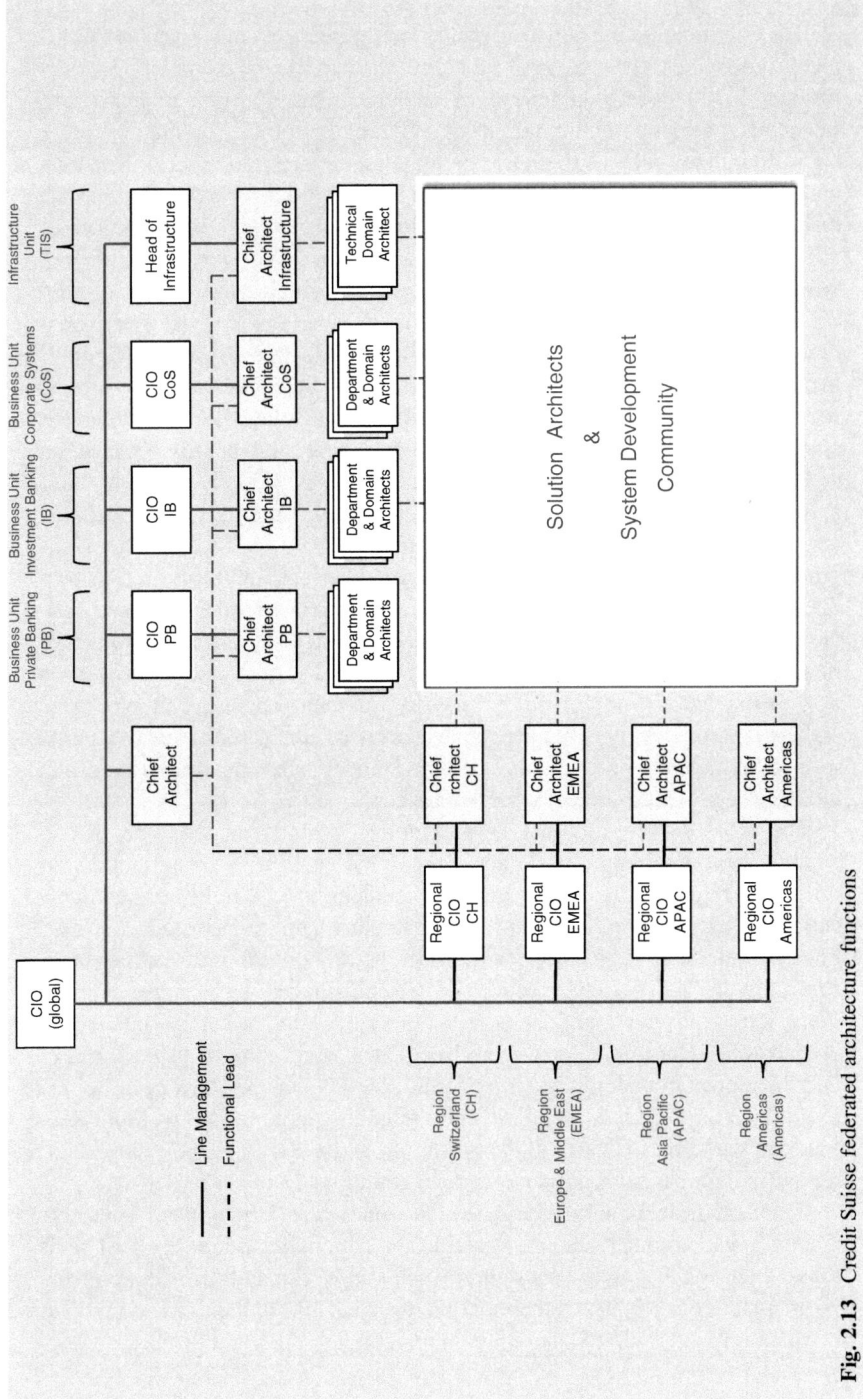

Fig. 2.13 Credit Suisse federated architecture functions

well as coordinating the departmental architecture programs. The chief architect is one of the CIO's two staff functions, the other being the chief operating officer (COO) mainly in charge of resource planning, risk management, financials, project portfolio, reporting and planning of the IT unit.

Furthermore, each of the business units mentioned above have their own architecture organizations, with a chief architect who reports directly into the business units' CIO with a functional management line into the bank's chief architect. The departmental chief architect runs a departmental architecture steering committee, in charge of setting departmental standards and guidelines according to the overarching guidelines. These groups run the day-to-day architecture implementation process by managing a departmental architecture program. Furthermore, they participate in a departmental project review board, reviewing all projects, thus ensuring adherence to all relevant standards. For the application oriented departments this mainly means data and application architecture. One particular case is the *infrastructure* chief architect, who is at the same time departmental chief architect of the technology infrastructure services department. In contrast to his application colleagues who cover the application domain model (see Side-Story 2.3) within their department, he covers the whole technical domain model (see Sect. 4.2). He has groups in charge of the technology portfolio and platform architecture managing the interface between applications and infrastructure, as well as system management architecture ensuring efficient operation of platforms and applications. As with his colleagues, infrastructure architecture maintains its own architecture program and enforces standards in infrastructure projects via the departmental project review board.

The most senior architect in a region – who is usually one of the departmental chief architects – acts as regional chief architect with a dotted line to the regional CIO. The regional responsibility is mainly for communication, culture and building up an architecture community in the region. Furthermore, he is responsible for finding synergy opportunities across business units from a regional perspective. Often it makes sense to use applications across business units in a local market, even if that isn't the case globally. Regional chief architects bring their unique regional perspective into the global architecture steering committee. Typical regional peculiarities in the banking business include local regulatory requirements or input on a function the region is particularly strong in, as for example the Asia Pacific region as a global software development center.

People in these functions are generally well-trained, experienced enterprise architects with strong technical, strategic and communication skills. As Credit Suisse believes that architects should be able to work hands-on, all architects on the first two levels have an obligation to spend 25% of their time on project work, often in the role of a solution architect in an important project.

2.9 Architecture Organization: Federated Architecture Process

The departmental chief architects have functional lines to the domain architects, which organizationally sit with the corresponding development and engineering departments. If the same domain is being worked on in multiple departments, each has its own domain architect. Domain architects of the same domain coordinate with each other. Appointing a lead domain architect has been considered in cases where there are particularly strong synergy opportunities among business units. Domain architects spend roughly 50% of their time in strategic planning, coordination and alignment of their domain, while they spend the other 50% on projects, typically as solution architect.

The *domain architects* in turn lead the solution architects responsible for architecture of the individual projects touching a domain. Each project has the role of an architect in charge of the solution design in the project. In large projects, solution architect is usually a distinct role, while a senior developer might take it on in smaller projects.

The organization described in Side-Story 2.9 is appropriate to Credit Suisse's IT unit with more than 10'000 headcount. For a smaller organization one layer less would be sufficient.

Chapter 3
Integration Architecture

Summary Integration architecture provides the key concepts, processes and mechanisms for the implementation of managed evolution. At the heart of integration architecture is the decomposition of the very large information system into manageable components and the decoupling of the components by managed interfaces with formal syntax and precise semantics. The managed interfaces are enriched by non-functional properties and thus form services which are governed by stable contracts between service provider and service consumers. Administration and management of the service inventory is a major task in a very large information system belonging to a large, complex organization. Service delivery is based on a dependable service delivery infrastructure, implemented as an enterprise service bus.

3.1 Enabling Managed Evolution

As has been explained in Chap. 1, systems age in such a way that some parts of it become structurally unfit to fulfill new requirements. Outdated data structures which are no longer appropriate to hold information are one typical example that is observed. This situation creates tension between IT and business, because the system can no longer be adapted fast enough to satisfy strategic requirements. At times, high IT *integration cost* for new functionality destroys the business case of a business initiative. One example of this is integrating standard software to support enterprise resource planning processes. Experience shows, that the integration effort in such projects often exceeds the financial limit for a good business case.

In such cases, the system needs major restructuring. Because we cannot replace very large information systems as a whole, we must restructure them part by part and add enhancements by integrating new parts. The parts must be small enough to be replaced in one go, without incurring disproportionate risk. With the size of the system its complexity grows because the number of parts and connections increases. This makes exchanging parts difficult because each connection creates a number of additional dependencies as shown in Sect. 1.2. The concept of *integration architecture* is required to define the parts and their connections in a systematic way with the aim to preserve maximum *agility* and minimize *integration cost*. First, we reduce complexity by reducing the number of parts. This approach is limited by the adequate size of a part such that it can still be replaced as a whole. In the logic of the discussion in Chap. 1, a very large information system therefore must consist of more than one part. This requires cutting the parts such that they contain blocks of functionality and information that are reusable in many contexts. Furthermore, it requires that the parts expose functionality in a way that makes reuse efficient. Second, complexity can be reduced by reducing the number of connections which in turn also reduces the number of dependencies. After reducing the number of parts and connections to the maximum extent possible, the third objective is to couple parts as loosely as possible along the connections ([Kaye_03]).

> "Software is the ultimate building material, infinitely malleable and incapable of wearing out. Economic forces lead us to build systems of increasing complexity and thus, because of human limitations in coping with complexity, we abstract. The history of software engineering is, therefore, the history of abstraction"
> Marc T. Sewell, 2002

Very large information systems as defined in Chap. 1 are typically comprised of thousands of applications which are partly in-house built and partly acquired from third parties. Many of the applications are legacy systems. The applications run on heterogeneous infrastructures, such as a variety of operating systems and databases. In addition, applications are built with different technologies, such as different programming languages, compilers and libraries.

In order to provide an *agile system* able to support common business processes and sharing data across applications throughout the organization, the applications and data need to be integrated. Integration must be enabled on all levels, such as infrastructure, applications and data, as well as processes. The concepts underlying integration are defined in *integration architecture*. Various solutions to integration architecture or enterprise architecture exist and are extensively described in the literature ([Hohpe_04], [Fowler_03], [Newcomer_05], [Lankhorst_05], [Krafzig_05]). Typical solutions include hub and spoke messaging, or various enterprise integration patterns.

The authors believe that integration based on *managed services* and a standardized *service delivery infrastructure* is best suited to managed evolution. This approach is commonly known as service oriented architecture (SOA) or Enterprise Service Architecture (ESA) as introduced, e.g., in [McGovern_06], [Pulier_06], [Erl_04], [Erl_05]. Integration architecture, therefore, needs to define processes, methods, tools and technologies to loosen the dependencies created by a connection. Integration architecture has to ensure that the large organization behind a very large information system is enabled to reach the architecture objectives outlined above. Economically speaking, successful integration architecture reduces integration cost. The ability to replace parts of, or add parts to, the system without excessive effort is important to the success of managed evolution. Consequently, the organization's ability to master integration architecture is fundamental to the success of managed evolution.

3.2 Challenges for Integration Architecture

In order to fulfill objectives set out in Sect. 3.1, integration architecture needs to define various elements and answer very challenging questions. The discipline of software engineering provides many answers, although the solutions provided by software engineering often do not scale to the level of very large information systems. In this chapter, the authors will discuss where traditional approaches to software engineering need to be extended in that context.

From a *software engineering* point of view, the parts of the system correspond to software components and connections correspond to interfaces. The reader will find various definitions of software components in the literature. The definition, which fits the purpose of this book best, is the definition by C. Szyperski and C. Pfister ([Szyperski_97]):

A software component is a unit of composition with conceptually specified interfaces and explicit context dependencies only. A software component can be deployed independently and is subject to composition by third parties.

For the remainder of this chapter we will use "component" according to this definition[1].

The responsible integration architects have to address questions such as the right size of components, generalization versus specialization and hierarchical structure of components. They have to come up with various ways of classifying components in order to master the complexity of a very large information system. Most importantly though, integration architecture has to take care of the individual interfaces by which components expose their state and functionality. Complexity increases primarily with the number of parts and the number of interfaces. In addition, complexity is also generated by the complexity of the individual interfaces, such as the number and complexity of parameters passed. The challenge here is to keep complexity at bay. Remember that the number of interfaces may increase more than linearly with the number of components if not properly managed (Sect. 1.2).

Changing a component may lead to changes in its own interfaces and therefore in other components depending on those interfaces. Due to the different pace of change of the various business areas, components have different lifecycles: Some components are modified weekly and other components remain stable for longer periods. If one of the faster changing components changes, the stable components may need to change too, if they are not properly isolated. Therefore, the challenge of integration

---

[1]Up to this point, the terms "application" and "component" were used less precisely.

architecture is to create interfaces in such a way that only components, which are currently interested in the change, have to adapt and that all other components can operate unchanged – and be modified later when change becomes relevant to them as well. Designing interfaces for

> "Enterprise Service Architecture (ESA) is our context for creating business value with Information Technology"
> Dan Woods, 2006

explicit, precise semantics, proper separation of fast and of slow changing components and backwards compatible extensibility is at the heart of good integration architecture ([Alesso_05], [Bussler_03], [Dietz_06], [Fensel_07]). It requires a very deep and broad understanding of the business and the underlying technology.

Integration architecture has to define methods to specify the functional and semantic aspects of interfaces. In very large information systems, *non-functional properties* such as service levels, maximum loads and cost accounting become very important aspects that go far beyond interface specifications. For the remainder of this book the authors will use the term *service* for the interface and the specification of all conditions for the use of the interface. Design principles on how to choose the right interfaces and build successful services will be introduced in Sect. 3.4.

Integration architecture has to define the technical implementation of services and provide the corresponding infrastructure. As an additional challenge, very large information systems have grown continuously over decades and build on a heterogeneous set of technologies. Substantial parts of the system exist and should be exposed as components although they were not built on modern component technology such as Java or .NET. Integration architecture needs to define how legacy applications can expose themselves as components and get access to components provided in other technologies.

The link between components and their implementation *infrastructure* leads to a further complication for integration architecture. If one component based on a specific technology moves to another technology, dependent components should not have to move. This is a particularly important challenge when we move a system component by component, towards a more modern implementation technology. The solution is to connect the components on a level that is independent of the implementation technology used by the components. A technical "lingua franca" (= common language) for applications to interact with each other has to be defined, without degrading system performance to the point where the system can no longer meet the required service levels. Sect. 3.7 will discuss the service delivery infrastructure in more detail.

Componentization of very large information systems leads to very demanding *runtime environments*. Even if the services are as *loosely coupled* as possible as shown in Sect. 3.4.1, complex *operational dependencies* among technically heterogeneous components are established.

Last, but not least, integration architecture is a *management challenge*. A complete and authoritative catalog of services, standards and tools to document services, compatibility rules, responsibilities and architectural decisions on service design are needed. This is a hard thing to achieve in a very large information system and typically requires federated implementation, aligned with the federation of the architecture process. Applying integration architecture on a global scale leads to a high number of services being developed and used by a large number of people in different parts of the organization. A common understanding of services as *contracts* with obligations and rights for both the provider and the consumer of a service helps build trust in the organization (see Sect. 3.5). This mutual trust is necessary for successful reuse of components as people have no longer end-to-end control over an application. As these contracts evolve over time, a well-defined process to create, modify, use and finally retire services is required. Sect. 3.6 illustrates the authors' view on how integration architecture should be organized.

Legacy systems were not built with components in mind. Therefore, componentization needs to start somewhere. In the process of turning an existing monolithic system into components, integration architecture first needs to define virtual components. Next, all elements, such as code or data, must be assigned to these virtual components without yet separating the components from each other through proper interfaces. Finally, component isolation is gradually introduced where needed. Therefore, the componentization process preparing the system for managed evolution is in itself an evolutionary process. To transform a system from a tightly coupled into a more modular one causes additional complexity requiring careful management. Otherwise, the attempt to reduce complexity by modularizing tightly coupled systems ends with a chaos of unmanageable components and services, which are even harder to develop and operate than the original system. The authors discuss the approach to decomposing monolithic systems in Sect. 3.9.

3.3 Composing Systems from Components

As established in Sect. 3.2, very large information systems well suited for managed evolution consist of flexible components, small enough to be replaceable as a whole, generic enough to be usable for future extensions and providing the right interfaces to avoid unnecessary dependen-

> "Contracts have emerged as an essential concept for component-based system engineering"
> Eric Baduel, 2009

cies. Defining the right components depends on how they should play together. One objective is to reach independence between presentation, process and business logic. Doing so allows presentation, that is the user interface, to be changed, without being forced to adapt process and business logic. Changing process logic should also be possible without making changes to the business logic. Adding the requirement to also integrate external systems, such as B2B relationships, leads to four *integration contexts* as shown in Fig. 3.1.

The most basic integration context in Fig. 3.1 is *functional composition*, where components use other components to build richer functionality. Useful components for that pattern provide interfaces that hide the internal implementation and data

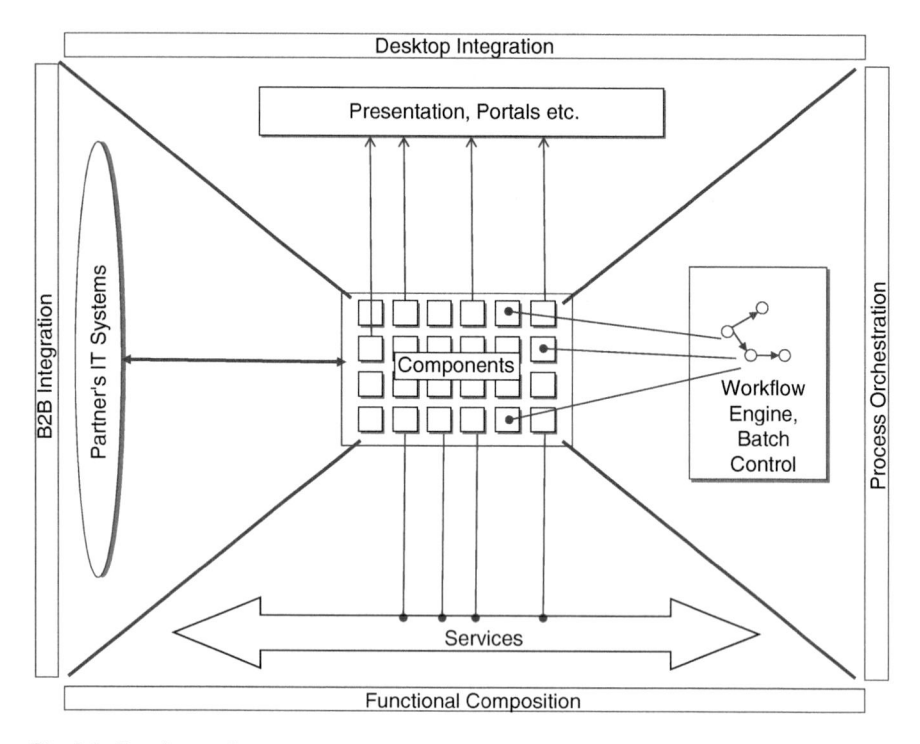

Fig. 3.1 Four integration contexts

representation and expose functional building blocks of generic usability to many situations. Richer, more specialized components reuse more generic ones to efficiently provide functionality. The purpose of *desktop integration* is to flexibly arrange components in the user interface while keeping a coherent user experience. *Process orchestration* integrates components along business processes. Finally, some of the functionality to be integrated into the very large information system may not be part of the system, but rather be provided from external service providers. *Business-to-Business (B2B) integration* logically corresponds to functional composition with components external to the system. This is different from the other three integration contexts insofar that it crosses the border of the system and thus requires a different approach to interface management, because the interface is only partially under control of the organization. Sect. 3.8 will describe this topic in detail.

3.3.1 Functional Composition

The purpose of modularizing business functionality and data is to enable a change of one component without affecting other components and to reuse components in different contexts without changing them. A typical example for a component well

3.3 Composing Systems from Components   85

chosen for functional composition is one that provides *customer information* to other components in the whole system. As most components need that information in one or the other way, providing it from a single component avoids functional redundancy and ensures consistency of customer information across the system.

The choice of component size and structure and the implementation of well-defined, stable interfaces on the business logic layer are of highest importance to successfully manage system complexity ([Bonati_06], [Woods_06], [Sandoe_01], [Ross_06], [McGovern_06], [Heuvel_07], [Herzum_00], [Evans_04], [Szyperski_02]). They are at the heart of successful integration architecture. An example of component design is given in Side-Story 3.1.

Good integration architecture on the business logic layer provides standards to define syntax and semantics of component interfaces, models that help align semantics across many interfaces, containers for components to execute in, rules and tools allowing interfaces to evolve over time and finally middleware that simplifies linking components across technical boundaries.

3.3.2 Desktop Integration

Many components expose themselves through a *user interface*. In the user interface, components should be freely composable into a common look and feel as well as being able to pass *context information* amongst each other. Very powerful examples of this approach are modern desktop operating systems, such as Microsoft's Vista (http://www.microsoft.com/en/us/default.aspx) or Apple's MacOS (http://www.apple.com/macosx). They offer rich libraries of predefined user interface components, clear guidelines for a good look and feel and powerful mechanisms to pass context across multiple components on the desktop. However, beside this local integration, in the context of integration architecture integrating business logic components into these modern desktop systems is a challenge.

User interfaces have to be of high quality since they have a direct impact on the usability and the end-user acceptance of a system. By reusing user interface components, on the one hand, redundancy is reduced and, on the other hand, consistency across the system is improved. Good decoupling of user interface components allows the end-user to establish a smooth flow of work while changing from one application to another. As many tasks require the use of different applications, the end-user will access applications in the context of some previous work. For a user-friendly work environment, the *context* must not be lost when switching over to another application, i.e. information input during one user operation must remain seamlessly available during the next user operation. This requires a data exchange between applications on the level of the user interface. A prime example of this is the clipboard functionality in modern desktop operating systems allowing the user to cut information from one component and paste it into another one in a meaningful way. However, with copy and paste the context of the information does not follow the information.

A typical example of desktop integration would be a customer service *portal* that brings together a number of user interface components in order to present the complete information about a customer. Portals allow the unified presentation and use of applications – usually through a web-frontend (see e.g. [Szuprowicz_00]). Integration architecture often defines portals as key elements for desktop integration.

3.3.3 Process Orchestration

As businesses change, they often need to use existing functionality provided by components in flexible business processes. A typical example for this is complaint handling, where depending on the kind of complaint and the customer, different processes must be followed, touching various components such as customer contact history, document archive and delivery tracking. Often we create, adopt and change processes faster than the underlying basic functions. Therefore, we need means to rearrange existing components easily in new or changing business processes. The integration context that arranges functions in sequences according to a process definition is called *process orchestration*. Integration architecture defines a language to define processes and an environment within which to execute process definitions in order to support this integration requirement. Processes may or may not include manual steps. The terms "straight through processing" for fully automated processes and "workflow" for mixed processes, which include both automated process steps and manual interactions, are used to distinguish between these two situations. It is important, however, that both cases follow the same pattern. Often, a process starts with many manual steps and is then automated gradually as the business continuously strives for improved operational efficiency. Good integration architecture supports *gradual process orchestration*, smoothly transforming workflows into straight through processes. Centralized process orchestration simplifies gathering data about process execution in a more straightforward and standardized way. This data, in turn is good input to the continuous optimization of processes. Note that "batch job scheduling" is also a form of process orchestration.

3.3.4 Layering Components

Components can expose themselves with interfaces on one or more *layers* – on the user interface layer, on the process layer and on the business logic layer – as depicted in Fig. 3.2. Component A is a component exposing interfaces on all three layers. Component B is a purely functional component including persistent data. It does not expose any interfaces for process or desktop integration. Component C offers interfaces on all layers without storing any persistent data. Component D in turn is a "headless" component exposing interfaces only on the lower layers.

3.3 Composing Systems from Components

This definition is in contrast to many common SOA concepts claiming independent components on each layer of Fig. 3.2. However, managed evolution practice has shown that existing systems are often tightly coupled between the layers and cannot easily be split into layered components. Therefore, a useful component concept in the context of legacy software cannot strictly enforce separate components on each layer.

Exposition on the different layers means the following:

- *Business logic layer*, including the persistent data layer: The component offers *services* as defined in Sect. 3.5 to other components which can access its encapsulated functionality and data,
- *Process layer*: The component offers hooks to the workflow infrastructure, such as the workflow engine shown in Fig. 3.1. Through these hooks it can be bound into a workflow orchestrated by the workflow infrastructure,
- *User interface layer*: The component provides a user-interface suitable for integration, such as a portlet (http://en.wikipedia.org/wiki/Portlet) that can be integrated into a portal. Components with their own user interfaces are often legacy components or commercial of-the-shelf software packages, whereas new components often deliver their portlets.

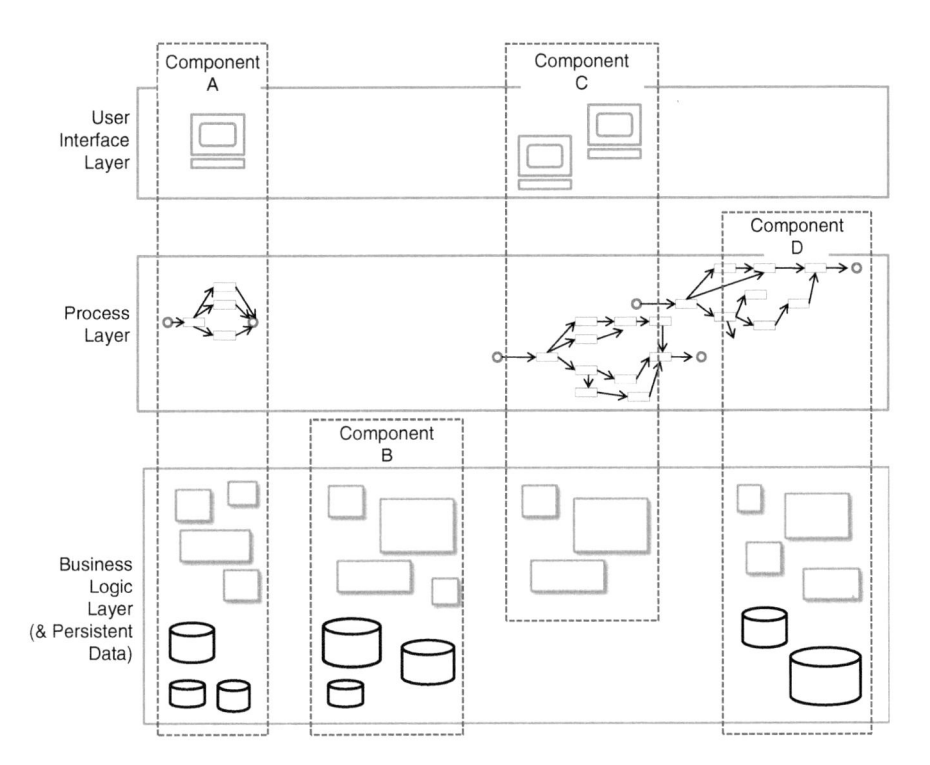

Fig. 3.2 Component layering

3-layer and 4-layer architectures can be found in the literature. In a 4-layer architecture the business logic and the persistent data form two separate layers. In the 3-layer architecture *data* is always exposed through the business logic layer, keeping business logic and data together. This is an important restriction for integration architecture in very large information systems. Often, legacy systems couple applications through a common database. This style results in very tight coupling across the system and is the root cause for many architectural issues. In practice, shared access to the same data should be restricted to components that are logically close, such as belonging to the same domain or subdomain, depending on the size of the system. For confidential data, such as client-identifying information, the access is protected by strong authentication in order to exclude misuse by unauthorized components. The set of authorized components is strongly restricted by the principle of "need-to-know". Logical layers as shown in Fig. 3.2 can easily be confused with technical tiers as in two- or three-tier architectures. They are, however, not the same because functional components are often deployed on many geographically distributed servers. In that sense, they constitute n-tier architecture.

Examples of components of type A are: Components providing services, a workflow infrastructure (WFI) interface and a portlet; a legacy application having its own GUI coded as part of the application; or a commercial of-the-shelf software packages with its own workflow control and GUI. An example of a component of type B is a tax calculation package, including the tax master data for the respective jurisdictions, which is only called via services from other components. An example component of type C implements a step in a mixed workflow based on an automated, stateless functionality and human interaction. An example component of type D implements business functionality and data and offers these to the workflow infrastructure and via services to other components.

Components should only interact among each other when they expose interfaces on the same layer, as shown in Fig. 3.3. In practice, you can find mainly the following components: Headless components exposing themselves only on the business logic layer (B) or on both the business logic layer and the process layer (D). Stateless components contain no persistent data (C). They can expose themselves on each layer. Legacy and stand-alone applications can be used as components, but they often can only be integrated on the business logic layer.

The three layers in Fig. 3.2 correspond to the three integration contexts "Functional composition", "Process orchestration" and "Desktop integration" shown in Fig. 3.1. "B2B Integration" may integrate external components on all layers. However, in "B2B Integration" only one side of the connection is under the control of the organization, the other side being specified, implemented and provided by the business partner.

Side-Story 3.1 describes a practical solution using layered components.

3.3 Composing Systems from Components

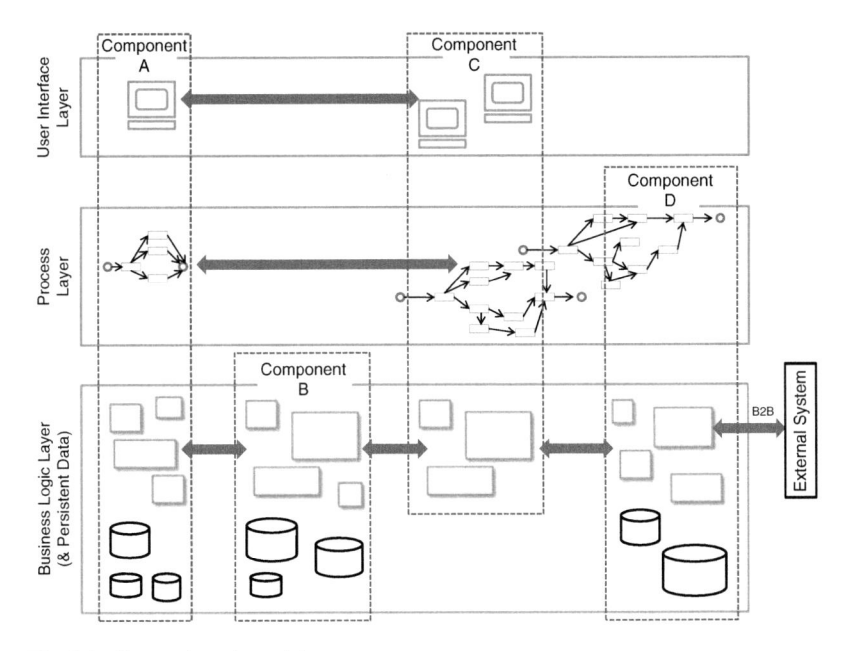

Fig. 3.3 Connections (usage) between components

Side-Story 3.1: Credit Suisse Global Front Systems

The *globalization* of Credit Suisse Private Banking and its markets has lead to a number of challenges for the information system. Traditionally, each location had its own information system, usually well adapted to the local environment and supported by a local vendor.

Business globalization created the need for *globally consistent business processes*, such as the customer advisory process and a global view of the customer's situation. This is not trivial, because a customer may maintain relationships with several business units of Credit Suisse. Customers may also communicate through different channels with the bank. Examples include through his relationship manager, through a trading desk, or via the Internet. In addition, the customer may use local products that are not available in another country. Subject to legal and regulatory restrictions, real-time, complete, consistent and up-to-date information on all aspects of the customer relationship have therefore to be available at any time and in any location where the customer wants to interact with the bank.

The solution envisage by Credit Suisse Private Banking is the use of *Global Front Systems* based on a mix of local and global components[2] accessing the local backend systems through the enterprise service bus (Fig. 3.4). The backend systems in this architecture expose their functionality and data via services over the enterprise service bus. The front systems come in two varieties: *global front components* and *local front components*. The global front components offer functionality and data that is used globally throughout Credit Suisse Private Banking, such as providing master data on securities and bonds or their current market value. The local front components implement location-specific functionality, such as the process required in a specific jurisdiction to register a new client. Both types of components have access to the backend systems[3]. Global and local front components are integrated on the GUI layer using portals and offer a unified look-and-feel for the user. The user can combine the required windows on his desktop, such as showing the total global assets and liabilities (customer portfolio) of the

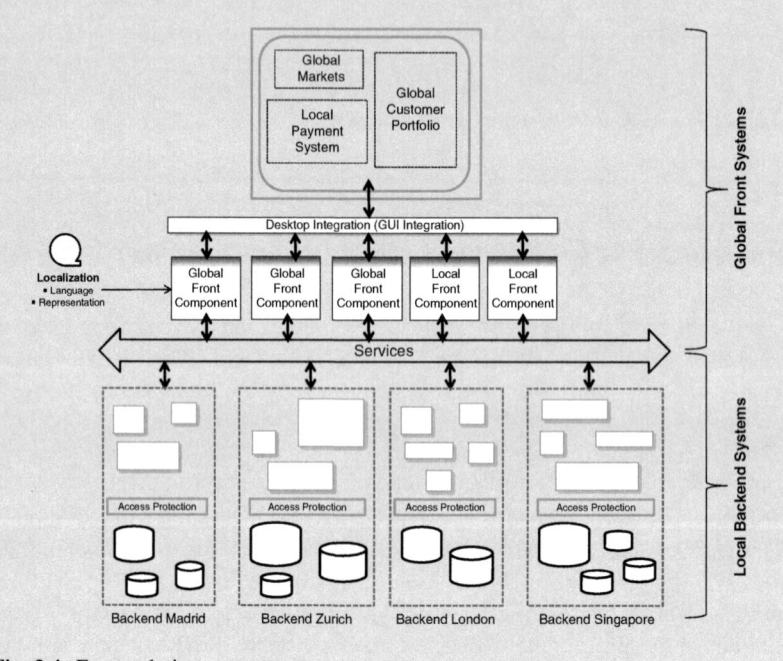

Fig. 3.4 Front solution components

---

[2]In banking traditionally the term "frontend" is used for functionality facing the users, and the term "backend" designates functionality and data executing the processing.

[3]Of course all data in the backend systems is well protected against unauthorized access. The security mechanisms are not shown in Fig 3.4.

customer, the global market data for a certain product segment and access to the local payment execution system. With this information, the relationship manager is able to give the expected service to the customer and immediately execute requested transactions.

The implementation of this solution is heavily based on integration architecture as shown in Fig. 3.3. Both global and local front components are highly reusable and configurable and can be deployed in any location because they run on globally available *application platforms* (see Sect. 4.3).

At the time of writing, all the necessary concepts and technical solutions have been piloted successfully in a number of applications. Developing and deploying global components is very challenging. It requires deep organizational and cultural changes for success. In the experience of the authors, it takes several years to globally roll out such a concept.

3.4 Choosing the Right Interfaces

As highlighted above, components expose their functionality and data through *interfaces*. The choice of the right interface is very important for managed evolution, because they should remain as stable as possible, in order to allow for independent development of the individual components. They should also hide the internals of the component implementation, such that implementation changes do not propagate across components. Topics here include information hiding, abstract data typing, etc. ([Szyperski_02], [Herzum_00], [Hohmann_03], [Clements_02], [Assmann_03]), which become even more important in larger systems. Well-designed interfaces foster reuse and decouple components operationally.

In the remainder of this section, some key design considerations for good interfaces are discussed. By choosing the right degree of coupling, we manage the trade-off between high independency of the components and operational efficiency. A very large information system may require different degrees of coupling depending on the *architectural distance* between provider and consumer of an interface. Architectural distance is small within the same component, medium within one domain and large across domains (See Sect. 2.5 for "domains"). Therefore, defining the scope of an interface is a key design consideration. Constructing systems from components is always about reusing components in different contexts and thus avoiding unnecessary functional and data redundancy. Avoiding redundancy completely is not a realistic design goal, however, as the coordination overhead wipes out the benefits, if we go too far. We need to design for *adequate redundancy*, where the focus is on avoiding unwanted and unneeded redundancy. One of the trade-offs is between operational efficiency and maximum reusability of interfaces. Often optimized design for reuse calls for very fine grained interfaces, which in turn is hard to implement efficiently. The right choice of *granularity*, thus, is another important design consideration. All interfaces must come with well-defined *formal syntax* and *precise semantics*, so that they are usable without implicit knowledge. As managed evolution leads to situations where two interacting components are implemented on different technologies, interfaces need to be technology-agnostic. Again, there is a balancing act between technology abstraction and efficient implementation.

3.4.1 Adequate Degree of Coupling

A major challenge in very large information systems is to find the adequate degree of coupling. This will, on the one hand, be a result of adequate architectural design. On the other hand this will heavily depend on the interface management process, balancing the project driven approach to deliver new interfaces in due time with overall alignment to a target architecture. This topic will be discussed in more detail in Sect. 3.6.

In order to discuss the adequate degree of coupling, we need to understand a number of interface types with different properties pertaining to the degree of operational coupling they establish between supplier and consumer of an interface.

The first integration type is the *exchange* (= synonymous with *synchronous* communications). This integration type exchanges information and control flow in a synchronous, request-wait-reply mode ([Pope_98], [Mowbray_97]). The consumer waits for a reply from the provider. Under the assumption that the provider can fail, this reply may never come. Therefore, the consumer needs a mechanism to determine when to stop waiting and what to do in that case. The consumer cannot be sure whether the exchange failed on the way to the provider or on the way back. In general, the consumer is not able to tell whether the provider ever knew of the exchange. This is very important if the exchange implies state changes within the provider. We can overcome this problem partly by adding a distributed transaction mechanism ([Weikum_02], [Newcomer_09]) to the exchange. In practice, this only works reliably in technically tightly coupled systems with predictable network delays and reliable connections. A more robust implementation style for exchanges that need to change the provider state is to implement *idempotent*[4] *operations*. This means that we can repeat an exchange as often as we want. As long as the input data is the same, we will always get the same state change at the provider. This allows the consumer to repeat the exchange until it gets confirmation of a successful state change. If it is logically difficult to design the exchange in an idempotent style, such as in an append operation, where each new exchange should append to the existing state of the provider, a good method is a two-step approach. First, the consumer gets a unique ID for his status change request either from the provider or from a generic service providing such unique IDs. The consumer then tags his request with the unique ID. By adding the unique ID to the input part of the exchange, we can turn any status changing exchange into an idempotent exchange. Exchanges are the

---

[4]Denoting an element of a set which is unchanged in value when multiplied or otherwise operated on by itself.

appropriate integration type if the consumer requests information from the provider without changing the provider state and if the consumer cannot continue without the information. We can implement state changing exchanges as shown above, but we should avoid doing so to the maximum extent possible. Synchronous exchanges establish a tight operational coupling between provider and consumer, as both sides and the network between them need to work correctly at the same time for the exchange to be successful. Typically, we implement this type on top of remote procedure call protocols, such as SOAP, IIOP ([Pope_98], [Mowbray_97]).

The second integration type is the *event*. This integration type communicates data or control in an asynchronous "store and forward" or "fire and forget" mode. As part of the interface, a component will declare that it either will send, or publish, specific events or will be able to receive or subscribe to specific events. Event-based integration is based on reliable delivery of messages for asynchronous program-to-program communication. There is no reply or exception returned to the sending component after the consumer accepts the message for processing. However, if replies are necessary, they can be implemented on the application level. After the underlying transport system accepts the message, there is no further information available to the sending component. A major advantage of this integration type is the better decoupling of provider and consumer of an interface. Once the event is sent, the consumer's responsibilities for successfully transmitting the data have ended. As part of the business logic, a component may still implement additional flow control, such as waiting for a confirmation message further along the process flow. The looser coupling comes at the cost of additional system management functions. Events that encounter difficulties in transmission end up in exception queues where they are logged, automatically re-sent, or brought to the attention of the operations staff for manual intervention. Because processing will happen outside the consumer's control, it is important that the events have a high probability for successful delivery and processing. This means that the sender bears additional responsibility to send only validated messages that can actually be processed at the receiver. As a rule of thumb, event integration should be preferred over exchange integration in order to loosen operational coupling. This is particularly true for state changing operations that are not time critical. That said, we should not forget that further decoupling comes at the cost of powerful transport and system management functions. Implementing a reliable, guaranteed delivery transport mechanism is very hard. Technically, events are implemented on top of products such as IBM MQ ([IBM_05b]), TIBCO ([http://www.tibco.com]), or Advanced Message Queuing Protocol AMQP ([http://www.amqp.org]).

The third integration type, *bulk transfer*, is a special case of the event type described above. It works in the same way as the event type, with the exception that the messages contain a lot of data. We often use files to transport bulk data among components. This is the typical integration style for offline batch processing. Where multiple records are processed en masse the data has to be forwarded from one component to the next. Bulk transfer is also useful to replicate data between components when the synchronization of the data takes place through mass updates rather than single updates. A typical property of batch interfaces is their ability to restart processing of a partially completed bulk transfer. The input data is usually so big that the probability that the processing completes without problems is very low. Therefore, the processing component takes snapshots of partially completed requests, so-called checkpoints. If the processing fails, everything rolls back to the last checkpoint and resumes from there.

The fourth integration type is *data sharing* whereby several components access the same logical database schema. This is a very tight form of coupling, since changes in the database schema have an immediate impact on all components accessing the database. We can partially loosen the dependency on a common database schema by providing specific *views* as an abstraction mechanism. This does not solve the challenge of data consistency, though. As accessing a common database provides only weak data encapsulation, each component has to implement the same validation logic to ensure semantic data consistency. To some degree, the database itself can implement consistency checks by applying constraints. In a very large information system, we should restrict this integration type to special situations. In our experience, it makes sense when providing a common database for flexible reporting, as in a data warehouse. It is also useful for efficiency reasons between components that are very closely related. One thing to avoid absolutely with this integration type is data sharing among multiple components with write access to the data. As logical data consistency is the responsibility of the writer, this will almost certainly lead to consistency problems. This is particularly true if data sharing is implemented in a distributed way with multiple databases replicating content to each other.

One good reason why we would like to share or replicate data is providing system-wide reference data to many components in a scalable, consistent and reliable way. The simple component architecture answer to this problem is to build a reference data component, with read-only, exchange type interfaces consumed by most of the other components. The naïve implementation of this is a centralized database encapsulated with an access layer providing the interfaces. This implementation easily fulfills the consistency requirement. However, due to its centralized implementation it often fails in terms of scalability and reliability. A better implementation of this component uses internal database replication and offers multiple instances of the read interfaces. It is often sufficient to have one instance of the update interfaces simplifying data consistency. This is a good way to profit from data replication capabilities of modern database systems, while keeping the desired encapsulation properties for a component.

3.4.2 Adequate Integration Scope

We should link the quality requirements to the visibility and the popularity of an interface. The broader the visibility of an interface and the higher its reuse, the more attention we must pay to its design quality. According to the domain model presented in Side Story 2.3, we can define interface visibility scope as within the

3.4 Choosing the Right Interfaces

same domain or subdomain, across the whole system, or even outside the system for Business-to-Business interfaces. In this book, we refer to interfaces with restricted visibility as *private interfaces*. Interfaces visible across the system are called *public interfaces* and the ones visible outside we name *Business-to-Business (B2B) interfaces*. Taking into account the federated architecture described in Sect. 2.9, it is clear that coordination across domains is harder than coordination inside a single domain and coordination across businesses is even harder. Likewise, coordination around an interface change that affects many consumers is also hard, leading to higher quality requirements for highly reused interfaces. Integration architecture, therefore, has to define design quality requirements according to visibility and popularity of interfaces. The defined standard may for example, support data sharing within the same domain, but not across domains. The required level of quality is also reflected in different levels of quality assurance required for public and private interfaces.

3.4.3 Avoid Redundancy

One of the complexity and cost drivers of very large information systems is unwanted or unknown *redundancy*: This includes redundancy in functionality, in data and in interfaces. In many cases such redundancy was created – and is possibly still being created – by high pressure from business on time to market and by a lack of transparent and adequate architectural governance. A good portfolio of components in a very large information system is ideally free of unmanaged redundancy. Each function or data object is provided by exactly one component. With the exception of justified cases such as business continuity, legal requirements or performance, the same functionality should only be developed once and the same data should be held in one place. It is important to reduce functional and data redundancy within the application landscape to an adequate level. This objective directly affects the flexibility since it reduces development and maintenance cost and avoids inconsistencies inevitable with multiple implementations of the same functionality or data. One reason for unavoidable redundancy is integration of third party software, where architectural control is limited. Redundancy in systems developed in a mix between in-house development and third party software can only be reduced if the whole industry shares the same architecture. Another reason for justified redundancy is the migration period when we replace a component and for a limited time both the old and the new version exist in the system. The challenge for integration architecture is to provide design guidelines for interfaces that allow maximum reuse, to define tools allowing existing functionality to be easily found and to run processes ensuring that no new redundancy is introduced in the system. In a very large information system all of this must be implemented in a federated way, with each domain controlling internal redundancy and a global mechanism on top.

3.4.4 Formal Syntax and Rich Semantics

Syntax is the set of rules for combining symbols to form valid expressions. This is applicable both to natural languages and to data storage and transport. Syntax of an interface must be defined in a *formal language* that lends itself to automatic checking and interpretation at run-time. A number of languages to define interfaces exist, such as CORBA-IDL ([Orfali_98]), XML-SCHEMA ([Daum_03a]) and WSDL ([Daconta_03]). These languages also allow for automatic generation of interface glue code, thus helping the developers write good quality implementation and considerably raise productivity.

Semantics defines the meaning of words, phrases and expressions and is applicable both to natural and computer-understandable languages ([Ogden_89]). A semantic definition can have different degrees of richness. It may just cover the basic meaning or it may define a term in high detail. As an example, consider the expression "sZZ'ZZZ'ZZZ.ZZ" for a signed ten digit decimal number with two digits after the decimal point. This number can have different meanings, depending on the specific context. Successively richer semantic definitions for this number could, for example, be:

- An arithmetical value expressed in decimal notation with a range of −99'999'999.99 to +99'999'999.99,
- An arithmetical value expressed in decimal notation with a range of −99'999'999.99 to +99'999'999.99 representing a monetary amount,
- An arithmetical value expressed in decimal notation with a range of −99'999'999.99 to +99'999'999.99 representing a monetary amount in Swiss Francs,
- An arithmetical value expressed in decimal notation with a range of −99'999'999.99 to +99'999'999.99 representing a monetary amount in Swiss Francs not including the Value Added Tax.

Rich semantics is defined as providing precise meaning in sufficient detail for the intended purpose, such as exchanging information between computers via services. Rich semantics is based on explicit representation of context without requiring implicit assumptions.

Rich semantics for an interface is harder to achieve than formal syntax. It is easy to write an interface that accepts unstructured data as an input, performs some operation on it and returns an unstructured result. This is the ultimate flexible interface. In such cases, all the semantics are based on implicit knowledge shared by the consumer and the provider of the interface. This is an obvious case of how *not* to do it. In the experience of the authors, that is exactly what often happens in less obvious ways, when interface designers want to keep the full flexibility and postpone the semantic integration problem to a later stage in development. The problem with this is that it breaks

> "Semantic interoperability is no longer a dream; it is the inevitable result of better engineering"
> Jeffrey T. Pollocks, 2004

3.4 Choosing the Right Interfaces 97

encapsulation and abstraction, because an interface can easily change its semantics without making this change obvious with a modified interface. At the heart of semantic integration is an explicit common understanding of semantic concepts shared among multiple components. *Semantic incompatibilities* and conflicts often result from naming conflicts in the form of synonyms - the same thing has different names - and homonyms - different things use the same name. Other sources of problems are lifecycle conflicts caused by different state models of information types and value domain conflicts with overlapping and incongruent sets or intervals of values. Identification conflicts caused by the use of different numbering systems are another challenge commonly found in this space. Conflicts can also occur in the interpretation of numerical data when two components assume different units or methods of measurement, such as meters or feet.

A strong method to deal with that challenge is to derive interfaces from *semantic models* shared by both sides of the interface. The authors had good experiences with using hierarchical business object models to solve the issue in a very large information system (Sect. 2.4 and Side Story 2.5). [Pollock_04] beautifully explores that topic. More modern approaches, such as ontologies look promising in that context, but the authors have no personal experience in applying them to a very large information system. Often widely understood standards help define the semantics of lower level concepts such as measurement units, numbering schemes and others. One example of this is the following Side-Story 3.2.

Side-Story 3.2: Semantic Color Specification

Formal semantic specification ([Portner_05], [Lacy_05]) is not obvious and not intuitive, but is of highest importance for the conceptual integrity of very large information systems. This side story therefore provides an example for a simple, intuitive formal semantic specification – for the color "red".

A good example of a semantic specification is the term "color red". Intuitively, everybody understands this term. However, a closer look reveals a rich space of interpretation. The "color red", therefore, needs a careful definition of its meaning. The human eye distinguishes about ten million color shades. How can we tell exactly which color we mean? One possibility is the use of RAL color charts. Since 1927, RAL (http://www.ral-ggmbh.de) has created a uniform language when it comes to color. RAL has standardized, numbered and named the abundance of colors (Table 3.1).

The statement:
<colour>rubyred
<RALcode>RAL3003</RALcode>
<brightness>67</brightness>
<saturation>50</saturation>
</colour>is syntactically and semantically precisely and unambiguously defined. Every human and computer program has exactly the same understanding (thanks to the RAL colour system specification).

Table 3.1 Semantic specification of "colour red"

Color	Red	RAL 3003: ruby red	Properties
The property possessed by an object of producing different sensations on the eye or different measurement values in an instrument as a result of the way it reflects or emits light [Oxford_98]	A color at the end of the spectrum next to orange and opposite violet, as of blood, fire, or rubies [Oxford_98]	Exactly specified in the RAL color metric system. Each color is represented by 7 digits, grouped in a triple and 2 pairs, representing hue (Farbton), brightness (Helligkeit) and saturation (Farbsättigung)	• Brightness (Helligkeit) • Saturation (Farbsättigung

One powerful instrument for syntax and semantic specification is *modeling*: Several models have already been presented in Chap. 2. A proven way of assuring rich semantics in a service is to base service definitions on the business object model (BOM). Such an example is given in Side-Story 3.3.

Side-Story 3.3: Service Definition Using Business Objects

As seen several times in this chapter, defining the semantics – the exact meaning – for the elements of an interface is a highly challenging task. The meaning for the elements of the interfaces – at least the ones used globally in Credit Suisse Private Banking – must be standardized and used uniformly. The standardization can be achieved with the help of systematic, semi-formal models, such as the *business object model* (BOM as introduced in Side Story 2.5).

The domain business object model of the domain CUS (CUS = Customer, see Side Story 2.5) contains the domain business object (dBO) "address". For the implementation of a global service providing create/update/read/delete functionality for "address", the developers first had to define the component business model (cBO), refining the dBO "address". This component business object model is shown in Fig. 3.5[5].

---

[5]Note that the *anchor object* is required for the management and searchability of the business object model repository.

3.4 Choosing the Right Interfaces

Fig. 3.5 Component business object "address"

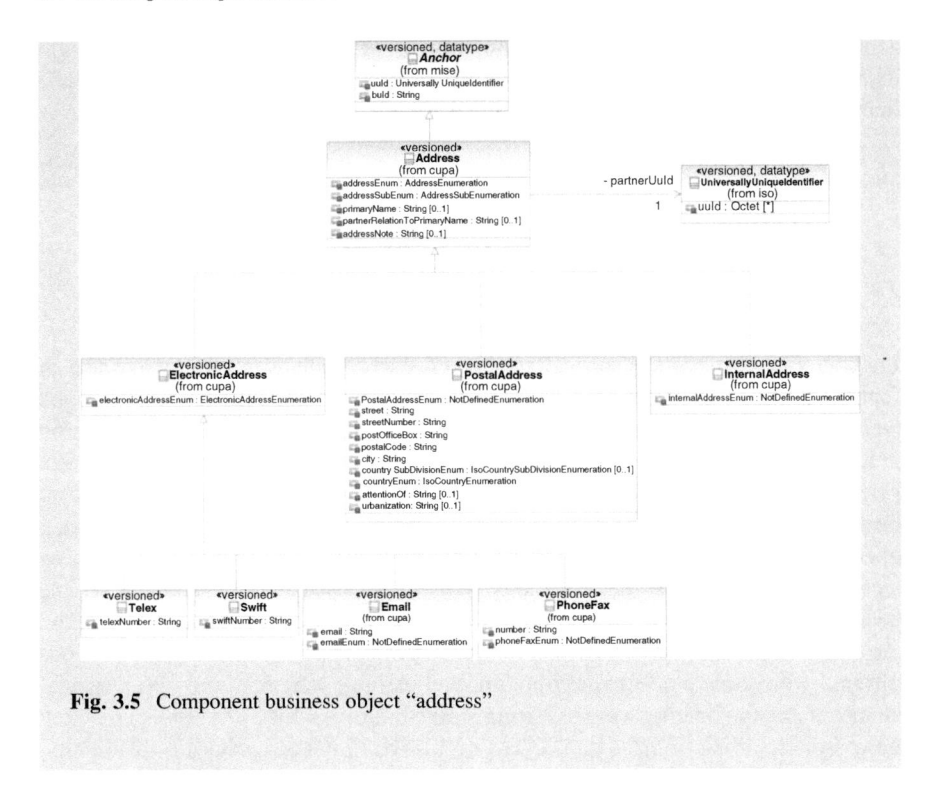

3.4.5 Adequate Granularity and Reuse

The adequate *granularity* of an interface or service is a widely discussed topic. If services are too fine-grained, they incur a lot of implementation overhead. If services are too coarse-grained they may not really be reusable. Usually we will find the answer to the granularity question by combining information in the business object model with the

> "It should be as easy to find good quality reusable software assets as it is to find a book on the internet"
> http://softwarereuse.nasa.gov

use-cases defined by the interface consumers. From the intended use of the interface and the attributes and operations belonging to the corresponding business object, the designer derives the adequate grouping and assembly of an interface. A reusable interface must fulfill a number of requirements under the general title "reusability" to be attractive to a developer.

The design principle is to choose an adequate granularity of interaction for performance. Since using interfaces incurs a certain amount of overhead an appropriate chunk of work needs to be processed. This design principle is in conflict with creating generic interfaces. For example, the most generic interfaces provide individual access to specific data elements. However, this interface style leads to a large number of very fine-grained interfaces in general. One good pattern to increase interface granularity is to provide *multi-valued interfaces*. Multi-valued interfaces accept a set of input values and deliver a corresponding set of results. By choosing the number of input values the consumer can steer the granularity.

3.4.6 Bridging Technical Heterogeneity and Network Distance

Integration architecture historically emerged early with *technical integration* in focus. As long as all components were running on the same computer and were using the same programming technologies no need for technical integration existed. With *distributed computing* emerging as a strong paradigm (see [Messerschmitt_00]), IT started to build systems spanning multiple hosts connected through a network. As these systems evolved, they embraced many different operating systems, computer systems, communication methods and programming technologies. Technical heterogeneity was the consequence. Suddenly simple basics like the codes used to represent characters could be different: EBCDIC on the mainframe and ASCII on Windows servers. The representation of strings differed with some platforms terminating the variable length string with a special character and the others giving the string length in the first byte of a string. Different processor families represented even multi-byte integer numbers differently, some storing the less significant bits in storage locations with lower addresses; others storing these the other way around. The big endian, little endian controversy was born.

Building distributed systems residing on heterogeneous platforms requires *transformations* of data to achieve interoperability. In the early days, this task was highly underestimated and led to many proprietary implementations. At that time, the term "middleware" was created and products appeared on the market to abstract the underlying network, facilitate the necessary transformations, provide additional services, such as security and bind the generic communication layer to the individual programming technologies. One early leading technology was CORBA ([Pope_98], [Mowbray_97]).

Good technical integration is decisive for the success of managed evolution. We can only evolve the system technically by moving one component after the other onto a new platform. This requires that components on the old platform remain transparently accessible from the new one until the last component has moved. Figure 3.6 joins the concepts of application and technical integration. Technical integration bridges heterogeneous platforms by providing a technical abstraction layer on each platform, depicted as inter-platform communication in Fig. 3.6 (Platforms are introduced in Sect. 4.3). Components use this layer to either connect to components on the same platform (arrow "2" in Fig. 3.6) or to a different one (arrow "1" in Fig. 3.6), transparently. Also different components on different platforms are bridged (arrow "3" in Fig. 3.6).

3.4 Choosing the Right Interfaces   101

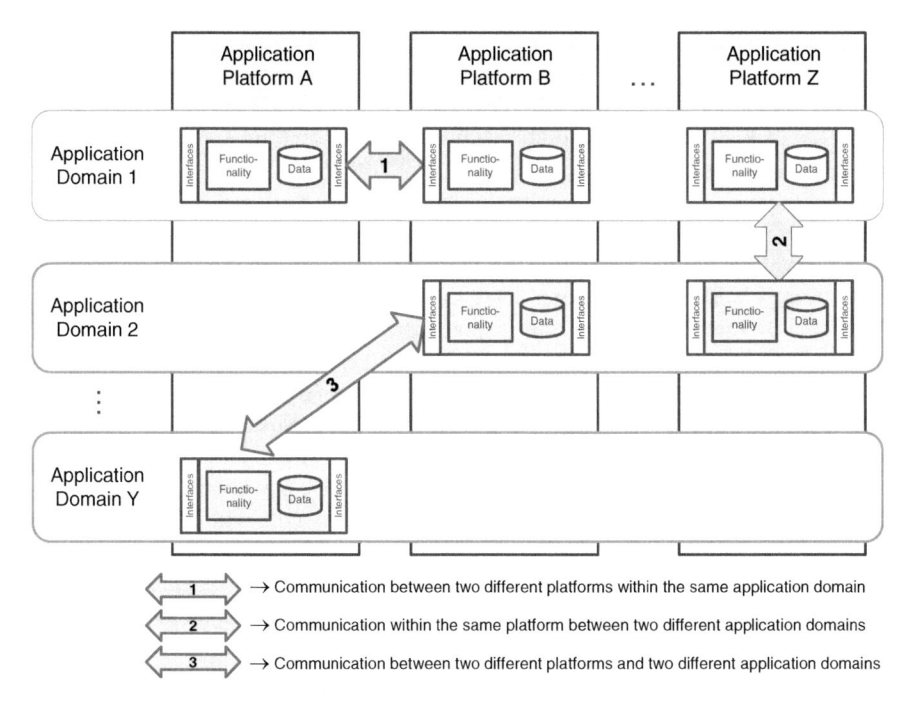

Fig. 3.6 Technical and application integration

In Chap. 4 (Infrastructure) we will show that the platform itself can also be seen as a "component" offering services to applications abstracting technical details and fostering reuse across many applications.

3.4.7 Use Industry Standards Where Applicable

In many industries there are well-established definitions in the form of message specifications or service definitions. Good examples of this are the standard ISO 20022 (http://www.iso20022.org) for messaging in the financial industry or the UN EDIFACT (http://www.unece.org/trade/untdid/welcome.htm) standard with all its domain specific specializations for various industries. It is, for example, of utmost value to the automotive industry with its fragmented value chain. Such standards may consist of high-level descriptions only; provide implementation fragments, security mechanisms, or naming schemes, all the way to a full messaging service on top of the standard. One example of a fully developed set of standards is SWIFT (http://www.swift.org). SWIFT (Society for Worldwide Information Transfer) is an organization of nearly all financial institutions which defines interchange standards and operates a worldwide, secure communications infrastructure. As standardization started well before the Internet was ubiquitous, the traditional standards rely on many different interfacing technologies. In the meantime, though, everybody sees XML as the de-facto interface standard. This leads to a rich collection of domain-specific standards on top of XML. The advantage of having everything on top of XML is that a common integration infrastructure is sufficient to handle most modern standards.

Clearly, such standards are indispensable for B2B interfaces. The organization behind the standard provides the necessary governance to ensure the longevity and future development of the standard. This is necessary, because in a B2B relationship, usually none of the partners have the power to control the evolution of the interface. Both rely on the standardization organization to provide that.

However, external interfacing standards are also useful to define internal interfaces for two reasons. First, the organization can save effort by just adopting a standard rather than defining its own. Often it is psychologically simpler to refer to an external standardization authority. Second, by using market standards, the business opens itself to external software and services, without incurring very large integration cost. This helps a lot to become more agile with business process insourcing or outsourcing.

In practice, the external standards do not fully satisfy the internal requirements. In such cases, it often helps to define standard extensions to the standard carrying, for example, security contexts, accounting information, or references to internal business objects. Having all standards defined in XML it is technically simple to add or remove such extensions when crossing the system border.

3.5 Interfaces and Service Contracts

Defining interfaces syntactically and semantically is not sufficient in very large information systems. We need more comprehensive contracts between providers and consumers of interfaces. In the large federated organizations building very large information systems many aspects behind interfaces need explicit clarity. As the system evolves, it is

> "Service orientation has become a viable opportunity for enterprises to increase the internal rate of return on a project-by-project basis, react to rapidly changing market conditions and conduct transactions with business partners at will"
> James McGovern, 2006

not enough to have clarity about the status of an interface. We need clear roadmaps to instill the necessary trust around the relationships established by interfaces. The overarching requirements to a complete service definition beyond the technical description of the interface are an underestimated pillar of integration architecture and managed evolution.

3.5.1 Interfaces and Services

Literature often uses the terms "interface" and "service" interchangeably. In the context of integration architecture for a very large information system, however, a distinction is useful (see also Fig. 3.7).

An *interface* is a specification and an implementation defining all the information necessary at design, development and operation time for accessing a component. It consists of text and formal definitions, such as usage instructions, syntactic descriptions of input and output parameters, pre- and post conditions, side-effects to the state of the component, version roadmap and functional descriptions. An interface is defined by a versioned interface specification. The same interface can be provided via different technical infrastructures such as an event or an exchange (see Sect. 3.4).

A *service* contains the interface, its implementation and specifications of conditions for the *use* of the interface, including performance restrictions such as throughput, response and latency times, and guaranteed behavior in case of failures, cost accounting rules, access control information and security guarantees. A service is defined in a versioned *service contract* between the provider of the service and the consumers of the service. The service contract includes the interface

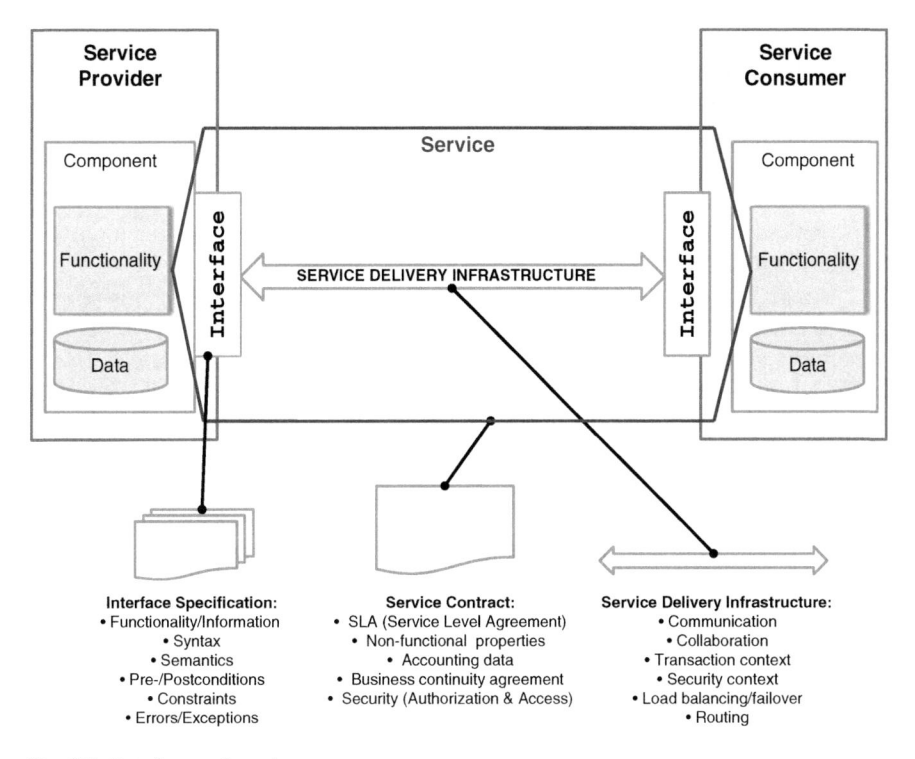

Fig. 3.7 Interface and service

specification as an integral part. Service contracts are related to specific instances and technical implementations of an interface. Many services can implement the same interface. Service contracts contain a "Service Level Agreement" (SLA). A service contract defines the relationship between the service provider and the consumer during development and operation of the system.

The relationship between the three elements "component", "interface" and "service" is shown in Fig. 3.7. The component contains and encapsulates the functionality and data, the interface provides the access; and the service requests and delivers the processing results or information from the component. The service contract covers additional agreements as described above and in Sect. 3.5.2. For any service, there is a service provider[6] and one or many service consumers.

As seen in Fig. 3.7 the service is delivered via a *service delivery infrastructure*.

An example of a formal *syntax* specification of an interface is given in Side-Story 3.4. The objective of Side-Story 3.4 is to demonstrate the effort and precision required to formally define syntax, not to explain any XML details.

Side-Story 3.4: Formal Syntax Specification of an Interface Using XML Schema

Credit Suisse operates a number of services that are used by a very large number of applications, the so-called cross-platform services. Apart from a high performance and dependability, such services need to be very well specified and be based on stable contracts. One example of such a service is used for any application requiring a *digital signature* attached to an electronic document, file or archive item. Digital signatures are used for integrity protection of documents.

Credit Suisse operates the Digital Signature Service (DSS) for this purpose: The DSS is called via a service "Request Digital Signature". The service call contains the information to be signed and some parameters. The DSS then applies a time stamp and the digital signature and returns the signed information based on a private key ([Feghhi_99]).

The service is offered as an asynchronous service (see Sect. 3.4.1) and the service is syntactically specified as an XML schema ([Skulschus_04]) which is partially shown in Table 3.2. The example demonstrates that formal syntax interface specifications of real-world services can become fairly complex. Good skills and a diligent process are required to achieve the necessary quality.

---

[6]Because of operational or availability reasons, a service may be provided by more than one provider instance.

3.5 Interfaces and Service Contracts 105

Table 3.2 Extract of the DSS service call syntactical specification (XML Schema)

```xml
<!--
###############################################################
        Service-Id:   DOC_1042
        Service-Name:   Request Digital Signature
        Technical Name:   Request Digital Signature for an electronic document or a data structure
        History: v0.1  03.06.2005   Draft
                 v0.2  08.06.2005
                 v0.3  15.06.2005
                 v0.4  23.06.2005
                 v0.5  23.06.2005
                 v0.6  24.06.2005
                 v1.0  01.07.2005   Final
###############################################################
-->
<xs:schema xmlns:xs="http://www.w3.org/2001/XMLSchema"
     xmlns:cs="http://www.cs-standards.org/schema/CS-BASE-1-0"
     xmlns:cif="http://www.cs-standards.org/schema/CS-CIF-BASE-1-0"
     xmlns:ebi="http://www.cs-standards.org/schema/CS-EBI-BASE-1-0"
     xmlns:dss="http://www.cs-standards.org/schema/CS-DSS-BASE-1-0"
     elementFormDefault="unqualified" attributeFormDefault="qualified">

    <xs:import namespace="http://www.cs-standards.org/schema/CS-BASE-1-0" schemaLocation="CS-BASE-1-0.xsd"/>
    <xs:import namespace="http://www.cs-standards.org/schema/CS-CIF-BASE-1-0" schemaLocation="CS-CIF-BASE-1-0.xsd"/>
    <xs:import namespace="http://www.cs-standards.org/schema/CS-EBI-BASE-1-0" schemaLocation="CS-EBI-BASE-1-0.xsd"/>
    <xs:import namespace="http://www.cs-standards.org/schema/CS-DSS-BASE-1-0" schemaLocation="CS-DSS-BASE-1-0.xsd"/>

    <!--
    ==============================================================
        ELAR Signature Request slot: 16 ELAR signature requests can be grouped into a single message.
    ==============================================================
    -->
    <xs:complexType name="RequestSlotType">
        <xs:sequence>
            <xs:element name="SlotStatus"     type="dss:SlotStatus"/>
            <xs:element name="BusinessUnit"   type="cs:businessUnitType"/>
            <xs:element name="HashtreeUUID"   type="cs:uuid20AsCharType"/>
            <!--
            -------------------------------------------------------
                Hash Control Loop:
                ==================
                To check the correctness of the internal hash function (on the
                ELAR mainframe), the last step of reducing the hash tree is
                reproduced by the DSS. This requires three values:
                The resulting root hash and the left and right 2nd level hash
                values. Each hash value itself is composed of a left and a right
                part, so a total of six values are passed in this message:

                ROOT:      [RootValueLeft][RootValueRight]
                2nd Level: [CheckLeftValueLeft][CheckLeftValueRight] || [CheckRightValueLeft][CheckRightValueRight]
            -------------------------------------------------------
            -->
            <xs:element name="HashtreeRootValueLeft"        type="xs:base64Binary"/>
            <xs:element name="HashtreeRootValueRight"       type="xs:base64Binary"/>
            <xs:element name="HashtreeCheckLeftValueLeft"   type="xs:base64Binary"/>
            <xs:element name="HashtreeCheckLeftValueRight"  type="xs:base64Binary"/>
            <xs:element name="HashtreeCheckRightValueLeft"  type="xs:base64Binary"/>
            <xs:element name="HashtreeCheckRightValueRight" type="xs:base64Binary"/>
        </xs:sequence>
    </xs:complexType>
    <!--
    ==============================================================
        Request a digitally signed timestamp for a hash value; the result
        is part of an evidence record structure (ELAR integrity protection)
    ==============================================================
    -->
    <xs:complexType name="EVR_Request">
        <xs:sequence>
            <!--
            -------------------------------------------------------
                Identifier for this message; used in a response message
                to relate (overall) result codes to the message sent.
            -------------------------------------------------------
            -->
            <xs:element name="MessageId" type="cs:uuid20AsCharType"/>
            <!--
            -------------------------------------------------------
                Define the hash and signature algorithms to be used for
                creating a response and to verify input data (control loop)
            -------------------------------------------------------
```

(*continued*)

Table 3.2 (continued)

```
-->
<xs:element name="HashtreeDigestAlgorithmLeft" type="dss:DigestAlgorithm"/>
<xs:element name="HashtreeDigestAlgorithmRight" type="dss:DigestAlgorithm"/>
<xs:element name="SignatureDigestAlgorithm"    type="dss:DigestAlgorithm"/>
<xs:element name="SignatureCryptoAlgorithm"    type="dss:CryptoAlgorithm"/>
<!--
    16 slots for timestamp requests (with control loop data)
-->
<xs:element name="Slot_0" type="RequestSlotType"/>
<xs:element name="Slot_1" type="RequestSlotType"/>
<xs:element name="Slot_2" type="RequestSlotType"/>
```

```
===================================================================
    Request a digital signature for a PDF document
===================================================================
-->
<xs:complexType name="PDF_Request">
    <xs:sequence>
        <!--
            Define the hash and signature algorithms to be used for
            creating a digital signature
        -->
        <xs:element name="SignatureDigestAlgorithm" type="dss:DigestAlgorithm"/>
        <xs:element name="SignatureCryptoAlgorithm" type="dss:CryptoAlgorithm"/>
        <!--
            Document related information and content
        -->
        <xs:element name="CifBusinessUnit"      type="cs:businessUnitType"/>
        <xs:element name="CifReceiver"          type="cif:cifNumberType"/>
        <xs:element name="DocumentUUID"         type="cs:uuid20AsCharType"/>
        <xs:element name="DocumentContent"      type="xs:base64Binary"/>
        <xs:element name="RequestAuthentication" type="xs:base64Binary"/>
    </xs:sequence>
</xs:complexType>
```

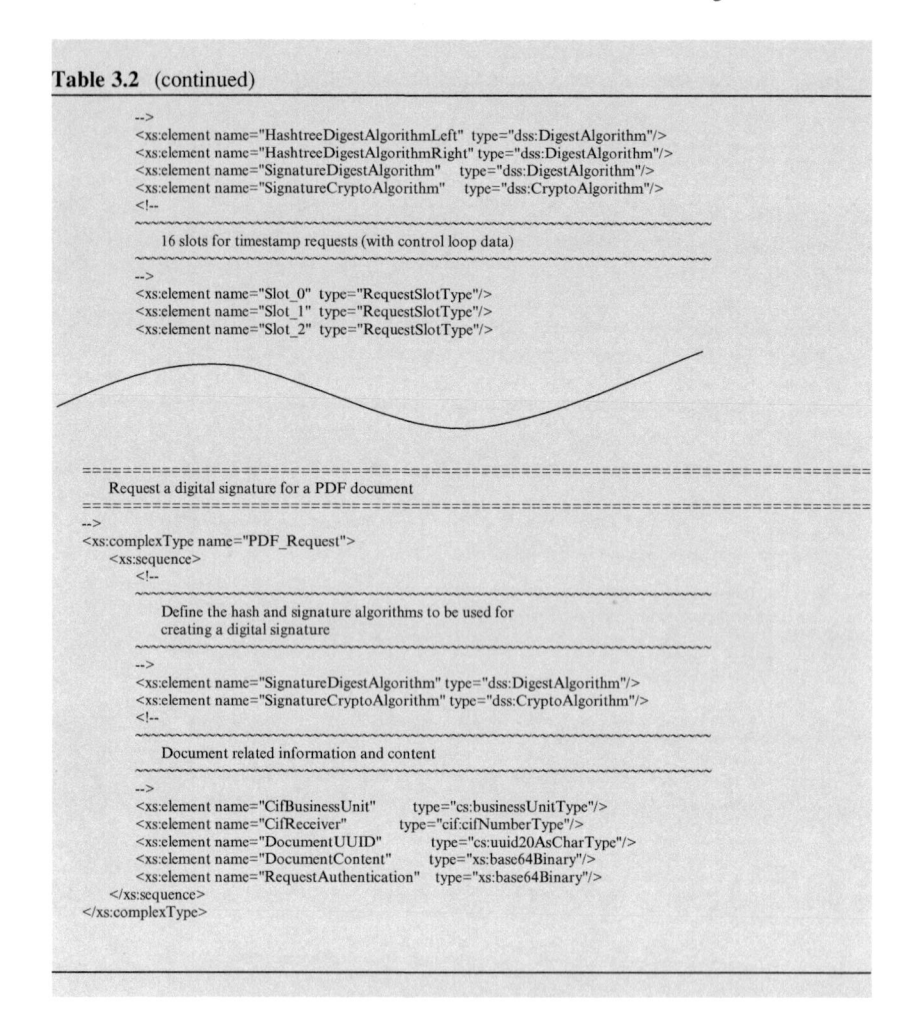

3.5.2 Non-Functional Properties of Services

A service contract for the use of an interface needs to contain more agreements than the interface specification; i.e. more than syntax, semantics, error and exception handling. These additional agreements cover the *non-functional properties* for the use of the interface. Non-functional properties include:

- *Performance*: Often the service contract defines maximum latencies, minimum throughputs, or both. Some contracts define absolute guarantees. Others define performance probabilities. Load and performance properties obviously depend on some conditions with the service consumer. Less can be guaranteed in the Internet than inside a data center.
- *Availability*: The service contract specifies minimum average availability for a service. Often, one only specifies availability at peak times or under special

circumstances such as a catastrophic event losing substantial parts of the system's capacity. At times, the contract defines availability in combination with performance. Performance degradation may be acceptable under some scenarios, for example if a part of the underlying network is not available.
- *Release cycle management*: In this area, the service contract may define minimum time windows for the client to move to a newer version, or a minimum advance notice by the provider to announce changes to the service.
- *Cost of use and accounting practice*: In very large information systems, we must account for service usage. The contract, therefore, must give pricing information for service usage. Depending on the accounting practices used, pricing schemes can be complex.
- *Security considerations*: The contract may include information about where the data is stored, how it is protected when stored and when transported. We need to define authentication and access control policies for the service.

Providing guarantees for the quality of functional, interface, and non-functional properties of a service (Or rather: the component offering the service) is based on the concept of *trustworthy components*[7] ([Meyer_98], [Meyer_03]).

Defining all these aspects of a service may sound as if it were a big effort. This is indeed the case if we elaborate these contracts from scratch, each time we build a new service. In a very large information system, we can simplify this by defining a number of service classes, each class standardizing a set of service definitions.

3.5.3 Contracts as Active Relationships

Service contracts play a crucial role in integration architecture. The central idea associated with a contract is its binding power between the provider of the service and the consumers of the service. The contract defines which interactions are possible, what is required in order to interact and what will be delivered as the result of the interaction. Each party relies on the longevity of the contract, so it should change only infrequently and under well-defined circumstances, governed by a mandatory process. This puts a special emphasis on service design: A service has to be designed in such a way that it is stable from the beginning and requires infrequent updates in the future. In the experience of the authors, stable interfaces result from a strong business object model (Side Story 2.5), rather than from individual requirements. Diligent interface quality assurance (see 3.6) reduces the need for frequent fixes to the interfaces. A precise *documentation* and design for

---

[7]Not to be confused with the notion of trust in secure computing. Guarantees for security properties are part of the properties of a trustworthy (or trusted) component, however, "trust" in trustworthy components extends to all quality factors ([Meyer_03]).

each service is required. Services have to be specified in business terms and with as much semantic information as possible. Using business terms for the description of the services facilitates the communication with the service consumer and enables reuse (see Sect. 3.6). This allows application designers to determine which services they can reuse and how to embed them into their solution. With badly designed and documented services, it will be hardly possible for application designers to understand meaning and behavior of the service, since they do not know the underlying implementation. In this case, reuse comes at unnecessary high cost, or not at all.

The component development methodology of "Design by Contract" ([Meyer_97], [Meyer_09], [Schoeller_06], [Abrial_10]) is a powerful concept for the design and implementation of correct software. Each component interface is specified with a set of preconditions and postconditions which guarantee their correct behavior. *Contract theories* are an important emerging field of research for component-based system engineering ([Baduel_09], [Raclet_09]). They assure formal correctness, composability and automatic checking capabilities for component interfaces.

Side-Story 3.5 gives an example of how to define non-functional properties of a service.

Side-Story 3.5: Example of a Credit Suisse Service Level Agreement

The service selected for this side-story is a synchronous CORBA-service delivering customer master data. When called with the customer information ID (CIF-ID), the service returns the customer information for 1 ... n customers, according to the number of input CIF-IDs. Because this service delivers confidential customer information, it is strongly protected against unauthorized access. The service description including the non-functional attributes, such as response time and throughput, is listed in Table 3.3. The main customer information database is located on the mainframe and is available to all properly authorized applications on all platforms via the CS enterprise service bus. Due to operational reasons, the CIF-component is redundantly deployed on different platforms and in different locations.

Table 3.3 SLA for the service "getCustomer"

Operation: getCustomer		
Topic	Attributes/Values	Remarks
Service Description	The service delivers the customer information for 1...n customers. The customers are identified by their CIF-ID (Customer Information File ID).	Synchronous service via CORBA
Operation	getCustomer	Interface formally specified in IDL

(*continued*)

3.5 Interfaces and Service Contracts

Table 3.3 (continued)

Operation: getCustomer		
Topic	Attributes/Values	Remarks
Properties	Public service General availability Read only Aggregated service (from single CIF reads)	Access restricted by fine-grained authorization rules, delivering more or less customer information, such as including customer balance
Service Owner	Hans Muster	Internal contact details
Service Developer	Sybille Beispiel	Internal contact details
In production since	Nov 9, 2007	
Estimated phase-out	No phase out planned	
Preconditions and return to call	• Consumer provides 1...n valid CIF-IDs • Consumer provides 1...n mixed valid, invalid and unauthorized CIF-IDs	• Service delivers the customer information for each CIF-ID • Service delivers the customer information for each valid and authorized CIF-ID. Service delivers an error code for all invalid and unauthorized CIF-IDs
Exceptions	*ExC02*: the following error occurred "xxxxxx" (standardized CS error codes) *ExC03*: Invalid value in field "yyyyy" *ExC01*: Customer information not found *ExC13*: Unauthorized access attempted	
Service Level	Roundtriptime: • Average: 500 ms • Minimum: n.a. • Maximum: 1,500 ms Throughput: • Average: 100,000 per hour • Average: 1,000,000 per day • Average: 20,000,000 per month	
First level support response time	Maximum: 1 h	
IN-Parameters	Formally defined in IDL	
OUT-Parameters	Formally defined in IDL	

3.5.4 Service Versioning

In very large information systems managing the large number of services is difficult. Service consumers rely on the service provider to fulfill the *contract* defined for the service. Only new versions of a service definition can introduce changes to the contract. In order to make sure that not all service consumers have to migrate to a new version of the service at the same time, usually some of the older versions are kept alive, in parallel.

There are various reasons to release a new version of a service, such as additional functionality, changes in existing functionality or repair of malfunctions. Whenever possible, the provider tries to change the service in a backwards compatible way. This means that the new version satisfies all specifications set by the contract for the old version. In practice that means that no additional input fields are required in the new version, that the ranges for the input fields are the same or larger than the ranges specified in the old version. For the output fields that mean that all fields specified by the old version must still be returned without extending the range of the fields. Moreover, we need to make sure that all the non-functional requirements defined in the old version are at least satisfied in the new version. If all of this is true, we call a new version backwards compatible and create a minor version. The property of a minor version is that the service provider can switch to it without violating the service contract with the consumers. Thus, we can update minor versions without notifying the consumers. If the contract needs to be changed in a way visible to the service consumer, we need to create a major version (see Fig. 3.8). For each major version, only the latest minor version implementation is in production, as it can be updated without involving the consumers. For technical reasons, such as non-extensible signatures in more traditional interface technologies, such as IDL ([Orfali_98]), it is often necessary to keep interface adapters to all minor versions, mapping those to the latest implementation. We would like to keep multiple major versions, however, to give the consumers time to adapt to the new contract. Integration architecture needs to set a policy about how many parallel

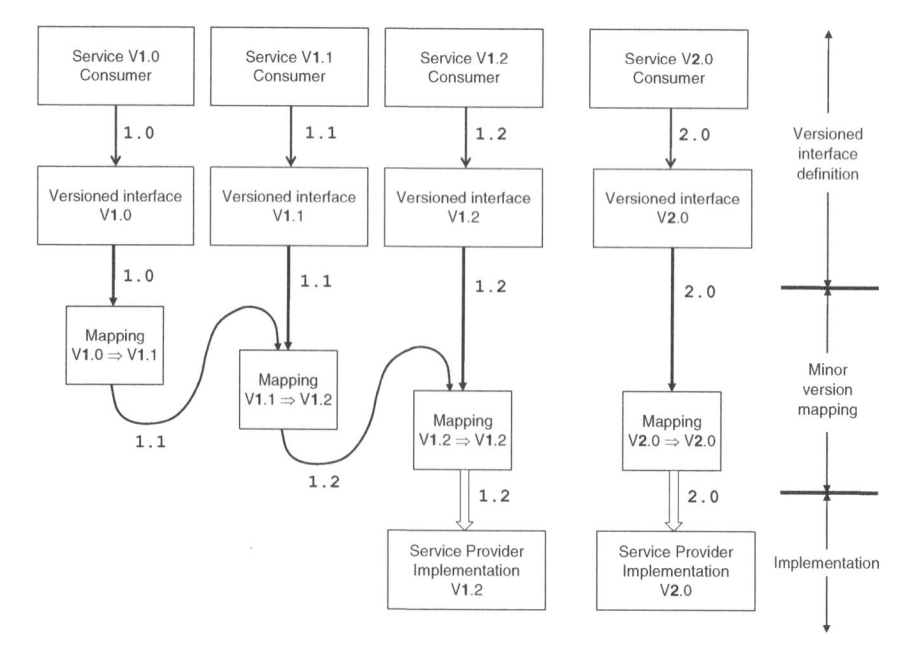

Fig. 3.8 Service versioning

major versions make sense. In the experience of the authors, about one new major version per year is released at the beginning of the lifecycle of a service. Later, this pace is slower. Three parallel versions have proven to be the right trade-off between provider complexity and pace of adapting to new major versions.

In a situation with many services, we will need a process steering the lifecycles and the dependencies between service consumers and providers. Using the architecture reviews, as shown in Sect. 2.8, all new projects are steered towards the latest version. Regular reports about consumers on old versions are produced in order to understand dependencies and to influence maintenance activity, with the objective to keep the number of parallel major versions limited.

For this process to be successful, a repository of services, versions and consumers is crucial. The whole service lifecycle around this repository needs careful management. This is the topic of the next section.

3.6 Service Management Process

Successful integration architecture relies on dependable services. In very large information systems, explicit and formal contracts define the relationship between the *service provider* and the *service consumer* for thousands of services. This requires a rigid management process supported by powerful tools. This "service management process" supports the following activities: Collecting requirements, specifying and designing a service and implementing and using a service. Finally, the process supports measurement of service architecture progress towards desired key performance indicators, providing figures for the number of services, SLA-adherence, usage counts and reuse characteristics.

A proven service management process is shown in Fig. 3.9. It shows the four phases (1) service requirements management, (2) service specification and design, (3) service implementation and (4) service use, as well as the overarching activity of service management and controlling. Between the phases (1) to (4) three *quality control gates*, QC0, QC1 and QC2, have to be passed when developing a service. The quality control is in the hands of a review board consisting of service and domain experts. It is based on formal deliverables to be presented by the provider of a service implementation. The full process must be supported by a powerful tool (see e.g. Side-Story 3.6).

In the spirit of "managed evolution," the service architecture evolves over time. Typically, the legacy system starts without services. First, the focus is on growing the number of services, as needed by the projects. This has to be counterbalanced by some architectural control in order to avoid redundant services without potential for reuse. Then potential consumers need incentives to use existing services, wherever appropriate. Finally, in a large environment, metrics help to steer in the right direction. The process shown in Fig. 3.9 supports the *service architecture* evolution in the context of a very large information system and then manages it in the long term.

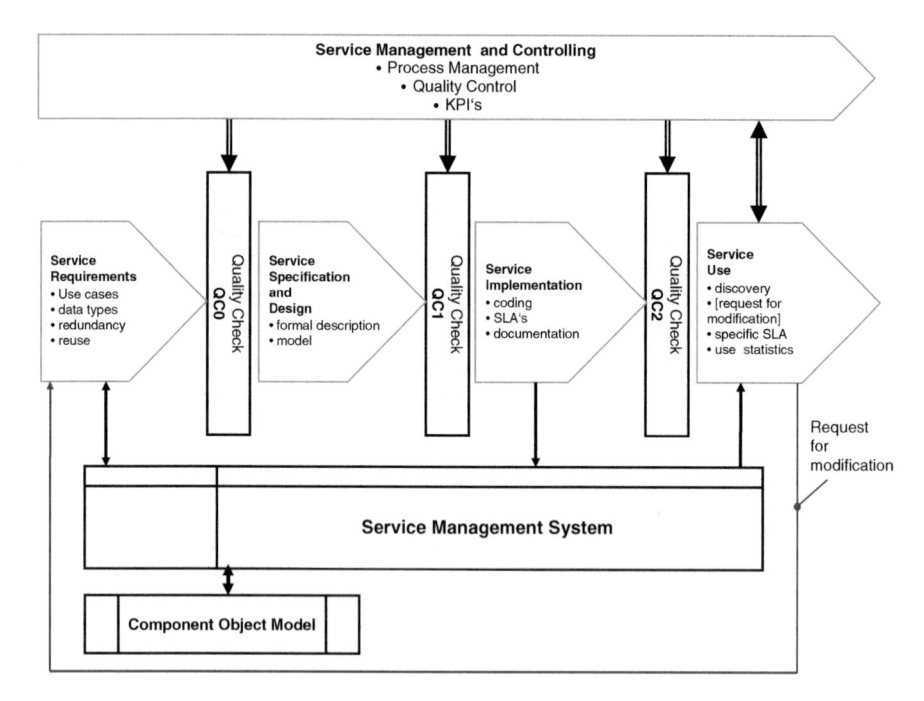

Fig. 3.9 Service management process

Providing a service starts with understanding and capturing the *requirements*, often in the form of documented use cases. In this first step, the major issue is to decide whether to extend or reuse an existing service, or build a new one. The service management tool supports requirements gathering and prioritization in a semi-formal way. It provides a good workflow to coordinate requirements gathering and review activities throughout the large organization. This is a collaborative effort between the service provider and its consumers. Often, the consumers come up with the requirements and the provider orchestrates detailing and prioritization of requirements. At this stage the planned service is integrated into the domain model and the business object model. This mitigates the risk that interface requirements go to the wrong domain and thus a possibly redundant service would be built. New global information types may need to be defined at this stage (see Side-Story 3.6).

The first prerequisite for successful service *reuse* is that a potential service consumer can find a suitable service for his purpose. The service management tool supports this with powerful search capabilities. Keyword searches, full-text searches and hierarchical searches are very useful. One possibility is to let the consumer browse the models in order to be able to find all services in a certain domain, all services acting on a specific business object, or those providing a certain information type as input or result. At that time the service consumer also needs to understand the non-functional properties of the service (see Sect. 3.5.2). Once an existing service is found, it often fulfills the requirements to an extent which is almost, but not quite, necessary. In this case the potential consumer can submit his

3.6 Service Management Process

requirements and start the process to create a new version of an existing service. It is necessary to understand how the quality characteristics provided by the service affect the overall quality of his application. In critical cases you need to analyze the load characteristics of the other consumers of a service in order to understand whether enough capacity is available. The tool supports that by giving information about all the consumers of a service and their usage characteristics. The first *quality check gate* QC0 checks the consistency and completeness of the *service requirements*, checks for redundancy creation, such as building a new or extended an existing service, enforces reuse and approves new information types if required.

The consolidated and approved service requirements form the base for the service design. During this phase, all details of the service, such as integration type, syntactic and semantic specifications of the interface and non-functional properties are fixed. At this stage, the tool needs integration with the models in the system to help place the service in the right domain and have clarity on syntax and semantics of the data passed in the service. For the precise specification of the service, the tool must provide template contracts, access to standard data types and import facilities in case some of the specification comes from a foreign source. Once the functionality of the service is documented, the next step is to design the service. The interface is architected, embedded into the existing landscape and modeled. If a new interface requires new information types, their syntax and semantics are carefully defined. For semantic integrity, all information types need to be linked to the business object model. The second quality check gate QC1 checks the *service specifications* with respect to requirements and reviews the formal, syntactical and semantic adequateness and completeness and approves the service model, including the formal service specifications.

Once the quality gate QC1 is passed, implementation work for the service on the platform can start. During the service *implementation phase* the component providing the service is implemented. To support this, the tool generates code fragments in the desired implementation technology (see Side-Story 3.6). A particularly powerful technology to do that is *model-driven architecture* ([Frankel_03]). Another important feature of the tool is a repository of test cases for services. This allows for automatic testing of the service contract, each time a new version is released. The final quality check gate QC2 reviews and approves the final implementation of the service. This is a technical review, including functional testing, non-functional testing and performance testing.

Once a version of a service is in production, its availability is published in the service repository with the complete contract information, including lifecycle information. The service *use phase* is the productive phase of the service. A new consumer discovers the service in the service repository and assesses the suitability for his purpose. In many cases, the service may be used unmodified. In other cases the user may submit a number of change requests to extend the existing service thus running through all phases of Figure 3-9 again. As the service provider releases new versions of the service and attempts to retire old versions, the process must support him identifying the users of the service, so that he can orchestrate the retirement of old versions. During maintenance, the consumer of a service is obliged to check the lifecycle information in regular intervals and update to new versions if his application consumes an old version (see Sect. 3.5.4).

The detailed implementation of this whole process depends a lot on the scope of the service in question. Services with global visibility need the most thorough quality assurance, as they potentially affect many consumers. Quality management can be relaxed for services visible only to their own domain or application.

In many organizations with emerging service architecture, services are created and built on demand by the projects. The advantage of this bottom-up approach is a quickly growing number of services driven by demand. In the experience of the authors, this is the only way to service-enable a very large information system. The potential disadvantage is redundancy and loss of architectural integrity, if not carefully managed. The process must, therefore, carefully balance the quest for minimum redundancy and consumer-oriented development.

On the level of the whole system, the service repository gathers important information to steer the whole process. Growth in the total number of services and reuse factor need monitoring. Large service growth with low reuse factor is dangerous, except in the early days of a service-oriented architecture. The overall tracking of service level agreements (SLA) provides information for accounting and gives early warning signals when certain services regularly violate the contract. Measuring the number of consumers sitting on deprecated service versions helps understand the overall lifecycle situation and steer maintenance investments towards areas lagging behind.

Side-Story 3.6: Credit Suisse Service Management System IFMS

In 2009 the number of managed services for general availability within global Credit Suisse was approaching 1,000 and was growing steadily. This tendency had been recognized already in 2006 and the necessity of a service management system (IFMS[8]) was recognized. Today the IFMS is in full operation and serves a wide community of users, including service users, service designers and service reviewers.

The elements of the IFMS are shown in Fig. 3.10. The first function of IFMS is the support of the complete *service management process* as presented in Sect. 3.6. All participants of the service management process are bound into a workflow and execute their tasks guided by the IFMS. Service designers are strongly supported by the IFMS and are forced to adhere to the service design guidelines.

---

[8]IFMS stands for Interface Management System which was the former name for the Service Management System.

3.6 Service Management Process

The second function is the *service repository*. The service repository contains all active services with their services and attributes and provides powerful search facilities. The service repository functionality supports the service portfolio management and reporting. Data from the service repository is exported to a number of downstream systems, such as the application landscape management system where services are connected to information flows.

The third function of the IFMS is the management of *information types*. The strict standardization, both syntactically and semantically, of data fields used in services on a global scale is of fundamental importance. The service designers must strictly use existing information types that are searchable in the IFMS. As an example the definition of the information type "date" is shown in Table 3.4. This information type must be used in all services containing a date-field. It is the task of the presentation layer to convert this date definition into the representation format, e.g. YYYY/DD/MM in the US or DD.MM.YYYY in Switzerland. If a specific information type for a new

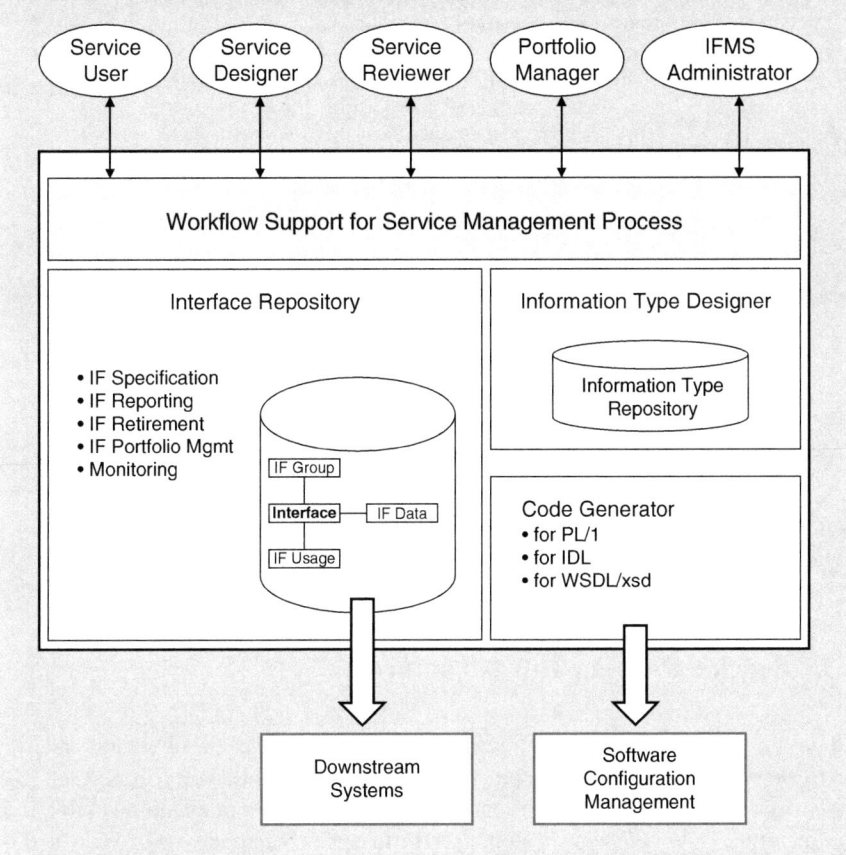

Fig. 3.10 Service management system elements

service is not available, the service designer requests it and the IFMS process will define it and make it available.

The fourth IFMS function is automatic code generation. The IFMS code generator generates code for PL/1, IDL and WSDL/xsd which can directly be used in the programming of the service. The generated code not only reduces time to market of a service considerably but, at the same time, increases the software quality significantly.

Table 3.4 Definition of the information type "date"

Name:	Date
Type:	string<8>
Attribute Types:	one
Description:	Date, based on the Gregorian calendar, represented according to the ISO 8601 standard in the basic format [YYYYMMDD]; dates prior 15 October 1582 ("15821015") are not valid, because of the introduction of the Gregorian Calendar by this date. Special semantic interpretation for following specific dates: "99991231" is interpreted as undefined in future See also: http://www.iso.org/iso/support/faqs/faqs_widely_used_standards/widely_used_standards_other/date_and_time_format.htm http://en.wikipedia.org/wiki/ISO_8601#Calendar_dates
Constraints:	1. Accepted characters: 0, 1, 2, 3, 4, 5, 6, 7, 8, 9 2. Exactly 8 characters must be entered 3. Range: 15821015 - 29991231, except 99991231 4. Further constraints: a) 01 <= MM <= 12 b) 01 <= dd <= 28 or 29 or 30 or 31, according to the Gregorian calendar c) Special value 99991231: nonterminating (infinite)/undefined
Domain:	BAS (Enterprise Base Solutions)
Subdomain:	GEDD (Generic Data Definitions)
Visibility:	AL
Status:	Reviewed - Accepted - Entered in IFMS
Review date:	27.02.2009
Review comment:	26.5.2008 Preliminary definitions accepted 2.2.2009 Updated according to the application architecture concept

3.7 Service Delivery Infrastructure

So far, the focus was on logical integration architecture. Nevertheless, the underlying *technology* to make integration architecture successful is very important. The main reason to make this section rather short is the plethora of available material in the literature on *middleware* ([Hohpe_04], [Erl_05], [Chappell_04], [Woods_03], [Britton_01]). The key requirements to the technical foundations enabling service architecture are the following:

3.7 Service Delivery Infrastructure

- Bridge network distance and technical heterogeneity, as described in Sect. 3.4.6 and hide these aspects to the maximum extent possible from the developer.
- Provide a registry of services for dynamic detection and addressing of services. Potentially add automatic failover to a replacement instance in case of failure. This service can be provided by name or by service property.
- Provide glue code to access services from within the programming environment understood by the provider or the consumer of a service. This can either be done by offering application programming interfaces or generated code.
- Transform messages according to rules on the application level in order to bridge syntactic or semantics gaps between provider and consumer. As mentioned above the authors consider this functionality as dangerous. If its use is not properly restricted, you end up with all the integration complexity as an unstructured heap of transformation rules in the middleware.
- Ensure adherence to the service contract from both consumers and providers. This can be done at run-time by measuring non-functional properties of the service and signal contract violations when appropriate. Depending on the implementation technology interface, syntax checking happens at compile time or run-time.
- Restrict access to services to authorized consumers. Protect data during transport from unauthorized access. Pass along a security context, so that the service provider can authenticate the consumer and decide on the service this consumer gets. Often, access to data through a service is restricted depending on the identity of the consumer. Log all activity on an interface in order to be able to prove that specific interactions have happened. This is particularly important in cases, where services have some commercial meaning.
- Collect data about service usage, contract adherence and other properties of the service architecture. Provide the results to accounting and quality assurance.
- Provide functionality for automatic recovery from service delivery failures. This includes restart of services, retries on undeliverable messages, automatic failover to other service instances in case of failure and distributed transaction management for tightly coupled services updating databases.
- Simulate service providers and service consumer for test purposes. This can go from very simple service stubs without a lot of business logic, for development purposes, up to a fully automated test case collection to test a service against the full extent of the contract, including non-functional properties. Often, you set up robot consumers constantly interacting with the service, in order to detect failures early.
- Finally, provide a service management tool with the functionality as described in Sect. 3.6.

Often an *enterprise service bus* (ESB, [Chappell_04]) provides a significant part of the functionality listed above. An ESB is a concept that provides dependable and secure communication and collaboration between components, enables their transaction and security context and executes data transformations and intelligent routing. In addition, service monitoring and managing functions are part of the

ESB. An enterprise service bus connects a significant number of diverse components running across the extended enterprise. Generally an enterprise service bus does not come "out of the box" from a vendor: It is a conceptual framework specifying the needs of the enterprise and it is implemented by a number of individual technologies such as network, messaging middleware, object broker and file broker. A number of enterprise service buses have been implemented in different enterprises. An example is shown in the Side-Story 3.7.

Side-Story 3.7: The Credit Suisse Integration Infrastructure CSXB

At the end of the 1990s, the complexity of the IT infrastructure reached a critical level with respect to flexibility, manageability and operability (see Chap. 16 in [Krafzig_05], [Hagen_03]). Credit Suisse decided at that time to introduce an integration architecture based on a service-oriented architecture. This required the design and implementation of an enterprise bus. The Credit Suisse architects were aware that this was a difficult task, because the requirements for an enterprise service bus are so diverse, that they cannot be covered by a single, homogeneous solution. In addition, the lifecycles for the underlying technical products and standards in this area tend to be short.

The first step was to introduce an information bus providing synchronous communications. This information bus successfully connected mainframe applications with application frontends running on different platforms and was a big step in the direction of integration and decoupling. Over time, asynchronous messaging, file transfers and portals were added. The evolving Credit Suisse enterprise service bus CSXB operates over the company intranet and is available worldwide on all locations and on all application platforms. The CSXB offers six basic functionalities to the applications (see Fig. 3.11): *Synchronous transactions* which are called *exchanges*. *Asynchronous messaging* which are called *events*. *File transfers* (also called *bulk transfers*) which consist of point-to-point file transfer and multi-point file transfers via file-broker. A number of support functions are provided by the *integration broker*, such as data replication and synchronization, stovepipe processing and multicast publish/subscribe[9]. Two additional important functions are the *portals* (portal infrastructure), which enable desktop integration ([Sullivan_03], [Szuprowicz_00]) and the *workflow infrastructure* providing support for the integration of mixed automated/manual business processes ([Van der Aalst_04]).

---

[9]See e.g.: http://www-01.ibm.com/software/integration/wbiadapters/library/infocenter.

3.8 Consuming Foreign Services

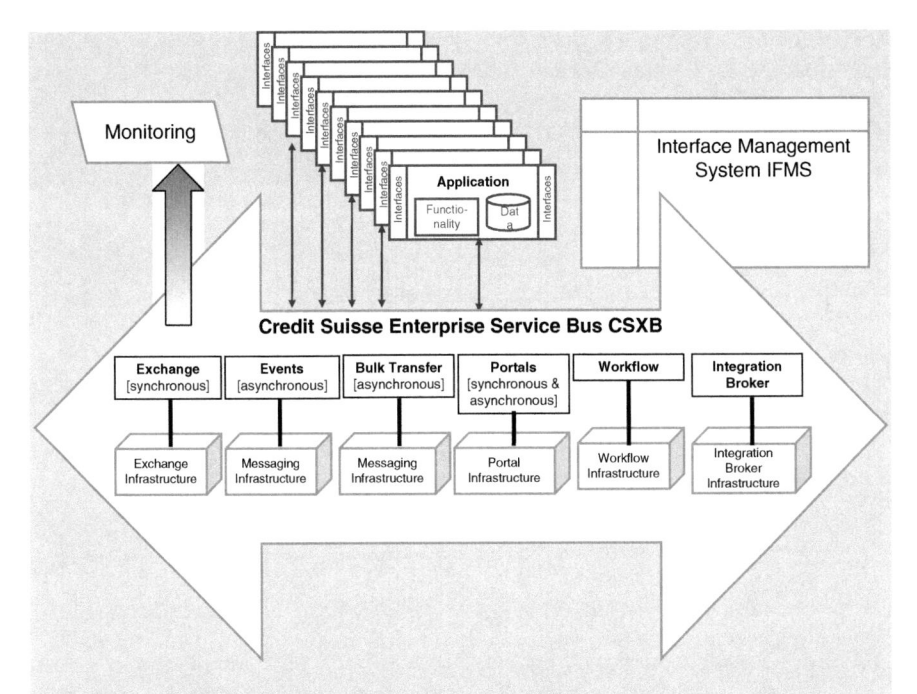

Fig. 3.11 The Credit Suisse enterprise service bus CSXB

An important part of the CSXB is the service management system (IFMS, see Side-Story 3.6): All public interfaces must be registered in the IFMS and can be found by any potential user. The registration process in IFMS also checks the conformity to the Credit Suisse interfaces standards; e.g. the adequate use of allowed information types. The CSXB is monitored at all times, thus allowing data to be collected on usage, performance, users, etc. of the CSXB. As an example, the usage of the exchange infrastructure is shown in Fig. 3.12. In 2008 approximately 800 public services were available and the number of synchronous CORBA calls (exchanges) was 4'525'000'000.

The CSXB also provides the basic *security infrastructure* for the service architecture ([Erl_05], [Hafner_09]). Security includes access control to services, forwarding of credentials, data transport encryption and generation of the necessary log files for audit trail generation.

3.8 Consuming Foreign Services

The key aspect of integrating *foreign services* – that is services not constructed and operated within the own organization – is that the contract is not fully under control of the organization owning the very large information system. The situation

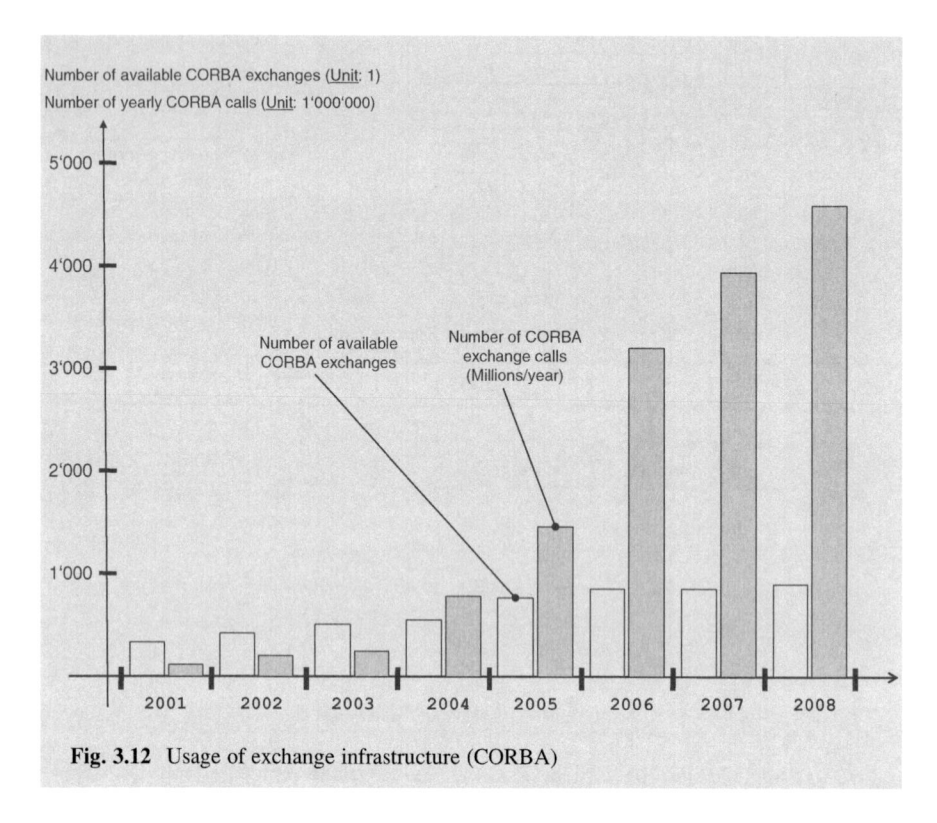

Fig. 3.12 Usage of exchange infrastructure (CORBA)

typically presents itself in two main forms. First, the system consumes services defined, implemented and operated by an external organization. We call this the *business-to-business (B2B) integration case*, which is the fourth integration context in Fig. 3.1. Second, if a piece of commercial off-the-shelf software (COTS) from the market is used, you neither define nor implement the services provided by the package, but you may operate it yourself. The difference is that in the first case, you don't control the service at all, while in the second case, you typically have control over the non-functional aspects of the service.

In the B2B case special attention has to be paid to mitigate all aspects of the dependency. This is a situation where it makes sense to employ the message transformation capabilities of the middleware to loosen the syntactic and semantic dependencies. If possible, B2B interfaces should implement market standards. This guarantees a level of independence from the service provider by externalizing some aspects of the contract to the standardization organization. Specialized integration mechanisms providing the necessary abstraction and security features are required to interact with the "outside world". The emerging protocol for B2B services are *web-services* ([Bussler_03], [Pulier_06], [Alesso_05]), which at least standardizes the technical level of the interface. In B2B relationships the service contract is often part of a commercial contract defining clear rules for service changes and bonus/malus payments depending on the service quality.

3.8 Consuming Foreign Services

The situation when integrating COTS into an existing very large information system is shown in Fig. 3.13: The challenge is that the owner of the existing information system has full control only over the interfaces in his system shown on the left part, which corresponds to only half of the service contract. The COTS may have different service standards, implementations and semantics. In most cases, the vendor of the software package is not able or not willing to adapt his services to the standards used in the existing system. Successful cooperation between the two systems therefore will need some transformations.

Integrating COTS into an existing application landscape, therefore, creates a big challenge on both the logical level of application integration and the level of technical integration.

With application integration there are two areas of concern: The COTS may use different terminology and different *semantics* for the entities processed and stored. This can be as simple as using the same name for a different concept or vice versa. On the syntactical level, the same data types may be defined with different value ranges or string length. Simple transformations, may lead to undesired loss of information. Differences may also be as subtle as different calculation rules, leading to inconsistent results in certain cases. Often, you need complex reconciliation mechanisms to deal with these challenges. The second challenge is that COTS may introduce *redundancy* in the form of overlaps of functionality and data with the existing application landscape. As most COTS are designed to be stand-alone, they come with a complete set of basic reference data, such as customer data or data about organizational structure. Unless the COTS becomes the leading system for this functionality, it is usually redundant.

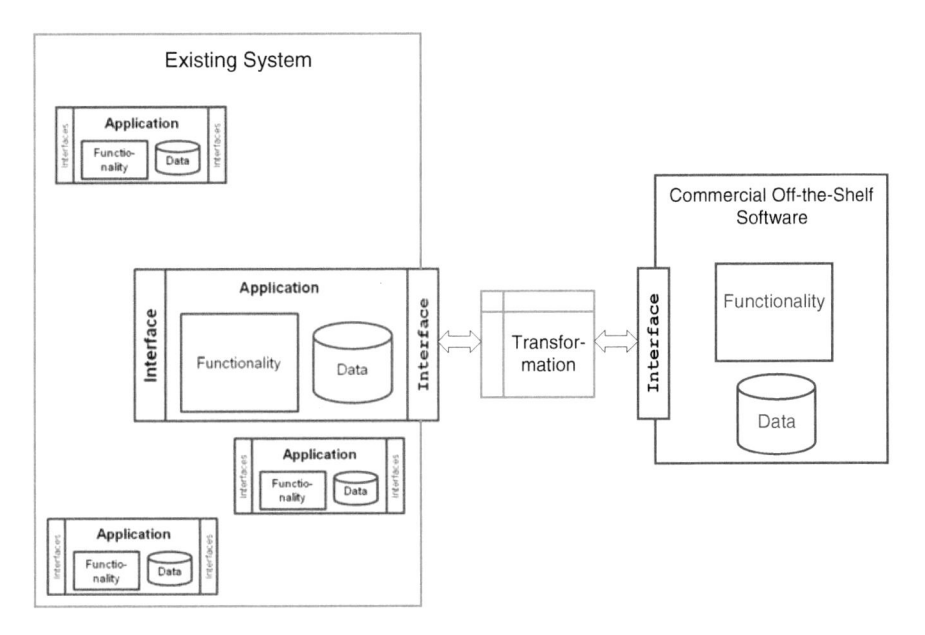

Fig. 3.13 Commercial off-the-shelf software integration

On the level of technical integration, COTS often require technical infrastructure that does not belong to the standard technology portfolio (see Sect. 4.2) of the organization or is at least not provided by the pre-integrated platforms (see Sect. 4.3). Often, this requires a specially engineered infrastructure leading to additional license cost and higher operations cost, because it cannot be operated in the factory. In addition to that, COTS often does not fulfill some of the key non-functional requirements such as security and systems management integration, needed in very large information systems. In the author's experience, successful COTS is often quite old and has its own share of legacy problems, which are carried over into the system when you integrate COTS.

Integrating COTS is fundamentally different from developing your own software. During the analysis phase, it has to be decided whether the "buy" strategy is indeed the best option. One important question in this evaluation is whether the integration cost exceeds the benefit from using COTS. In general, the more functionality a COTS covers and the less redundancy it creates with the existing system, the more likely a buy decision is financially successful. The reason for this is that the benefit of COTS is with the functionality provided and the architectural cost comes with integration and additional redundancy. Often COTS licensing models scale with the number of users or transactions, although development cost of software is independent of the volume.

Generally, this leads to a situation where COTS is not always economically attractive in the context of a very large information system with sound development practices. COTS vendors understand that point and invest into service architecture in order to help reduce the integration effort. In the experience of the authors, COTS is mainly useful where it can cover substantial parts of non-core domains in the very large information system. One way to improve the business case of COTS is collaboration between COTS vendors and customers towards joint service architecture. Side-Story 3.8 presents an example of this approach from the financial services industry.

Side-Story 3.8: Banking Industry Architecture Network (BIAN)

The *Banking Industry Architecture Network* (BIAN, [BIAN_08], http://www.bian.org) is a global, not-for-profit organization with an open intellectual property policy. It intends to bring together leading banks, vendors of banking applications and service providers in a joint community.

This community is convinced that contemporary information systems have to be improved by decoupling monolithic implementations. This leads to improved agility and flexibility, reduced complexity and lower cost of ownership. On the business side the drivers are value chain drivers as the improvement of time to market for new business requirements, market drivers

3.8 Consuming Foreign Services

such as industry consolidation and convergence (mergers and acquisitions), individualized customer needs and finally shareholder drivers like the need to implement new business and operating models.

The target of BIAN is to achieve practice-based results by collaborating on understanding the requirements for "banking enterprise services." The key deliverables of BIAN are the following:

- Create a standard banking services landscape,
- Ensure consistent service definitions, levels of detail and boundaries,
- Move from proprietary to standardized service models to enable commercially available products.

BIAN's vision is a SOA-enabled banking industry resulting in both internal and industry-wide agility and flexibility. BIAN focuses on the business functional definition of services; technical implementation is not in focus. BIAN respects and integrates existing interoperability standards. The majority of banks initiate SOA programs with an internal focus, which is a natural first step. BIAN supports banks to define their internal services based on industry collaboration and best practices. Through BIAN, banks can develop their service definitions on a standardized basis. BIAN intends to create a market for components and services based on its standards. The BIAN working mode is active participation of experts as members in working groups. The main fields of work are architecture, services and building blocks.

Service definition is the key deliverable. BIAN defines services from different viewpoints: The use case view, the business process view, the service landscape view, the business object view, the message view and the software view. The reason for this very systematic and comprehensive approach is to provide services that are sustainable and have the potential for standardization.

An architectural framework combining specific architectural artifacts supports systematic definition of services: The service landscape and the business object model are examples of such artifacts. The service landscape model is very important for defining the adequate delineations and granularity of interfaces. This service landscape is similar to a domain model and is structured in business areas, business domains and subdomains. The subdomains are the containers of functions and the basis for semantic interface definition.

The third set of intended deliverables is the *building blocks*. They help answer the following questions:

- Why SOA? (Strategic Business Scenarios),
- How to structure SOA? (Architecture and Service Definition),

- How to manage a SOA? (Governance, processes, tools, skills, KPI's, soft factors),
- Which scope of the SOA? (IT focus, Business/IT focus, Business to Business focus),
- How to implement SOA? (Implementation roadmaps).

Banks and solution providers are members of BIAN because they are convinced that the establishment of SOA standards for the banking industry will ultimately lead to an improved market for off-the-shelf software components in their sector. Due to the standardized services delivered by BIAN, the effort for integrating these banking components is expected to be lower in the future. Achieving such a global component market is desirable and probably no one will doubt its benefits. However, it will not emerge automatically and banks and software providers with a strong IT and large internal development capabilities think they have to contribute to make this happen.

BIAN is helpful for banks experienced with service architecture to benchmark the internal approach with other members. They use BIAN as a valuable network to exchange thoughts and ideas on a peer basis. Joining BIAN means a give and take of ideas, knowhow and resources. This cooperative approach is based on collaboration across banks and vendors, with the goal to accelerate maturity in service architecture for all members.

BIAN made available to the public its first results in July 2009 on the BIAN webpage (www.bian.org): The Service Landscape version 1.0 is an important artifact for supporting the definition and to ensure consistency and the right functional cuts of services. The BIAN Metamodel version 1.0 defines the types of architectural elements used in the architectural products of BIAN and defines the relationships among those elements. Objectives of the metamodel include: Ensuring consistency between BIAN's various architectural products; providing a common definition of basic concepts such that the different architecture groups can concentrate on their specific topic; and finally aligning activities and products of BIAN with comparable activities and products in the market. The first publication defines services for the *payments* domain and in the area of building blocks, the description of two processes: Service lifecycle management and service repository. BIAN intends to continuously publish new results for the banking industry in order to endorse any effort to realize standards in banking IT. The results are available to the public after registration.

3.9 Evolutionary Decomposition of Monolithic Systems

Modularizing a *monolithic system* starts by defining and implementing encapsulated components. Moving from a monolithic system into a componentized system is a multistep process. In a first step, you assign the existing functionality and data to

3.9 Evolutionary Decomposition of Monolithic Systems

components on a conceptual level, without changing anything in the software. Often this corresponds to the decomposition in the domain model. Depending on the desired granularity, you choose the level of sub-domains as the enterprise decomposition level. That is when managed evolution towards a component architecture starts. Each time that work is done on an interface crossing the sub-domain border, you introduce a new service as described in Sect. 3.5. Over time, this process leads to fully isolated components.

Componentizing a very large information system is a very long journey – depending on the starting situation, it can easily take a decade for a full transformation. In most cases, a specific business case is at the start of this journey: The first step is often to decouple frontend systems from backend systems, because the technology in the backend systems is not able to deliver applications to the Internet. Often backend decomposition follow as a next step for reasons, ranging from the intent to buy COTS, the ability to decompose the value chain, to stepwise migration away from outdated backend technology.

> "Implementing a SOA at the enterprise level is a significant endeavour that is likely to take many years. During this time, we probably will encounter many obstacles and will have to cope with frequently changing requirements. It is therefore essential that we look at a realistic road-map for rolling out our SOA"
> Dirk Krafzig, 2005

The *domain model* in most cases follows an evolution itself. Large IT organizations start with a proprietary domain model, which strongly reflects the structure of the legacy system. Over time, the requirements of the consumers, as reflected in a target business object model, drive the domain model, which is a strong prerequisite to support reuse and agility. Next, the models integrate market standards, where applicable. This is an important prerequisite to facilitate the implementation of COTS and to decompose the value chain.

Responsibility for service design shifts over time from a provider-driven service architecture to a stronger role for the consumer. First, architects and developers within a specific domain define interfaces, based on their knowledge of the domain, to be consumed from the outside. In the experience of the authors, depending on the kind of the domain, this does not deliver satisfactory results with respect to granularity and reusability. Hence, you need a more consumer-driven approach, as reflected in the process described in Sect. 3.6, where consumers are in charge of the *requirements*. Subsequently, enterprise architects are in charge of embedding the service into the overall landscape and the developers in the domain are responsible for the detailed design. Collecting requirements from multiple sources makes the services more sustainable and reusable.

Keep in mind that *architectural risk* is not the only reason why a service architecture cannot be built in one go. Another limitation is the change needed in the operations procedures. Operating a monolithic system is easier than managing a distributed, heterogeneous components landscape resulting from the process described above. Systems management needs to develop new methods, technologies and processes to cope with daily operations of such systems. More details about how to solve this problem are given in Sect. 4.4.

In addition to that, it takes time to develop skills, culture and governance, which are all indispensible success factors for service architecture. Clearly better modeling and design skills are necessary to succeed with the approach. On the technical side, more people need to understand how heterogeneous distributed systems work and even more importantly, what to do, if they do not work. Integration architecture is strongly based on the notion of a *contract* between the service provider and the consumer. In traditional IT organizations, the concept of end-to-end responsibility for a service is very strong. This is difficult to maintain in a service architecture. Therefore, you need a culture of mutual trust. Good governance helps this culture by providing transparency about the contracts and about whether the involved parties stick to the contract. In this book these aspects of managed evolution are treated in Chap. 6.

As mentioned when discussing the process, one key aspect is the balance between centralized control and consumer-driven development of the service architecture. In the experience of the authors this balance shifts over time. In the beginning, quite some freedom should be left to individual development, because at this stage you need to achieve a critical mass of services quickly. As the models mature and the approach is more accepted in the organization, governance needs to be more centralized in order to avoid the negative effects of pragmatic development.

You do not need completely implemented service architecture to achieve some pay back. As the managed evolution focuses the investments where they make most architectural sense, you will see better agility shortly after beginning the journey.

A special topic when managing a very large information system is the mainframe. Mainframe applications have often continuously grown over more than 30–40 years. During this time the complexity has grown massively and the applications became more and more entangled. Side-Story 3.9 shows how to improve such a situation with a targeted architecture program.

Side-Story 3.9: Disentangling the Mainframe Applications (DiMA)

In 2005 the mainframe application landscape at the Credit Suisse Zurich computer center consisted of 27 Million source lines of mostly PL/1 code. The monolithic structure of the mainframe had four severe disadvantages. First, implementation of new requirements took longer and longer and became more and more expensive (see Fig. 1.5). Second, the risk from changes was becoming higher, because any change could have unforeseen effects which were in some cases only detected after transfer to production. Third, even small changes required the recompilation and production transfer of very large portions of code. Finally, modernizing selected parts was difficult and time consuming because of the tight coupling. It became clear that the tightly coupled functions and data on the mainframe severely hindered the progress of enabling and supporting business growth.

3.9 Evolutionary Decomposition of Monolithic Systems

Therefore Credit Suisse decided in 2005 to start the "Disentangling the Mainframe Applications (DiMA)" program. The objective of DiMA was the implementation of a *component model* on the mainframe and of decoupling the components by *services* as shown in Fig. 3.14.

As a first cut for the component model the *subdomains* (Side Story 2.3) were used: Each mainframe module was analyzed and assigned to a unique subdomain according to the best fit of its functionality and data with the functional/data subdomain description. This required the analysis and assignment of approximately 140'000 mainframe software configuration units.

As a next step the *dependencies* between the modules located in different subdomains were identified. This was mostly done by automatic code analysis; however, some dependencies could not be found by the automatic code analysis and had to be searched for by manual code inspection. After this work had been completed, the mainframe application landscape had been *partitioned* with each component corresponding to a subdomain from the domain model, named a DiMA-component. Later it was experienced, that some of these DiMA-components had to be made more fine-granular, because the subdomains contained too many PL/1 modules – this resulted in a continuous refinement of the mainframe component model.

The DiMA team published a set of standards and guidelines for the construction of the interfaces and services between the DiMA components.

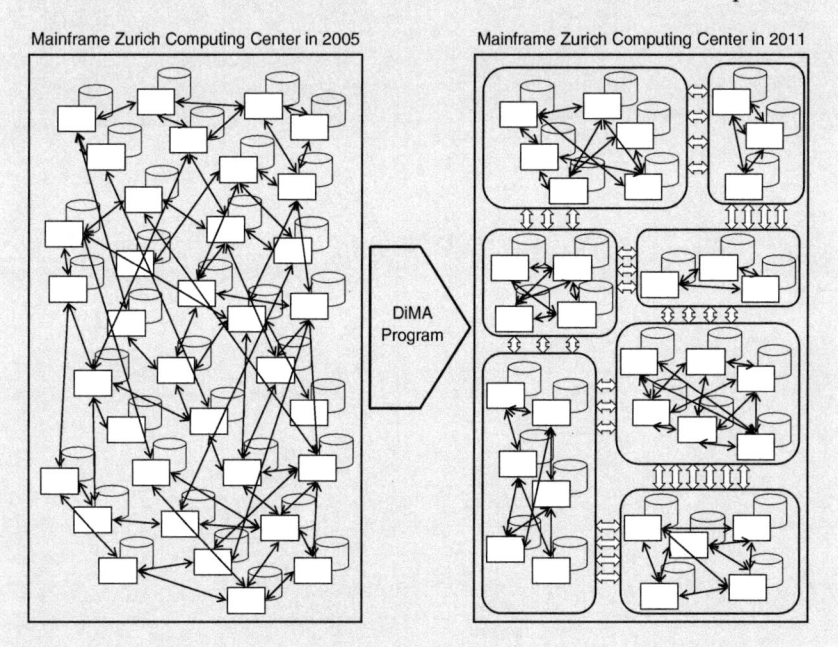

Fig. 3.14 Mainframe application disentangling

The components were successively decoupled. It was expected that 2'000–3'000 new services on the mainframe would have to be implemented. During 2008 five pilot projects introduced more than 40 services, leading to an estimate of the total effort required for the disentangling of the Zurich mainframe application landscape.

The large size of the disentangling program was only manageable with the help of the service management system IFMS (see Side-Story 3.6). IFMS forced the developers to formally define their interfaces and generated the high quality interface code stubs for them.

Chapter 4
Infrastructure

Summary Application software requires a powerful, advanced and dependable infrastructure to execute upon. Infrastructure must support the objectives of managed evolution: Most important is the decoupling of the applications from infrastructure. Infrastructure standardization and lifecycle management allow applications to be quickly developed and to follow their own lifecycles, only loosely coupled to infrastructure lifecycles. The key concepts to achieve successful decoupling are the management of the technology portfolio with respect to redundancy and to technology risk, the extensive use of platforms defined as sets of integrated technical components and processes for the development and operation of applications. Finally, an operations and system management which is specifically built in order to cope with a very large information system consisting of loosely coupled components is required.

4.1 Managed Evolution of Infrastructure

Very large information systems are based on very large infrastructures. Figure 2.1 shows the layered architecture of an information system: *Infrastructure* is the foundation layer. The infrastructure layer provides the *development environment*, the *test environment* and the *runtime environment* to the business applications. Any change in infrastructure may force changes in applications relying on the infrastructure. The large number of applications affected by infrastructure changes generates considerable risk and cost, and consumes significant development resources. However, it is not at all cost-effective to let each application develop and maintain its own infrastructure.

The last chapter has shown the importance of decoupling the different components of the system in order to provide high system agility. In order to be able to manage the applications and infrastructure layers independently from each other, one has to loosen the dependency between infrastructure and applications (Fig. 2.1). Applications and infrastructure are governed by very different evolution trends and forces and have different reuse and standardization opportunities. Whereas the evolution of applications is driven by business requirements, the evolution of infrastructure is mainly driven by technology market trends. Infrastructure optimization strategies are fundamentally different from optimization criteria for applications. Whereas in very large information systems applications are mostly developed in-house, infrastructure is a buy-and-integrate area. Infrastructure lifecycles are dictated by the vendors. Standardization and commoditization play important roles. This situation forces changes and adaptations in the infrastructure, even if the applications do not change. Examples of forced infrastructure changes are releases of new versions of technical products by vendors, new technology standards, emerging interoperability standards, increasing performance requirements and the appearance of better or more cost-effective technology components. Primarily, this means that the infrastructure must also follow managed evolution: Plan, evolve and control the infrastructure based on defined, strictly followed processes based on underlying principles, including technology risk management.

In order to achieve successful decoupling, four key *strategies* must guide the evolution and implementation of infrastructure. First, infrastructure must be *decoupled* from applications. The consequence of this first principle is the introduction of platforms (see Sect. 1.3) and of powerful integration mechanisms, such as the enterprise service bus.

Second, the *technology risk* must be managed. The negative impact a technology can have on the very large information system must be carefully assessed and handled. An important activity here is the proactive management of the *technology portfolio*.

Third, the infrastructure must provide a rich functionally to the applications relying on the infrastructure. This means implementing more and more functions used by many business applications in the infrastructure. This implies that the infrastructure is growing "upwards", taking over functionality that was traditionally seen in business applications, such as IT security. The boundary between infrastructure and business applications is moving upwards in Fig. 4.1 as more and more functionality is shifted "down" from the applications into the infrastructure. This results in a high degree of reuse of functionality as the functions are built and maintained only once in infrastructure, and are used by all applications. This also increases conceptual integrity, because important functions, such as security, systems management and logging are implemented and used in a consistent way. The infrastructure functionality must be provided in the form of contract-based *infrastructure services* with their own operational level agreements (OLA). An infrastructure service encapsulates the underlying functionality and makes changes, such as upgrades and technology product changes, in the infrastructure possible without requiring unwanted changes in the components and applications. The contracts (OLAs) must be centrally managed, thus avoiding unwanted redundancy, providing stability and allowing a long-term evolution of the contracts. Take advantage of *commoditization and sourcing*: Infrastructure technology is becoming more and more commodity, i.e. it is offered by many vendors in (roughly) the same way. Powerful international standards, such as Java, .NET, http:, FTPs, SQL force and guide this development. This reduces the amount of functionality which must be

4.2 Technology Portfolio 131

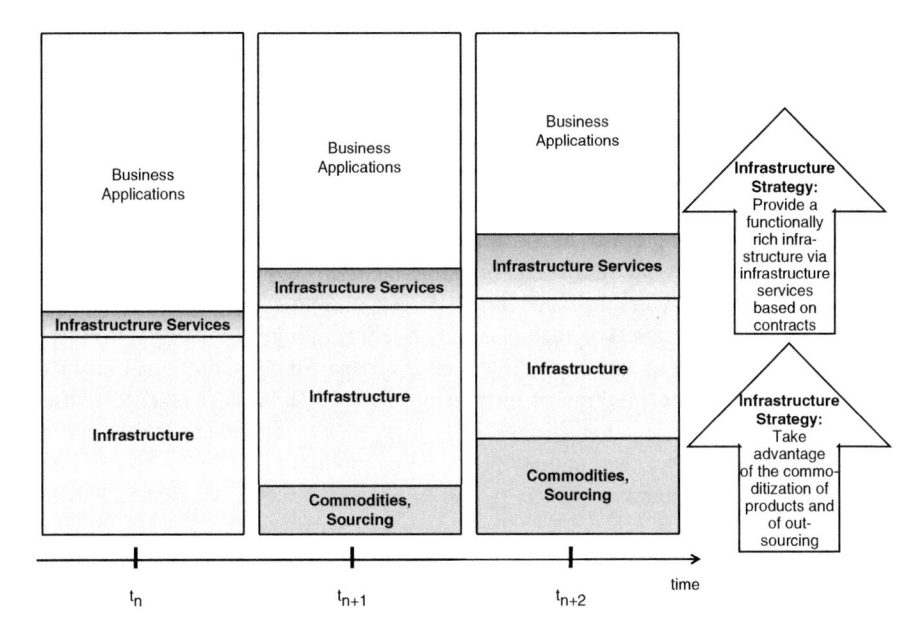

Fig. 4.1 Infrastructure strategy

built by the owner of the very large information system. At the same time, more and more infrastructure services are offered by third parties, i.e. they can be sourced under contract. Examples include telecommunications, Internet access provision, application providers, etc. The boundary between external providers and infrastructure owned and operated by the organization is moving upwards in Fig. 4.1.

Fourth, the infrastructure must guarantee stable *operation* of the applications in order to guarantee availability, dependability and other important non-functional properties of the very large information system.

4.2 Technology Portfolio

Infrastructure is composed of a set of *technologies*, including computing hardware, networking technology, operating systems, middleware, database systems, development environments and systems management applications. A very large information system relies on a considerable number of technologies to build its infrastructure ([Abramowicz_07], [Erl_04]).

Infrastructure technologies are implemented using *technical products*. Technical products are delivered by vendors and are governed by a lifecycle, expressed as *versions* of the technical products. At any time a large number of technical product versions are in use in the infrastructure of the very large information system. All technical products used in the system constitute the *technology portfolio*. The technology portfolio can be visualized as a rectangle with a width (y-axis) and a time window (x-axis) as shown in Fig. 4.2.

The *width* represents the set of technical product versions in operation at any time. The time window shows the *lifecycles* of the technical product versions in operation.

Managing the width of the technology portfolio includes controlling the *number* and versions of technical products in use. Any technical product generates cost, such as license cost, support cost and operations cost. The *width* of the technology portfolio should therefore be kept as small as possible. This also includes the avoidance of *redundancy*: For each task only one technology should be introduced and maintained, such as one message queuing system for asynchronous transmissions. When a new technology is introduced, the old technology should consequently be phased out. Due to the *longevity* of technology components infrastructure components once introduced and adopted by the applications need to have a long active lifecycle, because any change in infrastructure impacts all applications using the infrastructure.

An important activity is the careful assessment and management of *technology risk*. Technology risk is generated by products, vendors, standards and the marketplace. In the infrastructure of a very large information system no "exotic" technology

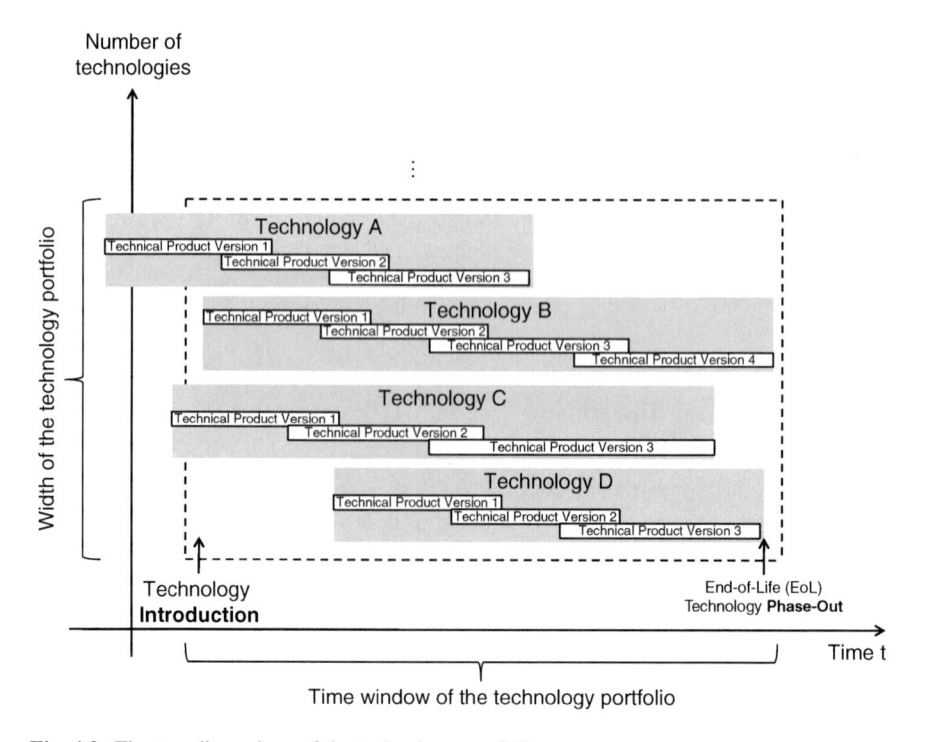

Fig. 4.2 The two dimensions of the technology portfolio

components should be used, but only proven mainstream technologies accepted by the marketplace are safe. Many properties of technologies and products – such as stability, reliability, interoperability, cost – are strongly dependent on market acceptance. Niche technologies or products may be attractive from the point of view of functionality, performance, or specific implementations. It is well known that often not the best technologies become widely used in the market. Because of the high cost and risk of phasing-in and phasing-out of a technology in a very large information system, staying in the technological "mainstream" is a safe decision. Note that this strategy applies also to the selection of standards. Figure 4.3 illustrates this concept: Each technology is positioned in a two-dimensional grid. One dimension denotes market acceptance and the other dimension importance to the system. The safe zone is along the diagonal in this grid. There market acceptance and internal importance are aligned. The problematic zone B is the lower right corner: There the system is heavily dependent on a technology with little market acceptance. This often happens for historical reasons, where a former mainstream technology loses its market acceptance. Depending on the severity of the situation, exit scenarios must be planned and executed for the affected technology. Another problematic zone A is the upper right corner: There the system makes little use of a mainstream technology. The reaction to this situation depends on the technology. If it provides a fundamental new capability, it needs to be introduced into the system. If it provides redundant capabilities to other, already used, mainstream technologies, no action is required.

Once introduced into operation, a technical product is very long lived. A number of versions or even product generations have to be kept productive. A key decision

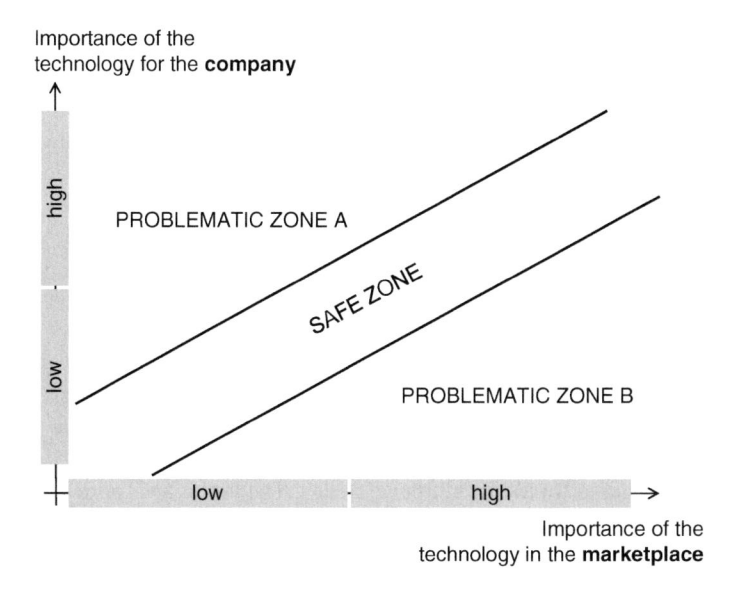

Fig. 4.3 Mainstream technology

for a specific technology is the adoption of either a single-vendor or a multi-vendor strategy. In a single-vendor strategy the best available technical product is selected as the single standard, whereas in a multi-vendor strategy at least two independent vendors for the technology are selected. Very often in specific areas, such as databases, the single-vendor strategy is used, whereas in the commodity area a multi-vendor strategy is better.

The *time window* in Fig. 4.2 refers to the usage time of technical products and their versions: The lifecycle of a technical product starts at the point in time when the product is introduced into productive use and ends at the point in time when it is phased-out. Note that before a technology or a technical product is introduced into productive use, a phase of evaluation, testing and risk assessment is needed. If a product or version is adopted too early, the early adoption risk exists, such as unstable behavior or unsatisfactory functionality. If a product or version is adopted too late, the useful life span is shortened which generates avoidable end-of-life efforts in the system. The question of when to adopt a technology into production is difficult to answer: Generally it is worthwhile to adopt key technologies somewhat earlier and take some technology risk. However, this must be embedded into an innovation strategy of the organization.

Successful management of the technology portfolio requires a formalized *technology portfolio management process*. The first instrument for technology portfolio management is structuring the technology portfolio using a *technical domain model*. The technical domain model partitions the technology portfolio to allow better management of complexity. In the technical domain model all the infrastructure technologies are grouped and assigned to their corresponding *technical domains* as described in Sect. 2.6 and is shown in Fig. 2.9.

Managing the technology portfolio is a continuous process. The objective of the *technology portfolio management process* is to implement the strategy presented above. The technology portfolio management process is a part of the architecture process and follows the same process steps (see Sect. 2.8) and uses the same roles.

The first step in technology portfolio management is the *development step*, consisting of two activities. All existing technical product versions are discussed and assessed. The result is either a confirmation or a change in both architectural status and/or lifecycle status, including phase-in of new and phase-out of old technical products (see Side-Story 4.1). The assessment follows a number of criteria, such as "fit for future", performance, cost, dependability, mainstream, interoperability and licensing. The other activity is the evaluation of new technologies or technical products. This activity involves a considerable research effort and in many cases the development of prototypes. The results of the development step are strongly influenced by the *technical domain strategy* presented by the technical domain architect. The inventory of all technical product versions with their associated architectural status and lifecycle status are published as infrastructure standards and are binding for all development teams. The larger and more federated the system becomes, the more importance must be given to the infrastructure standards

4.2 Technology Portfolio

base. The standards base must be easily accessible and comprehensive and must cover both implementation and evolution of the infrastructure.

The second step is *communication*: All standards are available in an online repository, including hints for their use and warnings. The standards are documented in a uniform way (see Side-Story 4.1). In a very large information system of global spread some differences in applicable standards are necessary, like a certain technical product may be mainstream in Europe but niche in the USA. An important part of the communication step is education: The understanding and acceptance of infrastructure standards differs according to the culture of the regions, some showing more and others less discipline.

After communication, *standards implementation* follows. Approved standards must be consistently enforced in the very large information system. The same methods as described in the architecture process (see Sect. 2.8) are used, with the main instrument being the *project reviews*. Project reviews done by experts check

> "The goal is to optimize, not minimize exceptions. Exceptions are a feature of the technology portfolio management, not a bug"
> Jennifer Costley, 2009

the project phase documents for adherence to standards. An important activity during implementation is the handling of *exceptions*. In justified cases, the project review board may grant an exception to a project, such as allowing the use of a non-standard technical product. Reasons for exceptions include specific functional requirements having a valid business case which cannot be adapted to be covered by a standard, or if the timing of a standard does not fit the project schedule. The former leads to a permanent exception permit, the latter to a temporary exception permit. All exceptions are recorded and managed. As part of the exception management, exception metrics are used. Exception metrics help to understand and manage standards and deviations from standards and support planning.

Because of the long duration of infrastructure provisioning – up to 18 months – for the support of a new standard, early investments in infrastructure are necessary. This is done through *infrastructure architecture programs*, both for strategic phase-ins and phase outs of technical products.

Finally, *technology portfolio management controlling* is necessary. This includes assessing the adherence to standards, exception management, maintaining the exception rate KPI and lifecycle management measurement, such as the number of applications still operating with old versions.

Defining and enforcing standards in a very large, global organization is a demanding task. It is important to involve all stakeholders in the process, to allow for cultural and national differences and to make good use of the available knowledge in the different geographical areas. Sometimes the loyalty of people to some sort of technology is amazing and it needs a lot of persuasion to make them abandon it. Finally, a good balance between consistent enforcement and exceptions is important.

Side-Story 4.1: Credit Suisse Technology Portfolio Management

The technology portfolio of Credit Suisse in 2009 contained 1'733 active technical product versions. This large number of technical product versions is assigned to the technical domains (Fig. 2.9). Each technical product is placed in exactly one technical subdomain.

Each technical domain is managed by its technical domain architect (see Sect. 2.6). The technical domain architect reviews all technical product versions each quarter with the assistance of his technical product owners. The review not only covers technical aspects, but also the non-functional properties and economic factors. Also regional and business unit impacts and their specific requirements are taken into account.

Each technical product version is managed and documented in the form of an "index card". The index card is of course not on paper, but is an electronically generated extract of the information in the technology portfolio on-line management tool. The index card contains the reference to the technical product version and the two important attributes:

- *Architectural Status*,
- *Lifecycle Status*.

These two statuses indicate the allowed usage of the technical product. The predefined values of architectural status and lifecycle status are shown in Table 4.1.

As an example, the record of a technical product version is shown in Table 4.2. All technical products have defined global statuses. The three business areas can restrict global statuses to their specific needs. This means that they can restrict the use of a standard technical product in their respective area. They may also define an earlier end-of-life date. In Table 4.2 for all three business areas the architectural status is "approved standard, invest" and the lifecycle status is "in production". However, business areas cannot unilaterally extend product life cycles or relax usage restrictions.

The technical product version record in Table 4.2 describes the lowest element in the technology portfolio: The *technical product version*. In the technology portfolio, all higher aggregation levels, such as runtime platforms and application platforms are shown with the active technical product version for each release of the platform. Platforms have their own lifecycle management (see Sect. 1.3.5) and all technical product versions are guaranteed to cover the full platform release lifecycle.

4.2 Technology Portfolio

Table 4.1 Technical product architecture and lifecycle status

Architectural Status	• Not examined	The technical standard/product is not considered
	• Under investigation	The technical product is being evaluated for fitness
	• Proposed for approval	Pending approval
	• Approved standard, invest	The technical standard/product will be further developed for use
	• Approved standard, maintain	The technical standard/product will not be further developed and has no plan for retirement
	• Approved standard, tactical	The technical standard/product is an intermediate step and has to be replaced by an approved standard
	• Approved standard, for restricted use	The technical standard/product remains active for a small population, not for general use
	• Retiring	The technical standard/product is scheduled to be retired in the near future (needs an estimated date)
	• No longer in use	The technical standard/product is removed from users and from infrastructure
	• Prohibited	Use of technical standard/product is not allowed
Lifecycle Status	• Initiation	Company, market and industrial research underway
	• Prototyping	Laboratory installation of technology, validation
	• Engineering	Preparing readiness for large scale deployment
	• Test	Full scale testing
	• Production Pilot	Production use for limited user populations, no defined SLA's or OLA's available
	• Production	Full production usage and fully supported
	• Retiring	No new initiatives should use this standard/product
	• End of support	Support agreements no longer exist
	• No longer in use	Product is no longer in use, no more instances are in production

Table 4.2 Technical product version record

Technical Product and Technical Product Release Name	*SUN Java Web Server/Sun Java Web Server 6.1SP2*			
Technical Product Description	Java Enterprise Server http://www.sun.com/software/products/web_srvr/index.xml			
Repository ID	ICTO-4368			
Owner	Barbara Beispiel			
Architectural Status	Global Status: Approved Standard, Invest	**PB** Approved Standard, Invest	**IB** Approved Standard, Invest	...[other units] Approved Standard, Invest
Lifecycle Status	Global Status: Production	**PB** Production	**IB** Production	...[other units] Production
Release Date, Planned	01.08.2006			
End of Life Date	01.10.2011			
Reference to Architecture and other Governance Decisions	Web Server Strategy			

4.3 Platforms

4.3.1 Platform Concept

As discussed in Sect. 3.3 decoupling components is of outmost importance for independent component lifecycles, and therefore for managed evolution. This is particularly true at the border between *infrastructure* and *applications*, as their lifecycles respond to different drivers. While ideally business requirements drive the lifecycle of applications, infrastructure mainly follows the market and technology developments. The technology portfolio (Sect. 4.2) provides managed lifecycles and an overall standardization on the level of single technical components. This is important, but not sufficient for effective infrastructure management, as this limits the view to single components without taking integration and non-functional properties of infrastructure services into account. If applications build their infrastructure directly from standardized technical components, this leads to silo-like ([Graves_08]) solutions based on individual integration efforts and one-off operating processes. This form of providing infrastructure may be necessary for certain cases. In the remainder of the chapter we will refer to these special cases as *special engineering*. For the majority of the applications, however, we can do better.

The key idea here is the *platform*. A platform provides a rich, standardized and pre-integrated set of *infrastructure services* for a certain class of applications. Applications see a platform as a "black box", presenting itself as a set of standardized, predefined and tested infrastructure services, tools and processes. Infrastructure functionality is offered to the applications via services based on contracts. Applications have no detailed knowledge about the implementation of the underlying infrastructure. The platform defines its services very carefully and under strict lifecycle control for the platform as a whole, very similar to the services described in Sect. 3.5. A change in the platform interface may have a big impact on many applications.

The platform approach can be compared to assembly lines or factories in manufacturing industries, where commodity goods such as cars, phones, or computers are assembled out of components according to pre-defined manufacturing processes. Depending on the commodity, the possibility to include features and options is kept. The analogy to factories in industry is platforms in applications development. Even though software development is more complex than commodity manufacturing, the general principles can be adopted. Platforms free development projects and application developers from most of the work related to infrastructure, since they are provided with pre-integrated infrastructure components. Projects are relieved from selecting and integrating components as well as from implementing and operating infrastructure elements. In the context of software engineering, this approach is related to *software product lines* ([Clements_02], [Linden_07], [Weiss_99]).

The decision to invest in building a specific platform depends on the number of applications expected to use it. Engineering a platform is significantly more expensive than performing these tasks for a single application. Experience shows that the critical mass to amortize platform development cost is in the order of magnitude of a hundred applications sharing a platform, which is only feasible in a large information system. Thus platform building starts with a business case demonstrating that the critical mass of applications exists or can legitimately be expected to exist. Success with platforms is closely related to effective architecture management practices (Chap. 2), on the one hand understanding the application portfolio and, on the other hand, being able to drive application development towards standards.

Once established, platforms provide powerful means to further increase infrastructure and operations efficiency. As many applications share infrastructure and operating processes, there is the critical mass to invest in standardization, better process automation or more sophisticated infrastructure. An example is capacity management, where platforms allow for much more aggressive resource sharing across applications than silo-like infrastructures. Stringent lifecycle management leads to automatic adoption of new platform versions by all applications. Technology end-of-life problems remain under control and applications automatically profit from platform improvements. Platforms also improve quality of service for applications. Infrastructure integration is better tested, both before a new platform version goes live and after that, because many applications use the same infrastructure in many different ways. Platforms can invest more into state of the art *systems management*, helping to stabilize the service. Finally, operations personnel can better react to problems, as they are more familiar with the standardized platform setup rather than individual infrastructure solutions. The author's experience with applying platforms in the very complex and quality sensitive area of Internet banking suggests that quality may well be the more important reason than efficiency to adopt a platform strategy.

4.3.2 Platforms as Infrastructure Service Providers

As explained in Sect. 3.5, *services* in general need to be governed by strong *contracts*. This is particularly true with *infrastructure services*, where a large number of applications depend fundamentally on the underlying infrastructure platform. In order to achieve the advantages of a platform, the platform contract specifies the following obligations for the service provider:

- Develop predictable platform roadmaps and stick to them,
- Keep a minimum useful lifespan of 3 years and higher for key infrastructure elements, to allow applications to follow the lifecycle as part of their periodic maintenance,
- Make services available across the whole system,
- Deliver high quality service, continuously optimize it,
- Take platform development decisions with full stakeholder involvement and use a transparent process.

Users of the platform also have some obligations:

- Use standard platforms whenever possible to generate volume,
- Include platform upgrades into periodic application maintenance to avoid additional lifecycle cost.

In addition to that, the contract contains the usual elements (see Sect. 3.5), such as service level agreements and precise interface description.

Platform services come in three groups for different clients of the platform. A first set of services provides services to application developers for efficient *development and deployment*. Once applications are deployed, a second set of services ensures flawless *platform operation* of applications according to the agreed service levels. Finally, the platform itself evolves as well. The third group of services ensures continuous evolution of the platform and makes sure that all applications follow the platform lifecycle (Platform management). Figure 4.4 shows the three service areas; Application development support, platform management and platform operations, as well as the necessary processes in support of the services. The processes are organized into process groups, such as platform product management, platform evolution management, platform development. Figure 4.4 shows that many process groups and thus processes overlap service areas.

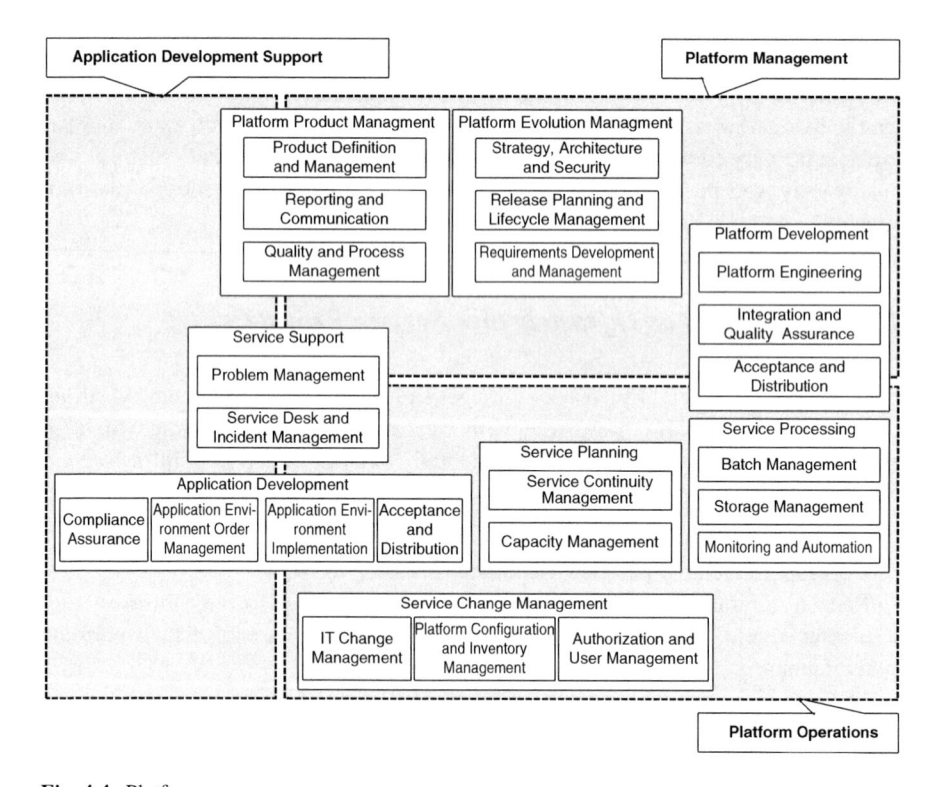

Fig. 4.4 Platform process map

4.3 Platforms   141

Throughout the remainder of this section the authors will refer to Fig. 4.4 to present the various aspects of a platform in context. Sections 1.3.3–1.3.4 will go through the three service areas and provide more details on each. By the end of Sect. 1.3.4 readers will have all the information to fully understand Fig. 4.4.

4.3.3 Application Development Support Processes

The key service to *application developers* is supporting them in using the platform. Each platform comes with a number of architecture guidelines, frameworks, tools, processes and technical components in order to support application development. Examples of architecture guidelines are security guidelines, coding standards and solution blueprints. Examples of frameworks cover data access, user interfaces and access to the integration infrastructure.

As platforms strive to provide rich functionality, a platform typically integrates a number of technical components as an ecosystem for applications to live in. Figure 4.5 shows the structure of *technical components* of a typical platform.

> "Virtualization is no longer an umbrella for disconnected niche technologies, but is rather what's seen by many as a necessity for increasingly complex information systems"
> Chris Wolf, 2005

Platforms on the lowest layer build on top of some server hardware, which may be hidden by a *virtualization layer* ([Wolf_05]) in order to make best use of shared *physical resources*. On top of the hardware or the *virtualization layer* there is an *operating system*. On top of the operating system the platform integrates a number of *technical components*. Some components have the character of middleware, directly necessary to run applications, such as communication middleware, databases, application servers, storage, network services and all the necessary frameworks and libraries to make this functionality accessible from application programs. Other components provide systems management functionality, such as monitoring agents and user directories. We will talk more about these in Sect. 1.3.4 (platform operations). Finally, there is a group of technical components only necessary at development and deployment time. These components belong to the ecosystem surrounding a platform. Components in this category include development environments, test environments including test cases, development tools, code and documentation repositories and quality assurance tools. Figure 4.6 shows a typical *development tool chain* for a platform.

The rich environment provided by a platform requires a lot of know-how, if developers want to properly leverage it. Therefore, the platform must provide documentation, training, developer support and finally code quality assurance to make sure that applications fit the platform. Projects need to have access to platform resources through an environment ordering and provisioning process. Once an application is complete and has passed all the necessary quality gates, platform

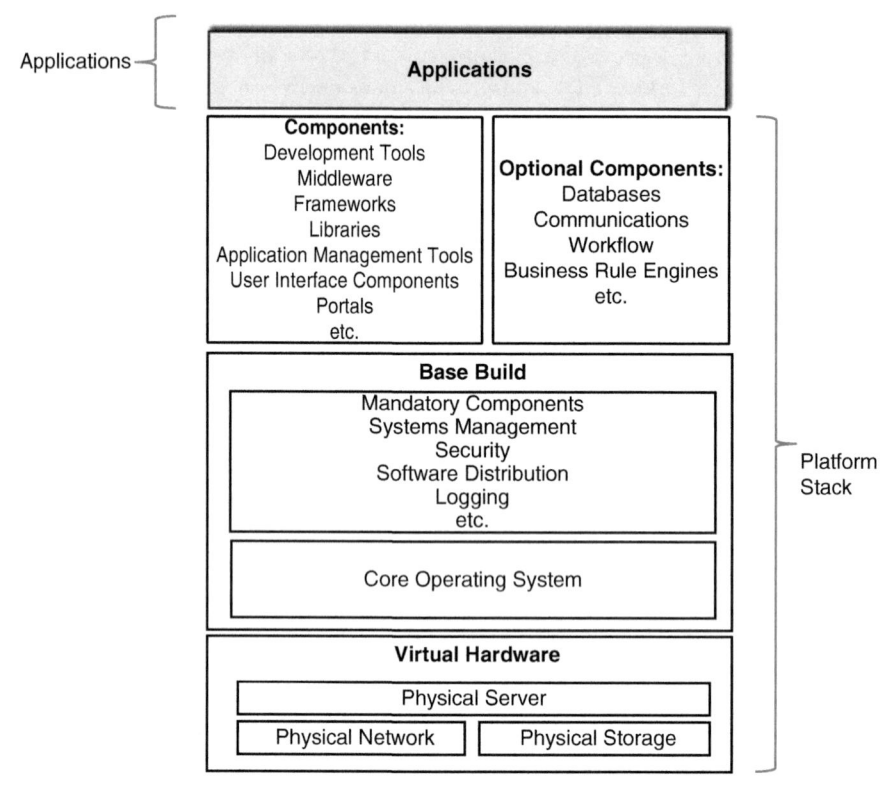

Fig. 4.5 Technical components of a platform

operations formally accepts the application for production and takes over responsibility. All of this is behind the *application development support* box in Fig. 4.4.

4.3.4 Platforms Operation Processes

Once applications are in production, there is one more interface between *application development support* and *platform operations*. When applications encounter problems in production, the platform defines a structured process to manage the incident and eventually solve the problem. This generally is based on a multi-stage escalation process, whereby operations directly solve the simpler problems, while application development takes care of the more complex ones. The *service support* box in Fig. 4.4 refers to this process.

Platform operation is more than reacting to problems, however. It comprises a number of processes to ensure operation of the platform and all the applications using it. A first process supports *change management* of *services*. Bringing new

4.3 Platforms

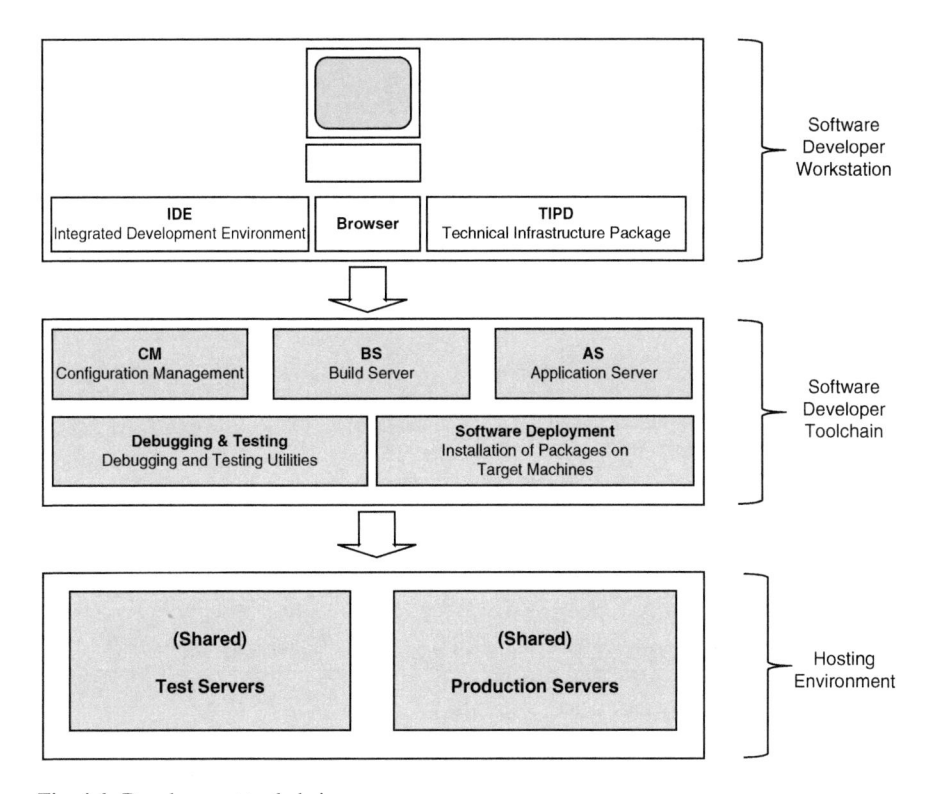

Fig. 4.6 Development tool chain

versions of an application into production is not the only change a platform has to handle. In a very large information system new infrastructure elements or users are added to or removed from the platform every day. Users get rights to access certain applications or data. Services need planning in order to have the necessary *capacity* ready to cope with the growth of demand within the promised service-levels. Often very large information systems support very critical business processes. Therefore, *service planning* is particularly important to ensure the agreed level of *business continuity* in emergency situations. Finally, platforms need to be operated on a day-to-day basis (*Service processing*). This includes monitoring, supervising batch jobs and ensuring backup of essential data. As platforms standardize the operating environment for a large number of applications, there is often a good business case to automate a lot of the day-to-day operations. As mentioned in Sect. 1.3.1 this reduces cost and increases quality by excluding human error.

All the processes described in this section are supported by an ecosystem of system management tools surrounding the platform. Figure 4.7 shows typical ecosystems elements of a large platform.

Platforms need basic functions such as naming services, user directory services, user access rights administration, e-mail systems, storage management systems,

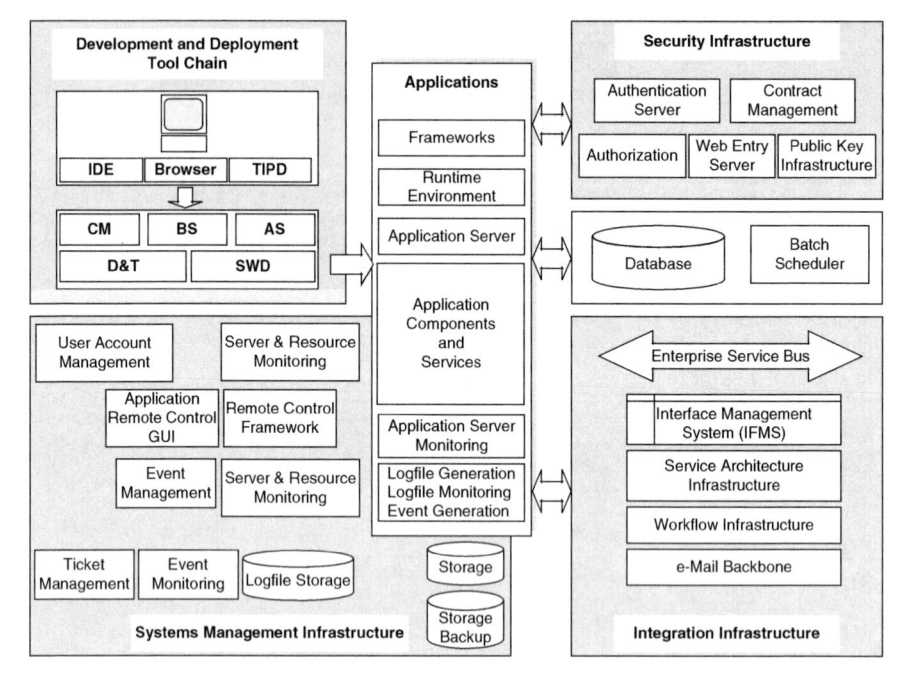

Fig. 4.7 Platform systems management ecosystem

inventory systems, monitoring systems and many more. The purpose of Fig. 4.7 is to illustrate that those platforms underneath very large information systems are based on complex ecosystems. Bundling and standardizing all ecosystem aspects simplifies application development and operation considerably.

The infrastructure provider must commit his level of service to the applications in a contract: The *operation level agreement* (OLA). Various levels of service exist and are specific to the organization providing and operating the infrastructure. OLAs must also be kept very stable, because each change of an OLA impacts a larger number of applications and their service level agreements with their users. An example of an OLA is given in Side-Story 4.2.

Side-Story 4.2: Credit Suisse Operation Level Agreement

The Java Application Platform (JAP) is introduced in Side-Story 4.4. JAP offers a number of different OLAs. As an example, the OLA "gold" is listed in the Table 4.3.

Table 4.3 OLA for JAP Application Platform

Java Application Platform: Operation Level Agreement "gold"	
IT Product Name	Application Platform JAP
OLA Level	Gold (A)
IT Product Manager	Hans Muster
Document Status	Version 1.2
Description	The Java Application Platform (JAP) is designed to be a cost effective, easy to maintain and well defined platform for Java based Intranet and Internet applications. JAP relies on widespread public standards (e.g J2EE) and supports the efficient operation of applications that are compliant with the CS architectural standards of Tower 1/2 and 4/5. The JAP OLA includes the infrastructure components of the layers 1 and 2. Each application running on the JAP infrastructure needs to be assigned to one of the JAP OLA levels. Since the JAP infrastructure is being shared by numerous applications, the application with the most demanding SLA category defines the overall standard of the respective environment. The 'Sharing Concept' defines the rules and guidelines, how applications are being grouped together on various JAP productive environments
Quality	*Service Times (on base of Swiss business hours)*
Default Product Quality	*Service Level Quality*
	• for production systems: 7 × 24 h
	• for Integration test (IT) systems: best effort
	• for Production Test and Acceptance (PTA) systems: best effort
	Maintenance Windows (Service down)
	• Planned (Production Systems) : Saturday: 23:00 to Sunday 06:00 h
	• Planned (IT and PTA Systems): by announcement
HW-Redundancy in % (if shared hardware used)	100%
	In the current JAP topology redundancy is accomplished by the concept of two parallel and load balanced server tracks and WLS clustering of certain application components (middle tear, business logic). In this case, a single track is still able to provide the complete service
Capacity Management	JAP provides system resources as required according to the users needs. To offer a lean and accurate service, capacity management needs on early and accurate performance data from the customer
Support times	1st Level: 7 × 24 h
	2nd Level: Mo–Fr. 07:00–17:00 h
	3rd Level: Mo–Fr. 07:00–17:00 h
Reaction Time IT Production	1st Level: 10 min
	2nd Level (after assignment of ticket):
	• Priority 1/2: 5 min
	• Priority 3: 15 min
	• Priority 4/5: 60 min
	• Priority 6: by agreement
Business Continuity Requirements	Class 11 (Credit Suisse internal Business Continuity Management class definitions)
	• Recovery time objective (RTO): 5 min–12 h
	• Recovery point objective (RPO): 0–12 h
Reporting (Service Quality and Usage)	Performance Measurement and Reporting for the various stakeholders
Costs	Cost Model "Leistungseinheiten" (Credit Suisse internal definition)
Contacts	IT Service Manager:...
	IT Product Manager(s):...
	IT Solution Manager:...
	Business CESA Controller:...
	IT Service Level Manager:...
	Data Owner:...
	Relevant third Parties:...
OLA Validity	1.1.2006–31.12.2010

4.3.5 Platform Management Processes

Platforms consist of an integrated set of technical components and processes. Platforms *evolve* over time with a different lifecycle than applications. Platform architects collect requirements from the application developers, platform operations and from the content of new standards for technical components as steered by the technology portfolio management (see Sect. 1.2). From the requirements they define a *platform strategy* that outlines new platform releases for the future. Most importantly, the platform strategy contains information about how the platform contract will change in the future (*product definition and management*). This platform lifecycle is then shared and agreed with all stakeholders.

The *platform lifecycle management* is of key importance for managed evolution. Platforms evolve according to their own *lifecycle* and are *engineered* by specialized infrastructure teams with planned deployment of new versions, each of them having a general availability and an end-of-life date as shown in the lower part of Fig. 4.8. Older versions remain in operation for some time, so that the applications do not immediately have to migrate to new versions of the platform. The upper part of Fig. 4.8 shows the synchronization between platform releases and application versions. The lower part shows the major releases of a platform, evolving from release 2.0 to release 6.0 over time. Within a major release, a number of minor releases, numbered 2.1, 4.2 etc. may go into operation. Minor releases need to be backward-compatible. Major releases are

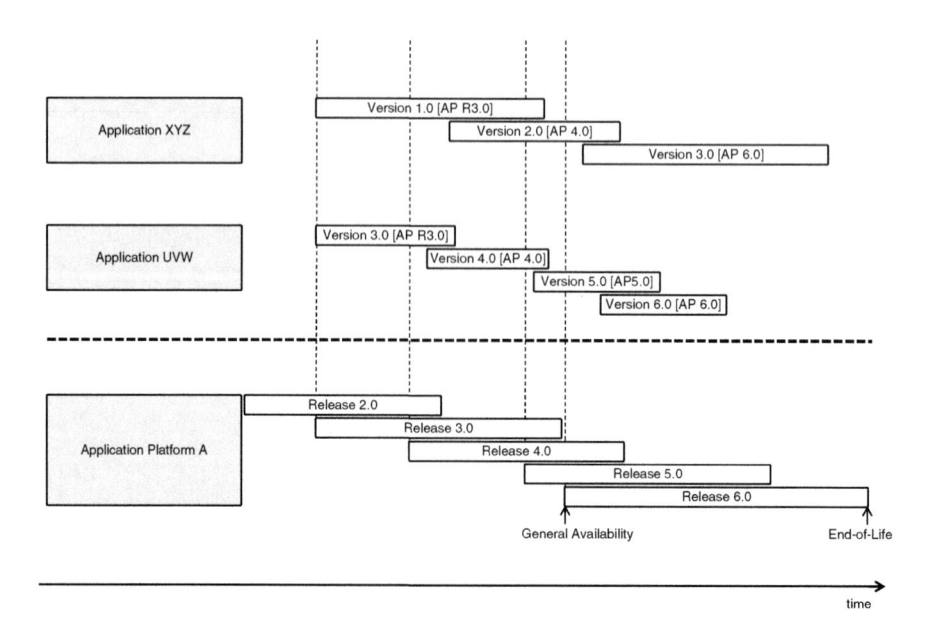

Fig. 4.8 Synchronized lifecycles of platforms and business applications

not backward-compatible and introduce significant new functionality, requiring adaptation of existing applications.

All applications using a platform release X must migrate to the latest platform release before the end-of-life date of release X is reached. Typically, applications upgrade to the latest platform release, each time they come out with a major release themselves. Experience of the authors shows that life spans of 3–4 years with new major platform releases every 12–18 months lead to the right balance of being able to include the latest technology into the platform, having enough lifespan of the underlying technical components to cover the platform lifespan, being able to join platform upgrades with functionality driven releases of applications and not having too many parallel platform versions in operation. Getting that balance right is key to successful managed evolution of infrastructure. An interesting question is how applications follow the platform lifecycle in practice. One example from Credit Suisse is given in Side-Story 4.3.

Two types of applications are shown in Fig. 4.8. Application XYZ is a stable application that has long upgrade times. It was created on the platform release 3.0, evolves over release 4.0 and skips the release 5.0, going directly to the release 6.0 after a major update. Application UVW has a shorter sequence of major updates and follows the platform release changes immediately.

This decoupling of the lifecycles of *business applications* and *infrastructure* (Fig. 4.8) is a powerful instrument of managed evolution: It allows two main elements of the very large information system – the infrastructure and the application landscape – to be moved forwards, independently of each other.

Platform product management also covers non-technical aspects. This includes pricing of services, reporting about platform health indicators and key performance indicators, facilitating communication with platform stakeholders.

Side-Story 4.3: JAVA Application Platform Adoption

The JAVA Application Platform (JAP) is introduced in Side-Story 4.4. JAP is evolved over time in *versions*. Each higher version of JAP offers substantial new functionality and extended services. Migrating from a JAP version to the next higher version requires some adaption work for most applications, such as implementing the new technical standards.

Because the adoption of a new JAP version is done gradually, the migration of the complete JAP application base requires some time. Several versions of JAP have therefore to be operated and supported in parallel. Figure 4.9 shows the adoption time for the JAP releases V3, V4 and V5 in the Zurich computing center. It can be seen that the migration of all applications requires nearly 2 years.

Fig. 4.9 JAP adoption history

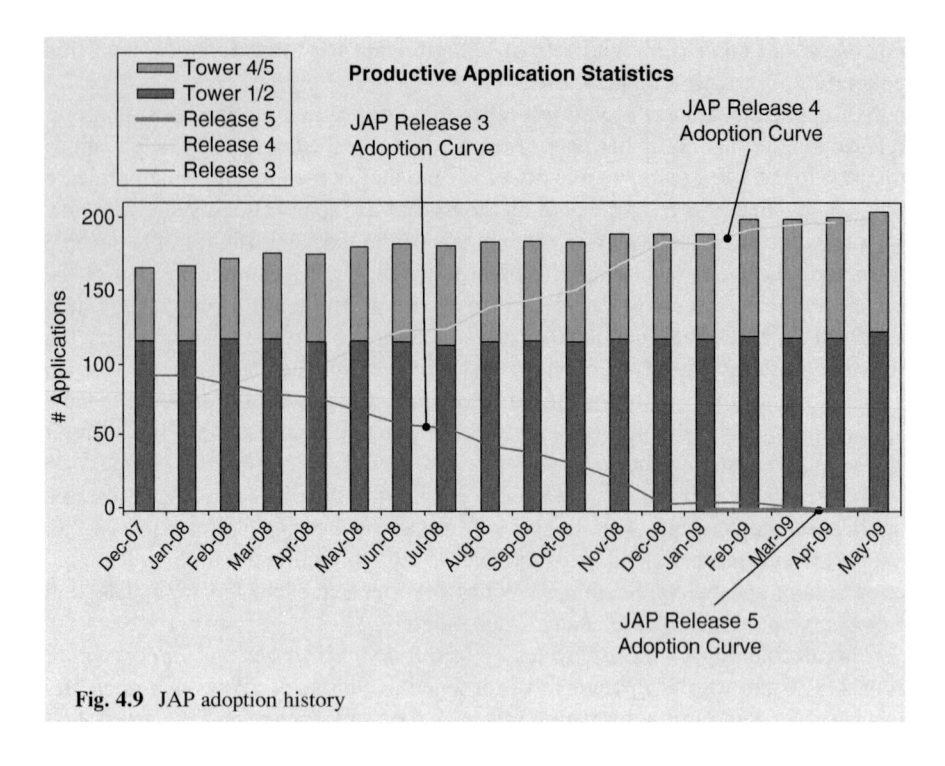

4.3.6 Application Platforms and Runtime Platforms

Two kinds of platforms are useful (Fig. 4.10). *Application platforms* implement the full extent of platforms as described in Sect. 1.3.2–1.3.4. The more basic platform is the *runtime platform*, which comprises a subset of services, providing no developer support, no application blueprints and little system management on the application level. In the component view (Fig. 4.5) the runtime platform contains the lower two layers.

As seen from Fig. 4.10, applications can either run on an application platform, a runtime platform, or assemble their own technology stack from the technical products in the technology portfolio using *special engineering*. Platform benefits are highest with the richest platform – the application platform. However, application platforms are more restrictive, because they prescribe much of the application design. Therefore, application platforms are suitable for in-house developed applications because these can adapt to the restrictions. Runtime platforms are intended to run commercial of-the-shelf software (COTS) and in-house developed applications that cannot be built within the restrictions of an application platform. In rare cases, an application may require a special infrastructure built from individual technical components. Valid reasons for special engineering include performance requirements, such as in a very low latency trading application, or COTS applications requiring specific hardware or software products. Special engineering solutions should still build from standard technology components. What they can't benefit from are all the processes and the integration

4.3 Platforms

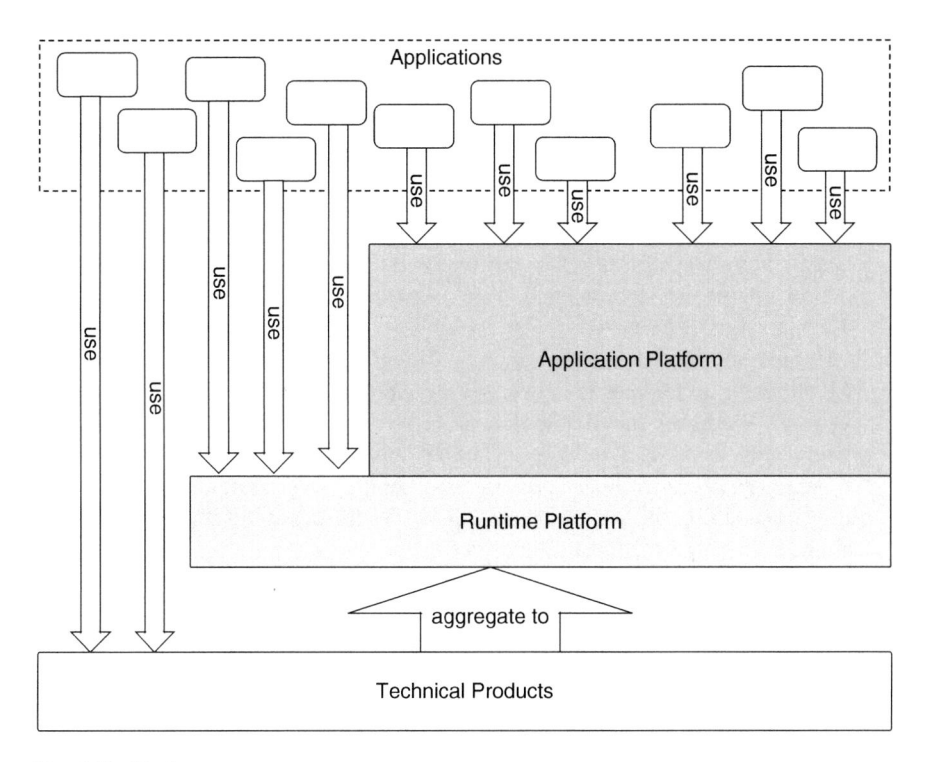

Fig. 4.10 Platforms

provided by platforms. Therefore, special engineering solutions will always require an initial engineering effort and a continuous effort with special purpose operations and lifecycle management. In the experience of the authors it is substantially more expensive to build and run special engineering infrastructure solutions. Experience with very large information systems shows that 80% of in-house built applications can use application platforms. Looking at all applications, in-house built and COTS, more than 90% should be based on a runtime platform. The remaining specially engineered technology stacks should drop below 10%.

Side-Story 4.4: Credit Suisse Java Application Platform (JAP)

Credit Suisse currently provides 4 application platforms to its application developers:

1. *Mainframe Transaction Processing*/Batch (MF TP/Batch) for transaction processing, based on IBM mainframes and Z/OS;

2. *Java Application Platform* (JAP) for client/server-style applications based on Java enterprise technology;
3. *Data Warehouse* application platform (DWH) for decision support applications;
4. *DotNet* application platform based on Microsoft Net-technology.

The *Java Application Platform* (JAP) is a standard Credit Suisse platform for client/server-style applications based on Internet technologies ([Cawsey_03]), both for Internet and Intranet and for high-performance transaction processing ([Richards_06], [Little_04]).

In this side-story we focus on the "Client/Server/Internet" architecture. JAP defines 5 archetypes for client/server applications, the so-called towers. Towers 1–4 address Intranet applications. Tower 5 is designed for the additional needs of *Internet facing applications* and is shown in Figure 4.11. The Tower 5 *reference architecture* separates applications into entry, presentation, application, service and data layers. It further defines the allowed communication protocols and security boundaries between these layers.

Whereas Figure 4.5 above shows the *technology components* used in the assembly of a platform, Figure 4.11 below shows the subset of technology components embedded in the data flow for an Internet application implemented on top of JAP. One of the main design considerations in Fig. 4.11 was the protection of information and applications against unauthorized access from

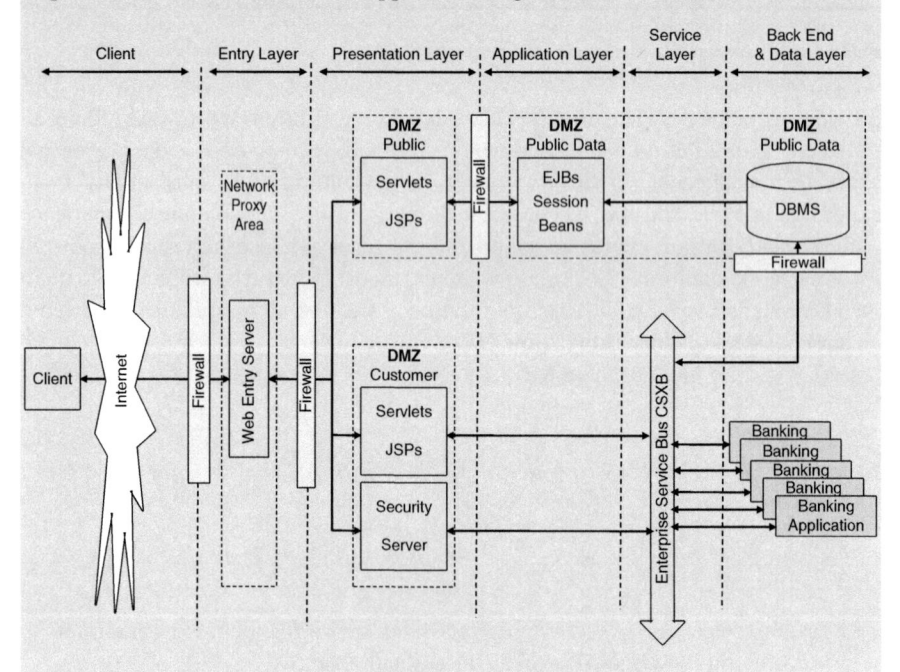

Fig. 4.11 Java platform reference architecture for Internet applications

the Internet. This is achieved not only by layers of firewalls, but also by a proxy and by specialized demilitarized zones (DMZ).

The architecture and technology of JAP is based on the Java Enterprise Technology, but restricts it to the key technologies. JAP defines a standardized software stack on top of the runtime platform CSS (Credit Suisse Solaris Platform) and bundles necessary components into so-called "Technical Infrastructure Packages" (TIP). For developers, the Technical Infrastructure Package for Development (TIPD) provides all the tools to develop, run and debug JAP applications on the developers' desktop machines (see Fig. 4.6). The TIP also contains the necessary software to access the different backend systems via the integration infrastructure. The infrastructure, security and system management is transparent to the applications through frameworks and integration into the JEE environment.

Applications on JAP typically run on shared hardware maintained and operated by the platform, but dedicated hardware is also obtainable. The available hardware covers the different Tower architectures and their security constraints. A demilitarized zone (DMZ) and a Web Entry Server are provided for Tower 5 in order to meet Internet security requirements. The servers can be scaled horizontally via network load balancer mechanisms. An application is typically deployed to two tracks residing in different Credit Suisse data centers, with mirrored databases. This covers fail-over requirements as well as business continuity management requirements.

In addition to the technical stack, JAP standardizes processes to efficiently support and automate key activities in operations and solution delivery. As an example, due to the standardization of how to configure, build, deploy and debug applications, JAP supplies developers with a fully integrated toolchain automating many day-to-day activities of developers. Similarly, the standardized runtime stack enables JAP to automate operational processes such as monitoring or performance management. Moreover, JAP facilitates all applications with a security concept and an operational manual, thus significantly reducing hand-over efforts to operations.

Most importantly, JAP provides *services* to its customer. Platform management (see Sect. 1.3.5) maintains the lifecycle for the entire platform ensuring stable environments over well-defined time frames. It further evolves the platform according to requirements of technology management, applications, security and operations. Standardization of runtime stack and lifecycle eliminates the usual conflicts with shared hosting and accelerates acceptance tests for applications. Because three major platform releases are always in operation, applications are not forced to migrate immediately to a new release. Applications benefit from reduced maintenance efforts, especially for third level support. Finally, JAP consultants guide projects through the entire development cycle shielding project managers from most infrastructure issues. JAP consultants significantly accelerate issue tracking and provisioning tasks.

The key non-functional parameters of a JAP installation, such as availability, support times, maintenance windows and downtimes are guaranteed to the application via an *operation level agreement* (OLA). Several operation level agreements exist, which provide different levels of service – and have different price tags for the application. An example of a JAP OLA is given in Side-Story 4.2.

4.4 Operations

A common requirement for very large information systems is to provide highly dependable services operated at competitive cost. This is a requirement for any very large information system, independently of the evolution strategy.

The infrastructure of the system provides basic mechanisms to support dependable operations. Technology portfolio management standardizes the infrastructure components simplifying operations. The consequent use of platforms (see Sect. 1.3) and the corresponding standardized processes lead to a further reduction of heterogeneity. This leads to better process automation and better quality implementation, further simplifying operations. Platforms provide pre-engineered, reliable solutions for redundancy, failover, load balancing, business continuity management, backup and more, leading to inherently more stable systems.

However, a reliable infrastructure alone is not sufficient for dependable operations: Failures and malfunctions may also occur on the application layer. Such failures have the same effect as technical failures: Either parts of the system become unavailable to their users or they produce wrong results.

The set of functionality ensuring smooth operation on all layers is called *systems management*. Systems management supports operations and change management by providing processes and tools for system configuration and installation. A dedicated set of specialized systems management applications runs in parallel to

> "IT components produced by high-tech companies over the past decades are so complex that IT professionals are challenged to effectively operate a stable infrastructure"
> IBM, 2006

the business applications and monitors any anomaly in the system. Systems management functionality ensures efficient use of infrastructure resources, such as network, processing power or storage capacity. Systems management processes identify causes of failures and react to them. Skilled IT professionals react to alerts delivered by systems management and take corrective actions. Contemporary systems management tools support the system managers in diagnosis and suggest corrective actions ([Schiesser_01]). The past progress in systems management tools and processes has shown a continuous trend to higher dependability and lower operations cost of very large information systems.

4.4.1 Operational Challenge of Managed Evolution

Interestingly, managed evolution introduces new challenges to operations, which cause traditional systems management some difficulties. The first challenge results from *componentization*. As shown in the previous sections (e.g. 2.3, 3.3, 3.5.1, 4.31), the information system is constructed from components which are as loosely coupled as possible and isolated from each other by services based on contracts. This approach has many advantages, such as reuse, reduction of complexity, life-cycle separation and decoupling – resulting in high agility and manageability of the system (see Sect. 1.5). However, it does lead to operational challenges: Naive componentization leads to single points of failure, performance bottlenecks and deadlocks and transactional integrity problems. A typical example is a component providing a master data service to a large number of consumers. If this component doesn't work, many business processes are stopped. Therefore, componentization needs to be architected with operations in mind right from the beginning. Systems management should evolve from a separate discipline with independent solutions into a property of all components, like security.

As a consequence of not being able to replace the system in one go, another undesired side-effect of managed evolution is a certain level of *heterogeneity*. The system is inevitably composed of a considerable number of technologies, with different lifecycles, (Fig. 4.2). This is true both for infrastructure components as well as for application development technologies, such as programming languages or middleware. This complicates system management, because the relevant practices vary widely for different technologies.

> "Systems management must become less of a separate discipline, but more a property of the system, like security"

4.4.2 Componentization for Operations

The individual application components and their interactions must be designed with *dependable operations* in mind. In very large information systems it can no longer be assumed that all components, communications channels and resources are available at all times. Because of the large number of parts and connections, failures become the norm, not the exception. A naïve approach, where each component counts on the availability of all components it depends on for proper operation, is no longer feasible, because the resulting availability, as experienced by the users, is not satisfactory in a very large system. The fundamental requirement here is that the system as a whole has better availability characteristics than its individual parts and connections ([Birman_05], [Berg_05]). A good example for this is the Internet, which is nearly 100% available, despite its unreliable components.

So far, this book has demonstrated how to cope with the *functional*, *semantic*, *temporal* and *technical* dependencies among components in a very large information system (as defined in Sect. 1.2). What remains are the *operational dependencies* (see also Sect. 1.2). We must identify and manage these in order to build highly dependable and cost-effective systems. Operational dependencies stem from data and control flows among components at runtime and by the dependency of applications on infrastructure, such as networks or computing platforms.

In the experience of the authors, a componentized very large information system resulting from managed evolution *can* be operated more dependably and at less cost if it is architected accordingly. Unfortunately, this area of knowledge is only just emerging and needs a lot of future work – both theoretical and practical. Some proven *architecture principles* supporting dependable operations of heterogeneous, highly componentized systems are:

- Build and deploy *multi-instance components* with replicated data underneath to cope with instance failures. Assure that the replicated data is properly managed and its quality is assured by consistency check mechanisms.
- Use *asynchronous coupling* to the maximum extent possible based on a dependable message queuing infrastructure in order to reduce immediate, temporal dependencies. Monitor and manage the queues to be able to react in time to malfunctions.
- Always use *defensive interface design* to avoid acceptance of illogical or inconsistent input data. This requires extensive plausibility checks at the interface by the component, not only on the type, syntactic and range level, but also on the applications and semantic level.
- Build components in such a way that they can cope with failures of partner components or connections, or non-availability of updates. This means built-in intelligent degraded modes of operation and consistency control loops for persistent data.
- Build components in such a way that they detect and mitigate operational problems by themselves. Escalate to the assigned system management component only in case of locally unmanageable situations.
- Build components in such a way that the components monitor their own service levels on all interfaces they provide and detect violations. Implement analysis functionality to diagnose service level agreement violations at the interface in the component. Escalate with the diagnosed reason of service level agreement violations to the higher hierarchical component or to systems management.
- Build components in such a way that they support only the interface versions approved for operation (see Sect. 3.5.4). This includes recognizing interface version changes and only accepting backwards-compatible versions, otherwise raising an alert.

4.4 Operations

- Build components in such a way that they detect wrong configurations of their runtime environments, such as missing technical components or inconsistent setups.
- Build components in such a way that they continuously optimize the setting of the internal parameters, such as database self-optimization.
- Use automatic discovery of components in the system to build the configuration management database dynamically.

The extensive use of componentization requires monitoring of *service level agreements* (SLA) committed to by the components and of *operational level agreements* (OLA) guaranteed by infrastructure. Appropriate systems management must detect and correct any violation of the service level or operational level agreement. SLA supervision is more straightforward for synchronous coupling, but somewhat more difficult for asynchronous coupling. In synchronous coupling both components are tightly coupled and therefore the consumer component immediately detects *SLA violations* by the provider component. In asynchronous coupling the sender component can only detect that the receiver component has not processed the messages when the queue is full. This requires additional measures, such as application level control loops and flow control.

SLAs can only be as good as the underlying integration infrastructure. Special attention must therefore be given to the reliability and availability of the enterprise service bus (see Sect. 3.7). The integration infrastructure therefore has to fulfill high standards with respect to dependability and systems management.

Two emerging fields promise support for the dependable operations of very large, componentized information systems: Autonomic computing (see Sect. 1.4.3) and new approaches to configuration management databases (see Sect. 1.4.4).

4.4.3 Autonomic Computing

In the opinion of the authors, there are three key concepts to operate very large, componentized information systems. First, we need a *dynamic infrastructure* providing a number of extended services, such as automatic failover, business continuity support and capacity management on demand. The components can then rely on a dependable set of high-availability infrastructure services. Second, the *individual components* need to be built for autonomous operation. Functions helping towards this objective include self-management to the maximum extent possible, degraded modes of operation in the case of failures with partner components or connections and intelligent handling of failures in the business logic or data. Third, the *connections* between the loosely coupled components must be engineered in order to tolerate unavailabilities, such as providing alternate communication paths, idempotent operation (Sect. 3.4.1) and rich diagnostics for the component to react accordingly.

The emerging discipline of *autonomic computing* ([Kephart_03], [IBM_06], [Hariri_06]) proposes some answers by defining *autonomic components* and an *autonomic system architecture*. Autonomic computing is an initiative started by IBM in 2001 ([IBM_04]). The objective of autonomic computing is to develop computer systems that manage distributed computing resources, self-adapting to unpredictable changes and failures whilst hiding their intrinsic complexity. An autonomic system makes decisions on its own, using high level policies: It constantly checks and optimizes its status and automatically adapts itself to changing conditions. The implementation of fully autonomic systems is far in the future. However, a number of key concepts can already be used in today's very large information systems. In fact, standards and vendor products supporting parts of autonomic computing are already available.

Although the authors do not (yet) propose to implement very large information systems according to the full autonomic system architecture, a short overview is given here (more information can be found in [Kephart_03], [IBM_06], [Hariri_06]), as the concepts really go in the right direction.

The essence of autonomic computing systems is *self-management*. Self-management frees system managers from the details of system operation and is intended to provide 7×24 availability of the very large information system at optimized peak performance. The concept of autonomic computing (see e.g. [Kephart_03]) proposes four aspects:

- *Self-configuration*: The autonomic system configures itself after any change or as a consequence of load changes automatically in accordance with pre-defined high-level policies. When a new autonomic component (see below) is introduced it will integrate itself seamlessly and the rest of the system adapts to its presence and interaction.
- *Self-optimization*: Autonomic systems continuously explore ways to improve their operation and efficiency. This includes tuning the large sets of parameters available from database systems, operating systems, middleware, etc.
- *Self-healing*: Detect, diagnose, localize and repair problems resulting from bugs in software and hardware using modern methods, such as regression testing or analyzing information from log files. Continuously analyze resource consumption, such as memory and databases in relationship to the load. Request more resources from the dynamic infrastructure and escalate if abnormal resource consumption patterns are detected.
- *Self-protection*: Maintain defenses against malicious attacks. Autonomic computing systems offer new possibilities of attack. Defending against such attacks needs a new sub-branch of security engineering.

These aspects are often referred to as self-* properties of an autonomic computing system. Virtually every aspect of autonomic computing is serious engineering, in some cases even an advanced research challenge. At the heart of the autonomic computing concept is the *autonomic component* (Fig. 4.12). An autonomic component consists of the *managed resource*, which in our case consists of business logic

4.4 Operations

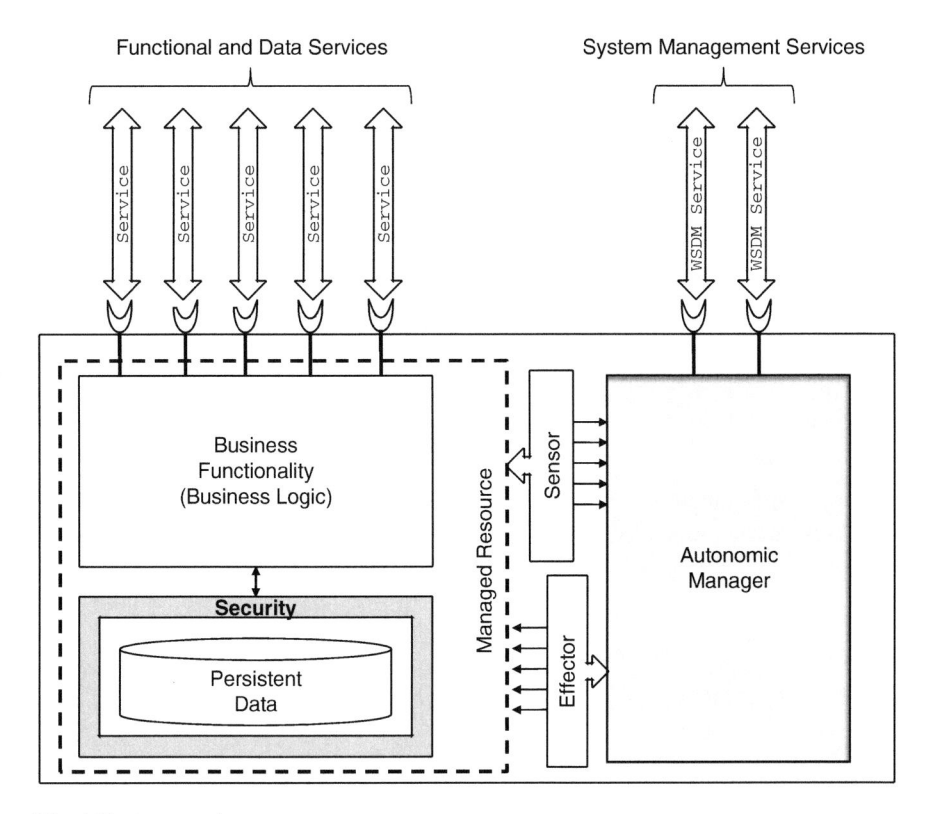

Fig. 4.12 Autonomic component

and persistent data. A managed resource, however, can be any element of the very large information system, such as a computing resource, a storage device or a network element. The *autonomic manager* building block within the component is the centerpiece of the autonomic architecture. It is responsible for automating the systems management functions. The autonomic manager is equipped with *sensors* and *effectors*. Via the sensors the autonomic manager receives information about the state of the managed resource and via the effectors the autonomic manager influences the managed resource. The autonomic manager communicates with other autonomic managers and with the system management environment via services, e.g. based on WSDM (= Web Services Distributed Management standard (see http://www.oasis-open. org) or other emerging autonomic computing standards).

> "The scale, complexity, and business demands require that the management systems be implemented in an automated manner with minimal or close to no human intervention. This requires the development and use of autonomic capabilities"
> Manish Parashar, 2007

The five primary functions of the *autonomic manager* are:

- *Monitoring*: Collect, filter and aggregate information from the managed resource.
- *Analyzing*: Extract events, patterns and correlations from the information received from the monitoring. Formulate request for action, such as provisioning more computing or network resources in case of increased load.
- *Plan*: Select a procedure to change attributes or elements of the managed resources.
- *Execute*: Schedule and execute the necessary changes to the managed resource. This also includes traceability; i.e. the possibility to follow the sequence of changes and to be able to undo them in case of problems.
- *Communicate*: Request and deliver system management information via system management services with other autonomic components or with system management facilities.

Autonomic computing is a promising approach for a dependable architecture of very large information systems. However, the authors so far have little practical experience in the implementation of autonomic computing concepts.

4.4.4 Configuration Management Database

A big challenge in managing a very large information system is to understand the current and the planned configuration of the system. The instrument to solve this is the *configuration management database* (CMDB). The CMDB should at all times reflect the true inventory and attributes of all active parts and connections in the system. Traditionally, this CMDB is maintained mostly manually through the change and configuration management process.

> "Implementing a CMDB is a hugely challenging project - and research shows the majority fail due to data quality issues"
> http://www.tideway.com, 2009

A configuration management database has two main purposes: First, mapping the "reality", that is the timely and reliable maintenance of the inventory of all components and dependencies that are active in the operational system. Second, use as a planning tool to support, document, and plan future system configurations.

In the context of managed evolution, the traditional approach shows some limitations. With the very large number of parts and connections, fragmented organizations and the high rate of change, a manually maintained CMDB lags behind actuality. This can be addressed by automatically detecting and identifying parts, connections and attributes in the real system. There are tools (see e.g. http://www.tideway.com) to discover *configuration items* (CI) across disparate technology layers, reaching from network switches to business applications. The same

4.4 Operations

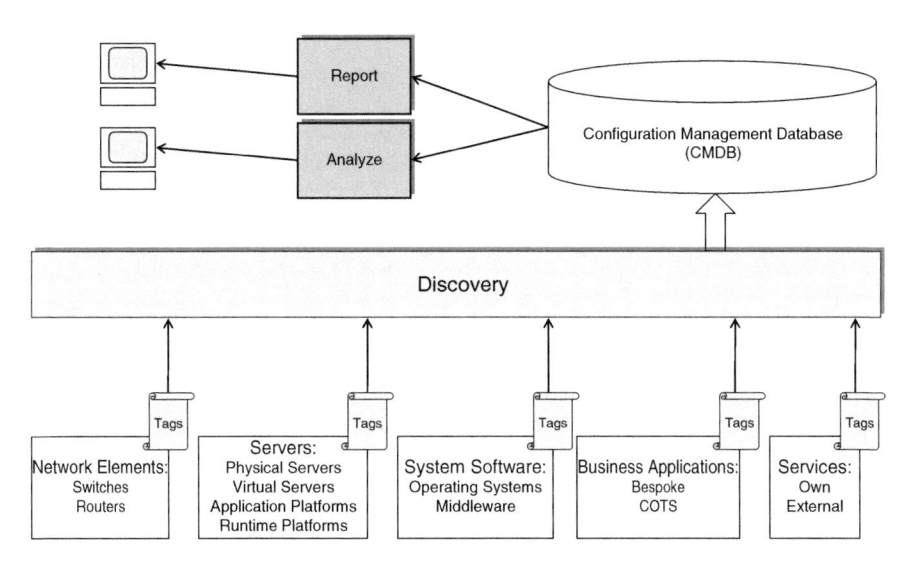

Fig. 4.13 Automatic discovery of components

tools also detect dependencies among the configuration items. This provides a consistent and up to date view of the system (Fig. 4.13).

Each configuration item is tagged: The tag contains information about the configuration item, such as the type, properties, versions, attributes and configuration. The tag contains sufficient data to automatically identify the component and provide the system-management relevant attributes, based on a system-wide tagging standard. The tag can be read by the CMDB detection/identification function and the information obtained is stored in the CMBD.

One part of the CMDB maintenance remains manual, however: The entry and use of *planned* items which are not yet operational. These are required to map and document planned, future configurations of the system. This approach resolves the issue of the CMDB lagging behind reality by directly representing reality in the CMDB.

Often current CMDB solutions are restricted to the technical layer. This is not sufficient for heavily componentized application architectures which are necessary for managed evolution. The CMDB needs to extend its reach to application level components and services. In the experience of the authors this is a weakness of the current approaches.

Part II
Organization and Management Processes for the Execution of Managed Evolution

Chapters 1–4 introduced challenges concerning properties, structure, and architecture of very large information systems. The focus was on understanding very large information systems and introducing the necessary tools and processes to shape such systems in the long run.

The second part of the book – starting with the chapter "Business-IT Alignment" – focuses on the organization owning the system. It presents the necessary cultural prerequisites, organizational concepts, governance models, and controlling mechanisms for the successful execution of managed evolution.

Chapter 5
Business-IT Alignment

Summary Managed evolution is based on an organizationally holistic approach. The relationship between business and IT plays a key role for the holistic view. A classical, that is a hierarchical and departmental, setup with its corresponding governance model and budget authority is not well suited to managed evolution. A new governance model, the domain-based model, is introduced and is shown to work best for managed evolution. The roles and processes for business-IT alignment, on the three layers of strategic alignment, project portfolio alignment and project alignment, are described in this chapter.

5.1 Managed Evolution and Business-IT Alignment

Sound *business-IT alignment* is a key prerequisite for business processes to be supported effectively by information technology, especially in large organizations. The main purpose of this alignment is to ensure that business requirements towards IT are defined by the business in a systematic and efficient way; that IT departments understand and accept these requirements; and that they provide adequate IT solutions fulfilling the requirements. This requires adequate processes, roles and organizational structures (see, e.g., [Wegener_07]). This chapter develops the elements and properties of business-IT alignment specific to very large information systems and managed evolution.

Each newly developed application will generally incur significantly more than its development cost for *maintenance* and *operation* throughout its entire life cycle. Moreover, due to increasing system complexity, the effort for operating and maintaining a growing application landscape may grow even faster than linear with the number of applications. Under the opportunistic approach (see Sect. 1.4.1) this inevitably leads to an ever increasing *"run the business"* spend, comprising maintenance and operation for both infrastructure and applications. The remaining *"change the business"* budget available to new projects, both initiated by business or IT, decreases. As a consequence, an ever larger portion of the total budget is eaten up he business". If the "change the business" budget should be maintained :vel in this situation, the total IT budget has to be increased every year. ds to tensions between business and IT because the business has to pay ame services every year. Therefore, the "run the business" spend needs to be limited, allowing for a sustainable "change the business" budget in the long run. Managed evolution is the way to achieve this: It balances the investment between business and IT initiatives as described in Sect. 1.5 and in Fig. 1.7. IT initiatives, especially *architecture programs*, improve the architectural quality of the system and thus contribute to complexity reduction. Complexity is reduced by architectural measures described in the previous chapters, such as partitioning the very large information system into domains eliminating redundancy, removing unused functionality and data, enforcing reuse, by consequently implementing service architecture and by architecting applications with maintainability and operability in mind. The result is the desired reduction of maintenance and operation cost.

> "As both business and software systems become more complex, the relationships between them become harder to keep in alignment"
> Roger Sessions, 2008

Managed evolution requires a method of business-IT alignment that ensures balanced investments in new business functionality and IT efficiency at the same time. Furthermore, good business-IT alignment means system-wide prioritization of requirements according to business and IT strategy, grouping requirements into projects with clear, non-overlapping scopes, twisting each project to make it contribute towards the target architecture (as shown in Fig. 1.7) and finally ensuring project delivery according to the plan. These objectives require close cooperation between business and IT. There is a strong relationship between business-IT alignment and managed evolution. In other words: Business-IT alignment is about finding and executing a strategically aligned portfolio of projects. This includes implementing business requirements according to strategic priorities, implementing the requirements only once where they architecturally belong and forcing each project to the maximum extent possible to contribute to a more efficient system. Furthermore, good governance ensures that the appropriate investments in IT efficiency take place in order to keep the whole system in the managed evolution channel, as explained in Sect. 1.5.

Due to the collapse of the Internet bubble at the beginning of this century, most IT budgets had to be cut, some of them dramatically. The same happened more recently in the financial markets crisis starting in 2008. High flexibility in reacting to *budget cuts* or *budget increases* is required. The continuous sequence of smaller efficiency investments characteristic to managed evolution makes it easier to manage these forced ups and downs in the IT budget. With managed evolution, it is possible to temporarily reduce the investments into the IT efficiency along with the other investments in a controlled way. In a greenfield approach (see Sect. 1.4.3), the budget strategy is much less flexible. Reducing the greenfield budget substantially jeopardizes the whole approach.

5.1 Managed Evolution and Business-IT Alignment

One key challenge of managed evolution is to define the appropriate *scope* for business-IT alignment in very large information systems. Determining the scope of the system means to decide which processes, applications and infrastructure components are within the system boundary. The scope of business-IT alignment must be chosen according to architectural criteria, mostly according to the level of coupling, as discussed in Sect. 1.3. Tightly coupled components have to be treated as part of the same system. This leads to well defined system boundaries, which at the same time define the scope of business-IT alignment. This seems to be obvious and not worth mentioning. But, looking at large organizations, this is often a real inhibitor to managed evolution. While it is essential to submit a single system to consistent governance, it is quite possible and practical to manage multiple systems under the same governance. This often makes a lot of sense if it is planned to merge different information systems over time and starts by reusing components and by joining business processes across systems.

A further challenge is to systematically capture and prioritize requirements across all stakeholders of the system. For managed evolution in particular, this means merging business and IT requirements. Over time, requirements mature from initial ideas to projects in various states of execution. The collection of all ideas and projects within the scope of the system forms the *project portfolio*. In very large information systems it is necessary to subdivide the project portfolio into *baskets*. Baskets are used to structure large project portfolios and consist of subsets of the project portfolio characterized by common properties. As we will see later in this chapter, the basket structure strongly impacts business-IT alignment because it will be used to federate *governance* and *budget authority* for the "change the business" spend.

Very large information systems have many stakeholders, often distributed over the world. Not only the large number of stakeholders is a challenge, but also the continuous change in both business and IT organizations. Frequent organizational and management changes affect important roles in business-IT alignment. In order to manage the number and diversity of stakeholders it is necessary to manage IT using a formal *governance model*. First and foremost, the governance model has to ensure productive collaboration of the stakeholders beyond personal relationships.

> First and foremost, the governance model has to ensure productive collaboration of the stakeholders beyond personal relationships

It must be resistant to the fact that stakeholders and organizational structures change continuously. The governance model defines processes and formal requirements management, because issues often cannot be discussed and solved informally. More specifically, it defines the *strategic business-IT alignment process*, the *project portfolio management process* and the *project management process* for individual projects. It clarifies roles and responsibilities of the stakeholders involved. The model sets clear rules for decision making. A good governance model is specifically designed to meet the strategic objectives of the organization (see e.g. [Weill_04] and Chap. 3 "SOA Governance" in [Bieberstein_08]). It clearly defines the scope and the federated structure of governance. In summary, business-IT governance has to be formal and systematic, but also very flexible in so as to absorb continuous changes on the business and IT sides. Managed evolution requires a very strong, multidimensional and sophisticated business-IT alignment, addressing culture, attitude, processes, roles and responsibilities.

In addition to business and IT in general, *architecture* is the second force in the business-IT alignment relationship. It has an overarching role, in spite of being managed by the IT department. In all the "change the business" processes, architecture management aims at focusing all investments towards the target architecture, both proactively on the level of strategic investment planning and reactively by influencing all projects, as described in Sect. 1.5. *Architecture management* plays an important role on each layer of business-IT alignment. Architecture management plays the role of custodian of the managed evolution and ensures architectural integrity in the evolution of the information system.

Strong architecture management is necessary, but not sufficient, for success in business-IT alignment. Adequately organizing IT is another key success factor. In this context, two aspects are relevant: First, the position of the IT organization within the enterprise and second, the internal organization of IT itself. For business-IT alignment, mainly the degree of "centralization" or "federation" across the enterprise matters. Large organizations with a federated IT organization may, for example, have a number of chief information officers (CIOs) individually reporting to the heads of the business units, without a CIO at the top of the organization. It is very hard to execute a managed evolution strategy across multiple units sharing the same information system in such a setup. The degree of autonomy of the different units, the lack of central architecture management and the missing system-wide project portfolio governance renders proper strategy execution impossible. The important observation here is that the scope of the governance model sets the boundaries for consistent managed evolution. In other words: Successful strategy execution depends on limiting the autonomy of IT functions in the units in the area of architecture management and project portfolio governance. Chap. 6 will discuss various aspects of how to organize the IT function in more detail.

> "Architecture management plays the role of *custodian* of the managed evolution and ensures architectural integrity in the evolution of the information system"

One key challenge is to bridge the gap between the high *rate of change* in the business organization and the inherently slow rate of structural changeability in a very large information system. One way to deal with it is to continuously adapt the governance model to the fast changes in the business organization. This approach jeopardizes the long-term continuity in the governance model necessary for managed evolution. The other possibility is to structure the business-IT alignment according to the *functional structure* of the information system and in this way aligns the governance model to the achievable rate of change in the information system. An adequate governance model manages these challenges. In the next chapter we will discuss the suitability of traditional *hierarchical IT governance* with respect to managed evolution.

5.2 Limitations of Hierarchical IT Governance

Common practice in many companies means individual IT strategy development by each business unit with little coordination at the corporate level. Strategic responsibility is decentralized. In this model, business unit heads decide on their IT budgets, within the constraints of the overall business unit budget. The budgets, on the one hand, cover business requirements, such as new products, new sales channels and optimized processes. On the other hand, it takes the cost of operation and the investments into infrastructure into account. Typically, the business head asks the IT department for an estimate of the total IT cost covering both. This estimate will then be challenged by the business and discussed until mutual agreement is reached.

Often infrastructure and operations are provided by a firm-wide unit. Cost of operation and the investments into infrastructure are decided by this unit and allocated to the business units according to some key. The business units manage this part of IT as a third party cost, which cannot be influenced throughout the year. The business units individually decide on the budget allocated to business projects. The company's IT strategy consists of different business unit strategies.

In this hierarchical governance model, business is strictly in the *sponsor* role and IT in the *provider* role. With this model it is very hard to sponsor the necessary IT life cycle investments or an architecture program. Many companies managed like this find it extremely difficult to make the necessary long-term investments for enterprise-wide service architecture. No business unit has a broad enough brief to finance such an investment. The infrastructure unit usually concentrates on the lower architecture layers in Fig. 2.1.

In the hierarchical governance model (Fig. 5.1) decision bodies basically correspond to the elements in the organizational hierarchy: Often the whole or a subset of the business unit management committee acts as a decision body on IT in general. There is very little coordination between the different IT investments of the business units. The role of the IT departments is to execute the divisional project portfolios under resource constraints. The whole IT project portfolio of the company consists of the different project portfolios of the business units. With multiple business units sharing the same system this model makes it very hard to avoid functional overlaps, redundancy and unnecessary complexity. Business and IT are strongly aligned *operationally* in this model.

The hierarchical governance model is not well suited for managed evolution, because the scope of investment planning does not cover the complete system and

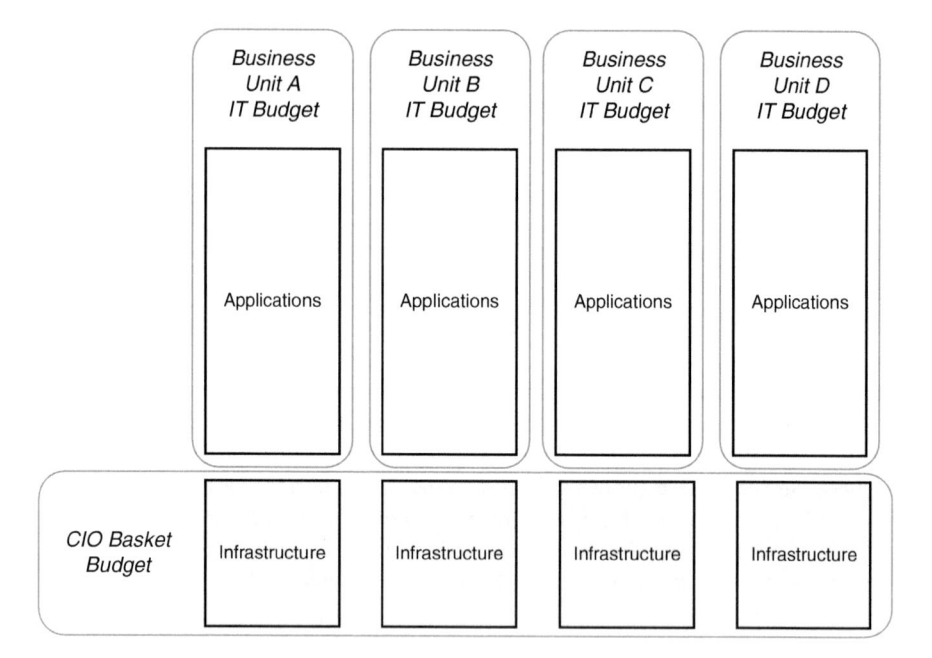

Fig. 5.1 Hierarchical governance model

the role of IT is not strong enough. In such a model it is likely that not enough investments in IT are made.

5.3 Matching Roles: Balance of Power

As mentioned above, one key aspect of successful IT governance in the context of managed evolution is a good *balance of power* between business and IT. This section describes a hierarchy of matching roles and joint decision making bodies, taking that delicate power balance into account.

The governance model enables business-IT alignment on three different layers: *Strategic business-IT alignment* ensures appropriate investment priorities on the corporate level with a long-term horizon; *project portfolio management* maps business requirements into projects and ensures proper execution and operational prioritization of thematically related projects; and *project management* turns requirements into adequate solutions within a single project, taking the environment into account. The governance model defines decision processes and bodies on all three layers. In this section the main focus will be on the appropriate decision making structures for managed evolution. The corresponding three processes will be described later in this chapter.

The first key aspect is that both business and IT are represented in decision making in a well-balanced way. This reflects the key idea of managed evolution – to

5.3 Matching Roles: Balance of Power

balance both investments into business value as well as into IT agility (Sect. 1.5). In practice, this means matching roles for business and IT participants on all layers and balanced representation of IT and business in all decision bodies. The idea behind this *dual representation* is to keep the power between business and IT well-balanced. The IT side represents the interests of an efficient and agile information system, while the business lobbies for additional functionality creating business value. Clearly, balancing the respective investments require balanced power in the decision process.

Second, managed evolution focuses strongly on developing and implementing a holistic IT strategy. This requires much deeper cooperation and more formal coordination on the strategic business-IT alignment layer. The old role model of business as a sponsor defining and prioritizing requirements and IT as a provider is no longer viable in this context. Both sides are jointly responsible for the sustainable development of the whole information system. The idea that business cares for business and IT cares for IT does not help to successfully manage very large information systems. Collaboration in joint committees fosters the understanding of IT managers for business requirements and of business managers for IT needs. Managing broad project portfolios jointly broadens the perspective of the individuals involved in governance, supporting a "think big, act local" culture. While dual, symmetric representation is necessary on the strategic level, it is still possible to have the traditional sponsor-provider relationship on the level of individual projects.

Figure 5.2 below lists the decision-making bodies on the different layers, including the respective business and IT representation.

The *executive board* is the ultimate authority in strategic business-IT alignment. It is responsible for all strategic decisions, like defining the overall IT budget, the change-the-business to run-the-business split and the number and size of the change-the-business baskets.

The *IT steering committee* decides on strategic project portfolio management issues. It manages the project portfolio throughout the year. In a highly volatile business environment, this task requires a lot of flexibility. Many new initiatives come up forcing reprioritization of the existing projects. At times, decisions on basket re-sizing have to be taken in order to accommodate larger, unplanned initiatives. The IT steering committee prioritizes the pro-

> "The combined effect of traditional approaches to IT development leads to a set of silos. Individually, the applications work fine. Together, they hinder a company's efforts to coordinate customer, supplier, and employee processes. And the company's data, one of its most important assets, is patchy, error-prone, and not up to date"
> Jeanne W. Ross, 2006

jects according to strategic priority criteria. This fine tuning of investments is a very important task serving to align business and IT operationally. Both the business representatives, as basket sponsors and the chief information officer, representing the CIO basket, have to demonstrate the strategic value of their respective projects. As an example, the CIO basket of Credit Suisse is described

Responsibility	Committee	Dual Roles		Process
		Business Representation	IT Representation	
Strategic Issues	Executive Board	Other executive board members	Executive board member in charge of IT (CIO, if member of the executive board)	Strategic Business-IT Alignment
Strategic Basket Issues	IT Steering Committee	Basket Sponsor	IT Basket Provider	Project Portfolio Management
Operational Basket Issues	Sponsor Meeting	IT Business Partner	IT Solution Provider	
Project Issues	Project Steering Committee	Business Project Leader	IT Project Leader	Project Management

Fig. 5.2 Committees, roles and processes in the governance model

in Side-Story 5.1. In addition to that project prioritization has to take dependencies among projects and capacity constraints into account. The chief information officer has to explain to his business colleagues why IT infrastructure investments are beneficial to the organization. In the experience of the authors, it makes sense to have an IT steering committee under a "neutral lead". The ideal person to lead this committee is the CEO. Often the role is delegated to the CFO. This may lead to a conflict of interest, as the CFO has his own basket with projects in the area of management information systems, accounting and compliance. Could the CIO lead the steering committee? The success of managed evolution highly depends on the proper balance between business and IT investments (as shown in Sect. 1.5). Thus, the chairperson of the IT steering committee should not own a large basket to avoid conflict of interest. This rules out the CIO, as the CIO basket is one of the largest baskets.

Side-Story 5.1: Credit Suisse Basket Governance Model for CIO Basket

The key objective of managed evolution is to balance investments between IT efficiency and new or improved business functionality. IT investments target risk reduction, agility improvements, innovation, process improvement and technology management. Examples related to IT risk are: Timely end-of-life replacements, clean-up of security issues and remediation of IT related audit issues. Technology portfolio reduction, removing unnecessary redundancy, completing unfinished migrations and implementing platforms all reduce complexity and improve agility. Introducing modern methods and technology contribute to the innovation of the information system. Improved processes and tools enable more efficient development and operation of the system.

5.3 Matching Roles: Balance of Power

All the investments into IT efficiency are managed in the CIO basket (Fig. 5.3). Credit Suisse has set up a *CIO basket governance*. The CIO basket governance includes all global IT functions. The governance model is based on four key principles:

- Strategy ("doing the right things"),
- Architecture ("doing the things right"),
- Delivery ("getting the things done well"),
- Value creation ("getting the benefits from the things done").

In order to do the right things, all investments are structured into initiatives, programs and projects leading to plans to be approved by sponsor meetings. All the proposals and projects are selected according to a value-driven portfolio management process ensuring overall IT strategy

> "Business strategy provides direction, an impetus for action. Most companies also act on strategy to guide IT investments. Accordingly, IT executives work to align IT and IT-enabled business processes with stated business strategy"
> Jeanne W. Ross, 2006

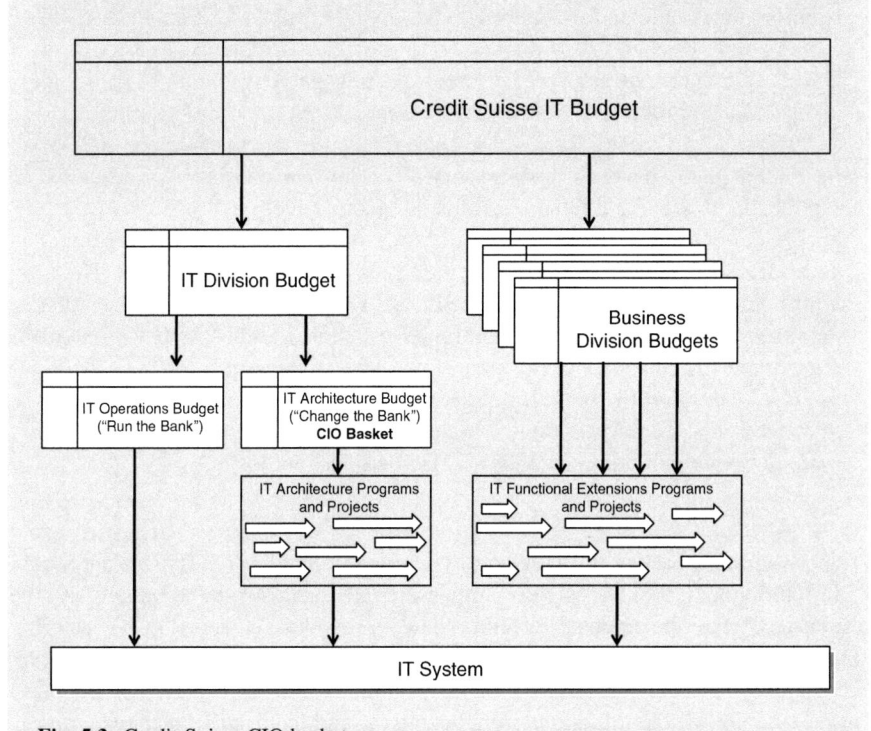

Fig. 5.3 Credit Suisse CIO basket

conformance. Each program has to present a *value case* demonstrating the strategic alignment, the benefits (financial and non-financial) and cost. Each project included into a program is documented as part of exactly one value case. The Credit Suisse CIO basket is split into 5 sub-baskets: The first basket is the "CIO cross-function" basket, sponsored by the CIO himself. The divisional CIOs are responsible for the 4 platform baskets: (1) Swiss and international private banking basket, (2) investment banking basket, (3) asset management basket and (4) shared services basket (including financial accounting, human resources and banking operations).

The Credit Suisse executive board decides on the allocation of the budget to the business baskets and to the CIO basket. The CIO sponsor meeting, more or less identical to the global IT management committee, then decides on the distribution of the CIO budget to the 5 subbaskets based on the global IT strategy.

One of the main targets of the CIO basket investments is to improve the architecture of the system. Therefore, a key principle is that each CIO-sponsored project is subject to the existing Credit Suisse IT project governance and has to fully support the architectural principles and standards (see Chap. 2, "Architecture Management").

The sponsor of a project is responsible for its professional delivery. The sponsor is accountable for adhering to the approved size of his subbasket. He or she approves each major phase of any project and releases the necessary budget. The sponsor tracks progress, ensures transparency about progress and takes action if progress is below expectations.

The process of benefit realization analysis makes sure that projects deliver benefits in line with their business case. The process consists of four steps: First, benefits are identified and estimated quantitatively in the "value case"; Second, after budget approval, the project delivers a detailed value case with an update benefits estimate and a value measurement control plan; Third, after completion of the project, benefits are reported and compared against the most recent estimates. Note that for investments into IT efficiency not all the benefits are financial, but some of them lead to indirect financial benefits because they contribute to complexity reduction or other architectural improvements leading to more efficient development or operation of the system. Such qualitative benefits are also demonstrated.

Projects within a basket are managed by a *sponsor meeting*. Sufficient autonomy within individual baskets is very important. Changes inside a basket are the responsibility of the sponsor meeting, led by the basket sponsor. IT steering committee and the IT sponsor meetings are both lead by a business representative. The sponsor meeting for the CIO basket is under the lead of the CIO. The CIO basket contains all the infrastructure investments and the *architecture programs*.

One key role in the governance model is the *basket sponsor*: The basket sponsor is usually a top manager from the business side, except for the CIO basket with the

CIO as the basket sponsor. The basket sponsor is responsible for strategically steering the basket. In this role he or she chairs the sponsor meetings, decides on initiating and implementing initiatives and optimizes allocations to sub-baskets if the basket structure is hierarchical. The sponsor's counterpart in the IT organization is the *basket provider*. The *basket provider* is usually a senior IT manager advising business representatives in sponsor meetings, deciding on funding issues up to a threshold and facilitating the sponsor meeting. The basket provider is responsible for accurate reporting on all projects in the basket and for escalating major issues to the sponsor meeting.

The next pair of matching roles is the *IT business partner* and the *IT provider*. The IT business partner comes from the business support organization and is responsible for channeling all business requests concerning a certain basket towards the IT provider. The IT provider is the development manager in charge of delivering the IT solutions. His organization typically executes the projects in the basket. IT business partner and IT provider handle all operational issues around the project portfolio in the basket.

Finally, there is a pair of matching roles on the level of the individual project: The *business project leader*; and the *IT project leader*. All the roles are described in more detail in the context of the business-IT alignment processes below.

5.4 Governance Models for Project Portfolio Management

Good business-IT alignment for managed evolution manages a portfolio of projects on multiple levels. It defines matching roles between business and IT. Decisions are made in carefully balanced groups. Besides a number of business baskets, the CIO basket is an important element in this governance model. Little has been said about how to structure the project portfolio into baskets.

In the *business basket governance model* (Fig. 5.4) the decision power is aligned with business structures and reporting lines. This is similar to the hierarchical governance model shown in Fig. 5.1. The important difference is that there is no direct allocation of IT budgets to business units. The overall IT budget and the split between "run-the-business" and "change-the-business" is decided at the top of the unit. The "change-the-business" budget is allocated to business unit baskets. The executive board of the company – business unit heads are members – approves an overall IT strategy with key actions, defined strategic priorities and a distribution of the "change-the-bank" budget into baskets. This could mean that from a corporate point of view a business unit investment proposal does not fit the corporate objectives and has to be postponed. The business units lose autonomy in their investment decisions, because they are bound to a common IT strategy in their project prioritization. Allocating basket budgets to individual projects and prioritizing projects within baskets are the responsibility of the company-wide IT

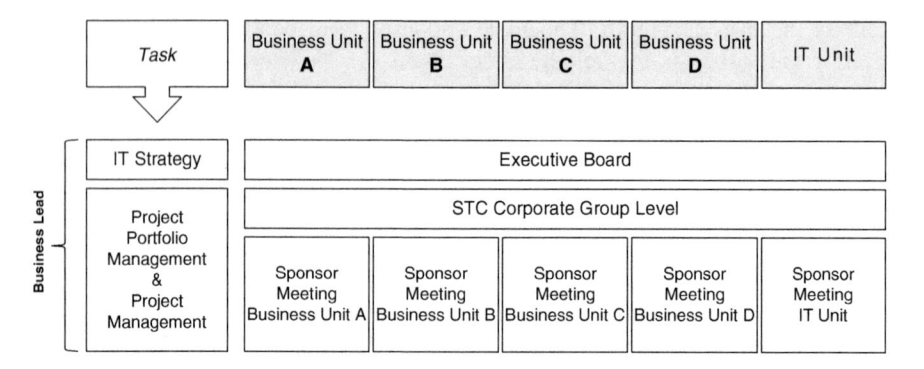

Fig. 5.4 Business basket governance model

steering committee. It acts on behalf of the executive board to balance business unit interests.

Typically the business unit head acts as the basket sponsor. Other members of the sponsor meeting represent other businesses affected by the projects driven by this sponsor, because they share the same information system. In this model, a business unit can react quickly to changes in the business environment by reprioritizing projects in its own basket. The basket provider and the business representatives from the other business units ensure that a wide range of interests are covered and that the same function is not implemented more than once. The basket provider may escalate to the IT steering committee, if such issues cannot be resolved within the sponsor meeting. The business unit baskets are matched by the CIO basket in this model, covering IT efficiency investments across the whole system.

From a managed evolution perspective this approach fosters balanced investments into business value and IT efficiency. It is still not the optimum setup, however. The business units are still too much focused on their own plans and not on the investments from a corporate perspective. Investments are optimized at best within each business unit. The advantage is that a clear reporting and escalation line is available. The disadvantage of this governance model is the risk of creating functional overlaps and to unnecessarily increase the complexity of the system. In the experience of the authors, one can often observe that this model leads to an overinvestment into visible systems, such as Web-portals and reporting systems. On the other hand, less visible systems, such as reference data, are neglected.

To sum it up: The business basket governance model is good enough, but not ideal, for managed evolution. It has its weaknesses, when it comes to coordination of requirements and avoiding redundancy. In large organizations this model is often used as a compromise that serves the purpose while still being acceptable to the business units.

The most sophisticated way to structure the project portfolio is along domains (introduced in Sect. 2.5) instead of organization. This *domain basket governance model* (Fig. 5.5), optimizes the cross-divisional coordination of IT investments into a single information system. To avoid the problem of too many baskets and

5.4 Governance Models for Project Portfolio Management

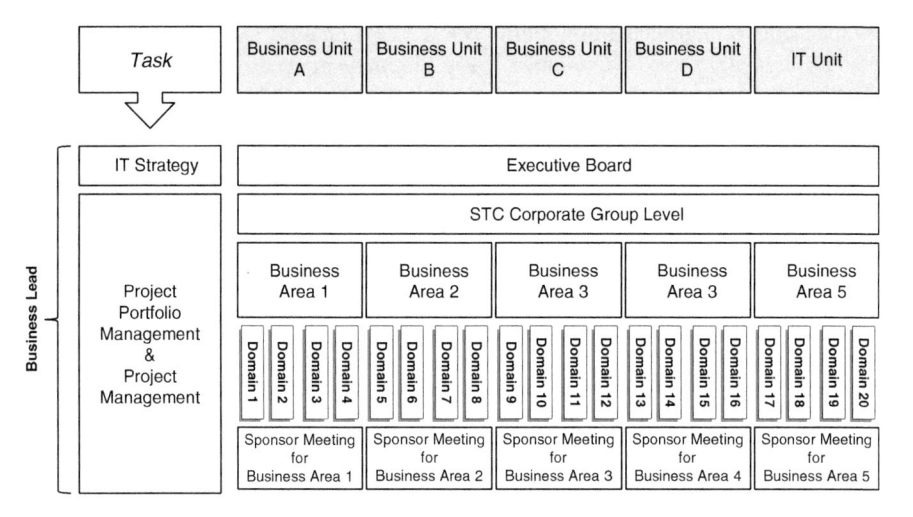

Fig. 5.5 Domain basket governance model

sub-critical basket size, the domains are often grouped into clusters as also shown in Fig. 5.5.

The group steering committee still has the task of managing the baskets and of prioritizing the initiatives according to the defined criteria. The biggest change compared to the business basket model is not on this level but one level below. The cluster basket sponsor meetings have to include all stakeholders affected by changes to functionality in the cluster. Often the main user acts as the sponsor in this model. As the IT provider should be in charge for all projects in a basket, the best fit is to organize *application development departments* along domains. This simplifies strategic resource planning. If the basket is significantly larger or smaller than the capacity of the corresponding organization, there is a problem. This leads to fewer escalations on resource conflicts among baskets. Less duplication and overlaps in the application portfolio are additional advantages of this model. It also supports a stable multi-year outlook on IT investments across a cluster independent of organizational changes. This fosters the necessary strategic investments. In contrast to that, the business basket model suffers from continuously having to adapt to the changing organization structure. A lot of administrative work and inconsistent investments may be two negative consequences of this.

The *domain basket model* convinces with its logical design. But is it feasible to implement this model in a rapidly changing environment characteristic of large organizations? Changing environments lead to changing organizations. Senior managers change jobs more often. How is it possible to implement and sustain a domain basket model in this fast changing environment? As very large information systems cannot be replaced in one go but have to be continuously developed over time, *stability in governance* is required. Stability is the key advantage of the domain basket model. The domain model is a stable model because it follows the logic of functional cohesion (Side-Story 2.3). This property does not change as fast as the surrounding organization. Furthermore, the domain basket governance model enables the paradigm shift from a *project approach* to a *product approach* in development. New functionality is delivered by new *product releases* according to a release plan. In that context the domain (or parts of a domain) is the "product" to be carefully evolved in the long term. New business requirements are managed by the sponsor and the basket provider as if they were product managers. They collect all requirements, prioritize them and finally allocate the requirements to one of the future product releases. The product is then released regularly, according to a predefined schedule, with requirements freeze, implementation, quality assurance and product release. Requirements that can't be handled in the next release are postponed to later releases. Each release is managed as a project. The IT development units mutate from project delivery organizations to "product providers", comparable with commercial off-the-shelf software vendors.

An important input to the domain-based budget planning is the yearly *domain assessment*: All applications in a domain are scrutinized for "fitness for purpose" and "fitness for future". This assessment gives an overall picture of the application landscape and allows discussions with business on the direction of investments. An example of a domain assessment is given in Side-Story 5.2.

Side-Story 5.2: Credit Suisse Domain Assessment 2009

The domain model (introduced in Side Story 2.3) forms the structural base for the management of the application landscape. Each domain contains a number of subdomains and all applications in the domain are assigned to subdomains.

Credit Suisse executes a yearly domain assessment, that on the one hand, allows the state of the application landscape to be explained to the business and, on the other hand, forms the base for investment planning. The domain assessment is carried out jointly by business and IT. The domain assessment is carried out as a "360° application domain analysis" (Fig. 5.6) resulting in a full assessment of all applications in the domain. The dimensions in the 360° analysis are the satisfaction of the business with the application, the architectural quality of the application, the comparison to competitive services and finally the sourcing and investment view.

Each application is analyzed according to a number of criteria along two main properties. The property *"Fit for Purpose"* uses the rating criteria *Business Functionality*, *Business Usability*, *Stability* and *Performance*. The property *"Fit for Future"* uses the rating criteria *Enhanceability*, *Maintainability*, *Database*, *Program Language*, *User Interfaces* and *Dependency on other applications*.

According to the outcome of the assessment each application is placed in the "Fit for Future"/"Fit for Purpose" grid as shown in Fig. 5.7. The example

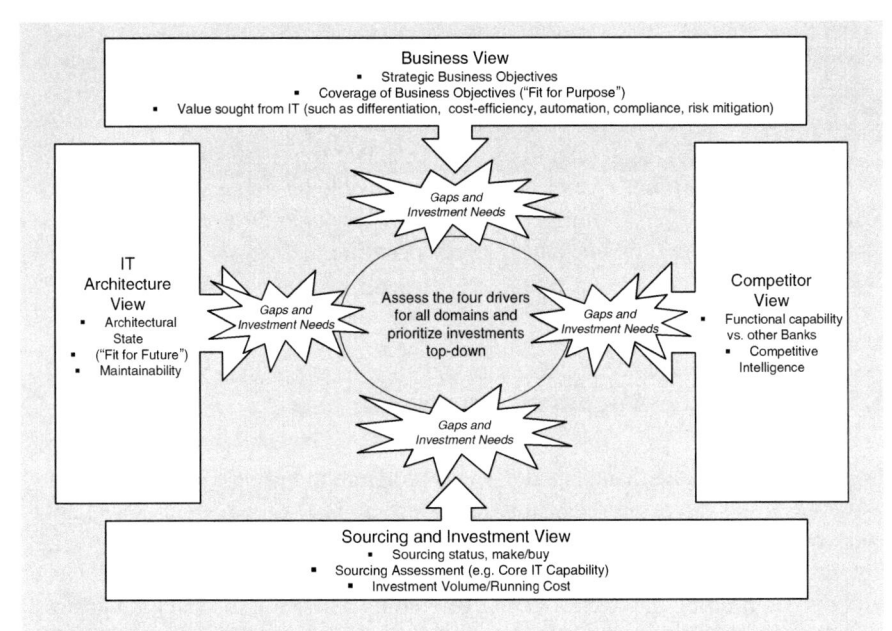

5.4 Governance Models for Project Portfolio Management

Fig. 5.6 360° Application domain analysis

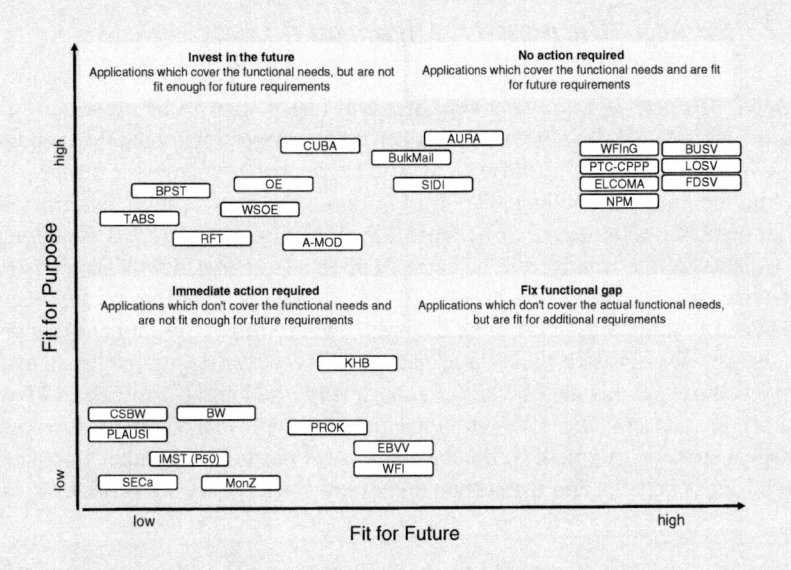

Fig. 5.7 Result of the domain assessment for domain BAS

> used in the figure shows the results for the domain Enterprise Base Solutions[1] as introduced in Side-Story 2.3. The resulting map provides a concise overview about the state of the domain and indicates the need for action.
>
> From the assessment map in Fig. 5.7 in a next step the individual actions required for the improvement or replacement of the application and their required budget are determined. This activity results in the proposed domain budget, including time line and resource planning.

5.5 Business-IT Alignment Processes

In addition to the governance model giving structure to business-IT alignment and assigning responsibility for decision making, there is a second, even more important, aspect of business IT alignment. The organization needs to define three key processes for business-IT alignment. The first is the *strategic business-IT alignment process* determining the overall IT budget and its allocation to "run the business" and the various "change the business" baskets. The second is the *project portfolio management process*, managing priorities and project progress across a single basket. Finally, the third process is the *project management process* ensuring results from the individual projects. The three processes correspond to the three levels of business-IT alignment: Whole enterprise, basket and individual project.

5.5.1 Strategic Business-IT Alignment Process

Strategic Business-IT alignment consists of different steps to be presented in this section. First of all, it is necessary to set a cost target for total IT expenditure. Second, one needs to define the desired ratio between the "change the business" and the "run the business" budget. The third important parameter to be determined on the strategic level is the ratio between IT efficiency and business functionality investments in the "change the business" budgets (see Sect. 1.7) This leads to an *investment plan* defining investments for each domain according to architectural fitness and functionality gaps to be covered. This results in investment targets for each basket. Within each basket a project portfolio covering the requirements and not exceeding the allocated budget is subsequently defined. Business and IT work together on the strategic level as equal partners with the common objective to manage a strategy-oriented, well balanced project portfolio that takes into account both business benefits and the sustainable optimization of the IT system.

---

[1]The short texts in the boxes identify the individual applications. This information is irrelevant in this context.

5.5 Business-IT Alignment Processes

Defining a cost target is an iterative process that approaches the right number from different directions. In order to determine the target from the bottom, all applications and all infrastructure components are assessed for architectural health and appropriate business functionality (Example in Side-Story 5.2). Reviewing applications from the business perspective, as well as the architectural perspective, is very important. Keeping the focus on new business functionality, only, may lead to a situation where parts of the application landscape become structurally and functionally obsolete over time. Typically this analysis is done domain by domain, leading to a list of requirements that are then assigned to *baskets*, grouped into projects and finally priced for execution. Additionally, a review of the *technology portfolio* is required. Outdated technologies have to be replaced and new technologies have to be implemented as described in Sect. 4.2. This analysis is based on a technology portfolio management strategy. All infrastructure and architecture investments, including release upgrades of existing technologies, are grouped in the CIO basket. Summing up the efforts for all necessary projects in all baskets results in a bottom-up estimate for the "change the business" budget, both for the business as well as the CIO basket. In the experience of the authors this sum is a bit higher than the actual spend on the projects later, as the project managers tend to estimate the project efforts on the safe side.

The other component of the complete IT budget is the "run the business" budget. The budget is based on the actual "run the business" spend from the previous year, with additional budget to cover increased volume, new functionality and inflation. Some of this increase can be offset by a reduction due to improved operational efficiency gains. Often large reengineering projects lead to intermediate situations, where operation costs are higher than in the target state. These effects have to be taken into account when calculating the "run the business" bottom-up estimate.

The other approach to determine the IT cost target is competitive analysis. Often, there are indicators from the market as to what the right IT spend in relation to revenue, overall cost or profit would be in a certain business segment. Taking into account top-down market estimates, bottom-up internal investment needs and overall business strategy, an overall IT cost target is set. Needless to say, the market estimate and the bottom-up estimate cannot be too far apart in the long run, otherwise the enterprise might be under-investing or be very inefficient with its investments. Target setting happens as an iterative process between business and IT. They have to agree to an IT cost target compatible with the overall planned cost of the organization in the budgeting process. It is possible that due to an economic downturn or a decrease in revenues the IT cost target has to be adapted during the year.

If the IT cost target is significantly below the bottom-up estimate, one usually has to reduce the "change the business" portion, because "run the business" budget cannot be compressed easily without investing into IT efficiency first in a well-managed organization. As mentioned a number of times in this book, this may lead to total paralysis in the extreme case, where the "run the bank" need exceeds the overall IT cost target. In such a case there is no more room for "change the business" investments. If this is the trend, one may want to increase the IT efficiency ratio at the expense of business projects. This in turn reduces the "run the business" spend and creates room for investments again. The alternative solution in this situation is to increase the overall IT cost target above the market estimate for a certain time period and spend the additional money on IT efficiency. The result of balancing all the factors described above leads to the total IT budget, the "change the business"/ "run the business" ratio and to the relative size of the CIO basket within "change the business". A well managed organization keeps these ratios more or less stable in the long run.

Systematically deriving business requirements from the business strategy is a prerequisite to bring requirements to a level of precision suitable to define projects in the project portfolio. First, strategic thrusts, which need IT investments, are identified. The more general strategic thrusts are then broken down into more specific actions. Then the actions are specified in more detail and assigned to planned projects or project ideas. The projects and ideas are then kept in the overall project portfolio. One of the risks in this process is functional overlap with existing applications or other planned projects. It is the task of *architecture management* to avoid such redundancy. Domain architects have exactly this responsibility. In the project review, they match the new requirements in a domain against each other and the existing functionality, to ensure maximum reuse and minimum unwanted redundancy. During planning, this check is simplified if baskets are aligned to domains, because all functionally similar requirements are then in the same basket.

For managed evolution it is important that allocation of funds to baskets starts from one common IT budget at the top of the organization. It is necessary to allocate the budget to baskets based on the business strategy, the domain assessment and the technology portfolio review. Defining the cost target, deriving business requirements from the business strategy, reviewing the application and technology portfolio and finally allocating funds to business and CIO baskets best happens in yearly cycles with a three year perspective in the experience of the authors. Given all the mutual dependencies, both the business strategy and the IT strategy process need to be aligned regarding both content and timing. Both strategies are developed in parallel requiring close interaction between the processes.

It is disputed within CIO circles if a formal, written *IT strategy* defined in a yearly revolving process has real value in a fast changing global environment. In the opinion of the authors, managed evolution is

> "Strategy is determined by what comes out of the resource allocation process, not the intentions and proposals that got into it"
> Clayton M. Christensen

hard to achieve without the overall framework of a formal IT strategy. Also, the necessary close alignment with business strategy is hard to achieve without a formal IT strategy process. Some key elements of an IT strategy are a written-down understanding of the long-term business requirements, a common understanding of market trends, the results of the assessment of the current situation, a long term business plan outlining the financials and all the "run the business" and "change the business" planning, as outlined above. The main value of a formal strategy is that it can be used to communicate the high level targets to the whole organization. Of course, the strategy needs to remain flexible in order to be able to absorb big events during the planning period, such as mergers or major market discontinuities. In such cases, the impact is often that either the cost target has to be reduced or the project portfolio undergoes a massive change to accommodate new priorities. The value of strategy in such cases is the priorities and the reasoning behind them. With all that information readily available, strategy can be changed more rapidly.

The value of an IT strategy for the business side lies in the systematic compilation of business requirements as seen by IT and of identifying major market and IT trends relevant for the organization. Within the IT strategy process it is important to analyze the external and internal situation and trends before defining the strategy. This analysis covers business-driven and technology-driven IT trends, as well as organizational, human resources and financial trends. Gaining an *overall perspective* on the IT situation within the company, positioning the "own IT" in relation to the market and industry and the alignment of IT with business requirements are further benefits.

The value of an IT strategy is also high for the IT organization internally. The IT strategy provides directions for all IT resources and functions within the company. For organizations with complex group, business unit and department structures, IT strategy defines the interaction between different business units and departmental IT organizations. With an IT strategy one can ensure better coordination and reap synergies across IT. From a communication and culture point of view, the strategy serves to ensure a common understanding about the future of the organization's information systems. The larger the organization is, the more it matters. Business context, application portfolio, technology infrastructure, funding, processes and organization are major topics in an IT strategy. Managed evolution impacts all of them simultaneously. Managed evolution does not only cover applications and technology. Human resources and their skills are also part of managed evolution. So is culture. In summary, we can say: Managed evolution is a proven approach, which gives IT strategy a comprehensive long term direction as an overall guiding principle. Managed evolution cannot be executed as an architectural paradigm or a program alone. It has to cover all elements of an IT strategy.

The IT strategy is the yearly result of the strategic business-IT alignment process. While the IT strategy is prepared by the whole IT and business organization, the final decision on it happens in the executive board. This underlines the strategic importance of this process. Architecture programs which serve to improve the architectural integrity and agility of the IT system are also defined as part of the IT strategy. As an example, the Credit Suisse Switzerland architecture program for the year 2009 is presented in the Side-Story 5.3 below.

Side-Story 5.3: Credit Suisse Switzerland Architecture Program 2010

The Credit Suisse *CIO basket* for the Private Banking (PB) business unit information system covers all the IT systems of the global private banking business. There is a clearly defined process for how to decide on the IT initiatives and on their priorities. In this side-story, the focus is on the content side of the IT initiatives. The initiatives in the CIO basket for 2010 are an important part of the implementation of the PB IT strategy and are based on the current architecture strategy with the three pillars *globalization*, *flexibility/reuse* and *modernization*.

In the *globalization* pillar it is planned to reuse solutions globally and to develop a global collaboration in application development. The *flexibility/reuse* pillar targets separation of application aspects, improved interface management and improving integration architecture. The *modernization* pillar contains all investments for reengineering outdated applications, for exits and replacement of obsolete technologies, for aligning to technology mainstreams and in focused innovation for security, integration and more efficient development. Selected examples for architecture initiatives 2010 are described in the following.

The initiative *application platform enhancements* contains projects to further develop the application and run-time platforms (see, e.g., Side-Story 4.4) and to roll out the platforms to locations outside of Switzerland. The objective is to provide an even higher level of standardization and development/runtime support and to enable applications to be deployed globally.

Data warehousing, often termed "corporate information factory ([Inmon_01])", is an important concept and a powerful technology for information systems. The initiative *DWH architecture improvements* advances the implementation of the Credit Suisse standard DWH architecture globally. The DWH architecture defines standards for feeders, data marts and analytic and business users with strong emphasis on information access control to protect confidential data in the DWH. Modeling, including semantic and data models, is also standardized and enforced and is based on the business object model (Side-Story 2.5). Another area covered by this initiative is metadata management. The objective is to implement a flexible, security-conscious, compatible data warehouse throughout all business units of Credit Suisse.

Application and service development consumes a large portion of the IT budget. Improving the productivity of the development cycle, i.e. producing more code with less resources, therefore has a significant impact on the efficient use of the application development budget. The IT initiative *enhanced development efficiency* contains projects to improve the development tool chain, the testing environment and the deployment mechanisms.

The objective of this initiative is to improve productivity, reduce time to market and, at the same time, provide higher software quality.

As shown in Sect. 4.4, systems management of componentized systems needs different approaches from traditional systems management. The IT initiative *system management improvements in Swiss banking IT platform* therefore contains projects to define, prototype, implement and deploy novel systems management tools. This includes IT services monitoring, logging and failure analysis. The objective of this initiative is to improve system stability and availability.

5.5.2 Project Portfolio Management Process

One level below strategy, *project portfolio management* is another important element of business-IT alignment. Project portfolio management serves the collective management of all projects and project ideas within a basket. It systematically collects information about progress, risks, dependencies, business cases and project effort across a whole basket. It serves the responsible managers of the basket to take decisions on funding, starting, stopping and reallocating resources to projects within the basket. Doing so best fulfils the strategic requirements as defined in the IT strategy.

When analyzing a traditional project portfolio management process, often certain weaknesses can be observed. A first weakness is that the project portfolio process is based on a static budget and managed in a yearly cycle, like the strategy. This may lead to situations that after half the year most of the projects are obsolete because business has changed in the meantime. While a yearly cycle is sufficient for business-IT alignment on the strategic level, project portfolio management is more dynamic. A second weakness is that all the projects of all baskets are planned at the same time in the same portfolio. This leads to micro-management and the management losing the overview. This is why project portfolio management has to happen on the level of the individual baskets with clearly defined responsibilities and standardized roles.

The group steering committee is responsible for the allocation of budgets to baskets (Fig. 5.2). The responsibility for the initial prioritization of projects and for changes in basket size during the year lies with the leading committee for project portfolio management, which is the basket sponsor meeting. All the business and IT representatives decide jointly on new requirements, initiatives, projects, prioritization and escalation.

The project portfolio of a basket can be further divided into sub-baskets depending on the size of a basket. The basket comes with several characteristics. First, it is defined by budget size. Second, it contains initiatives, programs and projects. Third, it is managed by the sponsor meeting and is governed by a set of roles such as: The basket sponsor and the IT business partner on the business side; and the basket provider and basket suppliers on the IT side. In the case of the CIO basket, both business and IT roles are filled by IT managers. For all other baskets, basket provider, basket supplier and the IT portfolio office are allocated to the IT organization.

Each basket has a *basket sponsor*. The basket sponsor decides on initiating, modifying and implementing initiatives, programs and projects. The IT business partner supports the sponsor as the main contact for all relevant business representatives regarding IT requests belonging to the basket. The sponsor manages the demand on the basket and leads planning, prioritization and aligning business and IT representatives. The basket provider role is assigned to a senior IT manager who advises business representatives in the sponsor meeting on IT services, on business opportunities enabled by technology and on synergy opportunities. The provider also coordinates one or more basket suppliers responsible for the delivery of IT projects.

The IT project portfolio office is responsible for the project portfolio administration as well as project accounting across the basket. An important task is to ensure consistency of project information between the level of the project portfolio and the level of the individual projects. This requires adequate tools, such as good project management and administration software. An additional task of the IT project portfolio office is to measure the success of projects; both ensuring that promised benefits really happen and that lessons learned in the course of the project are recorded and applied to future projects.

In very large organizations there may be a hierarchical structure of baskets and sub baskets with the respective sponsor meetings and roles defined for each basket or sub-basket. The sponsor meetings generally occur several times every year. This is generally sufficient to steer the individual projects. On the very low level, the project portfolio has to be adapted almost on a daily basis. Reporting information coming from the individual projects and new requirements coming from IT business partners have to be assessed in the context of the existing portfolio in order to prepare the necessary decisions in the sponsor meeting.

Experience shows that a project portfolio has to be defined iteratively, taking different views into account. One view stems from pro-actively discussing initiatives with the business and summarizing them as project ideas going into the portfolio. This helps the executive board to define the basket size and the IT cost target as discussed above. An additional challenge for project portfolio management is the large portfolio of projects, each in a different phase. Projects generally do not align nicely to planning cycles. So, planning has to take a number of running projects into account. Usually, as projects proceed, budgets become less flexible, due to signed contracts and allocated resources, for example. So, if priorities in the basket need to change, one has to take both priorities and the progress of the project into account, when shifting resources.

In a managed evolution approach, project selection is a big challenge. The organization needs to define clear selection criteria for projects. One approach that has worked for the authors was the following: Projects required due to legal and regulatory requirements or covering major operational risks get first priority. Next, projects are selected by business case. When analyzing business cases, it is important to differentiate between projects with measurable and committed cost savings or revenue increases and those with a positive, but not measurable, business case. Usually it is easier to measure cost reductions, whereas projects promising higher revenue have less reliable business cases in general. Which kind of business cases should be given priority depends on the economic environment and the priorities of the business strategy. In economically difficult times when cost has to be reduced, projects with a measurable business case have higher priority. When the strategy focuses on high business growth, the revenue projects are in favor.

Architecture provides the domain structure as an important prerequisite to project portfolio management. Throughout the process, the role of architecture management is to make sure that projects are properly allocated to domains. This is very important to foster reuse and reduce complexity, because redundant implementations can be avoided within the individual baskets. This is much easier in the domain basket governance model (Fig. 5.5) than in a business basket governance model (Fig. 5.4), because all redundancies can be detected and managed in the same basket. More importantly, it is easier to convince a single basket sponsor to align projects and change priorities for redundancy avoidance. Coordinating across multiple baskets is more difficult, even if redundancy is detected in the project reviews.

5.5.3 Project Management Process

The third level of business-IT alignment is the *management* of individual *projects*. On this level the relation between IT and business is a clear sponsor-provider relationship.

The biggest difference between project management that is adequate for managed evolution and general best-practice project management lies in the role of *architecture management*. Architecture management has to ensure that projects are executed according to managed evolution, driving the system in each project a little bit towards the target architecture as introduced in Sect. 1.5. The instrument for this is the *project review board*. The project review board, reviewing project deliverables after each project phase, assesses architectural quality and contribution to target architecture for each project. Sometimes compromises are necessary. This is, for example, the case if an urgent business requirement has to be implemented, violating architecture standards due to high pressure from the market. Architecture management cannot stop such projects, but has to suggest ways how the architectural problems introduced by such a short-cut project can be fixed later. It is up to the sponsor meeting to make sure that the corresponding architecture correction projects really happen at a later time.

On this level, the project portfolio management has clearly defined responsibilities both on the business and the IT side. For each basket there is one basket provider and several basket suppliers which are each responsible for a number of IT projects. Each project is lead by two people; the business project leader and the IT project leader. The business project leader reports to the IT business partner.

With that, joint IT/business responsibility is defined on all three levels of business-IT alignment. Basket sponsors relate to basket providers, business partners to basket suppliers, business project leaders to IT project leaders. Each team ensures business-IT alignment on their level. Going down level by level, a continuous transformation of the relation between business and IT can be observed: While it is a true partnership on the strategic level, it is a clear sponsor-provider relationship on the project level. Change management on all levels of business-IT alignment is a highly demanding task. Changes in the basket size have to be mirrored not only in the project portfolio but also in the individual projects. Realizing all the necessary changes in due time requires a highly agile organization.

This chapter completes with one final comment: Business-IT alignment is a challenge in very large information systems operated by very large organizations.

> "Today's IT agility is tomorrow's business agility"

The outcome of many surveys related to the relationship between business and IT show the same result: On the one hand, IT is seen as central to the organization's future ability to evolve the business and increasingly also as a source of competitive advantage. On the other hand, business managers see the current IT landscape as a barrier for fast adoption and speedy reaction to market needs. The increasing complexity of large organizations in many cases hinders IT in developing the ability to change and to shape the IT into the competitive tool the business requires. This may lead to tensions between IT and business. In a very large organization this becomes an even more severe issue. The reason for that is that very large information systems have many stakeholders. The importance to systematically manage and align the stakeholders increases with the size of the organization. As shown in this chapter, it is very important to find new ways of cooperation between the business side and IT, in order to overcome this vicious circle.

Chapter 6
People, Culture and Organization

Summary Very large information systems are built, maintained and operated by people and organizations. The quality of these systems is to a great extent defined by two factors: The skills and motivation of these people and the culture in which these people work and build their careers. The culture for a successful managed evolution is based on long-term thinking, sustainability and trust. Very large information systems need thousands of people – very often located in different countries – for their development. The management of such a large, distributed workforce requires a deep understanding of the principles of managed evolution, a strong, clearly communicated commitment to managed evolution and also the support of the business. People must be supported by an adequate organization, specifically designed for managed evolution.

6.1 People and Skills

Managed evolution requires many changes in technology, processes, people, methods and tools. Strategic business-IT-alignment, architecture governance and managing complexity, such as by modularizing and standardizing of systems and componentization, are examples of these new

> "The major problems of our work are not so much *technological* as *sociological* in nature"
> Tom DeMarco, 1999

elements giving managed evolution the right direction. In addition to these hard factors, *soft factors* play an important role. Soft factors are mainly skills and culture. In the same way as for the hard factors, soft factors need to be developed using an evolutionary approach, too.

To identify the soft factors, the characteristics of managed evolution must first be analyzed. Managed evolution has many faces, depending on which viewpoint is taken. At the heart of the managed evolution of the soft factors are carefully defined values. Defining the adequate and sustainable set of values is no simple task.

However, starting and executing the required cultural shift and embedding the defined values in a large organization which is often distributed geographically over the globe and thus encompassing a number of different mindsets and mentalities, are considerable challenges.

Existing *skills* in the organization are one of the most important assets of managed evolution because systems are built and developed by experienced and skilled *people* familiar with the existing systems. Because substantial parts of a very large information system always contain legacy subsystems (see Sect. 1.3), the knowledge and skills related to these legacy systems should be carefully hatched and protected. They are indispensable for the development and modernization of the very large information system. These special skills have to be managed carefully and maintained in the same way as other assets, in the very large information system, are. In parallel, a well-trained workforce of developers using new technologies must be built up. Both groups must cooperate well and value their mutual contributions to the success. It is noteworthy that the large scale change of the skills of a workforce takes time, effort and involves an element of risk. However, not all people with legacy skills will be able to make the transition to the new requirements.

A good example for new skills required is the ability to think and act strategically across the organization. A large percentage of the IT workforce must know, understand, accept and live the principles underlying the strategy. This knowledge will then enable them to make day to day decisions that positively contribute to the objectives of the managed evolution. A good example of how to develop these skills is described in the Side-Story 6.1.

Side-Story 6.1: Credit Suisse Strategic IT Training

In some companies "strategy" is a restricted area for some specialists and for the top management. If, however, an organization adopts managed evolution, the strategy has to be understood and lived to be successful. In order to communicate and motivate, the *Strategic IT Training* (SITT) was launched in Credit Suisse. Each year 30–40 mid-career IT professionals, both in technology and management roles, are invited to participate in the program.

> "The enterprise architecture provides a long-term view of a company's processes, systems, and technologies so that individual projects can build capabilities – not just fulfill immediate needs"
> Jeanne W. Ross, 2006

The training is delivered as a custom-tailored series of lectures and class work by a world-leading business school. Key topics include (see [Ross_06]):

> *Widening the Lens/Frontiers of IT: Driving Value, Driving Change*
> Few industry sectors outside of technology firms themselves and the military have been more directly affected by the information technology revolution than financial services. Technology products have become the primary business of banking. Technology managers must be able to identify the opportunities that offer the greatest strategic benefits for the firm and then mobilize the organization to ensure that it can deliver those benefits. The first block of this program focuses on the frontiers, i.e., the newest technological trends in information technology that are driving value and driving change in organizations.
>
> *From Vision to Reality: Strategies for Creating Value through IT*
> Strategy underpins the success of every company. The focus of block two is to enable skilled technical managers to think strategically about their business and to transform today's vision into tomorrow's reality. To do this they must understand the strategic issues confronting the firm, the impact of disruptive technologies on industry structures and be able to align IT strategies with the firm's business strategies. They need to have a solid "MBA-type" grounding in business strategy; to understand the concepts of strategic fit and strategic analysis; to understand how to make outsourcing decisions; and to understand the influence of strategy on organizational structure.
>
> *Linking Strategy and Implementation*
> Linking strategy with implementation requires a deep understanding of organizational reward systems, informal networks, elements of power and trust, the role of organizational culture, leadership and critical success factors for implementing change. The final block focuses on the frameworks and practical tools that IT managers need in order to implement new ideas and innovative change within the organization.
>
> A number of informal evening "fireside chats" with top level executives both from Credit Suisse IT and business completed the education. Substantial material used in the SITT lectures was published in 2006 as a book [Ross_06].

Given the importance of understanding the existing system, promoting internal talent and developing existing skills is the proven approach for success. This does, of course, not mean that recruitment from outside does not make sense in certain cases. In general, however, the human resources strategy for managed evolution is to continuously develop your own people instead of trying to solve difficulties by radical change. A very important tool to develop adequate in-house skills is a career and development plan. One key property of such a plan in an IT unit is to offer both a *management* and a *specialist career track*. Not offering both career opportunities leads to the situation where the best specialists are promoted to managers in order to progress with their careers. On the one hand, that often leads to unsuitable managers. On the other hand, much worse, it leads to a loss of senior specialist knowledge, dearly needed in the development of very large information systems. A successful example for *IT career tracks* is described in the Side-Story 6.2.

Side-Story 6.2: Credit Suisse Career Tracks

When starting with "managed evolution" around the year 2000, Credit Suisse realized that one of the key success factors would be to evolve the workforce along with the system. To manage this more proactively across IT and to provide a clear advancement path for the employees, a *career track system* was created. This side-story describes the main characteristics of this system. Over time this system was extended in scope from IT in Switzerland to functions outside IT (operations, for example) and IT as a global function. Today, careers of all employees of the global IT unit are managed according to the model below.

1) Career Tracks

The Credit Suisse career tracks serve both to rate and to develop employees. Career tracks define two dimensions:

- The *job family* describes the main working area of the employee. The available IT job families per career track are listed in Table 6.2.
- The *qualification band* rates individuals according to a number of IT competencies from the most junior (band 1) to the most senior roles (band 6).

Each employee belongs to a job family and to a qualification band corresponding to his/her current level of education and experience. An example for two employees is shown in Table 6.1. Each employee can apply for an upgrade to the next higher band in his job family every year. Depending on seniority he/she will then go through an assessment by more senior peers in the job family, resulting in a recommendation for band promotion. The assessment will include multiple dimensions, such as experience, education, current role and contribution to the advancement of more junior colleagues. As explained above, one of the key properties of this system is that line management is treated the same way as other job families (see Table 6.2).

To determine the qualification band of a specialist, *proficiency ratings* in several IT sub-competencies, such as core application systems, operational functions, IT environment, or application development tools are assessed.

Table 6.1 Employee rating in the Credit Suisse Career Tracks

Name	Job family	Band
Daniel Muster	Application Architecture and Development	3
Fritz Beispiel	IT Line Management	5

Table 6.2 The Credit Suisse career tracks

IT job family	Qualification band
Specialist Career Track	
Application Architecture and Development	1–6
Business Analysis and Engineering	1–6
Business Management	1–6
IT Operations	1–6
IT Risk Management	1–6
Quality Management and Testing	1–6
Project Management	1–6
Service and Delivery Management	1–6
System Architecture and Engineering	1–6
User and Production Support	1–6
IT Management Career Track	
IT Line Management	4–6

The proficiency rating ranges from level 1 (lowest, basic understanding) to level 4 (highest, subject matter depth and breadth). Each qualification band requires minimum proficiency levels in the corresponding IT sub-competencies.

2) *Application Architecture and Development Career Track*

As an example, the specialist career track "Application Architecture and Development" is described. The job family description reads as follows:

Individuals within the Application Architecture and Development job family are responsible for the technical analysis, design, architecture, development, implementation and support of software applications as well as for following established standards and procedures and for ensuring the smooth interoperability of their applications.

Senior Application Developers and Architects work with business and technical line managers, project managers, sponsors and other stakeholders to develop business and technical strategies, agree on project portfolios, develop application architectures and deliver applications that meet business requirements. They are responsible for tracking technical and business trends, assessing their impact and developing strategies to leverage this information to build solutions and mitigate risks.

> *Application Development professionals are responsible for working with their managers to assure their own continuing professional development and that of their teams. At the more senior levels, Application Developers and Architects are expected to train others, participate in company and industry working groups and encourage learning, sharing culture that supports development of innovative and effective business solutions.*
>
> *Application Development and Architecture professionals will develop a deep understanding of the businesses they support along with well-developed people and project management skills. They may apply these skills either within a narrow business focus or broadly across the firm.*

6.2 Culture and Values

Almost more important than skills are a number of *values* shared across the organization in support of the strategic objectives.

Managed evolution begins with an organically grown, very large information system. As explained in the chapters above, creating the necessary structures and prerequisites proceeds slowly, step by step. In the experience of the authors, it takes at least 3–4 years for the strategy to deliver significant results. As managed evolution may lead to very long component lifecycles, it is of outmost importance that people value legacy and, hence, build for the long-term. *Long-term orientation* and *continuity* are, therefore, key cultural values necessary for success. In today's fast changing world this is a serious issue. Rumor says that the average tenure of a CIO is 2 years, nowadays. The authors do not have the data to confirm this. But the fact is that top managers change their positions fairly often. Under these circumstances, it may be very hard to reach the necessary long-term orientation at the top level. It is a lot to ask from a manager to embark on a strategy where, it is clear from the beginning, that he/she won't be able to harvest the fruits of success. So, short-term orientation and a lot of management changes in particular jeopardize the success of managed evolution.

Managed evolution is a demanding journey over many years with many ups and downs. Internal influences, such as management changes, new business strategies and company crises or external factors, like economic downturns, mergers and acquisitions endanger the strategy. Therefore, a strong and clearly communicated commitment at all levels of the organization is required. *Perseverance* in steering the course under difficult circumstances is particularly important with the top management of both business and IT. Without this, managed evolution will almost certainly run out of steam. The organization will encounter many *conflicts* and setbacks during the managed evolution journey. These need high management attention in order to be resolved with the necessary long-term view. Such conflicts manifest themselves both in the relations between business and IT and within the IT organization. In the experience of the authors, the main resistance against managed

6.2 Culture and Values

evolution often comes from within the IT organization. The management hierarchy and people resist the required changes of culture, processes and skills. This sometimes requires difficult decisions to consistently support managed evolution. Often the conflict is between a local solution, quickly and cheaply delivered and a sustainable, global solution requiring a higher initial investment. As an example, developing the *integration architecture* (see Chap. 3) generates conflicts between the long term goals, such as reusable services and the short term requirements of hooking up two applications quickly. Another conflict is deviation from IT standards. Often a business project requires a specific new technology, which clearly violates the current IT standards. There are various reasons for such requests, such as fulfilling the prerequisites for a third party software package, which the business wants. Maintaining the necessary consistency between individual projects and the overall strategy is a challenging task. Perseverance in strategy must be strongly supported by stringent processes, appropriate decision channels and high levels of discipline across the organization. Incentives must be structured such that individuals are rewarded when they drive tasks systematically all the way to completion, taking a long-term perspective.

Discipline is a key prerequisite for certain concepts of managed evolution. Technology portfolio standardization only works if applications strictly adhere to the standards and follow the agreed life cycles. Project portfolio governance depends on all stakeholders to play their role appropriately, keeping the overall strategy in mind. It requires that all change-the-business activities are reported as projects. In integration architecture it is necessary that both service consumers and service providers adhere to the service contracts. Successful domain-based architecture relies on developers only building functionality belonging to their own domain and using functionality or data from other domains via services. Long-living applications demand complete and correct documentation. The necessary matrix organization (see Side Story 2.9) demands a culture that highly values the functional lines and responsibilities.

Leadership and commitment to managed evolution, with its requirement to coordinate across the whole organization, are required; especially in the transition phase from the traditional opportunistic approach where each development team could independently build their silo-ed applications. This transition will face a lot of resistance. Typical comments in this phase include: "Innovation and out-of-the-box thinking is killed", "Individual freedom becomes non-existent", "You are always hindered by other team's delays", "Architecture standards are inhibiting fast development" and many more.[1]

In managed evolution one of the key principles is building functionality and data only in the appropriate domain and to access it from other domains via well-defined services. This is particularly true for infrastructure (see Chap. 4) where applications

---

[1] Look at them as anecdotes and collect them for future amusement.

are expected to reuse the standardized platforms instead of building their own infrastructures. Developers have to integrate existing reusable components into their applications rather than developing their own modules. This way of working requires a high level of interaction in many new, not always easy, ways. Developers and project managers have to *trust* their colleagues providing the service to be used. In a large organization there may not even be a personal relationship between the user and the provider of a service. Developers may just go and grab a service description from the repository and build it into their application. This only works if the service contracts can be fully trusted. Often an application design relies on a service that doesn't even exist at design time. The only piece of information available is a specification and a roadmap that promises the service in the future. This exposes the project, using the service, to a risk. A delay in the promised delivery of the new service may negatively impact the committed schedule towards its client. In order to accept such dependencies across the organization, a fundamental level of *trust* must exist within the IT organization. Management must invest every effort to sustain this trust level, on the one hand, by having project teams deliver on time and, on the other hand, by accepting a project delay for justifiable reasons attributable to other teams. Important elements to foster this trust culture are transparency, accountability and institutionalized quality control. Everybody should document plans, keep updating them and finally deliver against the documented plans.

Lack of trust is an important reason for building *silo-ed applications*. Developing in silos offers a high independence on the side of people, tools, technology and processes. It also leads to substantial redundancy and inconsistency of data and functionality, as well as unnecessarily high maintenance and operations cost ([Graves_08]). Not surprisingly, remediating silo-ed architectures is a key topic in most architecture programs.

Often a matrix organization is necessary for managing very large information systems. A matrix organization can only be successful with *checks and balances* as an essential ingredient of the organizational culture. Balancing power is a prerequisite to managed evolution. Business-IT alignment is more than processes and bodies as described in Chap. 3. The *cultural* challenges are much more demanding. Closer cooperation between business managers and IT-managers and better checks and balances around investment decisions, leads to better results. There is a shift from managers having full power over their own area to a more cooperation-oriented culture. This does not mean, however, that *responsibility* is not clearly assigned and reflected in the incentive systems. To be successful, managed evolution requires strong *functional lines*, such as IT architecture. Strong architectural governance creates tensions within the IT organization because developers lose their independence in technology and methods decisions. Federated architecture management (Fig. 2.13, [Gartner_07], [Ironbridge_07]) mitigates this tension by delegating power to domain and departmental architects.

The CIO must manage the following internal conflict carefully. The three IT disciplines "development", "IT operations" and "architecture" have inherently

6.2 Culture and Values

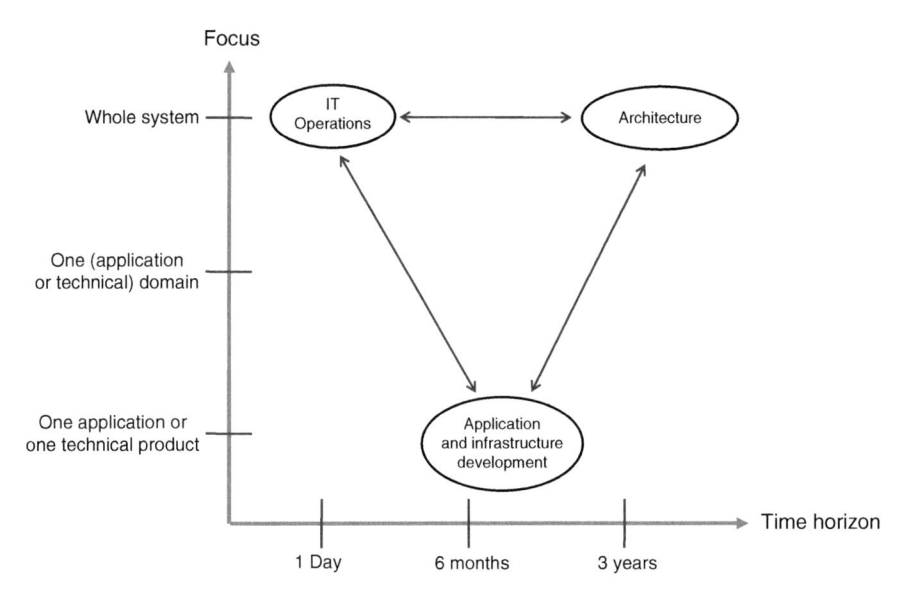

Fig. 6.1 Positioning of the three IT disciplines

different interests in terms of scope and time horizon (see Fig. 6.1). *Development* is focused on project delivery with a limited functional scope and a time horizon corresponding to the project duration of typically 6–12 months. In contrast to that, *IT operations* has the whole system in scope, because it needs to manage all the dependencies among the applications end-to-end. Its main focus is to have the system up and running all the time, leading typically to a shorter time horizon of hours to days in its management priorities. *Architecture* management, as the third function, again has the complete system with all the dependencies in scope. Its time horizon spans a full strategy period of multiple years. This is the time it takes to implement fundamental architectural change in a very large information system.

The success of managed evolution depends on a consistently implemented architecture across the whole system. The overall architecture results from thousands of micro-architecture decisions by the individual developers. Therefore, it is important that these specialists understand the overall strategy and that they are able and willing to contribute to it in their daily work. This means that they have to *think globally* and *act locally*. To support this value it is mandatory to communicate the big picture to each individual in the IT community. Valuable communications vehicles are town hall meetings, seminars and web-based communications and education tools (see Sect. 2.8).

The main success factor in managing *culture* is top management commitment and leadership to support these values. People watch decision-making and professional execution of decisions by the top management. The relevant saying for this is: "Walk the talk".

6.3 IT Organization

Success with managed evolution depends on some characteristics of the *organization* behind the very large information system. In this section we will analyze how the IT organization should be embedded into the overall business organization, how the main IT functions are best split into organizational units within the IT organization, how appropriate organizational choices strengthen the key processes and finally how organizational structure can strengthen the key cultural value of "checks and balances".

6.3.1 IT Organization Embedding

Very large organizations own and operate very large information systems and they have the corresponding requirements and the means to support such systems. By their nature, very large organizations are complex structures, divided into functional and regional sub-structures. When defining the *IT organization*, the first decision is how to embed the IT functions into the organization. The options range from a fully centralized IT department to fully federated IT functions embedded within the business areas they serve.

There are several ways to embed the IT function into the overall organization of large organizations. The right choice strongly depends on business strategy and the resulting overall organization. One often finds independent business units including the necessary IT functions for their business. In such organizations, central IT units may have the task to exploit global synergies. As an example, one often finds hybrid organizational structures where the application develop-

> "CIO leadership in a global organization is not just command and execute. We need to continually empower people with a vision and execution strategy, and position governance elements within a global framework. Part of the CIO's role is to ensure that we do not centralize too much and that our IT organization adapts to the different cultural environments we work in"
> Jeanne W. Ross, 2006

ment units report to their business units and a central CIO (Chief Information Officer) manages infrastructure and IT operations. If the organization, however, follows a more integrated strategy, one centralized IT unit is adequate. Large organizations often allocate their business functions according to customer segments, product lines, or regions. In order to ensure an adequate organizational *business-IT alignment* the IT organization should reflect the structure of the business.

This also means that the IT organization can be aligned *regionally*. In this setup, each region assumes the full responsibility for all IT functions in the corresponding region. This, obviously, does not simplify the development of global applications. If the business is organized in a *matrix organization*, IT has to reflect this complex structure as well. Because the authors restrict the discussion to the organizational

6.3 IT Organization

implications of *managed evolution* in this book, the reader is referred to existing literature about structuring global IT organizations in general (see [Weill_04], [Ross_06], [Bieberstein_08], [Calder_08] as good references).

Reuse, modularization and componentization lead to more dependencies and interaction among all IT units throughout the organization under the managed evolution strategy. Coping successfully with these dependencies is an important consideration when designing an IT organization and the corresponding governance model. The challenge is not only organizational, but also cultural. Managed evolution requires that all the IT units working on one information system follow the same strategy. The best organizational setup under these circumstances is to allocate all IT resources working on the same system to a single central IT organization with common business-IT alignment processes as described in Chap. 5. The responsibility of the central IT unit must be aligned with the system boundaries. A single, centrally managed project portfolio covers all projects modifying the same system. One architecture process covers all the IT functions contributing to the development, maintenance and the operation of the system. Cultural values necessary for managed evolution are shared across the whole organization. Skills are managed according to the same principles in the whole organization. In summary, the scope of the IT unit must be in line with the very large information system to be managed. This includes business-IT alignment, central architecture management, various application development units covering all domains and various other elements described in this book.

Often there is a desire to allocate application development closer to the business, despite the advantages of a centralized IT organization. This is possible if some preconditions are met. First, the *entire* information system must follow a single IT strategy accepted by all business and IT units. Second, it is essential to empower central architecture management and to ensure consistent project portfolio management, even if some budget authority is with

> "The consequence of a bad architecture is not constrained within the code. It spills outside to affect people, teams, processes, and timescales"
> Pete Goodliffe, 2009

the business units. A *matrix organization* with the application development units solidly reporting into business and a functional line to the central IT organization matches these ideas. It is possible to organize IT in such a way, but the authors do not recommend this for various reasons. One reason is that the direct line from the business to its development units renders a coordinated approach across the whole system more difficult. It also weakens the power of central architecture, typically leading to architectural damage. The underlying theme in choosing the appropriate organization is to find the right balance between the interests of the individual business units and the health of the overall system. It is harder to build a development organization around shared components because organizational frontiers are often cast in stone. One more reason why allocating application development units directly to the business is not advisable is that fast changing business organizations always have an impact on the IT organization. This is detrimental to the long-term orientation needed for managed evolution. With a centralized organization under a single management one can transform a business-aligned application development organization step by step to a domain-oriented organization, fostering reuse and long-term product ownership independent from organizational changes on the business side.

IT resources not linked to the very large information system may be allocated outside the central organization. One example for this is the IT of an independent branch only loosely coupled to the remainder of the organization. In such a case, responsibility for local IT is probably better with the branch manager rather than the central organization. Organizational centralization of IT does not only depend on the current structure of the systems. Often the organization is centralized first, if the strategy asks for tighter integration of formerly independent systems. This is, for example, the case immediately after a merger, when the strategy is to integrate the systems.

This concludes the discussion about the organizational relationship between business and IT. The next section discusses the inner organization of the central IT organization

6.3.2 Interaction of IT Functions

In large IT organizations we can mainly distinguish four core IT functions (Fig. 6.2):

1. Application development
2. Application maintenance and operations
3. Infrastructure development
4. Infrastructure operations

Extensive business know-how characterizes successful *application development* units in general. Deep know-how about legacy systems is particularly important to managed evolution, because understanding legacy systems is seen as the foundation for new solutions. However, know-how about legacy applications is scarce in areas with little new development, because the knowledge is continuously lost if it is not applied. In general, know-how about legacy systems is strongest in the responsible maintenance staff. This asks for combined organizational units covering both application development and maintenance within the same domain in order to foster legacy knowledge in new development projects. This is in contrast to a pure pool organization, where business analysts, application developers and IT project leaders are centralized and separated from the skills responsible for maintenance of the existing systems. This, in theory, leads to more flexible deployment of resources. In practice, however, full centralization is limited by the available know-how.

From a managed evolution point of view, it is advisable to pool different roles according to different criteria. As *project management* is a fairly generic skill, project leaders can be pooled on the level of the whole application development

6.3 IT Organization

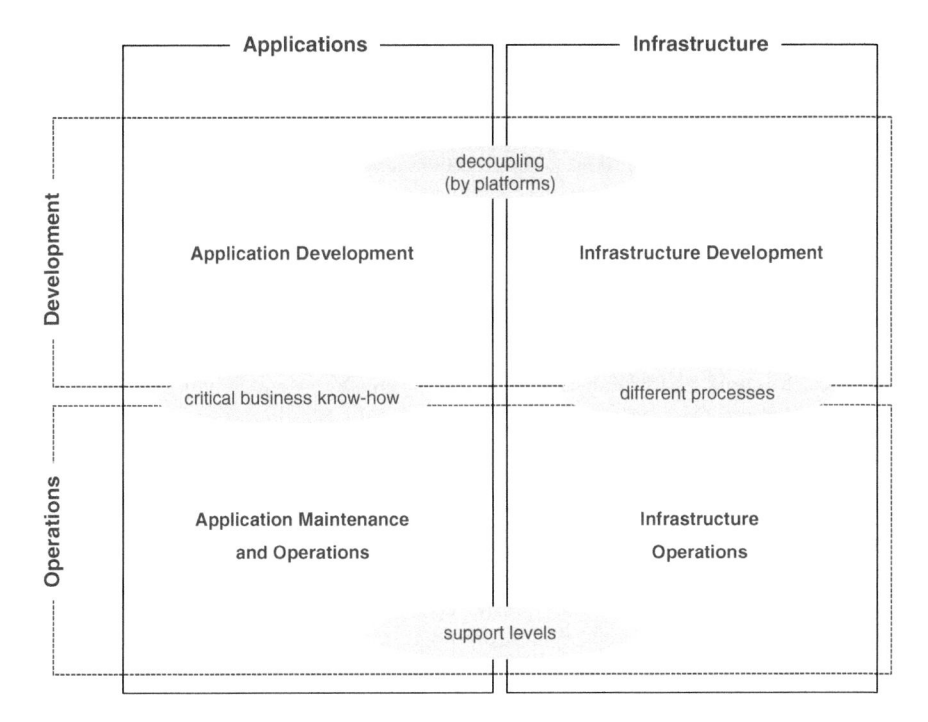

Fig. 6.2 Boundaries and interfaces between core IT functions

organization. Business analysts, application maintenance personnel and solution architects, however, should be pooled according to application domains or subdomains. Programming skills, finally, are best pooled along the application platforms (as introduced in Sect. 4.3). All pools need to maintain a critical size for flexibility. If they fall below that size, aggregation on the next higher level is needed. This set-up gives resource flexibility while maintaining key knowledge within the pools.

To support reuse and avoid redundancy, the authors advise dividing the application groups according to the *domain model* (see Side-Story 2.3) combining new development and maintenance across a domain in the same group. This best reflects the strategic intent captured in the domain model. It bundles all the know-how about a specific domain in a single unit. In practice, organizing application development along domains may create resistance, because it challenges existing structures and management hierarchies. Well settled business-IT relations and long established development teams with proprietary practices are the main barriers against the change to a domain-oriented organization.

As explained in Sect. 6.1, there are, ideally, multiple career paths in an IT organization. This also needs to be reflected in the organizational setup by involving senior project managers and technical specialists, side-by-side with the line managers, in the decision making process. This helps in making informed decisions, taking all aspects of the complex information system into account.

IT operations include both application operations and infrastructure operations. Not separating application development from application maintenance, for reasons explained above, impacts the boundary between application development and IT operations. All application maintenance functions are allocated to application development. This leads to a support process distributed across organizational units. In the widely used three level support model, IT operations covers the first two levels, while application development through its maintenance function is in charge of third level support. For infrastructure support the process looks similar, but with an interface between infrastructure development and IT operations.

The question of where to draw the exact line between infrastructure development and application development is highly debated in many IT organizations. In large organizations with a central infrastructure function and federated application development functions this question often turns into a political discussion about centralization rather than an architectural debate about the concept of infrastructure. In managed evolution, *infrastructure development* provides standardized platforms (see Sect. 4.3) and a systematically managed technology portfolio (as introduced in Sect. 4.2) to the applications. These two concepts basically determine the boundary between application development and infrastructure development and are based on architectural criteria. Historically, infrastructure is growing "upwards" continuously, taking over functionality traditionally seen as part of applications (see Fig. 4.1). This "battle zone" is called "middleware" in the market. Therefore, it is necessary to realign this boundary periodically to the evolving infrastructure concept driven by the market and architecturally captured in the platform definition.

Infrastructure development and infrastructure operations differ fundamentally in the processes they implement. Infrastructure development, on the one hand, is comparable to an IT product company with a main focus on life cycle management, versioning and release management. Its main objective is to strategically steer the technology portfolio (see Fig. 4.2)

> "Poor company structure and unhealthy development processes will be reflected in a poor software architecture"
> Pete Goodliffe, 2009

and deliver platforms in a predictable way according to strategy. Strategic technology portfolio steering and platform management is a particularly important function for managed evolution. Infrastructure operations, on the other hand, focus on operations processes such as problem management, incident management and monitoring. Often these processes are shaped according to the ITIL process model ([VanBon_07]). The main objective here is reliable service delivery and high efficiency. One key aspect here is that the organization supports an end-to-end service view of the system, hiding the complexity of component integration from the user. The focus on different processes, skills and priorities, in addition to the desire to explicitly manage the handover of responsibilities between development and operations, are the main reasons for the authors to recommend separating infrastructure development and operations into two different organizational units.

From a managed evolution point of view it is advisable to structure the core IT functions as described in Fig. 6.1 into three units: (1) One or multiple application development units, combining application development and application maintenance, structured according to the application domain model; (2) an infrastructure development unit managing the technology portfolio and the standardized platforms, organized according to the technical domain model; and (3) the IT operations unit, operating both infrastructure and application, structured according to the process model.

6.3.3 Strengthening System-Wide Consistency Through Organization

Besides the core functions discussed in the previous section, there are a number of key processes and functions instrumental to the success of managed evolution. In large organizations, such as the ones behind the very large information systems discussed in this book, well-defined processes are often more important than the mere structural information. Many IT processes remain untouched by the managed evolution strategy. This is, for example, the case for most of the operations processes. Some processes, however, need to be adapted or strengthened significantly for the managed evolution strategy to be successful. The two most important ones in this category are *architecture management* and *project portfolio management*. They are both instrumental to achieve and maintain system-wide consistency.

Currently, in many very large IT organizations, architecture management is an organically grown discipline without sufficient power to really steer architecture. In such organizations each development unit independently decides architecture with a central architecture group giving advice, at best. Strong architecture management requires adequate positioning of the function in the organization, reflecting its significance to all IT activities. Organizationally, this means a strong central architecture organization led by the Chief Architect. It is responsible for the architecture processes as described in the chapter Architecture Management (Chap. 2). The chief architect should directly report to the CIO to ensure the necessary power of execution and to support adequate checks and balances within the IT organization.

The other function highly relevant to managed evolution is Business-IT alignment as presented in Chap. 5. Strong alignment between *business* and *IT strategy* is the foundation for successful project portfolio management, ensuring strategy-oriented investments. Requirements are converted into a project portfolio in line with strategic priorities and available resources. This includes the IT organization planning its own CIO basket (see Fig. 5.3). As described earlier, project portfolio management is a continuous process at the heart of turning strategy into reality. Project portfolio management and other central IT management processes are best owned by an IT Chief Operating Officer (COO), again directly reporting to the CIO. This ensures the necessary weight and independence behind strategic planning and steering activities.

6.3.4 Checks and Balances

Managed evolution is about balancing priorities between business and IT needs, long and short-term considerations and local and system-wide aspects. This balancing act is helped by carefully *balancing power* throughout the organization. As shown in Fig. 6.1 the IT core functions have different priorities:

- *Application developers* are usually focused on a single project. This results in a scope of a few applications and a perspective of a few months, when the next large deliverable from the project is scheduled.
- *Infrastructure development* focuses on the life cycle of platforms and products in the technology portfolio. Similarly to application development, the focus of this organization is on the next release of a technical product, which often means a time-span of some months. Content-wise, the focus is on a single component or a technical domain at most. People tend to be fairly specialized in this function.
- *IT operations* has to maintain a system-wide focus in order to meet the end-to-end service expectations of the users. The time horizon is much shorter, however. There the focus is on the day-to-day operation of the systems.
- *Architecture*, similar to IT operations, needs to focus on the system as a whole. Unlike IT operations, it maintains a long-term perspective. Major architecture changes usually require multiple years for implementation.

Clearly, the different scopes and time horizons result in different views of the world. This leads to different priorities and, as a consequence, to conflicts. The clients of both IT operations and application development are mainly on the business side. Very strong client alignment may undermine the power of internally focused functions, such as infrastructure development and architecture. For managed evolution to be successful, the organization needs to establish a balance of power among the four core IT functions. It is one of the main challenges for the CIO to balance the different interests including the business in such a way that they all contribute to the long-term objectives of managed evolution.

To sum it up: In order to ensure integral management, the remit of the IT organization is at least the *entire* very large information system. Distributing responsibility for the same system across multiple, independent IT organizations hampers the managed evolution strategy considerably. IT organizations embarking on that journey should best separate development from IT operations. Maintenance remains with development in order to foster the necessary legacy know-how in development. Development is best split along domain boundaries promoting long-term product ownership and reuse. On the highest level this means a split between infrastructure and applications. Key management processes essential to managed evolution, such as architecture management and project portfolio management need to be well positioned in the organization. That and the need to balance power among development, IT operations and coordination functions suggest that the chief architect and the chief operation officer join the heads of the core functions in the management committee directly reporting to the CIO.

Chapter 7
Measuring the Managed Evolution

Summary In order to steer a very large information system in the desired direction, progress must be measurable. Measurements are required both on the strategic and the operational level. Agility as measured by the time to market and the cost to market for a given amount of functionality serves as a good strategic indicator to steer managed evolution. On the operational level, the progress of the system properties, such as the degree of standardization or the progress towards target architecture is tracked. In addition, measurements for the success of the change drivers, such as architecture, business-IT alignment, culture and skills are required. This chapter introduces some of the metrics deemed important by the authors for measuring managed evolution.

7.1 Introduction

It is not possible to steer a very large information system in a desired direction if the progress cannot be measured. Managed evolution requires a specific set of measurements to track its progress. In this chapter we introduce a number of specific *measurements*. The authors are aware that more measurements are necessary to manage very large information systems in general, such as

> "I often say that when you can measure what you are speaking about, and express it in numbers, you know something about it; but when you cannot express it in numbers, your knowledge is of a meager and unsatisfactory kind; it may be the beginning of knowledge, but you have scarcely, in your thoughts, advanced to the stage of Science, whatever the matter may be"
> William Thomsolvin, 1st Baron Kelvin, 1883

production quality measurements and operational cost measurements. The focus in this chapter is on the measurements specific to managed evolution, both on a strategic and an operational level as shown in Fig. 7.1. On the strategic level,

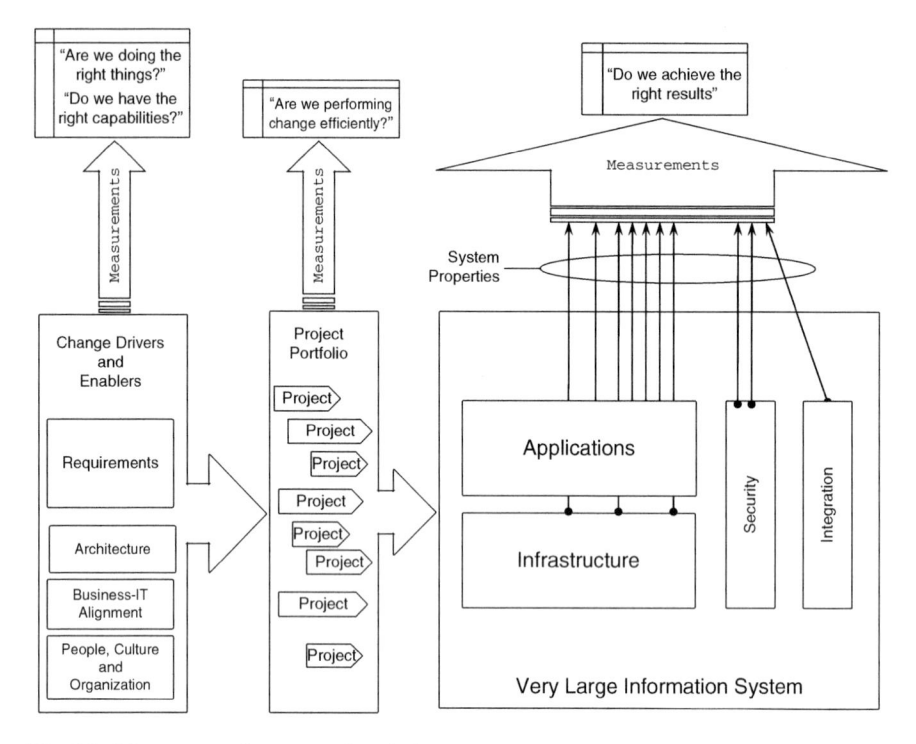

Fig. 7.1 Measurement for managed evolution

agility should remain constant or increase in spite of the continuously rising amount of functionality, increase in complexity and other factors as mentioned in Side-Story 7.6. On the operational level, measurement applies both to the change drivers and the system properties. This chapter is less precise in describing general issues in the main text and Credit Suisse specific material in side-stories, because most measurements are specific to managed evolution and, so far, only concepts from Credit Suisse are available.

Figure 7.1 shows the very large information system, represented as in Fig. 2.10. The system has a set of properties, such as size, complexity, redundancy of functions or data, the number of public services, the size of the technology portfolio, gaps between actual and target architecture, availability, performance, system value, operating cost and security features. Many of these system properties have been introduced in previous chapters. These *system properties* can be measured and their progress can be tracked using the measurement results. A number of system properties are important for managed evolution, especially architectural properties. Other properties, such as availability, performance, system value and security features are important for all large systems and do not contribute to managed evolution, although they also may contribute to system complexity. The qualities of processes that impact the system properties are also of high importance and contribute valuable measurements. Measuring system properties answers the

7.2 Measuring Change Drivers and Enablers 205

question "do we achieve the right results?" by comparing actual measurements either with earlier measurements or with target values for certain system properties.

The system is modified by *projects*. Figure 7.1 shows a project portfolio containing a set of projects that modify the system. Each modification of the system changes some of its properties. Examples include adding functionality and thus increasing size and complexity, or upgrading a number of applications to strong authentication, thus improving security. Properties of the project portfolio and of the projects can also be measured. Examples include measuring the development cost, the time to market and the amount of incremental functionality delivered by each project. Tracking the projects in the portfolio delivers planned and actual values for budget allocation, milestone dates and functional size of projects. From the basic data one can calculate a number of aggregated values, such as the investment split between architecture and business projects, investments per domain, time variance for delivery dates and finally agility, as defined later in this chapter (Sect. 7.4). Measuring project portfolio properties by comparing actual measurements either with earlier measurements or with target values answers the question "are we performing change efficiently?"

Projects are initiated, defined and selected by *change drivers* and *change enablers* as shown in Fig. 7.1. The main change driver is the *requirements* coming from the stakeholders of the system. This is the case for any evolution approach and mastering the requirements process is of great importance ([Robertson_99]). However, other change drivers, such as architecture or business-IT alignment (as shown in Chaps. 2 and 5) influence the content of the project portfolio. Performing changes to the system requires *change enablers*, such as people, skills, an adequate organization, tools and processes. If the change enablers are not adequate, the changes cannot be executed with the desired quality and speed, which restricts the project portfolio. Measuring change driver and change enabler properties answers the two questions "are we doing the right things?" and "do we have the right capabilities?" The change drivers and the change enablers therefore determine the content of the project portfolio.

> "In successful software organizations, measurement-derived information is treated as an important resource and is made available to decision makers throughout all levels of management"
> John McGarry, 2002

7.2 Measuring Change Drivers and Enablers

A number of measurements are required to cover all change drivers and enablers systematically. Measurements in this area often measure the quality and the efficiency of the underlying *processes*. Another key aspect is *portfolios*, such as the project portfolio or skills portfolio. In this section, a selection of measurements found to be particularly relevant in the context of managed evolution will be presented.

Architecture standards have a strong impact both on architectural integrity of the system and on the work of the development community. The set of architecture standards must continuously be adapted to the business strategy, the IT strategy and the relevant developments in the technology markets. Therefore, the architecture steering committee must review each standard periodically. Each standard defines a target date for the next review depending on the nature of the standard. While it may be sufficient to review generic principles every other year, technology portfolio standards need review every quarter, given the dynamic nature of the technology markets. This ensures that an up-to-date and usable standards document is maintained over time. A good measurement to be used here is the average delay of standards reviews performed by the architecture steering committee compared to the planned review dates. An example is shown in line 3.4 in the architecture scorecard (see Side-Story 7.3).

Communication between architecture and the remainder of the organization is very important to the success of architecture and therefore managed evolution as a whole. The relevant activity for this is the *architecture communication process*, as described in Sect. 2.8 and in Side-Story 2.7. Surveys have proven to be a good method to measure effectiveness of the architecture communication process, as well as other communication activities. Such surveys test the knowledge and acceptance of key architecture principles, strategies and standards with various groups of stakeholders, such as domain architects or solution architects. An example of an *architecture survey* is given in Side-Story 7.1 below.

Side-Story 7.1: Credit Suisse Switzerland Architecture Survey 2009

The objective of the architecture survey 2009 was to assess the perception, acceptance and penetration of architecture into the organization. The survey was conducted with the help of an intranet-based electronic questionnaire with 30 questions. Questions could be answered with 1 (very dissatisfied) to 10 (very satisfied). The selected participants were 56 architects (comprehensive survey), 241 Solution Engineers (= 20% random sample), 270 line managers (comprehensive survey) and 114 business project leaders and IT project leaders (= 20% random sample). The return rate in 2009 was 24.2% (152) of 628 persons invited. The results were grouped by role and by organizational unit. Some results are shown below.

The first interesting question is how much the different roles know about architecture and how they perceive the efficiency of the architecture communication process. Without knowledge of the standards, implementation by the development departments is not possible. The question asked was "How

7.2 Measuring Change Drivers and Enablers

satisfied are you with the information you receive concerning IT architecture?" The results to this question are depicted in Fig. 7.2 below. The initial results were not satisfying – as a reaction a special education program "Fit for Architecture" was started in 2007. All solution engineers had to participate in this 1-day education course.

Once architecture knowledge has been established across the organization, the next question is about the quality of collaboration between central architects and the various stakeholders. The result to the question "The *central* IT architects treat me as a partner" is shown in Fig. 7.3. To show the multi-year trend, results for 2007, 2008 and 2009 are included. Interestingly, nearly all roles see a better partnership with the central architects.

After the basic questions of *communication* and *collaboration* have been addressed, the architecture survey also serves as an instrument to gauge the acceptance of specific topics. As a further example, Fig. 7.4 shows the answers to the question "How satisfied are you with the IT architecture subject area *application platforms*?" The result was somewhat negative on a high level. The reason for the more negative feedback, especially from solution engineers, was a delay in application platform delivery that negatively impacted a number of projects.

The results of the IT architecture survey are used to improve the deliverables and the processes of central architecture.

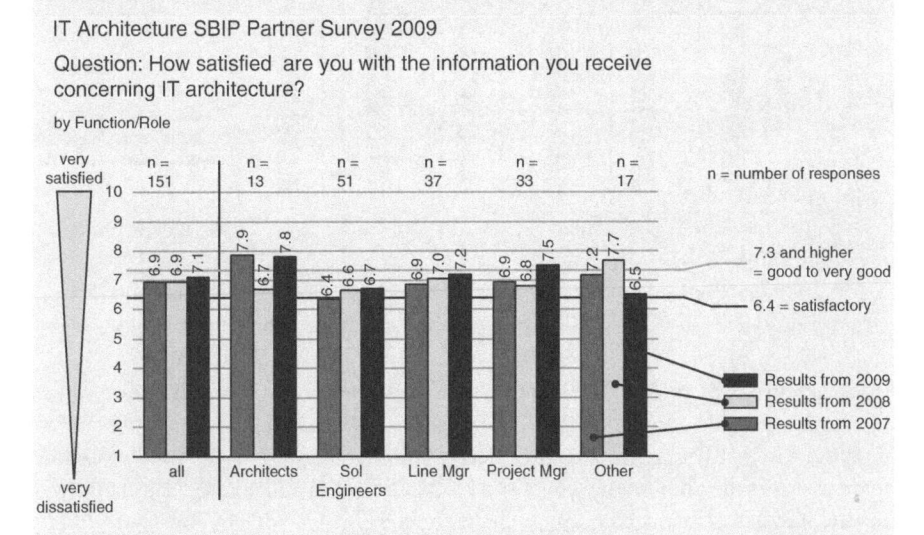

Fig. 7.2 Efficiency of the architecture communication process

Fig. 7.3 IT architecture survey result example 1

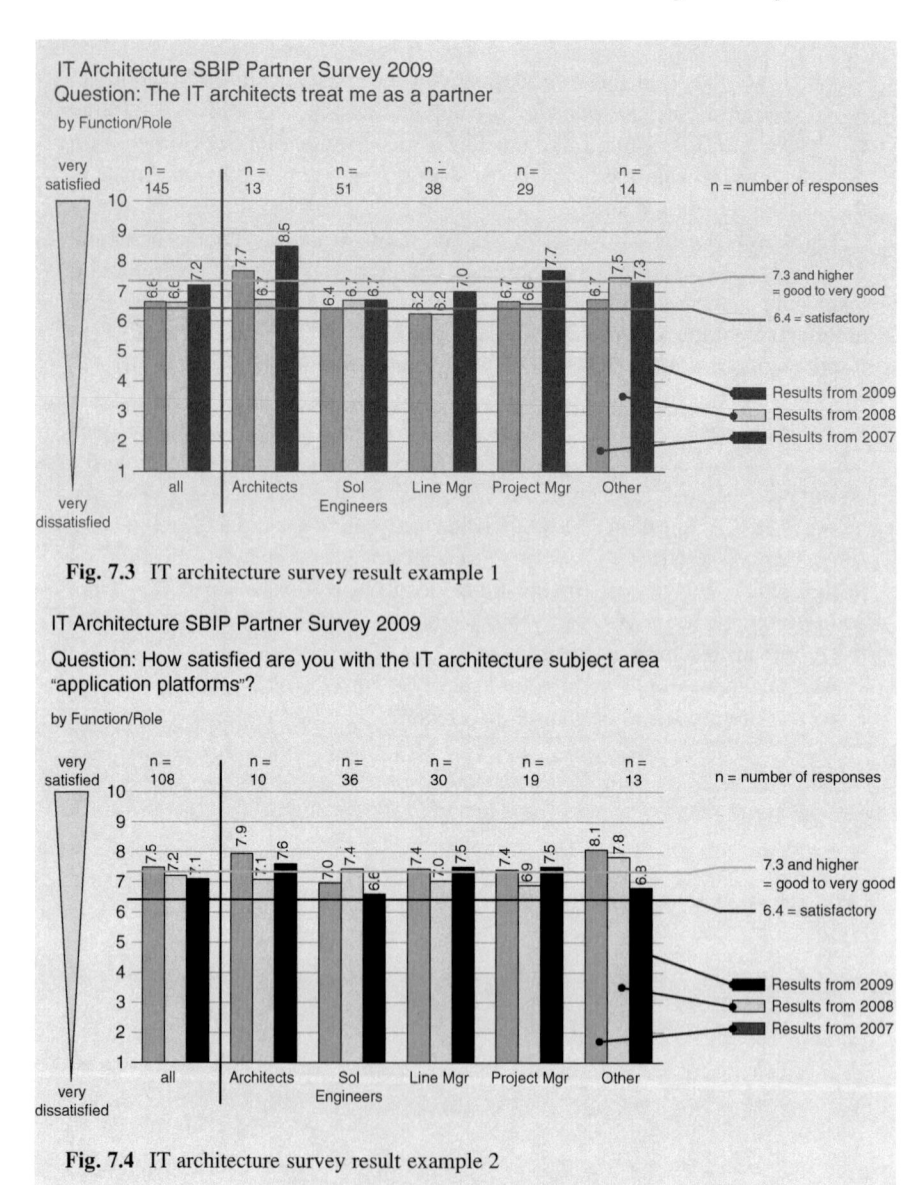

Fig. 7.4 IT architecture survey result example 2

Most development projects in Credit Suisse are quality-reviewed at each project milestone (see Side-Story 2.8). The quality review is executed by a team of experts, assembled in a project review board (PRB). Among other things, the project review board assesses the architecture proposed by the project team and requests changes if the architecture is inadequate. Such change requests are issued as formal *architecture obligations*. The obligations must be rectified by the project before the next review. If too many or severe obligations are issued, the project must rectify all

7.2 Measuring Change Drivers and Enablers

obligations before it is allowed to proceed. In certain cases, however, the best solution is not to follow some architecture standards. In such justified cases a formal *exception permit* is granted.

The project review process is best measured by calculating the average number of obligations and exception permits per project. Examples are shown in lines 3.1 and 3.2 in the architecture scorecard in Side-Story 7.3. Few *obligations* may hint at insufficient diligence in the review process. Many obligations may either be caused by inadequate standards or a problem in architecture communication. Few or no exceptions can be caused by an unnecessarily wide set of technology standards. Too many exceptions may be caused by inadequate standards.

Project portfolio reporting is a source of rich information. Projects report their planned and actual project data, such as development cost, infrastructure cost, manpower cost, cost assignments to organizational units and baskets, development time for each project phase, time-to-market, assignment to domains and amount of functionality delivered. The project data is used for many measurements. One key use of the data is to measure the gap between the planned and the actuals for each project and take the necessary corrective steps if the gap is too wide. On the strategic level, two uses of the project portfolio data are especially important. First, we can measure the overall efficiency of applying changes to the system via projects (time to market and development cost) and with that, indirectly the agility of the system. This will be explained in more detail in Sect. 7.4 below. Second, by assigning projects to baskets and domains, we can ensure the strategic business-IT alignment and measure whether the priorities set in the strategy are met in the real project portfolio.

With respect to *business-IT alignment* the following further measurements are important.

The *change the business – run the business* (CTB/RTB) *cost development* is an important indicator for the system health. The sum of CTB and RTB cost corresponds to the total IT budget (as explained in Chap. 5). If this ratio goes down it indicates that the operation of the information system becomes relatively more expensive and leaves less budget for the development of new functionality. However, it is important to compare the ratio with the IT cost target. A higher cost target improves the CTB/RTB ratio without progress in IT efficiency.

The development of system *maintenance cost* over time for individual applications, for groups of applications, for entire domains and for infrastructure yields interesting information. A disproportionate increase of maintenance cost for a domain may be an indicator that the applications in this domain are no longer fit for future (see Side-Story 5.2). An overall increase of maintenance cost together with other indicators, such as a lot of redundancy and a quick increase in the number of applications and components, hint at insufficient investments into architecture programs. Such quickly rising complexity leads to an increased maintenance effort. If this happens in a time of a decreasing overall budget, the CTB/RTB ratio may move quickly to a point where nothing is left for CTB, basically suffocating the system. So, although it may be unpopular, the only way to deal with that situation is to increase the budget and to spend it on architecture programs which reduce complexity, e.g., by eliminating redundant or unused functionality and data.

Balancing investments between projects developing new functionality and projects improving architecture is a basic principle of managed evolution, as shown in Sect. 1.5. The proportion of investments going into architecture programs is an important number to watch closely (see Sect. 1.6). Neglecting architecture improvement efforts has no immediate effect, but erodes architectural integrity and leads to the complexity trap as shown in Sect. 1.4 and in Fig. 1.5. As explained above, the complexity trap can be detected with a number of measurements. The clearest warning sign is a big increase in maintenance cost. In general, an architecture ratio of 20% is a good target to aim for. In practice, this proportion is dependent on the budget for CTB, the effectiveness of the architecture management, being able to avoid or fix architectural problems in the context of business projects and the history of the system. In a situation where little was done to manage the complexity in the past, a higher investment into architecture programs may be needed to get to a steady state. A large CTB budget may on the one hand cause a lot of additional system complexity. On the other hand, it offers many opportunities for architecture improvement in the context of individual business projects.

Another interesting aspect is the investment per domain, both into application domains (Side-Story 2.3) and technical domains (Sect. 2.6). There is a strong tendency to better fund domains with high visibility to the business, such as systems used by the sales organization or those systems supporting high revenue generating activities. Domains with less or no visibility to the business, such as infrastructure in general or basic reference data systems, tend to be funded less generously. This trend is dangerous, because it can lead to a starvation of these domains and in the long run will endanger the stability of the business operations. Tracking the investment per domain is an early warning indicator for timely investment decisions.

People and skills are important enablers of managed evolution. Lack of skills or inadequate skills not only hinder the evolution of the system, but are also the main source of quality problems. Measuring the skills portfolio is therefore indispensable for the planning of the required IT skills in the medium and long term. Skills management measurements are based on job families, technology or domain specialization within the job family where appropriate, seniority within the job family (see Side-Story 6.2), as well as the envisaged degree of outsourcing. Comparing the current staff demography to future needs as given by changes in the sourcing model, attrition, shifts in the technology portfolio, current weaknesses, future domain priorities and expected change in overall capacity, yields a target skills portfolio. Measuring the gap between the current and the target skills portfolio helps identify the necessary steps to close the gap. As the skills portfolio is probably the change enabler that is hardest to steer on short notice, careful long-term planning is necessary.

7.3 Measuring System Properties

While in the section above the focus was on measuring the change drivers and enablers, this section will measure the actual change in the system itself by monitoring a number of *system properties* relevant to managed evolution. These

7.3 Measuring System Properties

include *architectural properties*, such as system complexity, the amount of redundancy, the reuse of services, the number of technical products in infrastructure and the number of end-of-life technologies, among others. System properties come in two flavours. The first are fundamental properties that remain important for ever, such as the degree of standardization, reuse factors, system complexity and redundancy. The second set of properties is related to gaps between reality and target architecture. They are measured until the gap is closed. After that they are no longer important. Examples of such measurements include removing specific old technologies from the technology portfolio or the mandatory use of specific interfaces.

In this section, only a choice of system properties and their measurement will be discussed. They are grouped in properties related to application architecture (see Sect. 2.5), to integration architecture (see Chap. 3) and to infrastructure (see Chap. 4).

Management of the complexity of the *application landscape* is important. Experience shows a tendency to develop new applications and a certain reluctance to remove old applications from the system. Very often the reason is that a newly developed or bought application covers only parts of the functionality of one or several older applications, so that the older applications cannot be removed. Removing these older applications requires some additional investment, which is difficult to justify because no immediate business benefit is visible. However, the *system complexity* increases unnecessarily with each redundant application, leading to increased maintenance and operations cost. One way to measure application landscape complexity is the number of "net new applications". The net new applications number is defined as the difference of newly introduced applications minus the number of removed applications in a given time period. Limiting the number of net new applications is a powerful instrument to force the development departments to identify redundancy, unused functionality or data and obsolete applications. Once identified, standard software engineering methods, such as *refactoring* ([Fowler_99], [Feathers_07], [Fields_09]) can be used to clean up applications. In the experience of the authors, at the beginning of managed evolution (see Sect. 1.7) this is a very profitable activity with many low hanging fruits.

Another interesting measurement for the application landscape is the degree of adoption of specific, mandatory *standards*. Very often, historically grown application landscapes use different standards for the same function. Defining one standard as mandatory and forcing the applications to gradually convert to this standard has very positive effects on simplicity and transparency. In general, standard adoption is measured as the ratio of the number of applications implementing the standard to the overall number of applications to which the standard is applicable. This indicator should converge to zero over time. Often these measurements are temporary in nature, measuring the adoption of a new standard up to the point where it is fully implemented and the ratio has reached zero. Note that this measurement is not related to the project review process as shown above. It statically analyzes the current degree of standards adoption across the whole system. Not only exceptions, but also changing standards may lead to non-standard applications. This is typically the case with aging technology standards reaching the end of their life and being replaced by newer standards.

The yearly *domain assessment* (see Side-Story 5.2) gives a wealth of information about the individual applications, such as "fitness for future" and "fitness for purpose". The number of applications which are not "fit for future" or not "fit for purpose" in a domain is an important measurement and is one indicator for the required investments in the domain.

For *integration architecture*, the number of services, their runtime usage numbers and their reuse factors are good indicators. All services are registered in the service management system (see Sect. 3.6 and Side-Story 3.6). The registration also includes the provider and all consumers. Therefore, reliable numbers for reuse are available. The usage of services on the enterprise service bus is monitored for capacity planning and accounting purposes. As an example, Side-Story 7.2 presents the CORBA-based service reuse in Credit Suisse.

Side-Story 7.2: CORBA-Based Service Seuse

Credit Suisse measures the progress of integration architecture by monitoring a number of indicators across the different integration mechanisms (see Sect. 3.4). With measurement data reaching all the way back to the year 2000, the integration based on CORBA middleware ([Pope_98]) is a rich source of data to understand the long-term progress of service architecture.

Figure 7.5 plots a number of key indicators over the time from Q1/2005 to Q1/2009. The bars indicate the number of CORBA calls for the last month in each quarter. In December 2008, CORBA-based services account for 411 million calls. The continuous growth of this indicator demonstrates the widespread adoption of integration architecture.

The reuse of existing services is essential for the business case of integration architecture. The triangles represent the ratio of reused services compared to the total number of public services offered on the enterprise service bus. This curve is settling slightly above 50%, meaning that every second service is used by more than one application.

The bullets represent the average reuse factor. For each service the number of applications using it is counted. Each application counts only once, independently of how many times it uses the service. Intra-application reuse, i.e. if the service is used more than once within the same application, the calculation includes only the first use. This results in a reuse factor for each service. Averaging this factor across all services leads to the average reuse factor. This value is settling around 4. A deeper analysis of the reuse factor distribution shows that it is very uneven. A bit less then half the services aren't reused at all, while some services have reuse factors of more than 100 in an environment with some 100's of applications. The authors

7.3 Measuring System Properties

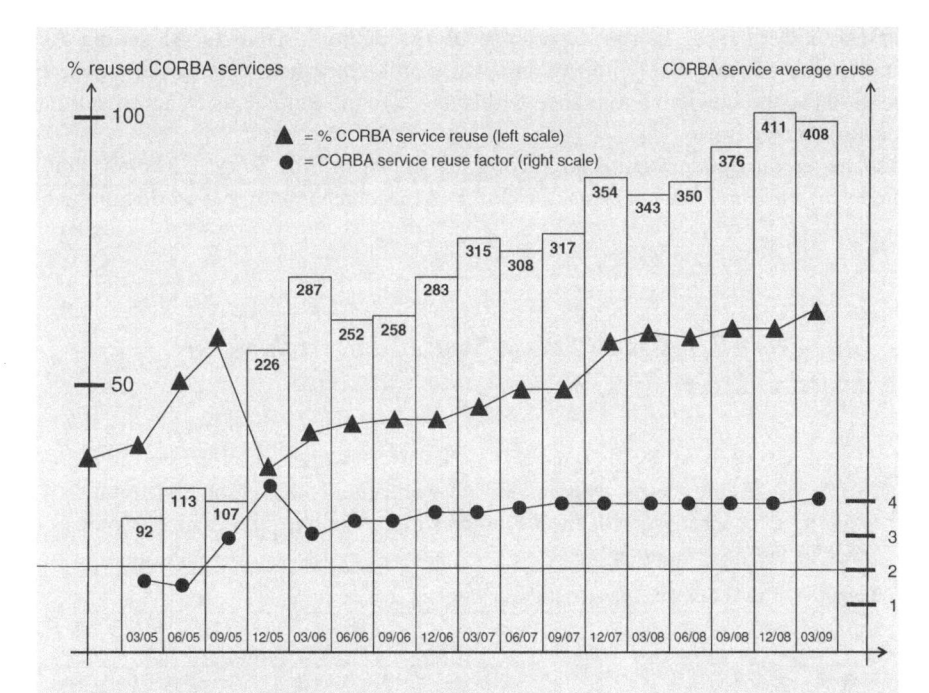

Fig. 7.5 CORBA-based services reuse statistics

believe that reuse factors could be higher, if the service architecture had not developed organically.

One number, that isn't shown on the graph, is the total number of different CORBA-based services. In Credit Suisse it has settled around a total of 1'000 services, representing the complete functionality of a universal banking system.

An important architectural property measuring efficient use of infrastructure is the *standard platform usage*: Applications can either be developed on standard platforms (see Sect. 4.3) or on special-engineered run-time environments. A strategic objective of managed evolution is to have a large number of applications execute on standard platforms for efficiency reasons and only allow special engineering in justified cases. Two useful metrics are the percentage of applications using standard platforms and the percentage of servers running standard platforms. Examples are shown in lines 1.1 and 1.2 in the architecture scorecard (Side-Story 7.3). The power of using application platforms is demonstrated quantitatively in Side-Story 7.6 below.

Some of the measurements mentioned above are based on subjective assessments. This has to be taken into account when measurements are used directly to assess performance. In the experience of the authors, naive target setting for individuals can negatively impact the quality of the measurements, because people tend to use the inevitable tolerance with subjective measurements to improve their performance report.

The Credit Suisse architecture scorecard shown in Side-Story 7.3 below illustrates the measurement concepts introduced in this chapter with real-world numbers.

Side-Story 7.3: Credit Suisse Switzerland Architecture Scorecard

The Credit Suisse Switzerland IT architecture scorecard is shown in the Table 7.1. Figures below refer to the IT organization in the region Switzerland. Due to a recent merger of the IT organizations, global figures for the other regions are not yet available.

Table 7.1 Credit Suisse Switzerland IT architecture scorecard

Key performance indicator	06/08	09/08	12/08	03/09	06/09
IT Architecture Scores					
Managed Evolution Strategy					
0.1 Agility	0.15	0.17	0.17	0.25	0.25
0.2 Cost per UCP (kCHF/UCP)	6.5	6.2	6.2	5.2	5.1
0.3 Time-to-Market per UCP (Days/UCP)	1.0	1.0	0.9	0.8	0.8
Use of Standard Application Platforms					
1.1 Percentage of application platform usage (%)	69.0	68.0	69.0	69.0	69.0
1.2 Servers on runtime platforms (%)	79.0	82.0	83.0	84.0	84.0
1.3 Applications on one single application platform	441	459	470	478	485
1.4 Applications on more than one application platform	84	81	86	90	89
Service Architecture Implementation					
2.1 CORBA exchanges reused (% reused)	52.2	54.6	53.7	56.2	56.7
2.2 Average reuse factor per CORBA exchange	3.8	3.8	3.7	4.0	3.8
2.3 Number of mainframe CORBA exchange calls per month (in Millions of calls)	350	376	411	408	393.1
2.4 Number of messages per month (in Millions of calls)	44	67	60	53	51
2.5 Number of applications using the standard workflow infrastructure	18	17	17	16	16
IT Security Standardization					
3.1–3.4: Four KPI's tracking the progress of security architecture implementation	–	–	–	–	–
IT Architecture Management and Process KPIs					
4.1 Average number of architecture conditions per project	1.551	1.512	0.673	0.816	0.824
4.2 Average number of architecture exception permits per project	0.000	0.003	0.041	0.026	0.029
4.3 Central architecture support for projects (% of architecture workforce)	31.3	33.3	36.6	34.1	36.4
4.4 Average delay of submission of concepts, models and standards to chief architect steering committee review (days)	–	15	42	30	45

7.3 Measuring System Properties

The individual lines in the scorecard have the following meaning:

- Lines 0.1, 0.2 and 0.3 contain metrics for the managed evolution (*agility*), such as cost and time to market per Use Case Point (UCP) and are described in Sect. 7.4 below. They are included here for the sake of completeness.
- Line 1.1: Percentage of applications using *application platforms* (see Sect. 4.3). This percentage shows how the adoption of application platforms is progressing over time.
- Line 1.2: Percentage of servers based on *runtime platforms* (see Sect. 4.3). This percentage shows how the adoption of runtime platforms is progressing. This percentage is always higher than the number in line 1.1, because all application platforms build on top of run-time platforms. So each application on an application platform automatically counts for the run-time platform, too.
- Line 1.3: Applications can have components on more than one application platform, such as a user interface on JAVA application platform (JAP, see Side-Story 4.4) and business logic on the mainframe. This number shows how many applications use only one single platform.
- Line 1.4: This number shows how many applications use more than one platform. The usage may be mainframe platform + Java application platform, or the mainframe + data warehouse platform + Java application platform.
- Line 2.1: Percentage of reused CORBA-based services. A service counts as reused if more than one application uses the same service. Intra-application reuse doesn't count on this level. As the adoption of service architecture and reuse progresses, this percentage increases.
- Line 2.2: Average reuse number per CORBA exchange. The progress of integration architecture can be measured by the *service reuse factor* ([Hagen_06]), shown in Side-Story 7.2.
- Line 2.3: Number of mainframe CORBA calls per month (in millions of calls). This is another indicator for the success of the integration architecture and shows the increasing usage of services by applications.
- Line 2.4: Number of messages transmitted per month (in millions of calls). This figure shows the increasing use of asynchronous messaging, indicating the success of the messaging part in the Credit Suisse Enterprise Service Bus CSXB (see Sect. 3.7).
- Line 2.5: Number of applications using the standard workflow infrastructure. This number declined because a family of applications started using their own workflow infrastructure.

3.1–3.4: Four (confidential) KPI's tracking the progress of ty architecture implementation.

4.1 Average number of architecture obligations per project. tecture obligations (see Side-Story 2.8) are conditions or binding recommendations imposed on a project by the project review board. This is an indicator for the quality of the architecture implementation process (see Sect. 2.8).
- Line 4.2: Average number of architecture exception permits per project. This is an architecture process indicator covering both architecture definition as well as architecture implementation.
- Line 4.3: Central architecture support for projects (% of architecture workforce). Central architects (see 2.9) primarily develop IT architecture standards. However, they are also supporting projects. This figure indicates what percentage of the work of central architects was dedicated to specific architecture project support.
- Line 4.4: Average delay of re-submission of standards to the chief architect steering committee review board. This figure indicates the average delay between scheduled resubmission date and actual resubmission date.

7.4 Measuring Managed Evolution Strategy

As introduced in 1.5, managed evolution is measured as an evolution curve in a coordinate system with the two axes *business value* and *agility* (Fig. 1.5). The two properties *"business value"* and *"agility"* of the system have been chosen by the authors as the key metrics for managed evolution. Note that this choice is typical for a profit-oriented organization with high dependence on its information systems, such as financial institutions.

Agility is used as the metric on the *y*-axis of the managed evolution coordinate system. The term "agility" in the literature covers mostly software development technologies and processes (see, e.g., [Shore_07]). In the context of managed evolution, "agility" must be seen in a wider context: Implementing new requirements in a very large information system involves not only software development, but embraces the entire system, such as infrastructure, applications, processes, governance, people and behaviour. To reflect this, the following definition holds in this context:

Agility is the ability to efficiently implement required changes.

Changes to the system are applied in the context of projects contained in the project portfolio. Each project incrementally changes agility and business value (Fig. 7.6). The contribution of an individual *project* to business value can be measured through its business case. Agility is a property of the whole system and

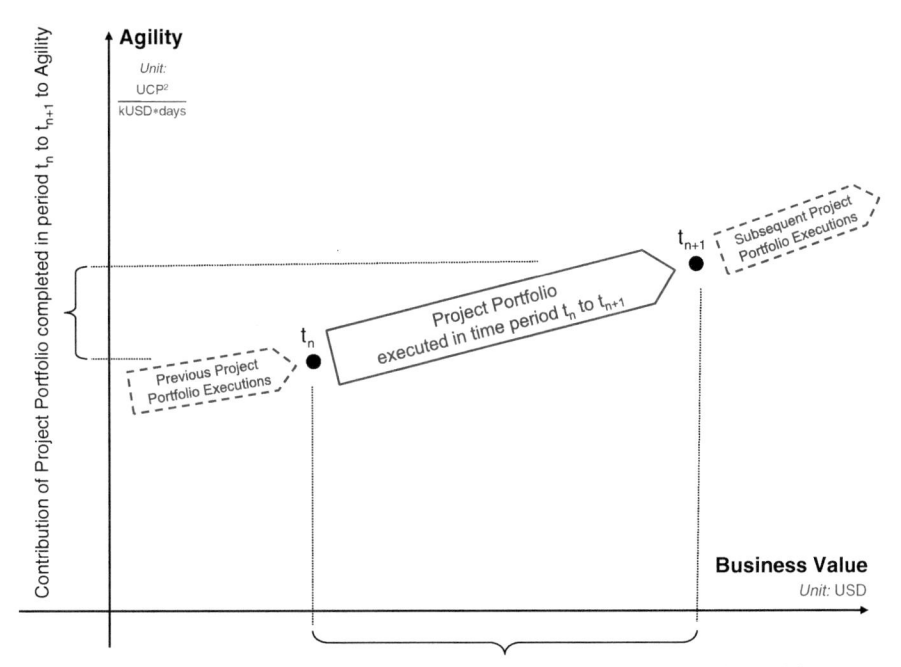

7.4 Measuring Managed Evolution Strategy

Fig. 7.6 System evolution mechanism

the corresponding IT organization. Agility can be measured by monitoring implementation efficiency across a representative *project portfolio*. The projects within that portfolio need to cover large parts of the system and the organization. Note that the contribution of an individual *project* to agility cannot be measured. The aim in the remainder of this section is to quantify the concepts of *business value* and *agility* and their measurement.

A representative project portfolio results in a certain business value and exposes the agility of the system. Both business value and agility can be quantified. The progress of business value and agility over time across the whole system shows the strategic success of managed evolution. As we are interested in seeing progress of the whole system over time, the project portfolios consist of projects completed within a given time period starting at time t_n and ending at time t_{n+1} as shown in Fig. 7.6.

One way of measuring *business value* is the *Net Present Value* (NPV). It is based on the fact that each project requires some up-front investment and that the deliverables from the project allow the business to either generate revenue or reduce cost. The NPV is the sum of all discounted cash flows

> "The software industry has become crucial to the global economy. It is a large and rapidly growing industry in its own right, and its secondary impact on the remainder of the economy is disproportionate"
> David G. Messerschmitt, Clemens Szyperski, 2003

attributed to the project. Details how to calculate NPV can be found in any financial management textbook, such as [Remenyi_00]. The sum of all NPVs of the individual projects in the project portfolio results in the business value of the project portfolio. In practice, the process of determining the business value of projects is faced with a number of challenges, such as pre- and post calculation, proper attribution of savings and revenues to projects and choosing the right interest rates when discounting the cash flows to properly reflect cost of capital and project execution risk. As this topic has been discussed in many other texts it will not be pursued further in this book.

Agility, the second dimension in the managed evolution coordinate system, is less easy to measure. The proposed measurement method is indirect. It is based on measuring how efficiently new functionality can be added to the system. For this we measure two properties of all projects in a representative portfolio:

1. The *time to market* of the projects
2. The *project cost*.

Important is the set of both values of *time to market* and *project cost* across the entire project portfolio. The system is *highly agile* if these values are low. In other words, new functionality can be introduced in short time and at low cost. If adding functionality requires much time and generates high cost, the system has a *low agility*. In systems with low agility all projects are penalized; in the worst case up to immobilization (see evolution curve in Fig. 1.6). Improving agility is therefore a worthwhile objective in an organization with intense development activity.

Time to market TtM for a project is measured as the number of *elapsed calendar days* between the formal start date of a project and the date when the project result is delivered and accepted (see Fig. 7.7). The unit of TtM is a calendar day.

The *project cost* DevC for a project is measured as the amount of all costs incurred by the project from the formal start date of the project to the end date of the project (see Fig. 7.7). DevC includes all internal and external costs, such as manpower, consulting, development system cost, software licenses, etc. This includes a warranty period of 3–6 months after delivery. During the warranty period the complete documentation must be delivered and all corrective maintenance for project results is charged to the project. The unit of DevC is kUSD (1,000 US $) or any preferred currency.

In practice, projects vary very much in functional *size*, i.e. some projects deliver a small amount of functionality and other projects deliver very large amounts of functionality. Therefore, the projects also show very different values for DevC and TtM. It would not lead to a useful metric to just sum up time to market and development cost. Therefore, project portfolios must be *normalized* by their *functional size* in order to become comparable. In order to calculate agility for a project portfolio we need to measure the three quantities "time to market", "development cost" and "functional size" for each project in the portfolio.

Measuring software attributes and properties, especially size, have a long tradition. It started by measuring and normalizing the number of *source lines of code* ([Boehm_00], [Fenton_97]), succeeded later by *function points* ([Garmus_01], [Ebert_07]). A more modern approach related to functional size but taking into

7.4 Measuring Managed Evolution Strategy

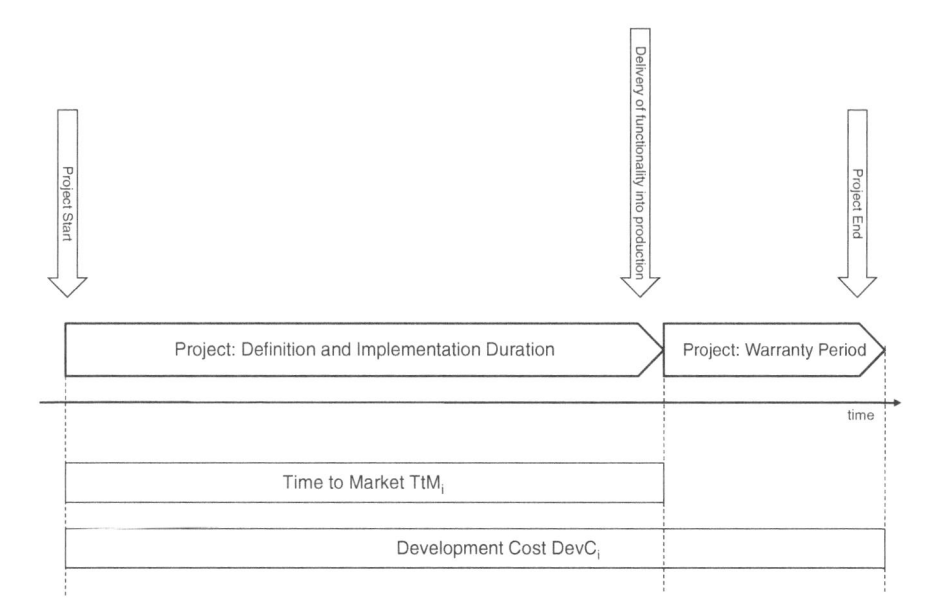

Fig. 7.7 Measurement periods for time to market and development cost

account modern software engineering methods are *use case points* (UCPs, [Fronhoff_06], [Fronhoff_07], [Fronhoff_08], [Anda_08]). Use case points are based on the notion of a *use case* ([Jacobson_92], [Schneider_98], [Cockburn_01], [Denney_05], [Fowler_04]). Use cases are an important part of requirements specifications in most modern project management methodologies. Once the use cases are carefully formulated, the *size* of each use case can be established by assigning the number of use case points according to a counting template. Various *measurement methods* can be found in the literature. However, each organization needs to adapt the measurement method to its own project types. An example from Credit Suisse Switzerland is shown in the Side-Story 7.4. The unit of size is the number of use case points (#UCP).

Side-Story 7.4: Credit Suisse Switzerland UCP Measurement

The Credit Suisse Switzerland use case point measurement method is shown in Fig. 7.8. Each new requirement is broken down into use cases and accesses to business objects. Once the use cases are fully documented, they are assessed. Each use case is classified as simple, medium or complex according to a list of assessment criteria. This assessment of each use case gives the first contribution to the unadjusted number of use case points (short: UC) for the use case. Next, the impact on business objects (creation, modification, number of attributes etc.) is determined, again classified as simple, medium or complex according to a list of assessment criteria. This result gives the second contribution to the unadjusted number of use case points (short: BO) for the same use case. The sum of UC and BO is the total unadjusted number of use case points for a certain functional specification defined in the respective use case.

Next, the technical complexity of the implementation is investigated. A number of predefined complexity factors, such as distributed data processing, required performance, reusability factor, portability and concurrency are assessed. Each complexity factor contributes to the system complexity and a *technical complexity factor* is computed, again from a list of assessment criteria and weights. The unadjusted number of UCPs, i.e. UC + BO from above, is then multiplied by the technical complexity factor (short: TC) leading to the total number of adjusted use case points #UCP. The total of #UCP for all the use cases implemented by a project is the functional size #UCP delivered by the project.

The #UCP is first calculated during specification and again after full implementation for the whole scope of the project. The calculation at specification time serves as an input to the cost estimate for the project. The post-calculation after implementation results in the real functional size of the project. This procedure, as applied in the IT organization in the region Switzerland, results in a functional project size for each suitable project.

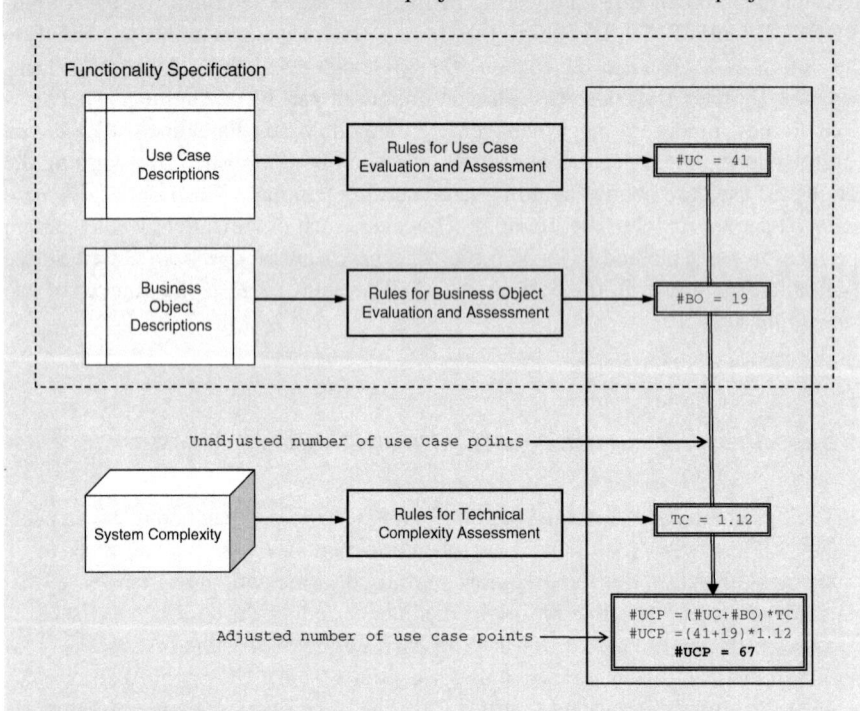

Fig. 7.8 Credit Suisse Switzerland use case point measurement method

7.4 Measuring Managed Evolution Strategy

There are two challenges with the UCP counting method. First, the number of UCPs is determined by a manual procedure. This leads to a certain level of subjectivity, which must be mitigated by training the people responsible for applying the method. Second, measuring UCPs depends on the type of project. For projects building new functionality in a typical application development context the method is well suited and produces a reliable count of UCPs. Other project types, like projects *replacing* existing functionality, projects integrating third party software, or projects developing infrastructure, are not well suited for this method. This is a problem, if we need sizes for every project in the portfolio. In order to determine agility it is, however, sufficient to work with a representative subset of the portfolio. So, taking only projects with a valid UCP count into consideration for agility calculation is sufficient.

The individual data points TtM_i, $DevC_i$ and $size_i$ of the projects can be seen as statistical variables with a significant random influence. The random influence is rooted in many contributing factors to these data points, such as variance in the skills and productivity of the people forming the project, variance in management attention for the project, variance due to unforeseen delays because of unavailability of infrastructure, or variance in the precision of specifications. To smooth out the variance, the individual data points in the project portfolio must be averaged. If the set is sufficiently large in number, the variance will be reduced and the averaged result becomes significant. Averaging is done by summing up the time-to-market and the development cost of all projects in the portfolio. To produce normalized results, allowing comparison of two portfolios, the total time-to-market and development cost is divided by the total amount of functionality produced by the portfolio. Averaged *time to market* $Av_{TPj}TtM$ for the projects P_i to P_{i+n} in the portfolio is:

$$Av_{TPj}TtM = (TtM_i + TtM_{i+1} + TtM_{i+2} + TtM_{i+3} + \ldots + TtM_{i+n})/(size_i + size_{i+1} + size_{i+2} + size_{i+3} + \ldots + size_{i+n})$$

$Av_{TPj}TtM$ is the measure for the average time to market for one unit (1 UCP) of functionality produced by the project portfolio P_i to P_{i+n}.

Averaged *development cost* $Av_{TPi}DevC$ for the projects P_i to P_{i+n} in the portfolio is:

$$Av_{TPi}DevC = (DevC_i + DevC_{i+1} + DevC_{i+2} + DevC_{i+3} + \ldots + DevC_{i+n})/(size_i + size_{i+1} + size_{i+2} + size_{i+3} + \ldots + size_{i+n}).$$

$Av_{TPi}DevC$ is the measure for the average development cost for one unit (1 UCP) of functionality produced by the project portfolio P_i to P_{i+n}.

The number and type of projects in the portfolio must be chosen in such a way, that the statistical values $Av_{TPj}TtM$ and $Av_{TPi}DevC$ have *statistical relevance* ([Rumsey_03], [Hill_06], [Spiegel_00]). Comparing individual projects on the basis of $TtM_i/size_i$ or $DevC_i/size_i$ does not make sense, as the variance – due to many factors – is too high.

The agility measured by the portfolio under consideration is computed as:

$$\text{Agility} = 1/(\text{Av}_{\text{TPj}}\text{TtM} * \text{Av}_{\text{TPi}}\text{DevC}).$$

The unit of agility is #UCP^2/(day*kUSD). The unit results from first dividing both TtM and DevC by size which results in day/#UCP and kUSD/#UCP, then multiplying both and finally taking the inverse.

Agility is *high* if (day*kUSD) is *low* per #UCP^2, i.e. if the time to market and the development cost per UCP are low. This is intuitively clear. Improving the agility of the very large information system thus gives lower time to market and lower development cost per unit of functionality. Agility is a very powerful metric: It covers the *complete* system, such as the development capability, the infrastructure provisioning speed, management and resource planning, effectiveness of development tools, skills of people etc. Any of these areas can introduce delays and/or additional cost and thus negatively influence the TtM and DevC measurements of the project under consideration. Representative results from Credit Suisse Switzerland are shown in Side-Story 7.5.

Side-Story 7.5: Credit Suisse Switzerland Agility Measurements for 17 Quarters

Note that in this side-story the unit for cost is Swiss Francs (CHF). The TtM/size and DevC/size measurements for 17 quarters in Credit Suisse Switzerland are shown in the Fig. 7.9. The *x*-axis is the time axis: 2005/06 denotes the second quarter of the year 2005 and so on. The *y*-axis shows the values of TtM/size and DevC/size. Each value represents the average over *all* projects completed in the 12 months before the date indicated, i.e. 2005/06 covers the time period 1.7.2004–30.6.2005. Proceeding forward in quarters on the time axis 2005/09 then covers the time period 1.10.2004–31.9.2005. This *averaging technique* is known as *sliding window* with a window size of one year and a shift period of one quarter. This method was chosen because looking only at the projects completed within the quarter would not have yielded a representative project portfolio and because the number of suitable projects was too low.

Calculating 1/[(TtM/size)*(DevC/size)] as explained above leads to the development for agility over time and is shown in Fig. 7.10. For the respective quarters the number of projects with dependable data[1] was between 24 and 38 (average: 31) and the implemented functional size was between 7'197 and 20'549 UCPs (average: 15'517).

---

[1] Only a small fraction of projects have dependable data at the time being.

7.4 Measuring Managed Evolution Strategy

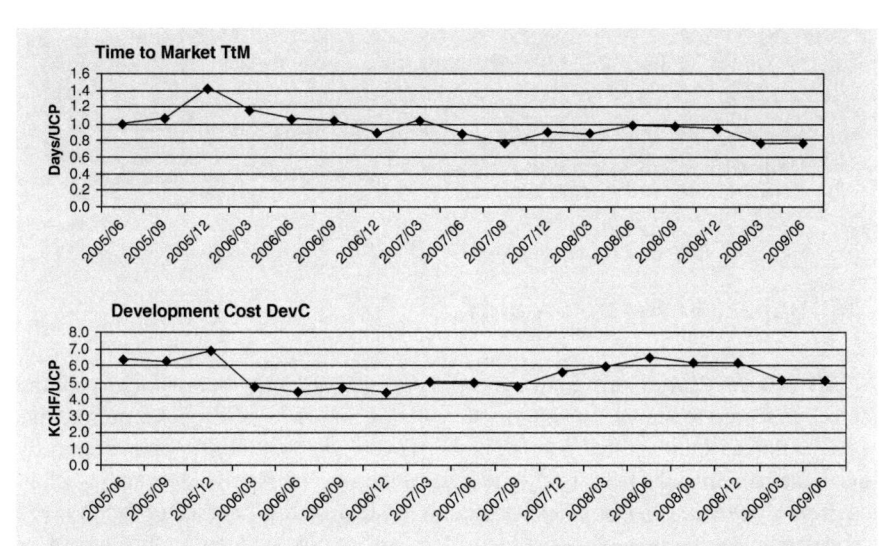

Fig. 7.9 Credit Suisse Switzerland time to market and development cost for 17 quarters

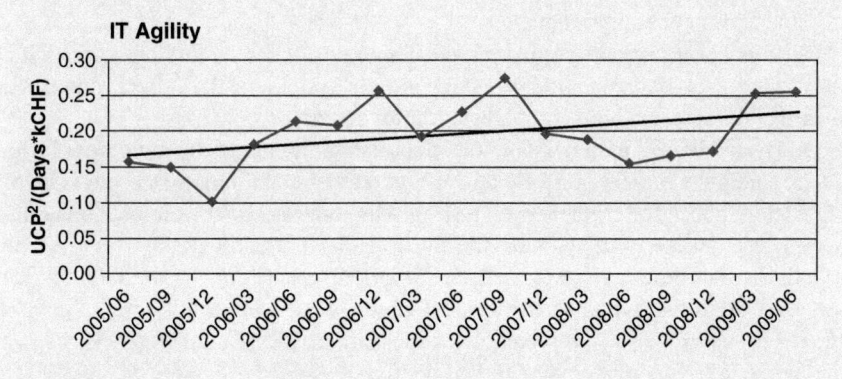

Fig. 7.10 Credit Suisse Switzerland agility measurements for 17 quarters

The measurements show continuous improvement of agility as illustrated by the trend line in Fig. 7.10. This positive result was achieved in spite of the growth in functionality, higher investments in quality assurance resulting in better system stability, impact of inflation and more consequent reporting of project overhead. On the other hand, activities like offshoring, better development tools and more stringent architecture management helped to improve agility.

The average number of projects per time period in Fig. 7.10 is statistically at the lower end to deliver stable results. This is manifest in the wide variance of the values in Fig. 7.9. Over the long run, however, the trend is stable. Reasons for this high variance include the different size mix of projects, process stability and the subjectivity of the size estimation (#UCPs).

Despite the challenges with measurement, the authors are convinced that the results are meaningful in the context of the overall system.

7.5 Impact Factors on Agility

Agility in a very large information system depends on a number of *factors*. Some factors expected to increase agility include the quality and stability of requirements specifications, highly skilled people, powerful development tools, good support by line management and a healthy architecture of the system. Applied research work in the area of *software development productivity* identified a number of factors (see e.g. [Boehm_00]). Factors assumed to decrease agility include badly defined or incompletely implemented processes, delays in infrastructure provisioning, insufficient standardization, unmanaged data redundancy, and - last but not least - unstable or fuzzy requirements.

Little is known about the quantitative impact of these factors on agility. Such knowledge would enable the organization to systematically direct investment towards the factors promising the best improvement.

One possible way to understand the quantitative impact of the individual factors is to segment the project portfolio into *sub-portfolios* according to one single factor. The factor chosen for segmentation reflects a hypothesis about its impact on agility. A typical example is to segment the portfolio by project size. By doing so, the hypothesis that time to market is better for large projects due to parallel work, can be tested. Also the hypothesis that development cost is lower for smaller projects due to less coordination overhead, can be tested. A significant difference in agility among the sub-portfolios may validate the hypothesis.

Agility calculations from such sub-portfolios must be interpreted carefully. First, the number of projects in any sub-portfolio must be large enough to deliver statistically relevant raw data. Second, many factors are *correlated*, which can significantly corrupt the interpretation of the calculations. Experience shows that the size distribution of a sub-portfolio strongly influences the resulting agility. Therefore, any segmentation according to another factor has to take size distribution in the sub-portfolios into account.

The method described above can be improved by using the statistical technique of *single factor analysis* (ANOVA, [Hill_06]). For analyzing correlated factors the *multivariate statistical factor analysis* based on the general linear model ([Dobson_02], [Ravishanker_02]) can be used. The multivariate statistical factor analysis returns the percentage of impact on agility for each factor and also shows if hidden factors are present. However, the authors have no significant results from applying this method.

7.5 Impact Factors on Agility

As an example demonstrating the single factor analysis approach, the impact of development based on application and run-time platforms (see 4.3) against development using special engineering is shown in Side-Story 7.6.

Side-Story 7.6: Credit Suisse Single Factor Analysis for Agility

For this side-story, all projects used for the agility calculation in Side-Story 7.5 were segmented into two project *sub-portfolios*: First containing all projects using standard application or run-time platforms; and second containing all projects using special engineering. The development cost per UCP and the time to market per UCP were then calculated separately for each project sub-portfolio, resulting in different agilities.

Note that agility calculation over a representative project portfolio as shown in Sect. 7.4 delivers the agility of the *entire* system and organization. When working with sub-portfolios which are segmented according to specific criteria, the agility calculation delivers agility comparisons with respect to these criteria and not for the entire system.

For the two sub-portfolios "platforms" and "special engineering" the results are shown in Fig. 7.11 ([Kradolfer_09]). Figure 7.11 shows, in an impressive way, the power of platforms: The sub-portfolio containing projects based on platforms shows an agility of 0.24 versus the sub-portfolio containing projects based on special engineering with an agility of 0.09. Thus, project portfolios implemented on platforms provide an advantage resulting

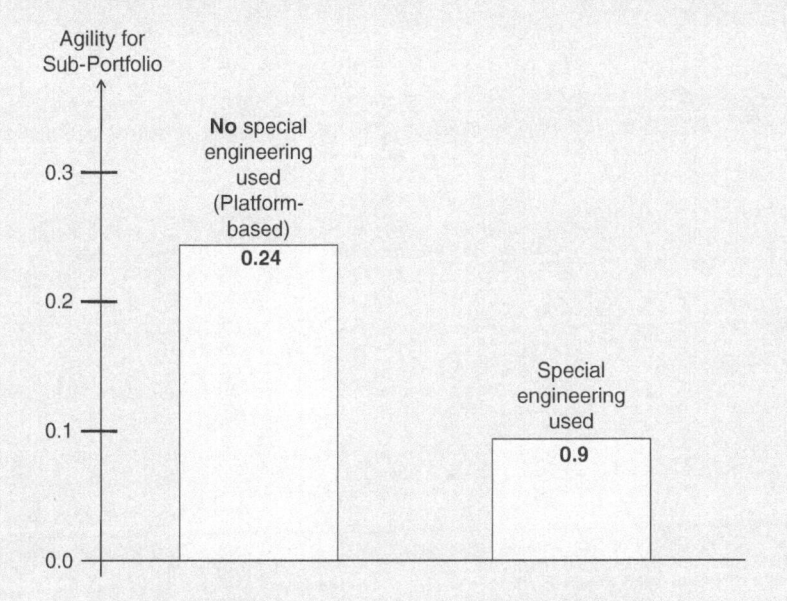

Fig. 7.11 Agility for projects using and not using special engineering

in better agility by a factor of 2.5 compared to project portfolios based on special infrastructure engineering!

The "application sub-portfolio" contained 133 projects and the "special engineering sub-portfolio" contained 19 projects. Due to the low number of projects with special engineering and a big variance of the single project agility values, the statistical significance of Fig. 7.11 (using the Mann-Whitney U-Test [Hill_06] with $n_1 = 103$, $n_2 = 12$, $U = 832.5$) results as $P = 0.048$.

Part III
Summary, Conclusions and Outlook

Chapter 8
Conclusions and Outlook

8.1 Summary of Key Points

Very large information systems have grown to a level of complexity, size and age, that except under special circumstances these systems can only be evolved and not replaced as a whole. *Evolution* implies that only a certain percentage of the system can be changed in any given time period.

If evolution takes place by just implementing a series of *business requirements*, the efficiency in operating and evolving the system decreases to a point where the system becomes unstable or requirements can only be implemented at disproportionate cost and risk.

The key idea of *managed evolution* is to steer the evolution such that the efficiency of developing and operating the system is preserved or even increased. This is done by maintaining a balance between the efficiency improvement investments and the purely business driven investments. This balancing of investments requires a different *governance* mechanism to steer prioritization and budget decisions in IT. First of all, this process needs to ensure the appropriate balance between efficiency and additional functionality investments. Second, investment decisions should be made, balancing the needs of multiple stakeholders of a certain application domain, to enable the reuse of applications by multiple business lines. Last, but not least, a balance between long-term and short term investments is needed, taking into account the long lifecycles of very large information systems.

> "Establishing the right architecture has helped some of the world's most successful companies not just survive but thrive despite increasingly tough global competition. These blockbuster companies excel because they've made tough decisions about which processes they must execute well, and they've implemented the information systems needed to digitize those processes. Result? Their information systems have become an asset rather than a liability, and have fostered unprecedented agility"
> Jeanne W. Ross, 2006

Architecture management is a key aspect of managed evolution. The system must be evolved towards the target architecture. The target architecture needs to be defined. Gaps need to be determined and used as inputs for architecture-driven investments. The key to architecture management of very large information systems is to break them down into a hierarchy of manageable pieces, so called *domains*. Usually the system is decomposed into the application landscape based on the application domain model and the infrastructure, based on the technical domain model. Besides technical architecture, depending on the nature of the system, other key architectures, such as security, data, integration, operation and development architectures need to be defined. In the spirit of managed evolution, the organization needs to manage architecture as a continuous two-step process, including architecture definition and architecture implementation.

First, in the *architecture definition* step, the target architecture is continuously being reviewed and adjusted to future needs. The results of this process are concepts, guidelines, standards, models and so on. A federated decision making process ensures broad involvement of stakeholders. Second, *architecture implementation* consists, on the one hand, of analyzing gaps, preparing investment decisions and driving architecture programs. On the other hand, it ensures alignment of projects to the target architecture by structured reviews. Organizationally, in our experience, a federated architecture organization with a small central architecture organization delivers the best results for a very large information system.

Good architecture management is based on successfully dividing the very large information system into manageable parts. In addition to that we need a joint language used by all participants in order to simplify communications. Both requirements are covered by a number of *structural* and *semantic models*, providing abstractions of the system on various levels for different purposes.

One particularly important element of architecture for the managed evolution is *integration architecture*. Integration architecture defines the appropriate coupling and decoupling of the system's components. At the heart of integration architecture is the interface management process that manages evolving interface contracts between producers and consumers of a service. Accepting that a very large information system cannot be replaced as a whole requires a component replacement strategy. For this, it is paramount that the interfaces are stable or at least evolve in defined, predictable ways. As very large information systems tend to develop some degree of technical heterogeneity, the technology to link components across multiple technologies is another key element of integration architecture. If a very large information system was built as a monolith, a first step of decomposing it into components may be necessary to begin the process of managed evolution.

One area often neglected is the *infrastructure technology portfolio* underneath a very large information system. It is essential for a long-lived system to continuously adapt to modern technology. If not managed carefully this leads to a very broad, expensive and hard to manage technology portfolio. One difficulty with technology portfolio management is that applications depend in many ways on the underlying technology. So, if the abstraction layer between infrastructure and applications is not managed with care, changes in the underlying technology portfolio can become

8.1 Summary of Key Points

extremely expensive. The authors found the approach of defining *platforms* that combine a technology stack with well-defined processes and services for running and developing applications to be a very powerful abstraction concept in this context. Operating a very large information system built from loosely coupled components poses new challenges compared to operating a traditional, rather monolithic system. Operational concerns must be addressed early, already when architecting and developing the applications.

A good and transparent *alignment* between business and IT is very important for managed evolution: Both business and IT stakeholders need to understand the long-term direction of managed evolution and the impact on their areas. Business has to support the investment split requested by managed evolution. Business and IT have to develop a joint governance model that supports strategic allocation of investments according to the managed evolution principles, ensuring the balance between efficiency and functionality investments and fostering reuse. By grouping the projects into strategic baskets and ensuring the balance of power within individual projects, the governance model makes sure that all project activities are properly aligned to strategy.

Structures, processes and methods are useful, but not sufficient for managed evolution. As important, if not more important, are certain *cultural values* in the organization behind the system. Because managed evolution is a continuous process, people must have a long-term orientation. Perseverance and discipline following the approach are required to be successful. Key to managed evolution is well-defined, dependable *interface contracts* fostering *reuse* of components. The corresponding cultural values are trust, reliability and transparency. If you want to overcome the "not-invented-here" syndrome plaguing many IT organizations, people need to trust in the quality and timeliness of the components they depend on for success. Transparency helps to instill that level of trust. As the overall direction of the system's evolution is driven by uncountable micro-decisions, all decision makers need to understand and support the overall direction. So, a "think big, act local" attitude is required. All involved parties need to understand and accept key strategic directions.

Very large information systems are generally being built by large teams with a lot of interaction among the members, due to the highly connected nature of such systems. While good skills and the right cultural values help to optimize individual contributions, good *organization* and mature *processes* help in getting the maximum out of the collaboration within the team. First of all, the IT organization needs to be properly embedded into the business they serve. It is very hard to manage the complex processes and dependencies necessary for managed evolution, if the IT organization working on a single system is distributed among many business lines. As a consequence, all IT resources working on a single system, ideally, directly report into one CIO. Within the IT organization, the key functions of developing and maintaining infrastructure and applications can be organized in many ways. Combining application maintenance and development in domain-aligned groups helps fostering reuse and provides the necessary legacy knowhow where it is needed for new developments. Centralizing infrastructure supports technology portfolio standardization and platform reuse. The two key strategic functions, *architecture* and *business-IT alignment governance*, need strong organizational positioning to underline the importance of the corresponding processes. A good organization creates a healthy level of tension between the interest for long-term strategic solutions, immediate delivery of individual solutions and stable operations.

Finally, big organizations and big systems only move in a certain direction if progress is *measured* and, in the case of insufficient progress, corrective action is taken. One can measure architectural progress on various levels. The simplest way is to measure the quality of the processes by measuring whether all standards are kept up to date, projects are properly reviewed and review results are followed through. The next level is to measure the progress towards the target architecture, by looking at adoption rates of technology standards or reuse factors of interfaces. The highest level is to measure whether the system makes progress towards better agility or not. There is a clear relationship between improved agility and business value of the system. What is less clear is the relationship between better process and better architecture and on the next level between better architecture and better agility.

8.2 Outlook

This book reflects the authors' experience in evolving a very large information system over more than a decade. The book summarizes the successful concepts as known to the authors so far. However, it is clear that each answer the book gives leads to new open questions. One of the main reasons for writing this book is to encourage others to find answers to the open questions and thus advance the craft of evolving very large information systems. True to this purpose, this last section of the book groups and summarizes the open questions that are known to the authors.

One key area of further development is the *measurement of agility* (introduced in Sect. 7.4) or productivity. Both *time to market* and *development cost* need to be normalized to a unit of functionality delivered. Traditionally, this has been done by counting the lines of delivered source code. This approach is limited in two ways: On the one hand, it only works for in-house development where we have the source code; on the other hand, it doesn't encourage reuse of existing functionality. This problem can be overcome by linking the amount of functionality delivered to the *requirements specification* rather than the implementation. This is the motivation behind using use case points in this book. This is better, but still not perfect for two reasons. While use case points are good at measuring traditional applications, they are of limited value for more modern concepts, such as flexible reporting applications or projects that consolidate functionality, such as reengineering projects. In these cases, project requirements cannot easily be expressed in use case points. Another limit of the method is a degree of subjectivity, where use cases need to be rated for complexity.

Once we can measure agility reliably, it remains difficult to link individual elements of the strategy to the overall success. This is less of a concern in the early days of managed evolution, when the key strategic thrusts are usually quite obvious. As the strategy evolves, however, more and more elements are added to it. It is, for example, not simple to decide whether it makes more sense to invest more into education in order to improve the skills portfolio or into better integration architecture. It is clear that a balanced investment into both is needed. But, the right balance is hard to analyze. In addition to that, more factors impact agility. Identifying the factors and determining their degree of impact is important to fine-tune the allocation of investments. One possible analysis method is multivariate statistical factor analysis, which has proven its value in other disciplines, such as economics and market research.

The whole book has mainly been written with the perspective of evolving a system by developing software. For many large legacy systems this assumption holds true for the time being. There is, however, the tendency to buy more and develop less software. The key challenge with buying application software and services is the *architecture clash*. Generally, systems as well as the third party components to be integrated have developed towards completely different target architectures up to the point in time where they need to be integrated. Most of the standard software vendors have recognized this problem and try to solve it by offering well-defined *interfaces* via services implemented in standard technologies. This usually helps in bridging the technological gap. The harder problem of *semantic integration* remains, however. The consequence of this is a lot of glue code, of redundant data and functionality, making the system less agile and more expensive to maintain and operate.

The authors see two ways of resolving that issue: We need *domain-oriented standardized application architectures* in order to overcome architectural misalignment and foster industry-wide coordination of architecture alignment. This has been successful in the area of infrastructure, but remains difficult on higher levels (see Fig. 2.1.). On the economic side, more creative pricing models by providers are needed, to make off-the-shelf software more attractive for integration into very large information systems.

One of the least understood areas of component architecture is *systems management*. Current systems management practices focus on separating systems management from the system itself. In a more distributed and dynamic environment, system management has to become part of the components themselves (see Sect. 4.4.). It has to move up the value chain from infrastructure management to service and application management. Application designs need to become more defensive, taking into account failure of components. As components are decoupled asynchronically, global message flow control becomes very important. In theory a lot of this is clear. It is, however, very difficult to implement such solutions in the context of a very large information system.

It is well known that individual productivity of developers varies very widely. Key to success with managed evolution is a culture that, on the one hand, accepts the need for coordination to avoid redundancy and heterogeneity and, on the other hand, is welcoming to highly productive individuals. The authors find this very hard to achieve. The key problem is the difference between organizational and individual productivity. A developer feels most productive with least coordination overhead. But, the sum of all individually productive developers is unfortunately not a productive organization, because it creates a lot of redundancy.

The authors see two very promising areas of progress in architecture methodology. Traditionally, IT has used architecture methods more than business. More recently, *architecture* has also been recognized by the business as a method value. This has partly been driven by advanced efficiency methods, such as business process reengineering and partly by regulatory developments, such as Sarbannes-Oxley ([Marchetti_05]) that force businesses to systematically understand and document their processes. For IT, this is an advantage, because it allows linking technical concepts, such as applications and data, to business concepts. Adequate models on each level are key to success in this area. This leads to the second promising innovation in architecture: *Model-driven architecture*. Once models exist on each layer, we can systematically transform models between layers and eventually generate implementations from business specifications. In general this remains a vision, but some good progress has been made in areas such as user interfaces, database access, interface code, business rules and business process automation. The authors see a lot of additional potential in this area.

> "You need to construct a solid foundation for business execution – an IT infrastructure and digitized business processes that automate your company's core capabilities"
> Jeanne W. Ross, 2006

References

Abramowicz_07	Abramowicz, W., & Mayr, H. D. (2007). *Technologies for business information systems*. Dordrecht, The Netherland: Springer. ISBN 978-1-4020-5633-8.
Abrial_10	Jean-Raymond Abrial (2010). **Modeling in Event-B – *System and Software Engineering***. Cambridge University Press, Cambridge UK, ISBN 978-0-521-89556-9
Adams_99	Adams, C., & Lloyd, S. (1999). *Understanding public-key infrastructure – concepts, standards, and deployment considerations*. Indianapolis, IN: MacMillan. ISBN 978-1-57870-166-X.
Adamsen_00	Adamsen, P. B. (2000). *A framework for complex system development*. Boca Raton, FL: CRC. ISBN 978-0-8493-2296-0.
Albin_03	Stephen, T. A. (2003). *The art of software architecture*. Indianapolis, IN: Wiley. ISBN 978-0-8493-0440-7.
Alesso_05	Peter Alesso, H., & Smith, C. F. (2005). *Developing semantic web services*. Wellesey, MA: A K Peters. ISBN 978-1-56881-4.
Alexiev_05	Alexiev, V., Breu, M., de Bruijn, J., Fensel, D., Lara, R., & Lausen, H. (2005). *Information integration with ontologies – experiences from an industrial showcase*. Chicester, UK: Wiley. ISBN 978-0-470-01048-7.
Allemang_08	Allemang, D., & Hendler, J. (2008). *Semantic web for the working ontologist – effective modeling in RDFS and OWL*. Amsterdam, The Netherlands: Morgan Kaufmann Publishers (Elsevier). ISBN 978-0-12-373556-0.
Anda_08	Anda, B., Dreiem, H., Sjoberg, D. I. K., & Jorgensen, M., *Estimating software development effort based on use cases – experiences from industry*, 2008. Retrieved from: http://www.bfpug.com.br/Artigos/UCP/Anda-Estimating_ SW_Dev_Effort_Based_on_Use_Cases.pdf
Antoniou_04	Antoniou, G., & van Harmelen, F. (2004). *A semantic web primer*. Cambridge, MA: MIT Press. ISBN 978-0-262-01210-3.
Assmann_03	Assmann, U. (2003). *Invasive software composition*. Berlin, Heidelberg: Springer. ISBN 978-3-540-44385-1.
Baduel_09	Baduel, E., Benveniste, A., Caillaud, B., Legay, A., & Passerone, R. (2009) *Contract theories for embedded systems – a white paper*. Deliverable D1.2b-Y2 from the European Project COMBEST
Baier_07	Baier, C., & Katoen, J.-P. (2007). *Principles of model checking*. Cambridge, MA: MIT Press. ISBN 978-0-262-02649-9.
Basilevsky_94	Basilevsky, A. (1994). *Statistical factor analysis and related methods – theory and applications*. New York: Wiley. ISBN 978-0-471-57082-6.
Ben-Ari_01	Ben-Ari, M. (2001). *Mathematical logic for computer science* (2nd ed.). London, UK: Springer. ISBN 978-1-85233-319-7.

Berg_05	Berg, C. J. (2005). *High-assurance design – architecting secure and reliable enterprise applications.* New Jersey: Addison-Wesley. ISBN 978-0-321-37577-7.
Bernstein_09	Bernstein, P. A., & Newcomer, E. (2009). *Principles of transaction processing* (2nd ed.). Amsterdam, The Netherlands: Morgan Kaufmann/Elsevier. ISBN 978-1-55860-623-4.
BIAN_08	BIAN Consortium. *Banking Industry Architecture Network (BIAN)*, 2008ff. Retrieved from http://www.bian.org
Bieberstein_08	Bieberstein, N., Laird, R. G., Jones, K., & Mitra, T. (2008). *Executing SOA – a practical guide fort the service-oriented architect.* New Jersey: IBM developer work series, IBM Press, Pearson plc. ISBN 978-0-13-235374-8.
Birman_05	Birman, K. P. (2005). *Reliable distributed systems – technologies, web services, and applications.* New York: Springer Science and Business Media. ISBN 978-0-387-21509-3.
Boehm_00	Boehm, B. W., Abts, C., Winsor Brown, A., Chulani, S., Clark, B. K., Horowitz, E., et al. (2000). *Software cost estimation with COCOMO II.* Englewood Cliffs, NJ: Prentice Hall. ISBN 978-0-13-026692-2.
Bonati_06	Bonati, B., Regutzki, J., & Schroter, M. (2006). *Enterprise services architecture for financial services.* Germany: Verlag Galileo Press GmbH. ISBN 1-59229-095-7.
Britton_01	Britton, C. (2001). *IT architectures and middleware – strategies for building large, integrated systems.* Boston, MA: Addison-Wesley. ISBN 978-0-201.70907-4.
Brodie_95	Brodie, M. L., & Stonebraker, M. (1995). *Migrating legacy systems – gateways, interfaces & the incremental approach.* San Francisco, CA: Morgan Kaufmann Publishers. ISBN 978-1-55860-330-1.
Bruegge_00	Bruegge, B., & Dutoit, A. H. (2000). *Object-oriented software engineering – conquering complex and changing systems.* Englewood Cliffs, NJ: Prentice Hall. ISBN 978-0-13-017452-1.
Buchanan_03	Buchanan, R. W. (2003). *Disaster proofing information systems – a complete methodology for eliminating single points of failure.* New York: McGraw Hill. ISBN 978-0-07-140922-X.
Bussler_03	Bussler, C. (2003). *B2B integration – concepts and architecture.* Berlin, Heidelberg: Springer. ISBN 978-3-540-43487-9.
Buxmann_08	Buxmann, P., Diefenbach, H., & Hess, T. (2008). *Die Softwareindustrie – Ökonomische Prinzipien, Strategien, Perspektiven.* Berlin, Heidelberg: Springer. ISBN 978-3-540-71828-4.
C:D	Sterling Commerce. *C:D.* C:D: "Connect Direct" (http://www.sterlingcommerce.com/Products/MFT/ConnectDirect
Calder_08	Calder, A., & Watkins, S. (2008). *Corporate governance – a managers guide.* London and Philadelphia: Kogan Page. ISBN 978-07494-4817-2.
Cawsey_03	Cawsey, A., & Dewar, R. (2003). *Internet technology and E-Commerce.* USA: Palgrave Macmillan. ISBN 978-0-3339-8999-9.
CERT_04	Carnegie Mellon SEI, CERT. (2004). *Illicit cyber activity in the banking and finance sector.* Pittsburgh, PA: Carnegie Mellon, CERT. http://www.cert.org/search_pubs/search.php?sort=pub_dated
Chappell_04	Chappell, D. A. (2004). *Enterprise service bus.* Sebastopol, CA: O'Reilly & Associates. ISBN 978-0-596-00675-4.
Charette_05	Charette, R. N. (2005) *Why Software Fails.* IEEE Spectrum, *42*(9), 42–49. Retrieved from http://www.spectrum.ieee.org/print/1685
Chrissis_06	Chrissis, M. B., Konrad, M., & Shrum, S. (2006). *CMMI – guidelines for process integration and product improvement.* New Jersey: Addison-Wesley. ISBN 978-0-321-27967-0.

References

Clements_02	Clements, P., & Northrop, L. (2002). *Software product lines – practices and patterns*. Boston, USA: (SEI Institute) Addison-Wesley. ISBN 978-0-201-70332-7.
Cockburn_01	Cockburn, A. (2001). *Writing effective use cases*. Boston, USA: Addison-Wesely. ISBN 978-0-201-70225-8.
Cummins_09	Cummins, F. A. (2009). *Building the agile enterprise – with SOA, BPM and MBM*. Amsterdam, The Netherlands: Morgan Kaufmann (Elsevier). ISBN 978-0-12-374445-6.
Daconta_03	Daconta, M. C., Obrst, L. J., & Smith, K. T. (2003). *The semantic web*. Indianapolis, IN: Wiley. ISBN 978-0-471-43257-1.
Daum_03a	Daum, B. (2003). *Modeling business objects with XML schema*. Amsterdam, The Netherlands: Morgan Kauffmann Publishers (Elsevier). ISBN 978-1-55860-816-0.
Daum_03b	Daum, B., & Merten, U. (2003). *System architecture with XML*. Amsterdam, The Netherlands: Morgan Kaufmann Publishers (Elsevier). ISBN 978-1-55860-745-5.
Deloitte_10	Deloitte Development LLC. (2010) *Cyber crime – a clear and present danger combating the fastest growing cyber security threat*. Whitepaper, Deloitte Development LLC, Center for Security & Privacy Solutions. Retrieved from http://www.deloitte.com/assets/Dcom-UnitedStates/Local%20Assets/Documents/AERS/us_aers_Deloitte%20Cyber%20Crime%20POV%20Jan25 2010.pdf
DeMarco_99	DeMarco, T., & Lister, T. (1999). *Peopleware – productive projects and teams*. New York: Dorset House Publishing. ISBN 978-0-932633-43-9.
Denney_05	Denney, R. (2005). *Succeeding with use cases: working smart to deliver quality*. Amsterdam, The Netherlands: Addison-Wesley Longman. ISBN 978-0-321-31643-1.
Dietz_06	Dietz, J. L. G. (2006). *Enterprise ontology – theory and methodology*. Berlin, Heidelberg: Springer. ISBN 978-3-540-29169-5.
Dobson_02	Dobson, A. J. (2002). *An introduction to generalized linear models* (2nd ed.). Boca Raton, FL: Chapman & Hall/CRC. ISBN 978-1-58488-165-8.
Dubrawsky_06	Dubrawsky, I. (Ed.). (2006). *Designing and building enterprise DMZs*. Rockland, NY: Syngress Publishing. ISBN ISBN 978-1-59749-100-4.
Duffy_04	Duffy, D. J. (2004). *Domain architectures – models and architectures for UML applications*. Chichester, UK: Wiley. ISBN 978-0-470-84833-2.
Duke_05	Duke, A. (2005). *ABC air traffic control*. Texas: Ian Allen, 2005. ISBN 978-0711030749.
Ebert_07	Ebert, C., & Dunke, R. (2007). *Software measurement: establish – extract – evaluate – execute*. Berlin, Heidelberg: Springer. ISBN 978-3-540-71648-8.
Eckey_02	Eckey, H.-F., Kosfeld, R., & Rengers, M. (2002). *Multivariate Statistik – Grundlagen, Methoden, Beispiele*. Wiesbaden, Germany: Verlag Dr. Th. Gabler GmbH. ISBN 978-3-409-11969-8.
Erl_04	Erl, T. (2004). *Service-oriented architecture – a field guide to integrating XML and web services*. Upper Saddle River, NJ: Prentice Hall. ISBN 978-0-13-142898-5.
Erl_05	Erl, T. (2005). *Service-oriented architecture – concepts, technology, and design*. Upper Saddle River, NJ: Pearson Education. ISBN 978-0-13-185858-0.
Evans_04	Evans, E. (2004). *Domain-driven design – tackling complexity in the heart of software*. Boston, MA: Pearson Education\Addison-Wesley. 7th printing 2006. ISBN 978-0-321-12521-5.

Farrell_08	Farrell, N. (2008) *US air traffic control grounded by computer glitch*. The INQUIRER, 2008, Retrieved August 28, 2009 from http://www.theinquirer.net/inquirer/news/906/1036906/air-traffic-control-grounded
Feathers_07	Feathers, M. (2007). *Working effectively with legacy code*. Englewood Cliffs, NJ: Prentice Hall. ISBN 978-0-13-117705-5.
Feghhi_99	Feghhi, J., Feghhi, J., & Williams, P. (1999). *Digital certificates – applied internet security*. Reading, MA: Addison Wesley Longman. ISBN 978-0-201-30980-7.
Fensel_04	Fensel, D. (2004). *Ontologies – a silver bullet for knowledge management and electronic commerce*. Berlin, Heidelberg: Springer. ISBN 978-3-540-34519-0.
Fensel_07	Fensel, D., Lausen, H., Polleres, A., de Bruijn, J., Stollberg, M., Roman, D., et al. (2007). *Enabling semantic web services – the web service modeling ontology*. Berlin, Heidelberg: Springer. ISBN 978-3-540-00302-9.
Fenton_97	Fenton, N. E., & Pfleeger, S. L. (1997). *Software metrics – a rigorous & practical approach* (2nd ed.). Boston, MA: PWS Publishing company. ISBN 798-0-534-95425-1.
Fields_09	Fields, J., Harvie, S., Fowler, M., & Beck, K. (2009). *Refactoring – ruby edition*. Amsterdam, The Netherlands: Addison-Wesley Longman. ISBN 978-0-321-60350-0.
Flood_93	Flood, R. L., & Cars, E. R. (1993). *Dealing with complexity – an introduction and application of systems science* (2nd ed.). New York: Plenum Press. ISBN 0-306-44299-X.
Fowler_03	Fowler, M. (2003). *Patterns of enterprise application architecture*. Boston, USA: Addison Wesley. ISBN 978-0-321-12742-0.
Fowler_04	Fowler, M. (2004). *ULM distilled – a brief guide to the standard object modeling language*. Boston, MA: Addison Wesley. ISBN 978-0-321-19368-7.
Fowler_99	Fowler, M., Beck, K., Brant, J., & Opdyke, W. (1999). *Refactoring – improving the design of existing code*. Amsterdam, The Netherlands: Addison-Wesley Longman. ISBN 978-0-201-48567-7.
Frankel_03	Frankel, D. S. (2003). *Model driven architecture – applying MDA to enterprise computing*. Indianapolis, IN: Wiley. ISBN 978-0-471-31920-1.
Fronhoff_06	Fronhoff, S., & Kehler, K. (2006) *Use case points in der industriellen praxis*, sd&m AG, Offenbach. Retrieved from: http://www.sdm.de/web4archiv/objects/download/pdf/sdm_pub_metrikon_frohnhoff.pdf
Fronhoff_07	Fronhoff, S., & Kehler, K. (2007) *Use case points Aufwandschätzung auf Basis unterschiedlicher Spezifikations-Formate*, sd&m AG, Offenbach. Retrieved from: http://www.sdm.de/web4archiv/objects/download/pdf/1/sdm_frohnhoff_ucp_spezformate.pdf)
Fronhoff_08	Fronhoff, S. (2008) *Grosse Softwareprojekte – Aufwandschätzung mit Use Case Points*. Informatik-Spektrum, Sonderheft "Management grosser Systeme", *31*(6), 566-577
ftps	Wikipedia. *ftps*. ftps: "file transfer protocol secure" Retrieved from (http://en.wikipedia.org/wiki/FTPS)
Gamma_95	Gamma, E., Helm, R., Johnson, R., & Vlissides, J. (1995). *Design patterns – elements of reusable object-oriented software*. Reading, MA: Addison Wesley Longman. ISBN 978-0-201-63361-2.
Garland_03	Garland, J., & Anthony, R. (2003). *Large-scale software architecture*. Chichester, UK: Wiley. ISBN 978-0-470-84849-9.
Garmus_01	Garmus, D., & Herron, D. (2001). *Function point analysis – measurement practices for successful software projects*. Boston, MA: Addison-Wesely. ISBN 978-0-201-69944-3.

References

Gartner_07	Burke, B. (2007) *Management update – managing a federated architecture*. Gartner Research USA, Report ID Number: G00153749, 26 December http://www.gartner.com/DisplayDocument?id=571109
George_04	George, M., Rowlands, D., & Kastle, B. (2004). *What is lean six sigma?* New York: McGraw Hill. ISBN 978-0-07-142668-X.
George_05	George, M., Rowlands, D., Price, M., & Maxey, J. (2005). *Lean six sigma pocket toolbook*. New York: McGraw Hill. ISBN 978-0-07-144119-0.
Gharajedghi_06	Gharajedaghi, J. (2006). *Systems thinking – managing chaos and complexity: a platform for designing business architecture* (2nd ed.). Amsterdam, The Netherlands: Elsevier. ISBN 978-0-7506-7973-2.
Glass_02	Glass, R. L. (2002). *Facts and fallacies of software engineering*. Amsterdam, The Netherlands: Addison-Wesley Longman. ISBN 978-0321117427.
Glass_97	Glass, R. L. (1997). *Software runaways - monumental software disasters*. Englewood Cliffs, NJ: Prentice Hall. ISBN 978-0-13-673443-7.
Goldfarb_98	Goldfarb, C. F., & Prescod, P. (1998). *The XML handbook*. Englewood Cliffs, NJ: Prentice-Hall PTR. ISBN 978-0-13-081152-1.
Gomez-Perez_04	Gomez-Perez, A., Gernandez-Lopez, M., & Corcho, O. (2004). *Ontological engineering*. London, UK: Springer. ISBN 978-1-85233-551-3.
Gorton_06	Gorton, I. (2006). *Essential software architecture*. Berlin, Heidelberg: Springer. ISBN 978-3-540-28713-1.
Graves_08	Graves, T. (2008). *Bridging the silos – enterprise architecture for IT-architects*. Colchester, UK: Tetradian Books. ISBN 978-1-906681-02-9.
Haase_06	Haase, P. (2006). *Semantic technologies for distributed information systems*. DE: Universitätsverlag Universität Karlsruhe. ISBN 978-3-86644-2.
Hafner_09	Hafner, M., & Breu, R. (2009). *Security engineering for service-oriented architectures*. Berlin, Heidelberg: Springer. ISBN 978-3-540-79538-4.
Hagen_03	Claus Hagen. Integrationsarchitektur in der Credit . Chapter 2 in: Stephan Aier, Marten Schönherr (Editors): Enterprise Application Integration – Flexibilisierung komplexer Unternehmensarchitekturen. GITO-Verlag, Berlin, 2003. ISBN 978-3-936771-17-0
Hagen_06	Claus Hagen, Alexander Schwinn. Measured Integration – *Metriken für die Integrationsarchitektur*. Chapter 9 in: Joachim Schelp, Robert Winter (Editors): Integrationsmanagement – Planung, Bewertung und Steuerung von Applikationslandschaften. Springer, Berlin, Heidelberg, 2006. ISBN 978-3-540-20506-3
Halle_06	von Halle, B., & Larry, G. (Eds.). (2006). *The business rule revolution – running business the right way*. Silicon Valley, CA: Happy About Publishing. ISBN 1-60005-013-1.
Hariri_06	Salim, H., & Manish, P. (Eds.). (2006). *Autonomic computing – concepts, infrastructure, and applications*. Boca Raton, FL: CRC. ISBN 978-0849393679.
Herzum_00	Peter, H., & Oliver, S. (Eds.). (2000). *Business component factory – a comprehensive overview of component-based development for the enterprise*. New York: OMG Press\Wiley. ISBN 0-471-32760-3.
Heuvel_07	van den Heuvel, W.-J. (2007). *Aligning modern business processes and legacy systems – a component-based perspective*. Cambridge, MA: MIT Press. ISBN 978-0-262-22079-9.
Hill_06	Hill, T., & Lewicki, P. (2006). *Statistics: methods and applications – a comprehensive reference for science, industry, and data mining*. Tulsa, OK: StatSoft. ISBN 978-1-884233-59-7.
Hite_04	Hite, R. C., Rhodes, K. A., & McIntyre, H. W. (2004). *Air traffic control: good progress on interim replacement for outage-plagued system, but risks can be further reduced*. USA: Diane. ISBN 978-0-7881-4073-0.

Hohmann_03	Hohmann, L. (2003). *Beyond software architecture – creating and sustaining winning solutions.* Boston, USA: Addison Wesley. ISBN 978-0-201-77594-8.
Hohpe_04	Hohpe, G., & Wolf, B. (2004). *Enterprise integration patterns – designing, building, and deploying messaging solutions.* Boston, USA: Addison Wesley. ISBN 978-0-321-20068-3.
Horn_01	Horn, P. (2001). *IBM's perspective on the state of information technology.* New York: IBM Research. http://www-01.ibm.com/software/tivoli/autonomic/.
Hubert_02	Hubert, R. (2002). *Convergent architecture.* New York: Wiley. ISBN 978-0-471-10560-0.
IBM_04	IBM Business Consulting Services (2004) *A practical guide to the IBM autonomic computing toolkit.* IBM Redbook, SG24-6635-00, Retrieved from www.ibm.com/redbooks.
IBM_05a	IBM Business Consulting Services. *Component business models – making specialization real.* IBM Global Services, Somers, NY, 2005. www.ibm.com
IBM_05b	IBM International Technical Support Organization. WebSphere MQ V6 Fundamentals. IBM Redbook, SG24-7128-00, November 2005. Retrieved from www.ibm.com/redbooks
IBM_06	IBM Business Consulting Services. *An Architectural Blueprint for Autonomic Computing. IBM Autonomic Computing*, 4th edition, June 2006. http://www-01.ibm.com/software/tivoli/autonomic/
IEEE_00	IEEE-SA Standards Board. (2000). *IEEE recommended practice for architectural description of software-intensive systems.* New York: The Institute of Electrical and Electronics Engineers. ISBN 978-0-7381-2518-0.
Inmon_01	Inmon, W. H., Imhoff, C., & Sousa, R. (2001). *Corporate information factory* (2nd ed.). New York: Wiley. ISBN 978-0-471-39961-2.
Inmon_08	Inmon, W., O'Neil, B., & Fryman, L. (2008). *Business metadata – capturing enterprise knowledge.* Burlington, VT: Morgan Kaufmann Elsevier. ISBN 978-0-12-373726-7.
Ironbridge_07	Ironbridge LLC. (2007) *Enterprise Architecture and a Federated IT Governance Model.* Ironbridge LLC, Retrieved from March 21 White Paper http://www.ironbridgeonline.com/library/Enterprise%20Architecture%20Federation%20-%20IB%20Whitepaper.pdf
Jacobson_92	Jacobson, I. (1992). *Object-oriented software engineering – a use case driven approach.* Harlow, England: Addison-Wesley. ISBN 978-0-201-54435-0.
Jacobson_97	Jacobson, I., Griss, M., & Honsson, P. (1997). *Software reuse – architecture, process and organization for business success.* Harlow, UK: Addison Wesley Longman. ISBN 0-201-92476-5.
Jones_95	Jones, C. (1995) *Patterns of large software systems: failure and success.* IEEE Computer, 28(3), 86-87, Retrieved from http://www.spectrum.ieee.org/xplore/2048
Kan_95	Kan, S. H. (1995). *Metrics and models in software quality engineering.* Reading, MA: Addison Wesley Longman. ISBN 978-0-201-63339-6.
Kaplan_06	Robert S. Kaplan, David P. (2006). Norton **Alignment – *How to Apply the Balanced Scorecard to Corporate Strategy*** McGraw Hill Professional, New York, USA. ISBN 978-0-15-9139690-1
Kaplan_96	Robert S. Kaplan, David P. Norton. **The Balanced Scorecard – *Translating Strategy Into Action*** McGraw Hill Professional, New York, USA, 1996. ISBN 978-0-875846514-4
Kaye_03	Kaye, D. (2003) *Loosely coupled – the missing pieces of web services.* RDS Press, 2003. ISBN 978-1-88137-824-1
Kelly_08	Kelly, S., & Tolvanen, J.-P. (2008). *Domain-specific modeling – enabling full code generation.* Hoboken, NJ: Wiley. ISBN 978-0-470-03666-2.

References

Kephart_03	Kephart, J. O., & Chess, D. M. (2003). *The vision of autonomic computing* (pp. 41–50). New York: IEEE Computer Society. http://www-01.ibm.com/software/tivoli/autonomic/.
Killmeyer_06	Killmeyer, J. (2006). *Information security architecture – an integrated approach to security in the organization* (2nd ed.). Boca Raton, FL: Auerbach Publications. ISBN 978-0-8493-1549-7.
Kim_78	Kim, Jae-On, & Mueller, C. W. (1978). *Introduction to factor analysis – what it is and how to do it*. Newbury Park, CA: Sage University Paper, University of Iowa, Sage Publications. ISBN 978-0-8039-1165-3.
Kleppe_09	Kleppe, A. (2009). *Software language engineering – creating domain-specific languages using metamodels*. New Jersey: Addison-Wesley. ISBN 978-0-321-55345-4.
Knittel_06	Knittel-Ammerschuber, S. (2006). *Architecture: the element of success. Building strategies and business objectives*. Basel, CH, Switzerland: Birkhäuser Verlag. ISBN 978-3-76437465-5.
Knöpfel_05	Knöpfel, A., Gröne, B., & Tabeling, P. (2005). *Fundamental modeling concepts – effective communication of IT systems*. Chichester, UK: Wiley. ISBN 978-0-470-02710-X.
Kradolfer_09	Kradolfer, C. *Wirksamkeit des IT-Architektur-Managements der Credit Suisse: Erfolg der Managed Evolution Strategie*. Diplomarbeit, Universität Zürich, Institut für Informatik, November 2009
Krafzig_05	Krafzig, D., Banke, K., & Slama, D. (2005). *Enterprise SOA – service-oriented architecture best practices*. Englewood Cliffs, NJ: Prentice Hall. ISBN 978-0-13-146575-9.
Kumar_09	Kumar, B. V., Narayan, P., & Ng, T. (2009). *Delivering SOA using the Java enterprise edition platform*. Amsterdam, The Netherlands: Addison-Wesley Longman. ISBN 978-0-321-492159.
Lacy_05	Lacy, L. W. (2005). *OWL – representing information using the web ontology language*. Victoria, Canada: Trafford Publishing. ISBN 978-1-4120-3448-5.
Lankhorst_05	Lankhorst, M., et al. (2005). *Enterprise architecture at work – modelling, communication, and analysis*. Berlin, Heidelberg: Springer. ISBN 978-3-540-24371-7.
Lhotka_08	Lhotka, R. (2008). *Expert C# 2008 business objects*. Berkeley, CA: Apress. ISBN 978-1430210191.
Liebhart_08	Liebhart, D., Schmutz, G., Lattmann, M., Heinisch, M., Königs, M., Kölliker, M., et al. (2008). *Integration architecture blueprint – Leitfaden zur Konstruktion von Integrationslösungen*. München, Germany: Carl Hanser Verlag. ISBN 978-3-446-41704-5.
Linden_07	Linden, F. J., Schmid, K., & Rommes, E. (2007). *Software product lines in action – the best industrial practices in product line engineering*. Berlin, Heidelberg: Springer. ISBN 978-3-540-71436-1.
Little_04	Little, M., Maron, J., & Pavlik, G. (2004). *Java transaction processing – design and implementation*. Englewood Cliffs, NJ: Prentice Hall. ISBN 978-0-13-035290-X.
Maier_02	Maier, M. W., & Rechtin, E. (2002). *The art of systems architecting* (2nd ed.). Boca Raton, FL: CRC Press. 3rd edition, 2009. ISBN 978-0-8493-0440-7.
Marchetti_05	Marchetti, A. M. (2005). *Beyond Sarbannes-Oxley compliance – effective enterprise risk management*. New Jersey: Wiley. ISBN 978-0-471-72726-5.
Marco_04	Marco, D., & Jennings, M. (2004). *Universal meta data models*. Indianapolis, IN: Wiley. ISBN 978-0-471-08177-9.
Marks_08	Marks, E. A. (2008). *Service-oriented architecture governance for the services driven enterprise*. New York: Wiley. ISBN 978-0-470-17125-7.
Masak_05	Masak, D. (2005). *Moderne enterprise architekturen*. Berlin, Heidelberg: Springer. ISBN 978-3-540-22946-9.

Masak_06	Masak, D. (2006). *Legacy-software*. Berlin, Heidelberg: Springer. ISBN 978-3-540-25412-6.
Masak_07	Masak, D. (2007). *SOA? serviceorientierung in business und software*. Berlin, Heidelberg: Springer. ISBN 978-3-540-71871-0.
McCarthy_03	McCarthy, L. (2003). *IT security – risking the corporation*. Englewood Cliffs, NJ: Prentice Hall. ISBN 978-0-13-101112-X.
McComb_04	McComb, D. (2004). *Semantics in business systems*. Amsterdam, The Netherlands: Morgan Kaufmann Publishers, Elsevier. ISBN 978-1-55860-917-2.
McGary_02	McGary, J., Card, D., Jones, C., Layman, B., Clark, E., Dean, J., et al. (2002). *Practical software measurement – objective information for decision makers*. Boston, MA: Addison-Wesley. ISBN 978-0-201-71516-3.
McGovern_06	McGovern, J., Sims, O., Jain, A., & Little, M. (2006). *Enterprise service oriented architectures – concepts, challenges, recommendations*. Dordrecht, The Netherland: Springer. ISBN 978-1-4020-3704-7.
Mens_08	Mens, T., & Demeyer, S. (Eds.). (2008). *Software evolution*. Berlin, Heidelberg: Springer. ISBN 978-3-540-76439-7.
Messerschmidt_00	Messerschmitt, D. G. (2000). *Understanding networked applications*. San Diego, CA: Academic. ISBN 978-1-55860-537-1.
Messerschmidt_03	Messerschmitt, D. G., & Syperski, C. (2003). *Software ecosystem – understanding an indispendable technology and industry*. Cambridge, MA: MIT Press. ISBN 978-0-262-63331-0.
Meyer_03	Meyer, B. (2003) *The grand challenge of trusted components*. ICSE 25 (International Conference on Software Engineering), Portland, Oregon. IEEE Computer Press, 2003. Retrieved from: http://se.ethz.ch/~meyer/publications/ieee/trusted-icse.pdf
Meyer_09	Meyer, B. (2009). *Touch of class – learning to program well with objects and contracts*. Berlin, Heidelberg: Springer. ISBN 978-3-540-92144-8.
Meyer_97	Meyer, B. (1997). *Object-oriented software construction* (2nd ed.). Englewood Cliffs, NJ: Prentice Hall. ISBN 978-0-13-629155-8.
Meyer_98	Bertrand Meyer, Christine Mingins, Heinz Schmidt. (1998) *Providing trusted components to the industry* IEEE Computer, Volume 31, No. 5, pp. 104 – 105.
Miller_98	Miller, H. W. (1998). *Reengineering legacy software systems*. Woburn, MA: Butterworht-Heinemann, Digital Press. ISBN 978-1-55558-195-1.
Montes_05	Monica Montes, José Bas, Sergio Bellido, Oscar Corcho, Silvestre Losada, Richard Benjamins, Jesus Contreras Case Study eBanking – *Financial Ontology* EU project FP6-507483. Data Information and Process Integration with Web Services (DIP), 2004-2006. Deliverable D10.3. Downloadable from: http://dip.semanticweb.org
Moser_07	Moser, R. (2007). *Business architecture. A handbook for modeling complex organizations and business processes*. München, Germany: Martin Meidenbauer Verlag. ISBN 978-3-89975600-5.
Mowbray_97	Mowbray, T. J., & Malveau, R. C. (1997). *CORBA design patterns*. New York: Wiley. ISBN 978-0-471-15882-8.
Murer_08	Murer, S., Worms, C., & Furrer, F. J. (2008). *Managed evolution – Nachhaltige Weiterentwicklung grosser Systeme Informatik-Spektrum* (Vol. 31(6), pp. 537–547). Berlin, Heidelberg: Springer.
Myerson_02	Myerson, J. M. (2002). *The complete book of middleware*. Boca Raton, FL: CRC Press LLC. ISBN 978-0-84931-272-4.
NASA_84	NASA Goddard Space Flight Center. An Approach to Software Cost Estimation NASA: Goddard Space Flight Center Maryland USA, February 1984 Report SEL-83001 http://ntrs.nasa.gov/archive/nasa/casi.ntrs.nasa.gov/19840015068_1984015068.pdf

References

Neukom_04	Hans Neukom. Early Use of Computers in Swiss Banks IEEE Annals on the History of Computing, July-September 2004 Available from: http://www.computer.org/publications
Neukom_09a	Hans Neukom. UBISCO – Analysis of a Failure IEEE Annals on the History of Computing, 31, 2009, pp. 31-43 Available from: http://www.computer.org/publications
Neukom_09b	Hans Neukom. UBISCO – Analyse eines Scheiterns In: Computergeschichte Schweiz – Eine Bestandesaufnahme (Geschichte der Informatik, Band 17), Hrsg.: Peter Haber, Zürich 2009, S. 59-94. ISBN 978-3-0340-0985-0
Newcomer_05	Newcomer, E., & Lomow, G. (2005). *Understanding SOA with web services.* New Jersey: Addison-Wesley. ISBN 978-0-321-18086-0.
Nicola_02	Nicola, J., Mayfield, M., & Abney, M. (2002). *Streamlined object modeling – patterns, rules and implementation.* Englewood Cliffs, NJ: Prentice Hall. ISBN 978-0-13-06639-7.
Nicolis_89	Nicolis, G., & Prigogine, I. (1989). *Exploring complexity – an introduction.* New York: W.H. Freeman and Company. ISBN 0-7167-1859-6.
Niven_06	Paul R. (2006). **Niven Balanced Scorecard Step-By-Step** – *Maximizing Performance and Maintaining Results* John Wiley & Sons, Inc., New York, USA, 2006. ISBN 978-0-471-78049-6
Northcutt_05	Northcutt, S., Zeltser, L., Winters, S., Kent, K., & Ritchey, R. W. (2005). *Inside network perimeter security* (2nd ed.). Indianapolis, IN: Smas Publishing. ISBN 978-0-672-32737-6.
Northrop_06	Northrop, L. (Ed.). (2006). *Ultra-large-scale systems – the software challenge of the future.* Pittsburgh, PA: Software Engineering Institute, Carnegie Mellon University. http://www.sei.cmu.edu, http://www.sei.cmu.edu/uls/files/ULS_Book2006.pdf.
O'Connor_02	O'Connor, P. D. T. (2002). *Practical reliability engineering* (4th ed.). New York: Wiley. ISBN 978-0470844632.
Ogden_89	Ogden, C. K., & Richards, I. A. (1998). *The meaning of meaning.* Sand Diego, CA: Harcourt Brace Jovanovich. ISBN 978-0-15-658446-8.
OMG_08	OMG Business Architecture Working Group (BWAG) (2008) *Business architecture.* OMG, http://bawg.omg.org/
Orfali_98	Orfali, R., & Harkey, D. (1998). *Client/server programming with Java and Corba* (2nd ed.). New York: Wiley. ISBN 978-.
Oxford_05	Hornby, A. S. (2005). *Oxford advanced learner's dictionary* (7th ed.). UK: Oxford University Press. ISBN 978-0-19431606-4.
Patel_03	Patel, N. (2003). *Adaptive evolutionary information systems.* London, UK: Idea Group Publishing. ISBN 978-1-59140-034-1.
Pollock_04	Pollock, J. T., & Hodgson, R. (2004). *Adaptive information – improving business through semantic interoperability, grid computing, and enterprise integration.* Hoboken, NJ: Wiley. ISBN 0-471-48854-2.
Pope_98	Pope, A. (1998). *The CORBA reference guide – understanding the common object request broker architecture.* Reading, MA: Addison Wesley Longman. ISBN 978-0-201-63386-8.
Portner_05	Portner, P. H. (2005). *What is meaning? – fundamentals of formal semantics.* Malden, MA: Blackwell Publishing. ISBN 978-1-4051-0918-1.
Proctor_02	Proctor, P. E., & Byrnes, F. C. (2002). *The secured enterprise – protecting your information assets.* Englewood Cliffs, NJ: Prentice Hall. ISBN 978-0-13-061906-X.
Pulier_06	Pulier, E., & Taylor, H. (2006). *Understanding enterprise SOA.* Greenwich, UK: Manning Publications. ISBN 978-1-932394-59-1.
Raclet_09	Jean-Baptiste Raclet, Eric Badouel, Albert Benveniste, Benoît Caillaud, Axel Legay, Roberto Passerone. Modal Interfaces – *Unifying Interface Automata*

	and Model Specifications. Proceedings of the 9th ACM IEEE International Conference on Embedded Software, EMSOFT 2009, Grenoble, France, October 12-16, 2009
Ravishanker_02	Ravishanker, N., & Dey, D. K. (2002). *A first course in linear model theory.* Boca Raton, FL: Chapman & Hall/CRC. ISBN 978-1-58488-247-6.
Remenyi_00	Remenyi, D., Money, A., & Sherwood-Smith, M. (2000). *The effective measurement and management of IT costs and benefits* (2nd ed.). Oxford, UK: Butterworth-Heinemann. ISBN 0-7506-4420-6.
Renkema_00	Renkema, T. J. W. (2000). *The IT value quest – how to capture the business value of IT-based infrastructure.* Chichester, UK: Wiley. ISBN 978-0-471-98817-0.
Reussner_06	Reussner, R., Stafford, J., & Szyperski, C. (Eds.). (2006). *Architecting systems with trustworthy components.* Berlin, Heidelberg: Springer, Lecture Notes in Computer Science (LCNS). ISBN 978-3-540-35800-8.
Richards_06	Mark, Richards. (2006). *Java transaction design strategies.* USA: C4Media. ISBN 978-1-4116-9591-7.
Robertson_99	Robertson, S., & Robertson, J. (1999). *Mastering the requirements process.* Harlow, England: Addison-Wesley. ISBN 978-0-201-36046-2.
Ross_06	Ross, J. W., Weill, P., & Robertson, D. C. (2006). *Enterprise architecture: creating a foundation for business execution.* Boston, MA: Harvard Business School Press. ISBN 978-1-59139-839-4.
Rumsey_03	Rumsey, D. (2003). *Statistics for dummies.* Indianapolis, IN: Wiley. ISBN 978-0-7645-5423-9.
Sandoe_01	Sandoe, K., Corbitt, G., & Boykin, R. (2001). *Enterprise integration.* New York: Wiley. ISBN 978-0-471-35993-9.
Schiesser_01	Schiesser, R., & Kern, H. (2001). *IT systems management – designing, implementing, and managing world-class infrastructures.* Englewood Cliffs, NJ: Prentice Hall. ISBN 978-0130876782.
Schmidt_99	Schmidt, B. (1999). *Data modeling for information professionals.* Englewood Cliffs, NJ: Prentice Hall. ISBN 978-0-13-080450.
Schneider_98	Schneider, G., & Winters, J. P. (1998). *Applying use cases – a practical guide.* Reading, MA: Addison-Wesley. ISBN 978-0-201-30981-5.
Schoeller_06	Bernd Schoeller, Tobias Widmer, Bertrand Meyer. *Making specifications complete through models* In: Architecting Systems with Trustworthy Components. Editors: Ralf Reussner, Judith Stafford and Clemens Szyperski, Springer-Verlag, Lecture Notes in Computer Science (LNCS), 2006. ISBN 978-3-540-35800-8 http://se.ethz.ch/~meyer/publications/lncs/model_library.pdf
Schöning_08	Uwe Schöning. Theoretische Informatik – *kurz gefasst* Spektrum Akademischer Verlag, Heidelberg. Hochschultaschenbuch, 5. Auflage, 2008. ISBN 978-3-8274-1824-1
Schultz_02	Schultz, E. E., & Shumway, R. (2002). *Incident response – a strategic guide to handling system and network security breaches.* Indianapolis, IN: New Riders Publishing. ISBN 978-1-57870-256-9.
Seacord_03	Seacord, R. C., Plakosh, D., & Lewis, G. A. (2003). *Modernizing legacy systems – software technologies, engineering processes, and business practices.* Boston, MA: Addision Wesley. ISBN 978-0-321-11884-7.
Sessions_08	Sessions, R. (2008). *Simple architectures for complex enterprises.* Redmond, WA: Microsoft Press. ISBN 978-0-7356-2578-5.
Sessions_09	Roger Sessions. The IT Complexity Crisis – *Danger and Opportunity* White Paper, November 2009. Downloadable from: http://www.objectwatch.com/whitepapers/ITComplexityWhitePaper.pdf

Sewell_02	Sewell, M. T., & Sewell, L. M. (2002). *The software architect's profession – an introduction*. Englewood Cliffs, NJ: Prentice Hall. ISBN 978-0-13-060796-7.
Shore_07	Shore, J., & Warden, S. (2007). *The art of agile development*. Sebastopol, CA: O'Reilly Media. ISBN 978-0-596-52767-9.
Simsion_05	Simsion, G. C., & Witt, G. C. (2005). *Data modeling essentials* (3rd ed.). Amsterdam, The Netherlands: Morgan Kaufmann Publisher (Elsevier). ISBN 978-0-12-644551-6.
Skulschus_04	Skulschus, M., & Wiederstein, M. (2004). *XML schema*. Bonn, Germany: Galileo Press. ISBN 978-3-89842-427-3.
Sowa_00	Sowa, J. F. (2000). *Knowledge representation – logical, philosophical and computational foundations*. Pacific Grove, CA: Brooks/Cole. ISBN 978-0-534-94965-7.
Spiegel_00	Spiegel, M. R., Schiller, J., & Srinivasan, R. A. (2000). *Probability and statistics*. New York: Schaum's Outlines, McGraw-Hill. ISBN 978-0-07-135004-7.
Spinellis_09	Spinellis, D., & Gousios, G. (Eds.). (2009). *Beautiful architecture – leading thinkers reveal the hidden beauty in software design*. Sebastopol, CA: O'Reilly Media. ISBN 978-0-596-51798-4.
Stewart_08	Stewart, D. L. (2008). *Building enterprise taxonomies*. USA: Mokita Press. ISBN 978-1-4196-9362-5.
Stuckenschmidt_05	Stuckenschmidt, H., & van Harmelen, F. (2005). *Information sharing on the semantic web*. Berlin, Germany: Springer. ISBN 978-3-540-20594-2.
Sullivan_03	Sullivan, D. (2003). *Proven portals – best practices for planning, designing, and developing enterprise portals*. Amsterdam, The Netherlands: Addison-Wesley Longman. ISBN 978-0-321-12520-0.
Szuprowicz_00	Szuprowicz, B. O. (2000). *Implementing enterprise portals - integration strategies for intranet, extranet, and internet resources*. U.S.: Computer Technology Research Corporation. ISBN 978-1-56607080-5.
Szyperski_02	Szyperski, C., Gruntz, D., & Murer, S. (2002). *Component software – beyond object-oriented programming* (2nd ed.). Amsterdam, The Netherlands: Addison-Wesley Longman. ISBN 978-0-201-74572-0.
Szyperski_97	C. Szyperki, C. Pfister. *Workshop on Component-Oriented Programming* In: M. Mühlhäuser (Editor): Special Issue in Object-Oriented Programming – ECOOP96 Workshop Reader, dpunkt Verlag, Heidelberg, 1997
Tracy_05	Tracy, L. W. (2005). *OWL: representing information using the web ontology language*. Victoria, Canada: Trafford Publishing. ISBN 978-1-4120-3448-5.
Ulrich_02	Ulrich, W. M. (2002). *Legacy systems transformation strategies*. Englewood Cliffs, NJ: Prentice Hall. ISBN 978-0-13-044927-X.
Umar_04	Umar, A. (2004). *Information security and auditing in the digital age – a practical and managerial perspective*. USA: NGE Solutions. ISBN 978-0-9727-4147-X.
Vacca_04	Vacca, J. R. (2004). *Public key infrastructure – building trusted applications and web services*. Boca Raton, FL: Auerbach Publications. ISBN 978-0-8493-0822-4.
Van der Aalst_04	van der Aalst, W., & Van Hee, K. (2004). *Workflow management – models, methods, and systems*. Cambridge, MA: MIT Press. New edition. ISBN 978-0-262-72046-5.
VanBon_07	van Bon, J. (2007). *Foundations of IT service management based on ITIL V3*. Zaltbommel, The Netherlands: Van Haren Publishing BV. ISBN 978-9-08753-057-0.
Vlissides_98	Vlissides, J. (1998). *Pattern hatching – design patterns applied*. Reading, MA: Addison Wesley Longman. ISBN 978-0-201-43293-5.

Vygotsky_02	Vygotsky, L. (2002). *Thought and language*. Cambridge, MA: MIT Press. 13th printing. ISBN 978-0-262-72010-8.
Warren_99	Warren, I. (1999). *The renaissance of legacy systems – method support for software-system evolution*. London, UK: Springer. ISBN 978-1-85233-060-0.
Weaver_48	Warren Weaver (1948) *Science and Complexity*. American Scientist, Vol. 36, p. 536
Wegener_07	Wegener, H. (2007). *Aligning business and IT with metadata – the financial services way*. Chichester, UK: Wiley. ISBN 978-0-470-03031-8.
Weikum_02	Weikum, G., & Vossen, G. (2002). *Transactional information systems – theory, algorithms, and the practice of concurrency control and recovery*. San Francisco, CA: Morgan Kaufmann Publisher (Elsevier). ISBN 978-1-55860-508-4.
Weilkiens_06	Weilkiens, T. (2006). *Systems engineering with SysML/UML – modeling, analysis, design*. Amsterdam, The Netherlands: Elsevier Publishing. German Edition: dpunkt Verlag, Heidelberg, 2006. ISBN 978-0-12-374274-2.
Weilkiens_06	Weilkiens, T. (2006). *Systems engineering with SysML/UML – modeling, analysis, design*. Burlington, VT: Morgan Kaufman\OMG Press. ISBN 978-0-12-374274-2.
Weill_04	Weill, P., & Ross, J. W. (2004). *IT governance – how top performers manage IT decision rights for superior results*. Boston, MA: Harvard Business School Press. ISBN 978-1-59139-253-8.
Weill_98	Weill, P., & Broadbent, M. (1998). *Leveraging the new infrastructure – how market leaders capitalize on information technology*. Harvard, MA: Harvard Business School Press. ISBN 978-0-87584-830-3.
Weinberg_01	Weinberg, G. M. (2001). *An introduction to general systems thinking*. New York: Dorset House Publishing. ISBN 978-0-932633-49-8.
Weiss_99	Weiss, D. M., & Lai, C. T. R. (1999). *Software product-line engineering – a family-based software development process*. Reading, MA: Addison-Wesley Longman. ISBN 978-0-201-69438-7.
Wieczorek_03	Wieczorek, M., Naujoks, U., & Bartlett, B. (2003). *Business Continuity*. Berlin, Heidelberg: Springer. ISBN 978-3-540-44285-5.
Wolf_05	Wolf, C., & Halter, E. M. (2005). *Virtualization – from the desktop to the enterprise*. Berkeley, CA: Apress. ISBN 978-1-159059-495-7.
Woodfield_79	S. N. Woodfield. *An experiment on unit increase in problem complexity*. IEEE Transactions on Software Engineering, Vol. 5, No. 2, pp. 76-79, March 1979
Woods_03	Woods, D. (2003). *Enterprise services architecture*. Sebastopol, CA: O'Reilly & Associates. ISBN 978-0-596-00551-2.
Woods_06	Woods, D., & Mattern, T. (2006). *Enterprise SOA – designing IT for business innovation*. Sebastopol, CA: O'Reilly & Associates. ISBN 978-0-596-10238-0.
Yang_03	Yang, H., & Ward, M. (2003). *Successful evolution of software systems*. Boston, MA: Artech House Publishing. ISBN 978-1-58053-349-3.
Zachmann_08	John A. Zachmann. The Zachmann Framework for Enterprise Architecture http://www.zachmaninternational.com/
Zeidler_07	Zeidler, A. (2007). *Event-based middleware for pervasive computing: foundations, concepts, design*. Germany: VDM Verlag Dr. Müller. ISBN 978-3-83641-309-1.

Glossary

The following *glossary* defines the important key words used in this book. The definitions for terms of general use have been taken from:

- Judy Pearsall (Editor): **The New Oxford Dictionary of English**. Oxford University Press, Oxford UK, 1998. ISBN 0-19-861263-X ([Oxford_98]),
- **Merriam-Webster's Collegiate Dictionary**, 10th edition, 2001. Merriam-Webster Inc., Springfield MA, USA. ISBN 0-87779-710-2,

Term	Definition	Remarks
Agility	Agility is the ability to efficiently implement required changes	Agility is a global property of a system which expresses its modifiability or resistance to change in a measurable way. Systems with a low agility resist changes, whereas in systems with a high agility changes can be implemented efficiently. Agility is measured by the execution of a typical project portfolio *Note*: This definition is specific to this book
Application	An application comprises a set of *functionality*, the corresponding *data*, and *interfaces* to other applications in order to achieve a specific business purpose. Applications consist of one or several software components designed to support business processes and to fulfill specific needs of users.	A component consists of programs, data structures, configuration information, and associated documentation.
Application Architecture	The fundamental organization of the application landscape,	

(*continued*)

Term	Definition	Remarks
	embodied in its applications and components, their relationships to each other, and to the environment, and the principles guiding its design and evolution	
Application Landscape	Set of all business-relevant applications (code, flow of execution, and data), their relationships to each other, and their relationships to the environment	
Architecture	The fundamental organization of a system embodied in its components, their relationships to each other, and to the environment, and the principles guiding its design and evolution	[IEEE_00]
Architecture Integrity	Property of a system based on sound, proven, unified, and consistently implemented concepts	
Architecture Principle	Explicit rule or best practice for constructing an information system	
Atomic Business Function	An Atomic Business Function is the lowest level of functionality in a system that is still recognizable to the business	[Sessions_09], [Sessions_08]
Autonomic Computing	A computing environment with the ability to manage itself and dynamically, adapt to change in accordance with business policies and objectives. Self-managing environments can perform such activities based on situations they observe or sense in the IT environment rather than requiring IT professionals to initiate the task. These environments are self-configuring, self-healing, self-optimizing, and self-protecting	http://www-01.ibm.com/software/tivoli/autonomic/
Balanced Scorecard	The balanced scorecard is a strategic planning and management system used to align business activities to the vision and strategy of the	

(*continued*)

Glossary 249

Term	Definition	Remarks
	organization, improve internal and external communications, and monitor organizational performance against strategic goals(http://www.balancedscorecard.org/)	
Basket	Baskets are used to structure large project portfolios and consist of subsets of the project portfolio characterized by common properties	
Business Architecture	**What is Business Architecture?** "A blueprint of the enterprise that provides a common understanding of the organization and is used to align strategic objectives and tactical demands" **Business Architecture Overview** Business Architecture defines the structure of the enterprise in terms of its governance structure, business processes, and business information. In defining the structure of the enterprise, business architecture considers customers, finances, and the ever-changing market to align strategic goals and objectives with decisions regarding products and services; partners and suppliers; organization; capabilities; and key initiatives http://bawg.omg.org OMG business architecture group (BAWG)	
Business Component Map	Structure for the allocation of business functionality	Business components are containers for related sets of business functionality Result of the IBM (http://www.ibm.com) business component modeling process
Business Functionality Map	Conceptual structure for the allocation of business functionality	General term for structured containers for related sets of business functionality
Complexity	Property of a system consisting of many different and connected parts	[Sessions_09], [Sessions_08]

(*continued*)

Term	Definition	Remarks
Complexity Trap	End result of an evolution approach which continuously increases system complexity until the system becomes unmodifiable	Typical result of an opportunistic evolution approach
Component	A software component is a unit of composition with conceptually specified interfaces and explicit context dependencies only. A software component can be deployed independently and is subject to composition by third parties	[Szyperski_97] A component consists of programs, data structures, configuration information, and associated documentation.
Coupling	Linking of two system elements, e.g. software or technical components, such that they are dependent on each other	*Tight Coupling*: *Conceptual*: Any change in a system element immediately and completely forces a change in the dependent system element. *Operational*: Information or control flow between the system elements is governed by stringent conditions, such as timing restrictions *Loose coupling*: *Conceptual*: Change in a system element only requires change in the dependent system element if it is desired by and beneficial to the dependent system element *Operational*: Information or control flow between the system elements supports the autonomy of the individual system elements *Architecture*: System design style which introduces the least possible restrictions when connecting system elements
Dependability	Global property of a system which guarantees desired values for the important non-functional properties, such as availability, reliability, security, safety.	
Domain	Specific subject area or area of knowledge	Application Domains define a structure for the allocation of business functionality and data Technical Domains define a structure for the allocation of technical functionality (infrastructure)

(continued)

Glossary 251

Term	Definition	Remarks
Domain Model	Structure for the allocation of functionality	Application Domains for business functionality and (persistent) business data Technical Domains for technical functionality (infrastructure)
Enterprise Service Bus	An enterprise service bus is a standards-based integration platform that combines messaging, web services, data transformation, and intelligent routing to reliably connect and coordinate the interaction of significant number of diverse applications across the extended enterprise with transactional integrity	[Chappell_04]
Evolution approach	Strategy and methodology for the development of information systems	
Integration Architecture	Set of concepts, methods, processes, and infrastructure for the definition of parts and their connections in a systematic way with the aim to preserve maximum *agility* and minimize *integration cost*	
Interface	Formal syntactical and rich semantical access specification to a component covering functional and non-functional properties, such as pre and postconditions, laid down in an interface specification. The term interface also includes the implementation	*Private interface*: Restricted to a limited number of consumers within the same application domain *Public interface*: Available to any registered and authorized consumer, also cross-domain
Interface Specification	Managed, life-cycle controlled agreement between the interface provider (provider component) and the interface user (client component) covering syntactical and semantical access specification to functionality	In integration architecture a distinction between *interface* and *service* is made. The interface specifies what is delivered, the service specifies how it is delivered
IT Governance	Specification and implementation of the decision rights and accountability framework to encourage desirable behaviour in developing and using information technology	[Weill_04]

(*continued*)

Term	Definition	Remarks
IT Operations	All activities to provide dependable, efficient and secure functionality of the IT system to its users	IT operations include both application operations and infrastructure operations
Legacy part	Part of a system which resists modification because it is difficult to change, its function is not known in detail or it is based on obsolete components	May frustrate sponsors because any change takes much time and is expensive
Managed evolution	Evolution approach which balances progress in functionality and agility of the IT system	
Metamodel	Exhaustive definition and specification of all modelling elements which can be used in a class of models	
Model	Formal representation of an abstraction of reality for a specified purpose. A model only presents the characteristics of reality which are important for the intended use of the respective model	In information system theory models are layered in conceptual models, logical models and physical models
Net Present Value	The net present value is defined as the difference between the sum of the values of the cash-in flows, discounted at an appropriate cost of capital, and the present value of the original investment	[Remenyi_00]
Portal	Technology to integrate the user interfaces of component systems	
Portlet	*Portlets* are pluggable user interface software components that are managed and displayed in a web portal. Portlets produce fragments of markup code that are aggregated into a portal page. Typically, following the desktop metaphor, a portal page is displayed as a collection of non-overlapping portlet windows, where each portlet window displays a portlet. Hence a portlet (or collection of portlets) resembles a web-based application that is hosted in a portal	Portlet standards are intended to enable software developers to create portlets that can be plugged in to any portal supporting the standards.

(*continued*)

Glossary

Term	Definition	Remarks
Project	Series of activities intended to implement a set of requirements. Projects are governed by a project methodology	A project has a defined start and end time. At the end of the project the project deliverables must be transferred to a permanent owner
Project Portfolio	Set of all projects grouped according to some characteristics, such as all projects completed in one quarter	
Semantics	Semantics defines the exact *meaning* of all concepts, terms and expressions used in the system. *Rich* semantics is defined as providing precise meaning in sufficient detail for the intended purpose, such as exchanging information between computers via services. Rich semantics is based on explicit representation of context without requiring implicit assumptions	Semantics can be modeled on different levels of consistency. The simplest form is a *glossary* of terms. Often used semantic definition instrument are *taxonomies*, which specify the hierarchy and the meaning of terms. A *business object model* defines semantics on an even higher level of consistency. All business entities are modeled as objects, including their definitions, attributes, operations and. The richest level of specifications is *ontologies.* An ontology is a logical model, defining all the objects, attributes, and relationships in a formal, machine-readable way.
Service	Delivery mechanism for the functionality and data offered by an interface of a component. Includes the interface and specifications of additional non-functional properties which are specified in the service contract	In integration architecture a distinction between *interface* and *service* is made. The interface specifies what is delivered, the service specifies how it is delivered
Service Contract	Managed, life-cycle controlled agreement between a service provider and service consumers covering interface specifications and the non-functional guarantees, specified in an service level agreement (SLA), such as performance guarantees, accounting rules or business continuity guarantees	
Service Delivery infrastructure	Standardized infrastructure for the delivery of services, including the management of services	

(continued)

254   Glossary

Term	Definition	Remarks
Service Level Agreement	Agreement between a service provider and the service consumers related to an interface contract, covering the non-functional properties, such as: • Availability (Latency, response time) • Performance (throughput, bandwith) • Business continuity • Lifecycle management	
Size	Measurable magnitude of an IT system or a part of an IT system.	Measurement units include number of source lines of code (SLOC), number of function points (FP) or number of use case points (UCP)
Solution Architect	Role in the application development departments with the responsibility of architecture specification in individual projects and for specific applications	
Syntax	Syntax is the set of rules for combining symbols to form valid expressions specified by a grammar	This is applicable both to natural languages and to data storage and transport. Syntax of an interface must be defined in a *formal language* that lends itself to automatic checking and interpretation at run-time
System Complexity	Topological system complexity, functional system complexity	[Sessions_08], [Sessions_09]
Target Architecture	Specification of an architecture of the information system to be achieved. Blueprint for the work of architects and developers	
Technical Architecture	The fundamental organization of the infrastructure, embodied in its technical components and technical products, their relationships to each other, and to the environment, and the principles guiding its design and evolution	
Technology Portfolio	Managed inventory of all technical components and technical products with directives for their lifecycle and use	
Trustworthy (trusted) Component	A trustworthy (or trusted) component is a reusable	Not to be confused with the notion of trust in secure computing.

(*continued*)

Term	Definition	Remarks
	software component possessing specified and guaranteed property qualities	Guarantees for security properties are part of the properties of a trustworthy (or trusted) component, however, "trust" in trustworthy components extends to all quality factors
Use Case	A use case captures a contract between the stakeholders of a system about its behaviour. The use case describes the system's behaviour under various condition as the system responds to a request from one of the stakeholders	[Cockburn_01]
Very Large Information System	Functionally rich, having a long development history, containing significant legacy parts which need to be replaced or reengineered, being exposed to a high rate of change, having high replacement cost, thus representing a high value to their owners, relying on heterogeneous technologies, being mission critical, having a large number of stakeholders resulting in a federated governance and often in a distributed IT organization	

Abbreviations

The *abbreviations* used in this book are listed below.

Abbreviation	Explanation
BAWG	OMG Business Architecture Working Group, http://bawg.omg.org
BCM	Business component map
BIAN	Banking Industry Architecture Network
BO	Business object
BOM	Business object model
BSC	Balanced scorecard
C:D	Connect: Direct (http://www.sterlingcommerce.com/Products/MFT/ConnectDirect)
cBO	Component-level business object
CDM	Combined domain model
CEO	Chief Executive Officer
CFO	Chief Financial Officer
CI	Configuration item
CICS	Customer Information Control System (an IBM product, http://www.ibm.com)
CIO	Chief Information Officer
CMDB	Configuration management data base
CMMI	Capability maturity model integration
CMMI	Capability maturity model
COO	Chief Operating Officer
CORBA	Common Object Request Broker Architecture (OMG)
COTS	Commercial of the shelf system
CPU	Central processing unit
CS	Credit Suisse AG
CSXB	Credit Suisse Enterprise Service Bus
CTO	Chief Technology Officer
dBO	Domain-level business object
DevC	Development cost
DiMA	Disentangling the Mainframe (CS Strategic Iniﬁative).
DMZ	Demilitarized zone (= Security element in the Internet architecture)
DSL	Domain-specific language
DSM	Domain-specific modeling
DSS	Digital signature service
eBO	Enterprise-level business object

(*continued*)

Abbreviation	Explanation
EIA	Enterprise integration architecture
ERP	Enterprise resource planning
ESA	Enterprise security architecture
ESB	Enterprise service bus
FP	Function point
ftp, ftps	File transfer protocol (http://en.wikipedia.org/wiki/FTPS)
IBAN	International Banking Account Number
IBASEC	Interbank security server
IBM	International business machines
IBM	International business machines
IDL	Interface Definition Language
IEEE	Institute of Electrical and Electronics Engineers
IMS	Information Management System (an IBM product, http://www.ibm.com)
ISO	International Standards Organization (http://www.iso.org)
IT	Information technology
ITIL	IT Infrastructure library (http://www.itil.org)
JAP	Java application platform
KPI	Key performance indicator
NPV	Net present value
OMG	Object Management Group
OMG	Object Management Group (http://www.omg.org)
PKI	Public Key Cryptography ([])
PTC	Prices, Terms, and Conditions
RSA	Rivest, Shamir, Adleman Inc. (http://www.rsa.com)
RTP	Run-time platform
SIC	Swiss Interbank Clearing (http://www.sic.ch)
SITT	Strategic IT Training (Credit Suisse education program)
SLA	Service level agreement
SLOC	Source Lines of Code
SOA	Service oriented architecture
SRAS	Secure remote access system
SSO	Single Sign-On
STC	Steering committee
SWIFT	Society for worldwide interchange of financial transactions
TCO	Total cost of ownership
TDM	Technical Domain Model
TOTAL	Target Operations and Trading Application Landscape (CS)
TtM	Time to market
UC	Use case
UCP	Use case point
UML	Unified Modeling Language (OMG)
VM	Virtual machine
WSDL	Web Services Definition Language
XML	Extensible Markup Language

Index

A

abbreviation, 259–260
abstraction, 54, 96
abstraction layer, 30
accountability, 64
acquisition, 19
aggregation, 54
agility, 15, 23, 32, 33, 36, 74, 80, 126, 129, 218, 222, 249, 253
ANOVA, 226
application, 5, 218
application architecture, 29, 41, 62
application development, 140, 198
application development environment, 59
application domain, 45
application domain architect, 73
application landscape, 30, 44, 45, 48, 60, 62, 70, 121, 213
application platform, 144, 201
application portfolio, 74
architectural atatus, 136
architectural distance, 91
architectural governance, 95
architectural integrity, 16
architectural leadership, 33
architectural risk, 126
architectural standard, 71
architecture, 29, 35, 36, 166, 171, 172, 202
architecture boot camp, 67
architecture clash, 235
architecture communication, 66
architecture communication process, 67, 208
architecture controlling, 70
architecture definition process, 65
architecture events, 67

architecture framework, 71
architecture implementation, 31
architecture implementation process, 67
architecture investment, 76
architecture leadership, 29
architecture management, 29, 30, 166, 180, 185, 197, 201, 232
architecture obligation, 210
architecture organization, 71
architecture principle, 37, 154
architecture process, 36, 65
architecture process group, 73
architecture program, 31, 36, 181
architecture project review, 70
architecture standard, 71, 208
asynchronous messaging, 118
atomic business function, 51
audience, vii
audit issue, 170
authentication, 64
authorization, 64
automation, 3
autonomic component, 156
autonomic computing, 156
autonomic manager, 157
autonomic system architecture, 156
availability, 26, 107
averaging, 222
averaging technique, 224

B

B2B, 83, 84, 102, 120
balance of power, 168, 202
balanced power, 194
balanced scorecard, 70

259

Banking Industry Architecture Network, 122
basket, 165
basket provider, 173
basket sponsor, 173
BCM, 44
BIAN, 122
black box, 138
BOM, 53, 57, 98
BOU, 40
Bruno Bonati, xiii
budget authority, 165
bulk transfer, 93, 118
business architecture, 41–43, 62, 236
business component, 44
business component map, 42–44, 51
business component modeling, 44
business functional map, 41, 44
business functionality, 43
business functionality map, 43
business logic layer, 87
business object, 47
business object model, 42, 53, 57, 98, 99, 255
business operation unit, 40
business process engineering, 43
business requirement, 31
business services, 44
business strategy, 31
business value, 15, 23, 32, 219
business-IT alignment, 30, 46, 163, 197, 211, 233
business-to-business integration case, 120

C
career track system, 190
CDM, 48
CFO, 170
change, 5, 11
change driver, 207
chief architect, 71, 76
CI, 158
CIO, 71, 166, 170, 202
CIO basket, 171, 182
CMDB, 158
cohesion, 46
complexity, v, 5, 7, 10, 17, 26, 48, 79, 83, 231
complexity management, 47
complexity trap, vi, 17
component, 30, 47, 81, 83, 104, 127, 138, 153
componentization, 82, 197
conceptual integrity, 97
configuration item, 158
configuration management database, 158
conflict, 193, 195

connection, 5
continuity, 192
contract, 83, 110
contract theory, 108
control, 32, 33
control flow, 5
COO, 202
CORBA, 100
CORBA-IDL, 96
core idea, 25
correlation, 226
cost, vi, 107
COTS, 120
Coupling, 46
Credit Suisse, vii
Crisis, 32
CTB/RTB cost, 211
Culture, 33, 196, 235

D
data, 45, 46, 88, 249
data base, 60
data flow, 5
data security, 64
data sharing, 94
data type, 113
dBO, 54
dBOM, 54, 57
defensive interface design, 154
degree of decoupling, 92
dependency, 5, 7, 25, 46, 80, 127, 154
design by contract, 108
design noise, 4
development cost, 222, 234
development environment, 129
development tool chain, 141
discipline, 193
distributed computing, 100
domain, 73, 198, 232
domain architect, 73, 77
domain assessment, 176
domain basket model, 174, 175
domain business object model, 54, 57
domain model, 30, 41, 43, 46, 48, 51, 73, 125, 199, 201
domain specific language, 47
domain specific modeling, 47
domain-oriented application architecture, 235
domain-specific architecture, 47
DSL, 47
DSM, 47
dual representation, 169
dynamic infrastructure, 155

Index 261

E
eBO, 54
effector, 157
efficiency, vii
encapsulation, 96
end-of-life, 134
enterprise architecture, 41
enterprise level BOM, 54
enterprise service bus, 118
ESA, 80
ESB, 118
event, 93, 118
evolution, 8, 15, 23
evolution channel, 24, 25, 31
evolution step, 25
evolution strategy, 18, 152, 197
evolutionary approach, 23
exception, 135
exception permit, 211
exchange, 92, 118
executive board, 169

F
failed system, 15
federated architecture organization, 48
federated organization, 166
file transfer, 118
financial institution, vii
foreign services, 120
formal language, 96, 256
framework, 42
Frank J. Furrer, xiii
function point, 220
functional composition, 83
functional dependency, 5
functional line, 195
functional size, 10
functionality, 15, 45, 46, 249

G
global front system, 89
globalization, 39, 89
glossary, 53, 249, 255
governance, 11, 21, 27, 33, 48, 165, 171, 172, 197, 231
governance model, 44, 165, 168, 171
granularity, 99
greenfield approach, 18, 22, 26, 164

H
heterogenity, 153
human resource, 22

I
IFMS, 114, 119
impact factor, 226
information architecture, 43
information bus, 118
information flow, 51
information technology, 3
information type, 116
infrastructure, v, 5, 30, 76, 82, 129, 152, 218
infrastructure architecture program, 135
infrastructure service, 130, 138, 139
infrastructure technology portfolio, 232
initial funding, 34
innovation portfolio, 72
integration, 3, 27
integration architecture, 30, 60, 76, 80–82, 88, 107, 111, 117, 118, 193, 232
integration broker, 118
integration context, 83
integration cost, 19, 79, 80, 253
integration software, 59
interface, 30, 45, 62, 81, 83, 98, 102–104, 249
interface contract, 233
interface management, 62
interface management system, 119
interface use, 113
international standard, 130
Internet applications, 150
investment, 25
investment plan, 31, 178
IT architecture, 47
IT career track, 190
IT governance, 4
IT management, 47
IT organization, 166, 196
IT steering committee, 169
IT strategy, 27, 171, 180–182, 201–202
IT strategy conformance, 24
IT system, v
IT target architecture, 30

J
JAP, 147, 150
Java application platform, 150
job family description, 191

L
layer model, 41
lead domain architect, 73
leadership, 33, 193
legacy, 125
legacy application, 47

legacy code, 10
legacy part, 15
legacy subsystem, 188
legacy system, 4, 33
life cycle, 15, 59, 81, 146
lifecycle management, 29
lifecycle status, 136
long term orientation, 192

M
Mainframe, 126
mainstream technology, 133
maintenance, 163
maintenance cost, 211
managed evolution, vi, vii, 9, 23–25, 27, 29, 30, 32, 37, 64, 70, 83, 147, 170, 187, 188, 190, 195, 200, 202, 218, 231
managed evolution strategy, 32
managed interface, 30
managed resource, 156
management process, 65
matrix organization, 197
meaning, 53, 255
measurement, 32, 205
merger, 19, 26, 34
metadata, 182
metamodel, 124
metric, 25, 218, 222
microarchitecture, 37
middleware, 57, 100, 117, 200
mission criticality, 11
model, 39, 48, 73, 98
model checker, 57
model consistency, 41, 57
model-driven architecture, 236
monolithic system, 30, 125
multidimensional optimization, 25
multivariate statistical factor analysis, 226, 235

N
naming conflict, 97
net present value, 219
non-functional property, 107
NPV, 219

O
OLA, 130, 152
OneBank, 48
ontology, 53, 255
operating cost, 17
operating system, 141
operation, 131, 152, 167

operational dependency, 7, 17, 82, 154
operational level agreements, 130, 144, 152, 155
opportunistic approach, 17, 163
organization, 12, 27, 31, 196, 233

P
part, 5
partition, 128
people, 188
performance, 107
performance indicator, 71
Perseverance, 193
persistent data layer, 87
physical resource, 141
platform, 30, 59, 138, 200, 215, 233
platform architecture, 30
platform management, 140
platform operation, 140, 142
portal, 86, 87, 119
portfolio, 30, 207
portfolio management process, 171
portfolio of modifications, 25
principles of managed evolution, 25
process, 30, 48, 218, 233
process layer, 87
process orchestration, 86
process quality indicator, 71
project, 207
project cost, 220
project management, 165
project management process, 178
project portfolio, 34, 165, 178, 185, 218
project portfolio management, 29, 30, 165, 183, 201
project portfolio management process, 178
project portfolio reporting, 211
project review, 67
project review board, 185
property, 9

Q
qualification band, 190
quality attribute, vi
quality check gate, 113
quality control gate, 111

R
rate of change, 23, 25, 166
rearchitecture program, 29
redundancy, 47, 48, 91, 95, 122, 132
refactoring, 213
reference architecture, 150

Index

regional alignment, 197
replacement approach, 18, 20
requirement, 207, 218
requirements specification, 221
reuse, 51, 112, 233
review, 111, 135
rich semantics, 96
risk, vi, 11, 29, 170
runtime environment, 129
runtime platform, 59, 148

S

Sarbannes-Oxley, 236
sBO, 54
scope, 33, 165
security, 62, 107, 119
security administration, 64
security architecture, 62, 63, 76
security monitoring, 64
self-configuration, 156
self-healing, 156
self-management, 156
self-optimization, 156
self-protection, 159
semantic, 53, 91, 96, 121, 235, 255
semantic dependency, 6
semantic model, 53, 232
semantics, 42, 96, 235
sensor, 157
service, 82, 83, 87, 104, 114, 124, 127
service architecture, 111, 214
service consumer, 104, 111
service contract, 103, 107
service delivery infrastructure, 104
service implementation, 113
service layer, 29
service level agreement, 155
service management process, 115
service management system, 114
service oriented architecture, 47
service provider, 104, 111
service repository, 115
service reuse factor, 217
service specification, 113
silo-application, 17, 193, 194
silo-thinking, 31
simplification, 8
SITT, 188
size, 220
skill, 188
SLA, 104
SLA violation, 155
sliding window, 224

SOA, 80, 87
software engineering, 81
software product line, 138
solution architect, 73
solution delivery budget, 32
source lines of code, 220
sourcing, 131
special engineering, 138, 148
sponsor, 172
sponsor meeting, 171, 172
standard, 67, 97, 98, 101, 213
standard software package, 19
statistical relevance, 222
Stephan Murer, xiii
strategic business-IT alignment, 165, 178
strategic business-IT alignment
    process, 178
strategy, 31, 32, 171, 188, 234
strategy development, 167
structural model, 41, 53, 232
subdomain, 45
sub-portfolio, 227
SWIFT, 101
synchronous communication, 92
synchronous transaction, 118
syntax, 91, 95, 104, 256
syntax specification language, 96
system architecture, 39, 42
system complexity, 213
system evolution strategy, 15
system management, 76
system property, 206, 212
systems management, 60, 139, 152, 235
systems management architecture, 62
systems theory, 5

T

target architecture, 31, 36, 65
taxonomy, 53, 255
technical architecture, 42, 57, 62
technical component, 5, 141
technical dependency, 7
technical domain, 57, 134, 136
technical domain architect, 57, 73, 136
technical domain model, 59, 134, 201
technical domain strategy, 134
technical integration, 100, 122
technical product, 131
technical product version, 136
technology, 72, 117, 131, 193
technology base, 11
technology portfolio, 17, 30, 38, 57, 74,
    132, 179

technology portfolio management, 130, 134
technology portfolio management controlling, 135
technology portfolio management process, 134
technology risk, 38, 130, 132
temporal dependency, 7
test environment, 129
time to market, vi, 220, 222, 234
trade-off, 37
transparency, 47
trust, 194
trustworthy component, 107

U
unit of change, 16
use case, 98, 221
use case point, 220
user interface, 85
user interface layer, 87

V
value, 11, 192, 233
value case, 172
value creation, 171
version, 131, 146
vertical architecture, 60
very large information system, v, vi, 4, 5, 12, 14, 22, 30–33, 37, 57, 80, 92, 97, 102, 110, 111, 121, 125, 152, 154, 188, 202, 218, 231
view, 94
virtualization layer, 30, 141

W
waterfall model, 69
web-service, 121
workflow infrastructure, 119
workforce, 188

X
XML, 102
XML-SCHEMA, 96

Printed in France by Amazon
Brétigny-sur-Orge, FR